Launching the Imagination

A Comprehensive Guide to Basic Design

fourth edition

Mary Stewart

Connect
Learn
Succeed™

Published by McGraw-Hill, an imprint of The McGraw-Hill Companies, Inc., 1221 Avenue of the Americas, New York, NY 10020. Copyright © 2012, 2008, 2006, 2002. All rights reserved. No part of this publication may be reproduced or distributed in any form or by any means, or stored in a database or retrieval system, without the prior written consent of The McGraw-Hill Companies, Inc., including, but not limited to, in any network or other electronic storage or transmission, or broadcast for distance learning.

This book is printed on acid-free paper.

1 2 3 4 5 6 7 8 9 0 DOW/DOW 9 8 7 6 5 4 3 2 1

ISBN: 978-0-07337924-1
MHID: 0-07-337924-7

Vice President Editorial: *Michael Ryan*
Publisher: *Christopher Freitag*
Associate Sponsoring Editor: *Betty Chen*
Director of Development: *Rhona Robbin*
Developmental Editor: *Cynthia Ward*
Editorial Coordinator: *Sarah Remington*
Executive Marketing Manager: *Pamela S. Cooper*
Senior Production Editor: *Carey Eisner*
Design Manager: *Preston Thomas*
Interior Designer: *Linda Robertson*
Cover Designer: *Bill Stanton*
Lead Photo Research Coordinator: *Alexandra Ambrose*
Photo Researcher: *Deborah Anderson*
Buyer II: *Tandra Jorgensen*
Media Project Manager: *Bethuel Jabez*
Composition: *10.5/14 Palatino Roman by Lachina Publishing Services*
Printing: *70# Sterling Ultra Web Dull, R.R. Donnelley & Sons*

Cover: Top right: Suzanne Stryk, *Genomes and Daily Observations (woodpecker)*, 2005. Courtesy of Suzanne Stryk; Center: Tara Donovan, *Untitled* (Styrofoam Cups), 2008. Photograph by Raymond Meier. Courtesy of Tara Donovan and PaceWildenstein Gallery; Left: Edgar Degas, *Frieze of Dancers*, c. 1895. The Cleveland Museum of Art. Bequest of Leonard C. Hanna, Jr., 1946.83; Middle: Eva Hild, *Lamella*, 2008. © Eva Hild, Courtesy of Gallery Bienvenu; Bottom: Bill Viola, *Slowly Turning Narrative*, 1992. Photo by Gary McKinnis. Courtesy of artist and James Cohan Gallery.

Library of Congress Cataloging-in-Publication Data

Stewart, Mary, 1952-
  Launching the imagination : a comprehensive guide to basic design / Mary Stewart. — 4th ed.
     p. cm.
  Also issued in parts titled: Launching the imagination : a comprehensive guide to two-dimensional design, and Launching the imagination : a comprehensive guide to three-dimensional design.
  Includes bibliographical references and index.
  ISBN-13: 978-0-07-337924-1 (softcover : alk. paper)
  ISBN-10: 0-07-337924-7 (softcover : alk. paper)
  ISBN-13: 978-0-07-737980-3 (softcover : alk. paper)
  ISBN-10: 0-07-737980-2 (softcover : alk. paper)
  ISBN-13: 978-0-07-737981-0 (softcover : alk. paper)
  ISBN-10: 0-07-737981-0 (softcover : alk. paper)
  1. Design. I. Title. II. Title: Comprehensive guide to basic design.
  NK1510.S74 2011
  745.4—dc22
                                        2010045154

The Internet addresses listed in the text were accurate at the time of publication. The inclusion of a Web site does not indicate an endorsement by the authors or McGraw-Hill, and McGraw-Hill does not guarantee the accuracy of the information presented at these sites.

www.mhhe.com

Launching the Imagination:
A Comprehensive Guide to Basic Design
is dedicated to Dr. Richard Siegesmund

dedication

Launching the Imagination treats *design* as both a verb and a noun—as both a process and a product. By covering the process of creative and critical thinking as well as presenting the elements and principles used in creating a product, this book offers a unique resource for foundations courses.

The title *Launching the Imagination* suggests the goals of this book and of the foundations year as a whole. Through an immersion in 2-D, 3-D, and 4-D concepts and problems, students are encouraged to develop ways of thinking visually that will serve them throughout their studies and careers. They learn that design is deliberate—a process of exploring a wide range of solutions and choosing the most promising option for further development. And they find inspiration in the work of others, analyzing the art of the past and the present for insights

into how composition informs communication. This book supports these goals in the following ways:

UNIQUE COVERAGE OF "PROCESS" AS WELL AS "PRODUCT"

Every artist/designer faces challenges in getting started, generating and evaluating visual ideas, managing long-term projects, working with others, and handling critiques. **Part Two: Concepts and Critical Thinking** offers practical advice and examples that students can consult at any point in the course. Chapter Eight in Part Two also explores the question of meaning in art from the artist's perspective.

APPLICATIONS TO STUDIO PRACTICE

For the practicing artist/designer, it is not enough to recognize the elemtns and principles in the work of others. **Key Questions** throughout the book challenge students to apply concepts to their own works in progress. **Studio project ideas** on the book's Web site invite a hands-on exploration of chapter topics. A list of some of these studio projects can be found at the end of each chapter.

CONVERSATIONS WITH PRACTICING ARTISTS AND DESIGNERS

Just as guest lecturers enrich the classroom by contributing different perspectives on how and why we make art and create designs, so the **artist and designer profiles** at the end of each chapter add other voices and experiences to the text. In these interviews, students learn about working processes and career choices from a remarkable group of professionals, including designer Adam Kallish, photographer Samuel Yates, illustrator Bob Dacey, metalsmith Marilyn da Silva, sculptor Kendall Buster, and ceramicist David MacDonald.

Profile:
Kendall Buster, Sculptor
Biological Architecture

Kendall Buster's large-scale "biological architecture" projects have been exhibited at Artist's Space and the American Academy of Arts and Letters in New York City; the Hirshhorn Museum and the Kreeger Museum in Washington, DC; the Kemper Museum in Kansas City; Suyama Space in Seattle; the Nevada Museum of Art in Reno; and the KZNSA Gallery in South Africa. Buster has created commissioned sculptures for the Washington, DC, Convention Center; Massey Cancer Center in Richmond, VA; and the Agave Library in Phoenix. Current projects include commissions for the new chemistry building at Princeton University, Johns Hopkins University, and the Indianapolis Museum of Art.

MS: Microbiology was your initial academic passion, and you worked in this field for twelve years. What attracted you to microbiology, and what did you learn from it?

KB: Peering into a microscope gave me access to an intricate and beautiful world that was beyond ordinary perception. As I learned more, I became increasingly interested in the architecture of natural forms—the way cells are constructed to maximize efficiency or the permeability of a particular cell wall. The sculptures I now create begin with an internal skeleton that I wrap in a fabric or plastic skin. And, I am still fascinated by shifts in perception, from very small scale to very large scale. For me, art and science are simply aspects of the same impulse.

MS: How do you translate your ideas into large-scale objects? Most of your recent projects could fill an entire gymnasium!

KB: Ideas often occur just as I am waking up. At this point, they are more intuitive than intentional. I begin to record possibilities through pencil drawings. Drawing is crucial—it is the first step in getting the idea out of my head and into the world. I then move to what I see as three-dimensional sketching, using carved Styrofoam, wire, or various types of board.

Further work is done with an entire team of collaborators. Computer-aided design helps us explore variations further and analyze the structural requirements and possibilities of the forms. With my studio team, I create physical models of the building in which the artwork will be placed in order to study

the ways in which the sculpture converses with the site. I have a project coordinator who communicates with the client on the architectural particulars of the site and a rigger who is an installation specialist.

MS: How are the pieces actually constructed?

KB: My large-scale sculptures are made with many interlocked parts, and so creating patterns for the parts is critical. These patterns, both computer generated and hand drawn on the studio floor, are used for shaping and welding the steel frames or cutting planar material. The frames are professionally powder-coated, and when the frames are covered in cloth I might work with as many as ten to twenty helpers in a marathon "screening party."

MS: Please talk us through *New Growth*, installed in the Boise Art Museum.

KB: *New Growth* is an inventory of architectural models that function like biological systems. In this imagined city, old forms generate new forms through processes that suggest germination, budding, merging, hybridization, or absorption. The model city is conceived as a single organism constructed from many interdependent parts. Some structures are connected by passageways that suggest either umbilical cords or parasitic invasions. Contiguous membranes create distinct regions in the city, and the transparency of these membranes allows inner layers to be visible through the outer shell.

Architectural structures form and re-form the fabric of cities over time. To evoke this process, I wanted

to build a structure that seems to be based on a precise blueprint, while at the same time contradict this idea by creating a structure that seems dynamic, continually changing. I am also interested in exploring the tension between what is revealed and what is concealed; how windows link interior space with exterior place to create shifting sight lines; how narrow entryways or low passages act in direct confrontation with the body; how space is compressed and movement directed; how one is at times hidden, and at times exposed.

New Growth is also a response to the particulars of the Boise Art Museum site. On my first visit I visualized a kind of floating cityscape made up of forms that behaved both as individual structures and as a continuous membrane. The sculpture that I finally built connected to the exhibition site in unexpected ways. Curved rooftops in my architectural models seemed to echo the arched beams in the ceiling, and the ever-changing light penetrating through the floor-to-ceiling windows created subtle shades of white and gray on the transparent layers of fabric.

Scale shifts between the viewer's initial "panoramic" overview and the more closely observed details were also important. At one moment, the viewer is dwarfed by the artwork; at another, the artwork reads as a model that the viewer can command. As a result, the viewer is enveloped, embraced, and engaged—all at the same time.

MS: What advice do you have for beginning students?

KB: I have three bits of advice. First, realize that each of us has our own work process and embrace the process that is right for you. Second, find the right balance between conceptual breadth (lateral thinking) and conceptual depth (vertical thinking). Too much lateral thinking can result in superficiality, while too much vertical thinking can narrow your possibilities. Finally, embrace the idea of an ongoing and preferably daily studio practice. Complex ideas and structures don't happen overnight!

Kendall Buster, *New Growth*, 2007. Dimensions variable, as installed in Boise Art Museum.

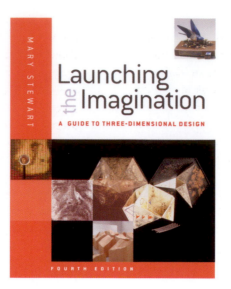
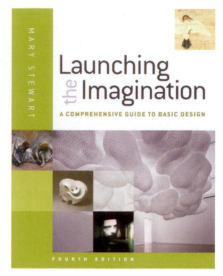

AN UNMATCHED VISUAL RESOURCE

By looking closely at as many outstanding illustrations as possible, students can build a mental library of images that can then serve as a launching pad for their own work. The **650 color reproductions** in this book encompass contemporary and traditional art, craft, media arts, and design, from both Western and world cultures. In addition, instructors who adopt the book can tap into **Connect Image Bank,** a way to easily browse and search for images and to download them for use in class presentations.

THOROUGH COVERAGE OF DESIGN VOCABULARY

A carpenter stocks his shop with a variety of tools, including a table saw, band saw, jig saw, and radial saw. Each has distinct capabilities and uses. Similarly, when students master the visual and verbal vocabulary of basic design, they can more eloquently express their ideas using a variety of tools. *Launching the Imagination* covers all of the topics common to most foundations courses, thus offering a coherent approach to a full-year curriculum.

Key terms are clearly explained and illustrated within the text, with at least one visual example provided for each concept. Students can review these terms in a Key Terms list at the end of each chapter and can test their understanding in an online flashcard and quiz program. A glossary of terms starting on page 372 serves as a comprehensive resource.

FLEXIBLE FORMATS

As in the past, *Launching the Imagination* is available in three formats so that professors can choose the coverage that best fits their curriculum:

1. A **comprehensive volume** for full-year courses. This volume covers 2-D, 3-D, and 4-D time design, plus creativity and problem solving (Parts One to Four).
2. A **2-D volume** that also includes chapters on creativity and problem solving (Parts One and Two).
3. A **3-D volume** that also includes chapters on creativity and problem solving (Parts Two and Three). This volume has been substantially expanded to better serve the 3-D classroom.

CourseSmart, a new way for faculty to find and review eTextbooks, is also a great option for students who are interested in accessing their course materials digitally and saving money. CourseSmart offers thousands of the most commonly adopted textbooks across hundreds of courses from a wide variety of higher-education publishers. It is the only place faculty can review and compare the full text of textbooks online, providing immediate access without the environmental impact of requesting print examination copies. At CourseSmart, students can save up to 50 percent off the cost of a print book, reduce their impact on the environment, and gain access to powerful Web tools for learning, including full text search, notes and highlighting, and e-mail tools for sharing notes among classmates.

Craft your teaching resources to match the way you teach. With **McGraw-Hill Create, www.mcgrawhill create.com,** you can easily rearrange chapters, combine material from other content sources, and quickly upload content you have written such as your course syllabus or teaching notes. Find the content you need in Create by searching through thousands of leading McGraw-Hill textbooks. Arrange your book to fit your teaching style. Create even allows you to personalize your book's appearance by selecting the cover and adding your name, school, and course information. Order a Create book and you'll receive a complimentary print review copy in 3–5 business days or a complimentary electronic review copy (eComp) via email in about one hour. Go to www.mcgrawhillcreate.com today and register. Experience how McGraw-Hill Create empowers you to teach your students your way.

NEW TO THE FOURTH EDITION

Working with invaluable feedback from other foundations teachers and my students, I have made the following improvements to the text:

- **Expanded and improved coverage of 3-D design.** The coverage in Part Three, Three-Dimensional Design, has been improved in several ways. Topics such as "form," in Chapter Nine, have been reorganized to work better as a unit of study. Coverage of 3-D elements and principles has been expanded, and Part Three has 12 additional examples of concepts, for a total of 200 full-color images. Every image has been carefully evaluated to ensure that it clearly illustrates the concept, and more than 30 examples have been replaced. Many more examples of contemporary sculpture have been included, representing works by artists such as Ann Hamilton, Kiki Smith, Ned Kahn, Nick Cave, Liza Lou, Olafur Eliasson, Jaume Plensa, Xu Bing, and Tara Donovan.
- **Refined existing coverage of color and strengthened discussion of its implications for art and design.** The writing has been tightened up, and seven more examples have been added.
- **Reorganized and streamlined Part Two, Concepts and Critical Thinking.** The chapters in Part Two have been resequenced to align more closely with the steps in the design process. The first chapter in this part, Chapter Five, focuses on strategies for initiating a project. Tips for cultivating creativity as a daily practice and suggestions for managing creative projects from start to finish are now covered in Chapter Six. As in

past editions, Chapters Seven and Eight cover critical thinking and constructing meaning in art. New image choices create a stronger balance between 2-D and 3-D examples representing both art and design.

- **Increased focus on contemporary art.** The focus on contemporary art and artists has been increased throughout, with a particularly strong emphasis on sculptural works. There are 40 new examples by artists and designers, including works by Devorah Sperber, John Paul Miller, Petah Coyne, William Kentridge, and Dan Sutherland.
- **New artist profiles.** Painter Suzanne Stryk discusses the value of the close observation of nature and connections between her sketchbooks and more developed artworks (Chapter Six), while sculptor Kendall Buster discusses her large-scale public art projects and the collaborative process through which they are made (Chapter Seven).

SUPPLEMENTS

Led by Mathew Kelly from Central College, a remarkable team of collaborators has developed an extensive online Instructor's Manual and an accompanying Web site. Advice on course construction, critique skills, and technical resources are included, along with more than 70 assignments. Divided into sections on Two-Dimensional Design, Three-Dimensional Design, Four-Dimensional Design, Color, Creativity, and Digital Design, this manual provides the basic information on which the teacher can build a rich and informative course.

Online Learning Center at www.mhhe.com/stewart4e

The Online Learning Center offers resources for each chapter of the text, including chapter objectives, vocabulary flashcards, activities, and studio projects. For instructors, lecture PowerPoints and an Instructor's Manual filled with advice on course construction, critique skills, and technical resources are available, along with assignment ideas.

MyArtStudio at www.mhhe.com/ArtStudio

Students have access to MyArtStudio, a rich and comprehensive Web site with interactions that allow students to study and experiment with various elements and principles of art and to view videos of art techniques and artists at work. Exercises on the Online Learning Center guide students to MyArtStudio at appropriate points in the text.

ACKNOWLEDGMENTS

Images are at the heart of this book. I would like to thank all the artists and designers who granted permission for use of their artworks and the galleries, museums, archives, and private donors who provided the high-resolution images. Photo researcher Deborah Anderson was remarkably tenacious in pursuing each permission and inventive in suggesting alternatives when necessary. Recommendations by developmental editor Cynthia Ward greatly improved the structure in Part Three and improved overall clarity; fine-tuning by copyeditor Mary Roybal improved consistency. At McGraw-Hill, I would like to thank production editor Carey Eisner, marketing manager Pamela Cooper, and, especially, sponsoring editor Betty Chen—truly the model of grace under pressure. Eric Zeiter did an exemplary job with the layout of this challenging book and William Stanton again created the beautiful covers. Thank you to Denise Wright and her team at Southern Editorial Publication Management, LLC, for all of their hard work with the supplements.

The artists I interviewed have been remarkably generous and supportive. In this edition, I would particularly like to thank Kendall Buster and Suzanne Stryk. At Florida State University, I would like to thank Dean Sally McRorie for all of her support and her relentless work in the service of the arts.

This book is dedicated to three of my colleagues. The comprehensive version is dedicated to Dr. Richard Siegesmund, from the University of Georgia, in recognition of his exemplary work with Integrative Teaching International, a nonprofit college teaching organization. The 2-D split edition is dedicated to Adam Kallish, who has served as both the catalyst for action and the designer for the same organization. The 3-D split edition is dedicated to Jeff Boshart, in recognition of over 25 years of service to F.A.T.E. (Foundations in Art: Theory and Education) and his repeated contributions as a reviewer for various editions of this book.

For the Fourth Edition:

The following reviewers provided valuable insights and suggestions:

Donald Barrie, *Seattle Central Community College*
Nicholas Bonner, *Northern Kentucky University*
Jeff Boshart, *Eastern Illinois University*
Keith Bryant, *University of North Carolina at Charlotte*
Marie Bukowski, *Louisiana Tech University*
Jessica Calderwood, *University of Wisconsin, Oshkosh*

Ben Cunningham, *Millersville University*
Eileen Doktorski, *Utah State University*
Scott Dooley, *Wittenberg University*
Frankie Flood, *University of Wisconsin, Milwaukee*
Paul Gebhardt, *University of Maine at Fort Kent*
David Griffin, *Eastern Illinois University*
Dan L. Henderson, *Art Institute of Atlanta*
Kevin W. Hughes, *Missouri State University*
Dawn Hunter, *University of South Carolina*
Imi Hwangbo, *University of Georgia*
Rosalie Rosso King, *Western Washington University*
Casey McGuire, *Metropolitan State College*
Erik Miller, *The Community College of Baltimore County*
Alan Moss, *Kent State University*
Gary Nemcosky, *Appalachian State University*
Jane Nodine, *University of South Carolina Upstate*
Laura Prange, *University of Southern Mississippi*
Ann Coddington Rast, *Eastern Illinois University*
Laura Ruby, *University of Hawaii*

For the Third Edition:

Scott Betz, *Winston-Salem State University*
Denise Burge, *University of Cincinnati*
Holly Earhart, *Full Sail Real World Education*
Sarah Gjertson, *University of Denver*
Marth McLeish, *Indiana State University*
Julia Morrisroe, *University of Florida—Gainesville*
John Nettleton, *Ontario College of Art & Design*
Gayle Pendergrass, *Arkansas State University*
Renee Sandell, *George Mason University*
Kyle Trowbridge, *University of Miami*
Jeremy Waltman, *Florida State University*
Peter Winant, *George Mason University*

For the Second Edition:

Kathleen Arkles, *College for Creative Studies*
Donald Barrie, *Seattle Central Community College*
Julie Baugnet, *St. Cloud State University*
Donna Beckis, *Fitchburg State College*
Nancy Blum-Cumming, *University of Wisconsin—Stout*
Debra K. D. Bonnello, *Lansing Community College*
Jeff Boshart, *Eastern Illinois University*

Jacquelin Boulanger, *New College of Florida*

Stephanie Bowman, *Pittsburgh State University*

Peter Brown, *Ringling School of Art*

John Carlander, *Westmont College*

Steven Cost, *Amarillo College*

Michael Croft, *University of Arizona*

Cat Crotchett, *Western Michigan University*

Claire Darley, *Art Academy of Cincinnati*

Anita M. DeAngelis, *East Tennessee State University*

Beverly Dennis, *Jones County Junior College*

Tracy Doreen Dietzel, *Edgewood College*

Jim Doud, *American University*

Clyde L. Edwards, *Valdosta State University*

James Elniski, *School of Art Institute at Chicago*

Jane Fasse, *Edgewood College*

John Ford, *Labette Community College*

Corky Goss, *Cazenovia College*

Arlene Grossman, *Art Institute of Boston at Lesley University*

Danielle Harmon, *West Texas A&M University*

Christopher Hocking, *University of Georgia*

Carol Hodson, *Webster University*

Sara M. Hong, *University of Arizona*

Lorie Jesperson, *Lake Michigan College*

C. Ann Kittredge, *University of Maine—Presque Isle*

Deborah Krupenia, *Endicott College*

Michelle La Perriere, *Maryland Institute College of Art*

In Shile Lee, *Tompkins Cortland Community College*

Richard F. Martin, *New York Institute of Technology*

Christine McCullough, *Youngstown State University*

Julie McWilliams, *Sussex County College*

Nancy Morrow, *Kansas State University*

Byron Myrich, *Jones Junior College*

Kelly Nelson, *Longwood University*

Soon Ee Ngoh, *Mississippi State University*

Lara Nguyen, *California State University, Long Beach*

Grace O'Brien, *Purdue University*

Mark O'Grady, *Pratt Institute*

Sally Packard, *University of North Texas*

William Potter, *Herron School of Art–IUPUI*

Patsy C. Rainey, *University of Mississippi*

Gerson M. Rapaport, *New York Institute of Technology*

Cherri Rittenhouse, *Rock Valley College*

Gil Rocha, *Richland Community College*

William B. Rowe, *Ohio Northern University*

Kim Schrag, *Tompkins Courtland Community College*

Jean Sharer, *Front Range Community College*

Todd Slaughter, *Ohio State University*

Robert Smart, *Lawrence University*

Karen Spears, *Eastern Kentucky University*

Mindy Spritz, *The Art Institute of Atlanta*

Teresa Stoll, *Lake City Community College*

Katherine Stranse, *University of Arkansas—Little Rock*

Rob Tarbell, *Limestone College*

William Travis, *Rowan University*

Linda Vanderkolk, *Purdue University*

Carolynne Whitefeather, *Utica College*

Reid Wood, *Lorain County Community College*

Marilyn H. Wounded Head, *Mesa State College*

Alice Zinnes, *NYC College of Technology, CUNY*

For the First Edition:

Scott Betz, *Weber State University*

Jeff Boshart, *Eastern Illinois University*

Peter Brown, *Ringling School of Art and Design*

Brian Cantley, *California State University, Fullerton*

Laurie Beth Clark, *University of Wisconsin, Madison*

Michael Croft, *University of Arizona*

John Fillwalk, *Ball State University*

David Fobes, *San Diego State University*

Albert Grivetti, *Clarke College*

Imi Hwangbo, *University of Louisville*

Michelle Illuminato, *Bowling Green State University*

Ann Baddeley Keister, *Grand Valley State University*

Margaret Keller, *St. Louis Community College*

Dan Lowery, *Southwestern Illinois College*

Karen Mahaffy, *University of Texas at San Antonio*

Richard Moses, *University of Illinois*

Gary Nemcosky, *Appalachian State University*

Helen Maria Nugent, *Art Institute of Chicago*

Rick Paul, *Purdue University*

Ron Saito, *California State University, Northridge*

Karen Schory, *Johnson County Community College*

Susan Slavick, *Carnegie Mellon University*

Paul Wittenbraker, *Grand Valley State University*

William Zack, *Ball State University*

part one

xi

part three

Author Mary Stewart with *Labyrinth* book.

Mary Stewart is currently Director of Art Foundations at Florida State University. She has received two grants from the Pennsylvania Council on the Arts and has participated in over 95 exhibitions, nationally and internationally.

From 1994 to 2004, Stewart worked with Greek philosophy as a primary source for her images. In Plato's famous dialogues, Socrates led his students through a series of conversations on the nature of beauty and the role of memory in developing knowledge. For Socrates, life was a process of self-discovery, a search for essential truths remembered from a pre-birth state. Unlike Aristotle, who argued that knowledge was derived from experience, Socrates suggested that knowledge was inherent and universal. *Labyrinth,* shown in the top photo, is composed of 11 etchings based on cave paintings, fragments of early writing, and Greek sculpture. When collapsed, the book presents a cohesive composition; when opened, the images become fragmented, creating a sense of mystery.

In her current work, Stewart constructs invented landscapes from her digital photographs. Based on multiple north Florida sites, *Stormfury #4* presents a world that is both treacherous and awe-inspiring. Line, shapes, textures, and colors expand, compress, and collide within an apocalyptic panorama.

Mary Stewart, *Stormfury #4,* 2008. Digital photocopy with prismacolor and acrylics, 90 × 44 in. (228.6 × 111.76 cm).

i.1 **Bill Viola,** *Slowly Turning Narrative,* **1992.** Bill Viola's *Slowly Turning Narrative* consists of a large, rotating screen onto which moving images are projected. One side of the screen is a mirror, which reflects distorted images back into the room.

BEGINNER'S MIND, OPEN MIND

You are ready to embark on a marvelous journey. New technologies and exhibition venues offer dazzling new ways to produce, perform, and publicize visual ideas. Contemporary art has expanded to include performances, earthworks, and installations (i.1). Metalsmiths now use everything from plastics to precious metals to create inventive small-scale sculptures (i.2). Graphic designers develop many forms of visual communication, from shopping bags and exhibitions (i.3) to Web sites, logos, and brochures. Film and video are becoming increasingly integrated with the Internet, which promises to extend visual communication even further (i.4). The opportunities for exploration are endless (i.5). It is a great time to be studying art and design!

i.2 **Keith E. LoBue,** *Where Music Dwells,* **1993.** A broken pocket watch can become an evocative artwork when images and words are added.

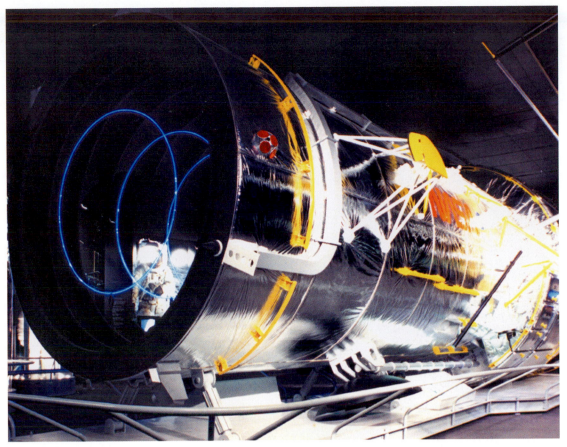

i.3 Bill Cannan & Co., NASA's Participating Exhibit at the 1989 Paris Air Show. To suggest the mystery of space travel and highlight individual displays, this NASA exhibition used dramatic pools of light within a mysterious dark setting.

i.4 Hans-Jürgen Syberberg, *Parsifal,* 1982. Syberberg combined live actors with oversized projections of dreamlike landscapes in his filmic interpretation of Richard Wagner's opera.

i.5 Xu Bing, *A Book from the Sky*, 1987–91. Hong Kong Museum of Art. Mixed mediums.

A journey of a thousand miles begins with one step. As a beginner, your first steps are especially important. Free of the preconceptions or habitual patterns that can paralyze more advanced students, beginners enter the learning experience with an open mind and an intense desire to explore new ideas. With no reputation to defend, they can more easily make the mistakes that are so essential to learning. Having taught students at all levels, I have found that beginners of any age are the most courageous by far. The open, unencumbered "beginner's mind" is wonderfully receptive and resilient. As a result, remarkable changes can occur during your first year.

DEFINING DESIGN

As a verb, *design* can be defined four ways:

- To plan, delineate, or define, as in designing a building

- To create a deliberate sequence of images or events, as in developing a film storyboard (i.6)

- To create a functional object, as in product design (i.7)

- To organize disparate parts into a coherent whole, as in composing a brochure

i.6 Harold Michelson, Storyboard for Alfred Hitchcock's *The Birds.* Storyboards are used to plan the sequence of events and compose the specific shots in a film. Alfred Hitchcock, who began his career as an artist, preplanned his films with exacting care.

i.7 Designworks/USA, Home Pro Garden Tool Line. These five gardening tools are all based on the same basic combination of handle, blades, and simple pivot. Variations in proportion determine their use.

As a noun, *design* can be defined as

- A plan or pattern, such as the layout for a garden (i.8)
- An arrangement of lines, shapes, colors, and textures into an artistic whole, as in the composition of a painting or sculpture (i.9)

Design is deliberate. Rather than hope for the best and accept the result, artists and designers explore a wide range of solutions to every problem, then choose the most promising option for further development. Even when chance is used to generate ideas, choices are often made before the results are shown. Design creates a bridge between artistic intention and compositional conclusion. As painter Joseph Albers noted, "To design is to plan and to organize, to order, to relate and to control."

Two-dimensional compositions are constructed from lines, shapes, textures, values, and colors that have been arranged to create a unified whole (i.10). Lines, planes, volumes, masses, and space are the basic components of a three-dimensional composition (i.11). Time design (including video, photography, performance, kinetic sculpture, and the book arts) is based on the juxtaposition of images and events (i.12). A great idea never saved a bad painting. Art and design are visual forms of communication: without careful composition, a great idea may be lost.

Developing a wide range of solutions to every problem is the quickest way to master composition. Small, quick studies are often used to explore the possibilities. By translating a mental image into a rough sketch, you can immediately see whether the idea has potential. Furthermore, the best way to have a good idea is to have a lot of ideas. By selecting the best rough composition from 20 sketches, you will have a better beginning point for your final design.

In the pages that follow, the basic elements, principles, and implications of design are explored in depth. Over 650 images supply visual examples from many cultures and in all areas of art and design. Fifteen interviews with living artists provide insight into the creative process.

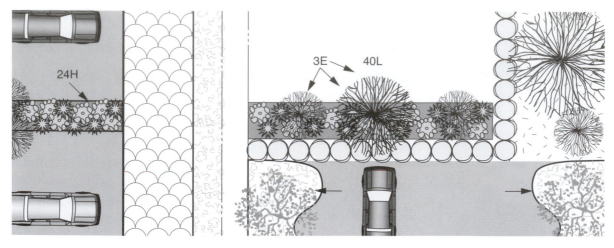

i.8 Garden Design. An extensive layout is generally used for planning a garden. Matching the plants to the soil conditions, setting, climate, and overall intent saves money and improves results. In this case, the design is not an artwork in itself but, rather, a plan of action.

i.9 Claude Monet, *Waterlily Pond (Le Bassin des Nymphéas),* **1904.** Impressionist Claude Monet moved to the village of Giverny in 1883 and built an extensive water garden. The waterlilies he grew there inspired his last major series of paintings. Monet combined lines, shapes, textures, and colors to create a compelling illusion of a shimmering space.

i.10 Sam Francis, *Flash Point,* 1975. Surrounded by explosive energy, the white square in the center of this painting provides a unifying focal point.

Reading this book, however, is just the first step. True understanding comes through your own efforts, combined with the direction your teachers can provide. Remember that basic drawing and design courses provide the foundation on which all subsequent courses are built. You are a college beginner only once in your entire life: this is not a rehearsal. By using your time well, you really *can* get the rocket off the launching pad.

i.11 Alice Aycock, *Tree of Life Fantasy: Synopsis of the Book of Questions Concerning the World Order and/or the Order of Worlds,* **1990–92.** Inspired by the double-helix structure of DNA and by medieval illustrations representing the entrance to paradise as a spinning hole in the sky, Aycock has combined a linear structure with a series of circular planes and a lot of open space. The resulting sculpture is as open and playful as a roller coaster.

i.12 Paul Jenkins and Jae Lee, from *Inhumans*: "First Contact," March 1999. Comic books, like films, rely on the development of characters, the use of "camera" angles, and the organization of multiple images.

Wassily Kandinsky, *Several Circles,* **1926.** Oil on canvas, 55¼ × 55⅝ in. (140.3 × 140.7 cm).

Two-Dimensional Design

On a personal level, making art heightens our attention, engages our emotions, and provides a sense of accomplishment. Creating objects and images is engrossing and exhilarating. These personal rewards make art one of the most popular hobbies.

A career in art and design demands more from us. As art and design professionals, we must translate our personal insights into public communication. The ideas and emotions a professional wishes to express must engage an audience, whether the encounter occurs in the silence of a museum or in the chaos of a city street.

This ability to communicate visually is developed through years of study plus relentless practice. Artists and designers must develop their visual awareness, create new concepts, and master various techniques. They spend hours in the studio, refining ideas and inventing alternative solutions to each visual problem. Creating the most powerful image is their compelling goal.

The elements and principles of design are the building blocks from which images are made and ideas are expressed. Line, shape, texture, and value are presented in Chapter One. Chapter Two is devoted to the characteristics and compositional impact of color. Chapter Three introduces a wide range of basic organizational strategies, known as the principles of design. These basic principles are expanded in Chapter Four, which is devoted to the illusion of space and the illusion of motion.

Part One

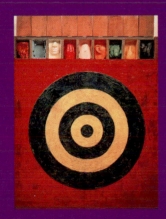

Basic Elements

Line, shape, texture, value, and color are the building blocks from which two-dimensional designs are made. Just as oxygen and hydrogen are powerful both individually and when combined as H_2O, so these visual **elements** operate both independently and in combination. In this chapter, we will explore the unique characteristics of the four most basic elements and analyze their uses in art and design. Color, the most complex element, will be discussed in Chapter Two.

LINE

Defining Line

Line is one of the simplest and most versatile elements of design. Line may be defined as

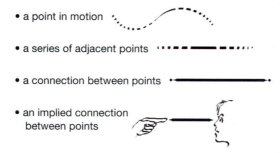

- a point in motion
- a series of adjacent points
- a connection between points
- an implied connection between points

1.1 Line definitions.

The inherent dynamism of line is embodied in the first definition. The remaining three definitions emphasize the connective power of line. Lighter and more fluid than any of the other visual elements, line can add a special energy to a design. Simply by drawing a line, we can activate a space, define a shape, or create a compositional bridge.

Line Quality

Each line has its own distinctive quality. This quality is largely determined by the line's orientation, direction, and degree of continuity, and by the material used.

Orientation refers to the line's horizontal, vertical, or diagonal position. Diagonal lines and curving lines are generally the most dynamic (1.2A, 1.2D). Charged with energy, they suggest action and movement. Horizontal lines are typically the most stable, or static (1.2B). Vertical lines imply *potential* change. When verticals adhere to the edge of the design, they become tethered and thus

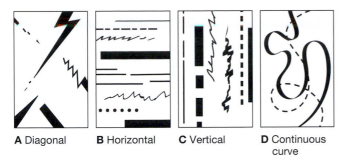

A Diagonal   **B** Horizontal   **C** Vertical   **D** Continuous curve

1.2A–D Line orientation and continuity.

lose mobility. Free-floating verticals, on the other hand, seem ready to topple at any moment (1.2C).

Direction refers to the implied movement of a line. Line weight can be used to accentuate direction. Generally, a swelling line suggests forward or outward movement, while a shrinking line suggests inward movement. Notice how the top and bottom diagonal lines in figure 1.2A seem to push forward as they become thicker.

Continuity, or linear flow, can enhance direction. As shown in figure 1.2D, a continuous line tends to generate a stronger sense of direction than a broken or jagged line.

Each **medium,** or material, can be used to produce a range of distinctive lines. Metallic graphite can be used to produce modulating lines of varying thickness. A felt pen produces a crisp, clean, emphatic line. Charcoal and chalk are soft and highly responsive to each change in pressure and direction. Brush and ink offers even wider variation in line width, continuity, and darkness. By experimenting with the range of marks each instrument can produce, we can use each medium more expressively.

A strong match between line quality and the expressive intent is essential. The network of agitated lines Giacometti used in figure 1.3 suggests anxiety, while the fluid lines in figure 1.4 express movement and playful energy. Barnett Newman used two very different lines in *Stations of the Cross: Lema Sabachthani, The First Station* (1.5). The solid black line is stabilized along the left edge of the painting. In contrast, the line on the right is surrounded by open space and agitated strokes of paint along its edges. In this painting, Newman used just two lines to express both spiritual strength and human fragility.

1.3 Alberto Giacometti, *Annette*, 1954. Pencil on paper, 16⅜ × 11¾ in. (41.59 × 29.85 cm).

1.4 Frank Thomas and Ollie Johnston, original sketch of Walt Disney Mickey Mouse Cartoon, 1938. © Disney Enterprises, Inc.

1.5 Barnett Newman, *Stations of the Cross: Lema Sabachthani, The First Station,* **1958.** Magna on canvas, 6 ft 5⅞ in. × 5 ft ½ in. (1.98 × 1.54 cm).

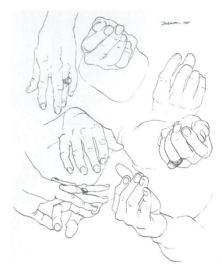

1.6 Eleanor Dickinson, *Study of Hands,* **1964.** Pen and ink, 13⅛ × 10⅛ in. (34 × 26 cm).

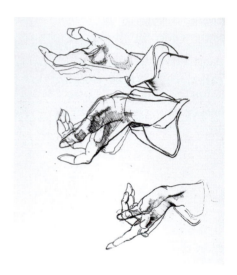

1.7 Rico Lebrun, *Hand,* **1964.** Pen and ink.

1.8 Rembrandt van Rijn, *Two Women Helping a Child to Walk,* c. 1635–37. Red chalk on paper.

Actual Lines

Actual lines can describe complex forms simply and eloquently. In figure 1.6, Eleanor Dickinson presents different views of hands using **contour lines.** Contour lines define the edges of a form and suggest three-dimensionality. In this study, the complex anatomy was distilled down to a few simple lines. Similarly, Rico Lebrun's **gesture drawing** of a hand (1.7) captures essential action rather than describing every anatomical detail. We focus on what the hand is *doing* rather than on what the hand *is.* As shown in figure 1.8, Rembrandt often used economical lines to describe the spheres and cylindrical volumes from which figures are made. Because it communicates information using

1.10 Wu Guanzhong, *Pine Spirit*, 1984. Chinese ink, color on paper, 2 ft 3⅝ in. × 5 ft 3½ in. (70 × 140 cm).

1.9 Attributed to Tawaraya Sôtatsu, calligraphy by Hon'ami Koetsu, *Flying Cranes and Poetry*, Edo period (1615–1868). Ink on gray-blue paper, gold flecked, 7⅝ × 6⅜ in. (19 × 16 cm).

1.11 Jerome Witkin, *Kill-Joy: To the Passion of Käthe Kollwitz* (Kreischerville Wall) detail, 1975–76. Oil on canvas, 74 × 79 in.

basic volumes, this type of line drawing is often called a **volume summary.**

Calligraphic lines can add even more energy to a drawing or a design. The word *calligraphy* is derived from two Greek words: *kalus*, meaning "beautiful," and *graphein*, meaning "to write." Like handwriting, the calligraphic line is both personal and highly expressive. In figure 1.9, words and images are combined in a celebration of flight. Painter Tawaraya Sôtatsu and calligrapher Hon'ami Koetsu used variations in line weight and continuity to suggest the graceful motion of birds. This exploration of movement is pushed even further in *Pine Spirit*, by Wu Guanzhong (1.10). Fluid ink lines record the movement of the artist's hand while simultaneously creating an abstract landscape. There is a wonderful economy in each of these drawings. As in poetry, a rich story is told using minimal means.

Organizational lines are often used to create the loose linear "skeleton" on which a composition can be built. Ideas can be developed quickly through line, and compositional changes can be made easily. As shown in the Giacometti drawing in figure 1.3, these skeletal drawings have great energy and may be presented as artworks in themselves. In other cases, organizational lines provide the framework for elaborate compositions. In Jerome Witkin's *Kill Joy: To the Passion of Käthe Kollwitz* (1.11), the linear sidewalk, curb, street, and car divide the image into horizontal bands of explosive energy. The gray wall extending from the top to the center, the strip of gray at the far right, and the two mannequins in the foreground create strong vertical divisions. Diagonal streaks of white and a gray arrow on the street pull us toward the woman in red positioned near the center of the painting, while the blue and yellow shapes in the upper-right corner send us ricocheting back out again. German artist and antiwar activist Käthe Kollwitz (1867–1945) fought against injustice and violence through her artwork: see figures 2.61, 2.62, and 2.63 on pages 61 and 62. Like Kollwitz, the woman in red provides solace to the wounded in a world that is filled with indifference and shattered glass.

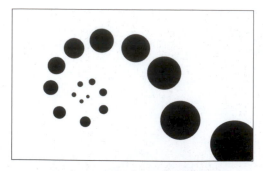

1.12 A series of dots can create an implied line.

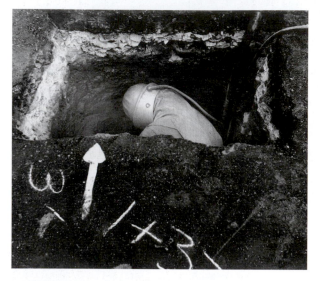

1.13 Minor White, *Sandblaster,* **San Francisco, 1949.** Gelatin silver print, 10⁷⁄₁₆ × 11⁷⁄₁₆ in. (26.51 × 29.05 cm).

A

B

1.14A and B Caravaggio, *The Deposition,* **1604.** Oil on canvas, 9 ft 10⅛ in. × 6 ft 7⅞ in. (3 × 2.03 m).

Implied Lines

Lines can play a major role in a design even when they are implied rather than actually being drawn. Because **implied lines** simply *suggest* connections, the viewer becomes actively involved in compositions that use this type of line.

Fortunately, we have a natural inclination to seek visual unity. Given enough clues, we will connect separate visual parts by filling in the missing pieces. The visual clues may be quite obvious. For example, we can easily link the circles in figure 1.12 to create a linear spiral. In other cases, the clues are subtle. In Minor White's *Sandblaster* (1.13), the white arrow implies a connection between the numbers in the foreground and the worker's helmet.

This inclination to connect fragmentary information is called **closure.** "Lost and found" contours require an elegant form of closure. In a "lost and found" composition, the edges of some shapes are clearly defined, while other shapes appear to merge with the background. When presented with such an image, the viewer must create a mental bridge between the resulting islands of information.

Caravaggio's *The Deposition* (1.14A) uses closure extensively. A contour drawing of this image has many gaps, as details are lost in the shadows (1.14B). Used skillfully, this loss of definition becomes a strength rather than a weakness. Connections made through closure can stimulate the viewer's imagination and encourage a more personal interpretation.

Linear Networks

Multiple lines can add detail to a design and create a convincing illusion of space. **Hatching** produces a range of grays through straight parallel lines. An even wider range of grays can be produced through **cross-hatching,** in which

1.15 Jacques Villon, *Baudelaire*, c. 1918. Etching, printed in black, plate 16⁵⁄₁₆ × 11 in. (41.4 × 28 cm).

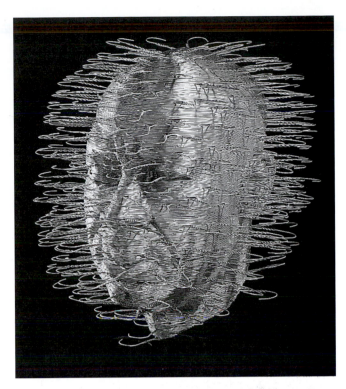

1.16 David Mach, *Eckow*, 1997. Coathangers, 2 ft 2¼ in. × 1 ft 11½ in. × 2 ft 5½ in. (67 × 60 × 75 cm).

multiple lines are placed at various angles to one another. Jacques Villon used both hatching and cross-hatching in his portrait of poet Charles Baudelaire (1.15). The head is divided into a series of faceted planes. Hatching defines each shift in the surface of the head, while cross-hatching creates the shadows.

Cross-contours can create an even more powerful illusion of three-dimensionality. Often created using curving parallel lines, cross-contours "map" surface variations across shapes or objects. In figure 1.16, David Mach created a cross-contour sculpture by bending coat hangers into the shape of a human head. In two-dimensional design, we can use drawn lines to produce a similar effect.

Hatching, cross-hatching, and cross-contour are often combined. In *Head of a Satyr* (1.17), Michelangelo used all of these techniques to visually carve out the curves and planes of the head.

1.17 Michelangelo, *Head of a Satyr*, c. 1620–30. Pen and ink over chalk, 10⁵⁄₈ × 7⁷⁄₈ in. (27 × 20 cm).

1.18 Jackson Pollock, *White Light,* **1954.** Oil, enamel, aluminum paint on canvas, 48¼ × 38¼ in. (122.4 × 96.9 cm).

Linear networks play an equally important role in abstract and nonobjective art. Jackson Pollock dripped and spattered house paint to produce *White Light*, shown in figure 1.18. Seeking universal meaning rather than conventional representation, Pollock spontaneously generated many layers of lines on a large piece of canvas. He then trimmed the canvas, discarding the weaker sections of the design. The remaining lines seem to flow in and out of the painting. Clusters of silvery enamel form swirling, textural masses that are punctuated by explosions of red and yellow.

1.19 PATH Station Maps, Louis Nelson Associates, Inc., NY. Graphic designer: Jennifer Stoller.

Using Line

Line can be used to define, enclose, connect, or dissect. Line serves all of these purposes in a New York City subway map (1.19). A curved line has been combined with an angular line to define the wheelchair logo. Another line encloses this logo within a square, emphasizing its importance. Diagonal lines connect the subway entrance to the elevators, while vertical lines dissect the drawing to highlight the location of the elevators. Using this map, a person in a wheelchair can navigate through a busy station and catch the right train.

In a sense, the first line we draw is actually the *fifth* line in a rectangular composition. In his *Self-Portrait* (1.20), Joel Peter Johnson used drawn lines to echo the four pre-existing edges of the composition. His head breaks out of this linear boundary. As a result, the portrait appears to extend beyond the painting's edge and into the world of the viewer.

Lines can serve many purposes at once. In an advertisement for the American Institute of Graphic Arts (1.21), vertical dotted lines at the upper left and lower right highlight the speakers' schedule. A horizontal line creates a connection between the *D* and *B* in the "design to business" logo and separates the top and bottom of the overall layout. Even the columns of text can be read as vertical and horizontal lines.

1.20 Joel Peter Johnson, *Self-Portrait.* Oil on board, 9 × 8 in. (22.86 × 20.32 cm).

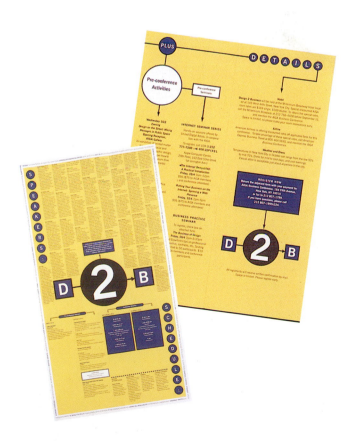

1.21 Brochure from an American Institute of Graphic Arts Conference "Design 2 Business, October 5–6 '96 NYC." Design Firm: Pentagram, NY.

When orientation, direction, continuity, and medium are effectively employed, line can be used to create compositions that are both sophisticated and thoughtful.

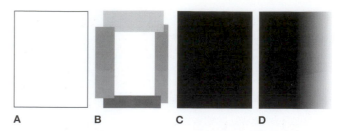

1.22A–D Any form of enclosure can create a shape.

Key Questions
LINE

- What is the dominant orientation of the lines in your design—diagonal, vertical, or horizontal? What is the expressive effect?
- What happens when lines are repeated or when lines intersect?
- How would the composition change if one or more lines were removed?
- Consider using line to direct attention to areas of compositional importance.

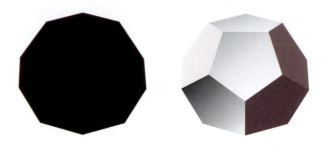

1.23 Variations in lighting can transform a shape into an illusory volume.

SHAPE

Defining Shape

A **shape** is a flat, enclosed area (1.22A–D). Shapes can be created by

- Enclosing an area within a continuous line
- Surrounding an area by other shapes
- Filling an area with solid color or texture
- Filling an area with broken color or texture

A three-dimensional enclosure is called a **volume.** Thus, a square is a shape, while a cube is a volume. **Gradation,** or **shading,** can be used to make a two-dimensional shape appear three-dimensional, or volumetric. For example, in figure 1.23, a flat, circular shape becomes a faceted polyhedron when a series of gray tones is added.

Both flat and gradated shapes can be used to create an arresting image. In Aaron Douglas's *Aspects of Negro Life: From Slavery Through Reconstruction* (1.24), flat silhouettes combined with transparent targets create an energetic panorama. We can

1.24 Aaron Douglas, *Aspects of Negro Life: From Slavery Through Reconstruction*, **1934.** Oil on canvas, 5 ft × 11 ft 7 in. (1.52 × 3.5 m).

1.25 Diego M. Rivera, *Detroit Industry, North Wall,* **1932–33.** Fresco, 17 ft 8½ in. × 45 ft (5.4 × 13.7 m).

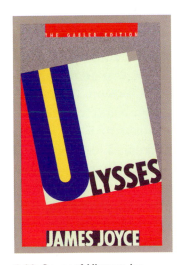

1.26 Cover of *Ulysses*, by James Joyce, 1986. Designer: Carin Goldberg.

1.27 Cover image from *The Penguin Pool Murder*, a Hildegarde Withers Mystery, by Stuart Palmer. Art Director & Designer: Krystyna Skalski; Illustrator: John Jinks.

1.28 Gustav Klimt, *Salomé*, 1909. Oil on canvas, 70⅛ × 18⅛ in. (178 × 46 cm).

almost hear the speaker in the center and feel the movement of the crowd. In Rivera's *Detroit Industry* (1.25), a combination of size variation and shading suggests volume and increases the illusion of space. One-point perspective (which will be discussed at length in Chapter Four) has been used to increase visual depth even further.

Graphic designers are equally aware of the expressive power of both flat and gradated shapes. In a cover for *Ulysses* (1.26), Carin Goldberg used crisp, simple shapes to create a design that evokes the modernism of Joyce's novel. Primary colors, combined with the slanted title block, immediately attract attention. Krystyna Skalski and John Jinks used a very different approach for their cover for a mystery novel (1.27). Here, the graduated, figurative shapes and swirling green bands suggest a complex and twisted plot.

Gustav Klimt combined flat and volumetric shapes to create *Salomé* (1.28). In this horrific tale from the biblical New Testament, John the Baptist has been imprisoned for his criticism of the royal family. Salomé, the king's niece, performs a stunning dance and the delighted king grants her a single wish. In revenge, Salomé asks for John's head. The tall, vertical shape of the painting is similar to the size and shape of a standing viewer. Flat patterns and color surround the volumetric figures, while two curving lines add a sinuous energy to the center of the design.

Types of Shape

The size and shape of a soccer field are very different from the size and shape of a tennis court. In each case, the playing area defines the game to be played. It is impossible to play soccer on a tennis court or to play tennis on a soccer field.

Similarly, the outer edge of a two-dimensional design provides the playing field for our compositional games. The long, horizontal rectangles used by Douglas and Rivera create an expansive panorama, while the vertical rectangle used for Salomé compresses the sordid drama into a

1.29A–D Various figure/ground relationships. When centered, the figure tends to be static. As it moves to the bottom left, it becomes more dynamic, and becomes even more so when it is diagonally positioned near the top or bottom edge.

narrow, claustrophobic column. Thus, creating a dialogue between compositional shapes and the surrounding format is our first concern.

Figure and Ground, Positive and Negative

As shown in figure 1.29A, a shape that is distinguished from the background is called a **positive shape,** or **figure.** The surrounding is called the **negative shape,** or **ground.** Depending on its location relative to the ground, the figure can become dynamic or static, leaden or buoyant (1.29B–D).

In traditional paintings such as Caravaggio's *The Deposition,* the entire composition is treated like a window into an imaginary world. To increase this illusion, the canvas texture is sanded down before the paint is applied, and heavy brushstrokes are kept at a minimum. We are invited to see *into* the painting, rather than focusing on its surface.

When a shaped format is used, we become more aware of the artwork's physicality. The 9-foot-tall teacup in Elizabeth Murray's *Just in Time* (1.30) is monumental in size and loaded with implication. The painted shapes connect directly to the shaped edge, emphasizing the crack running down the center of the composition. This is no ordinary teacup. For Murray, this crack in everyday reality invites us to enter an alternative world.

When the figure and ground are equally well designed, every square inch of the composition becomes supercharged. In Bill Brandt's photograph (1.31), the brightly lit arm, face, and breast dramatically divide the black ground, creating three strong, triangular shapes. These triangles energize the design and heighten our awareness of the compositional edge.

1.30 Elizabeth Murray, *Just in Time,* **1981.** Oil on canvas in two sections, 106 × 97 in. (269.24 × 246.38 cm).

1.31 Bill Brandt, *Nude,* 1952. Gelatin silver print.

An ambiguous relationship between figure and ground can add surprising energy and power to a design. In Paul Cézanne's *Rocks Near the Caves above the Chateau Noir* (1.32), the trees and cliffs begin to break apart, creating a shifting pattern of planes and spaces. Completed just one year before Einstein published his special theory of relativity, this painting served as a springboard into a new art movement known as Cubism.

Figure/ground reversal pushes this effect even further. **Figure/ground reversal** occurs when first the positive then the negative shapes command our attention. As shown in a fragment from *Metamorphosis II* (1.33), M. C. Escher was a master of figure/ground reversal. The organic shapes on the left become an interlocking mass of black and white lizards. The lizards then evolve into a network of hexagons. Combined with the figure/ground reversal, this type of metamorphosis animates the entire 13-foot-long composition.

Figure/ground reversal requires a carefully balanced dialogue between opposing forces. Escher generally achieved this balance by using light and dark shapes of similar size. In figure 1.34, Sam Francis achieved a similar balance

1.32 Paul Cézanne, *Rocks Near the Caves above the Chateau Noir,* 1904. Oil on canvas, 21.3 × 25.6 in. (54 × 65 cm).

1.33 M. C. Escher, part of *Metamorphosis II,* 1939–40. Woodcut in black, green, and brown, printed from 20 blocks on three combined sheets, 7½ × 153⅜ in. (19 × 390 cm).

1.34 Sam Francis, *Flash Point*, 1975. Acrylic on paper, 32¼ × 22⅞ in. (82 × 59 cm).

between a very small white square and a much larger red rectangle. The crisp boundary and central location strengthen the square. Despite its small size, it holds its own against the larger mass of swirling red paint.

Graphic designers often use figure/ground reversal to create multiple interpretations from minimal shapes. In figure 1.35, David McNutt used a single white shape on a black ground to create the head of a master and a servant within the outline of Africa. Used to advertise a South African play, the poster immediately communicates a dramatic human relationship within a specific cultural context.

Rectilinear and Curvilinear Shapes

Rectilinear shapes are composed from straight lines and angular corners. **Curvilinear shapes** are dominated by curves and flowing edges. Simple rectilinear shapes, such as squares and rectangles, are generally cooperative. When placed within a rectangular format, they easily connect to other shapes and can run parallel to the compositional edge (1.36A). Curvilinear shapes, especially circles, are generally less cooperative. They retain their individuality even when they are partially concealed by other shapes (1.36B). As a result, curvilinear shapes can be used as targets that emphasize areas of special importance in a design.

Aubrey Beardsley (1.37) combined rectilinear and curvilinear shapes to create another interpretation of the Salomé story, described on pages 11–12.

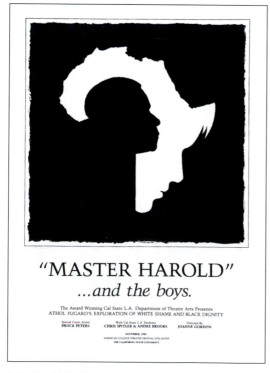

1.35 David McNutt, *"Master Harold" . . . and the Boys*, 1985. Poster.

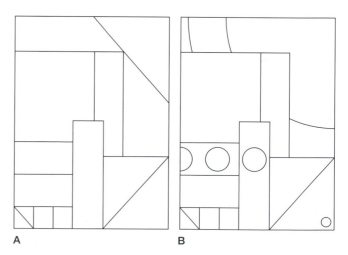

A   B

1.36A and B **Rectilinear and curvilinear shapes.** Rectilinear shapes can easily be fit together to create a unified design. Curvilinear shapes tend to be more individualistic.

players is surrounded by layered rectangles to the right, left, and bottom. A solid line extends from the catcher to the top edge. Vigorous brushstrokes add power to the painting. Occupying only a small fraction of the composition and surrounded by vigorously painted shapes, the circle *still* dominates the design: we *have* to keep our eyes on the ball!

Geometric and Organic Shapes

Geometric shapes are distinguished by their crisp, precise edges and mathematically consistent curves. They dominate the technological world of architecture and industry, and they appear in nature as crystalline structures and growth patterns. In Valerie Jaudon's *Tallahatchee* (1.39), geometric shapes provide a clarity, harmony, and universality comparable to a musical composition. **Organic shapes** are more commonly found in the natural world of plants and animals, sea and sky. As shown in Helen Frankenthaler's *Interior Landscape* (1.40), organic shapes can add unpredictable energy, even when the composition as a whole is based on rectangular shapes.

1.37 Aubrey Beardsley, *Salomé with the Head of John the Baptist*, 1894. Line block print, 11 × 6 in. (27.9 × 15.2 cm).

Using an internal boundary line, he emphasized the composition's rectangular shape. Within this boundary, curving black and white shapes create a series of complex visual relationships. A bubble pattern dominates the upper-left corner. In the upper-right corner, Salomé clutches Saint John's head. Extending from the head down to the flower, a white line follows the transformation of the dead saint's blood into a living plant. This line creates a conceptual and compositional connection between the top and bottom edges.

A very different combination of rectilinear and curvilinear shapes activates Robert Rauschenberg's *Brace* (1.38). The central image of three baseball

1.38 Robert Rauschenberg, *Brace*, 1962. Oil and silkscreen on canvas, 60 × 60 in. (152.4 × 152.4 cm).

1.39 Valerie Jaudon, *Tallahatchee*, 1984. Oil and gold leaf on canvas, 6 ft 8 in. × 8 ft (2 × 2.4 m).

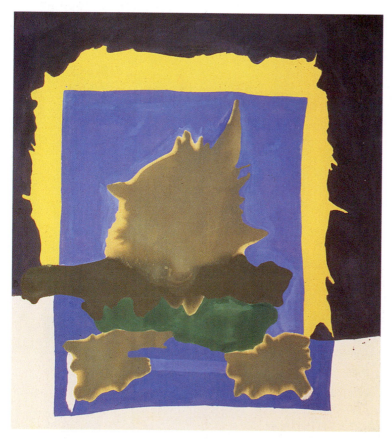

1.40 Helen Frankenthaler, *Interior Landscape*, 1964. Acrylic on canvas, 8 ft 8⅞ in. × 7 ft 8⅝ in. (266 × 235 cm).

Degrees of Representation

Nonobjective or **nonrepresentational shapes,** such as circles, rectangles, and squares, are **pure forms.** Pure forms are shapes created without direct reference to reality. Artists often use pure form to embody elusive emotions or express universal meaning. For example, in *Several Circles* (1.41), Wassily Kandinsky sought to express his complex spiritual feelings. For him, the simple circular shapes were as poignant and expressive as music.

Representational shapes are derived from specific subject matter and strongly based on direct observation. Most photographs are representational and highly descriptive. For example, in Ansel Adams's *Monolith, The Face of Half Dome, Yosemite Valley* (1.42), each variation in the cliff's surface is clearly defined.

Between these two extremes, **abstract shapes** are derived from visual reality but are distilled or transformed, reducing their resemblance to the original source. In *Seventh Sister* (1.43), Robert Moskowitz deleted surface details from the rocky mountain. His abstracted cliff is a general representation of a vertical surface rather than a descriptive painting of a specific cliff.

Reference to reality is a traditional way to increase meaning in an artwork. Drawing on their experience in the physical world, viewers can connect to the illusion of reality presented in the painting. In a nonobjective image, lines, shapes, textures, and colors must generate all of the meaning. Because there is no explicit subject matter, some viewers find it more difficult to understand nonobjective images.

By contrast, abstract images can combine the power of association with the power of pure form. Charles Demuth's *. . . And the Home of the Brave* (1.44) demonstrates this. A factory has been turned into a series of lines and geometric shapes. Variations on red, white, and blue add a symbolic connection to the American flag. Painted during a period of nationwide unemployment, the factory is dark and

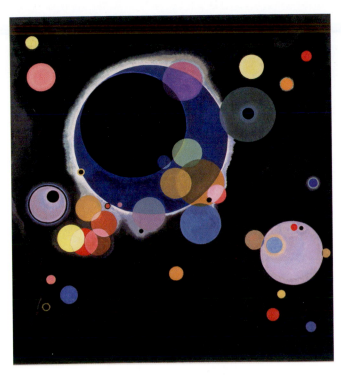

1.41 Wassily Kandinsky, *Several Circles,* 1926. Oil on canvas, 55¼ × 55⅜ in. (140.3 × 140.7 cm).

1.42 Ansel Adams, *Monolith, The Face of Half Dome, Yosemite Valley,* 1927. Photograph.

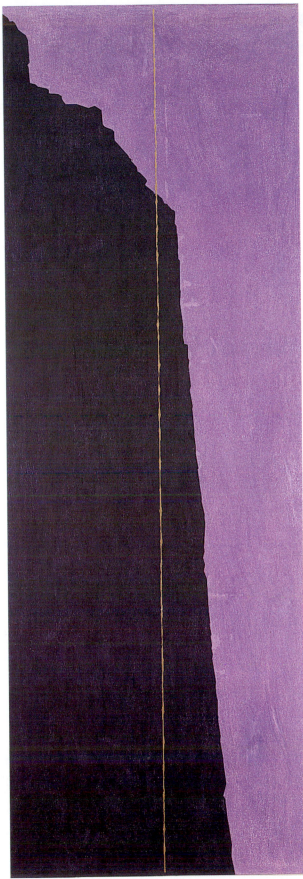

1.43 Robert Moskowitz, *Seventh Sister,* 1982. Oil on canvas, 108 × 39 in. (274.3 × 99 cm).

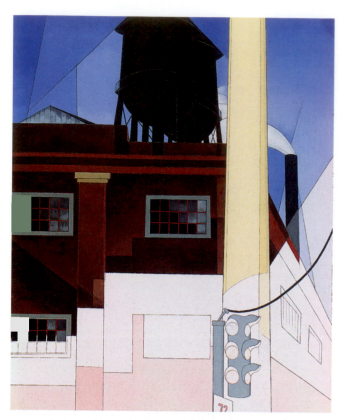

1.44 Charles Demuth, . . . *And the Home of the Brave*, 1931. Oil on composition board, 29½ × 23⅝ in. (74.8 × 59.7 cm).

1.45 William Klein, *Gun 1, New York*, 1955. Gelatin silver print, 15¾ × 11¾ in. (40 × 29.8 cm).

forbidding. The ironic title (which is based on a line from the American national anthem) adds a subtle political statement.

Degrees of Definition

Definition is the degree to which a shape is distinguished from both the ground area and the positive shapes within the design. **High definition** creates strong contrast between shapes and tends to increase clarity and immediacy of communication. For this reason, the diagrams used in this book generally feature black figures on a white ground. **Low-definition** shapes, including soft-edged shapes, gradations, and transparencies, can increase the complexity of the design and encourage multiple interpretations.

Definition is an inherent aspect of photography. In addition to variations in focus, the photographer can choose finer-grained film and slick paper to create a crisper image, and coarser-grained film and textured paper to create a softer image.

Variations in photographic definition can substantially affect meaning. We normally expect to see high definition in the foreground and low definition in the background. In *Gun 1, New York* (1.45), William Klein reversed this expectation. Pointed directly at the viewer's face, the gun itself is blurred, menacing, and monstrously large. Even more disturbing, however, is the scowling face of the boy holding the gun. Fierce and sharply focused, his face epitomizes both fear and rage.

Definition also plays an important role in drawing. Many mediums, including graphite and charcoal, can be used to create strong, clear lines as well as soft, fuzzy shapes. In Sidney Goodman's *Man Waiting* (1.46), charcoal was used to create a mysterious figure in a threatening space. The darker, more clearly defined shapes in the upper torso seem to push toward us, while the legs, hips, and chair dissolve into the background. Similarly, in Juan Muñoz's *Raincoat Drawing* (1.47), simple white lines create a frame above the couch, suggesting an unexpected interior space. The shading used in the staircase increases the illusion of space. Encouraged to fill in the details, the viewer becomes actively involved in both drawings.

1.46 Sidney Goodman, *Man Waiting,* **1961.** Charcoal on paper, 25⅝ × 19⅛ in. (65.1 × 48.7 cm).

1.47 Juan Muñoz, *Raincoat Drawing,* **1992–93.** Mixed media on fabric, 49³⁄₁₆ × 40⅛ in. (124.94 × 101.92 cm).

Using Shape

Simple shapes are often used when clear, direct communication is needed. Gary Goldsmith used just two shapes in an ad for an antidrug campaign (1.48). The text on the left reads "The average high induced by cocaine lasts thirty minutes." The text in the black shape on the right reads "The average death induced by cocaine lasts slightly longer." When these two sentences are compositionally combined, the narrow white band and the large black rectangle suggest the division between life and death.

More complex shapes are often used when the message is subtle or contradictory. **Collage** is one method for creating such complex shapes. Constructed from visual fragments initially designed for another purpose, a collage combines two kinds of shapes: the shape of each piece of cut paper and the shapes created by the information printed on the paper.

In Romare Bearden's *The Dove* (1.49A), the outer edges of each cut fragment create a lively pattern of curvilinear and rectilinear shapes. The lines and textures printed on these photographic fragments create a second set of shapes. A linear diagram of this artwork demonstrates the complexity of the resulting composition (1.49B). Combining his perceptions of contemporary Harlem with childhood memories, Bearden used this interplay of the cut edges and printed textures to create a rich composition from the shifting shapes.

In *Target with Plaster Casts* (1.50), Jasper Johns combined simple shapes with sculptural objects to create an equally complex composition. A series of concentric circles creates a clearly defined target at the center of the painting. Nine sculptural fragments of a human figure line the upper edge—an ear, a hand, a mouth, and so forth. To add further complexity, scraps of newspaper were embedded in the colored wax from which the painting was constructed. Equally attracted to the representational body parts above and the symbolic target below, we must reconcile two very different forms of visual information.

The average high induced by cocaine lasts thirty minutes. The average death induced by cocaine lasts slightly longer.

Citizens Against Cocaine Abuse

1.48 Ad by Citizens Against Cocaine Abuse: "The average high induced by cocaine lasts thirty minutes. The average death induced by cocaine lasts slightly longer." Art Director & Designer: Gary Goldsmith; Copywriter: Neal Gomberg; Agency: Goldsmith/Jeffrey; Client: Citizens Against Cocaine Abuse.

1.49A Romare Bearden, *The Dove*, 1964. Cut-and-pasted paper, gouache, pencil, and colored pencil on cardboard. 13⅜ × 18¾ in. (34 × 47.5 cm).

1.49B Romare Bearden (compositional diagram). Printed and cut shapes work together to create a complex composition.

1.50 Jasper Johns, *Target with Plaster Casts,* **1955.** Encaustic and collage on canvas with objects, 51 × 44 × 2½ in. (129.5 × 111.8 × 6.4 cm).

Key Questions

SHAPE

- Experiment with rectilinear, curvilinear, geometric, and organic shapes. Which shape type will best express your idea?

- What happens when you combine flat, solid shapes with gradated shapes? Or fuse negative and positive?

- Contrast adds interest. What happens when two or more shape types are used in a composition?

TEXTURE

The surface quality of a two-dimensional shape or a three-dimensional volume is called **texture.** Texture engages our sense of touch as well as our vision, and it can enhance the visual surface and conceptual meaning of a design.

Types of Texture

Physical texture creates actual variations in a surface. The woven texture of canvas, the bumpy texture of thickly applied paint, and the rough texture of wood grain are common examples. **Visual texture** is an illusion. It can be created by using multiple marks or through a simulation of physical texture. Albrecht Dürer's *The Knight, Death and the Devil* (1.51) employs both visual and physical texture. The knight's armor, the horse's glossy hide, the dog's furry coat, and other details were created through cross-contours, cross-hatching, and patterns of dots called **stippling.** All are examples of visual texture. Furthermore, this print is an **engraving.** Each dot and line was carefully carved into a thin sheet of copper. Ink was pressed into the grooves, and the surface metal was wiped clean. The plate was then positioned faceup on a printing press, and damp paper was laid over it. Both were cranked through the press, transferring the ink and creating a subtle embossment. As a result, physical texture accentuates the visual texture in this image.

Invented texture is one form of visual texture. Using invented texture, the artist or designer can activate a surface using shapes that have no direct reference to perceptual reality. Bruce Conner used invented textures from many sources to construct his paper collage *Psychedelicatessen Owner* (1.52). Floral patterns, visual gemstones, and cross-contours were combined to create a witty and improbable portrait. By contrast, Brad Holland drew all of the textures in figure 1.53, using pen and ink. As the density of the marks increases, the face dissolves into dark masses of pure energy.

Creating Texture

When creating any type of texture, we must take two basic factors into account.

First, every material has its own inherent textural quality. As shown in figure 1.46, charcoal is characteristically soft and rich, while a linocut, such as Beardsley's *Salomé* (see figure 1.37), creates crisp, distinct edges. It is difficult to create soft, atmospheric textures using linocut or to create crisp textures using charcoal.

Second, the support surface contributes its own texture. This surface may be smooth, as with most photographs, or quite bumpy, as with the canvas and embedded collage Jasper Johns used for his *Target* (see figure 1.50, page 22). Thus, work

1.51 Albrecht Dürer, *The Knight, Death and the Devil*, 1513. Engraving, 11 × 14 in. (28 × 36 cm).

1.52 Bruce Conner, *Psychedelicatessen Owner*, March 31, 1990. Paper collage, 8 × 6 in. (20.32 × 15.24 cm).

1.53 Brad Holland, *Illustration for Confessions of a Short-Order Artist, Persönlich,* 1997. Pen and ink.

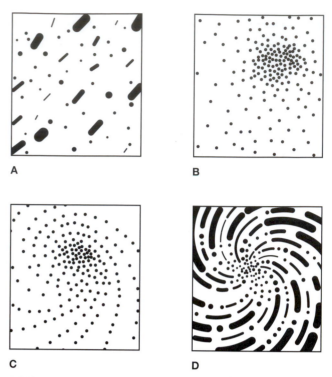

A

B

C

D

1.54A–D Examples of textural size, density, and orientation.

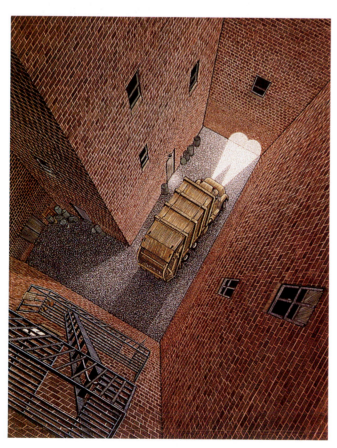

1.55 Douglas Smith, *No Turning,* 1986. Scratchboard and watercolor, 11¼ × 15 in. (29.2 × 38.1 cm).

1.56 Robert Indiana, *The Great American Dream: New York (The Glory-Star Version),* 1966. Wax crayon on paper, Sheet: 39¹³⁄₁₆ × 26⅛ in. (101.1 × 66.4 cm).

with texture requires a heightened sensitivity to both the support surface and the medium used to create the design.

Texture and Space

Visual texture is created whenever lines, dots, or other shapes are repeated. Variations in the size, density, and orientation of these marks can produce different spatial effects. Larger and darker marks tend to advance outward (1.54A). Finer marks, tightly packed, tend to pull us inward (1.54B). In figure 1.54C, the marks have been organized into a loose spiral. The overall impact is strongest when size, density, and orientation are combined, as in figure 1.54D.

In figure 1.55, Douglas Smith combined texture and linear perspective to produce a dramatic illusion of space. The lines of mortar between the bricks all point toward the truck in the center, while the bricks themselves diminish in size as the distance increases. The truck at the bottom of the wall of bricks seems to be trapped in a claustrophobic space.

By contrast, Robert Indiana's *The Great American Dream: New York* (1.56) is spatially shallow. Indiana constructed a three-dimensional model of a coin or medallion from layers of cardboard. He then laid his drawing paper on top of the construction and made a rubbing, using colored pencils. This seemingly simple composition can be interpreted in at least three ways. First, creating a design through rubbing can remind us of the coin rubbings we may have made as children. Second, in many cultures, rubbing coins evokes wealth or good luck. Finally, the rubbing itself creates the *illusion* of the coin or medallion, not the reality. Perhaps the Great American Dream is an illusion, ready to dissolve into economic disarray.

Both spatial and flat textures can be created using letters, numbers, or words. Variations in size, density, and orientation can strongly affect the meaning of these verbal textures. In figure 1.57, African-American painter Glenn Ligon repeatedly wrote, "I feel most colored when I am thrown against a sharp white background" on a gallery wall. As the density of the words increases, the words begin to fuse together, creating variations in the visual texture while reducing verbal clarity.

1.57 Glenn Ligon, Untitled *(I feel most colored when I am thrown against a sharp white background)*, **1990.** Oilstick and gesso on wood, 6 ft 6 in. × 30 in. (2 m × 76.2 cm).

1.58 Richard Haas, trompe l'oeil mural on Brotherhood Building, Cincinnati, OH.

1.59 Claudio Bravo, Detail of *Package*, 1969. Charcoal, pastel, and sanguine chalk, 30⅞ × 22½ in. (78.42 × 57.15 cm).

Trompe L'Oeil

Taken to an extreme, visual texture can so resemble reality that a deception occurs. This effect is called **trompe l'oeil,** from a French term meaning "to fool the eye." Trompe l'oeil can become a simple exercise in technical virtuosity or can significantly alter our perception of reality. By simulating architectural details, Richard Haas created an amazing dialogue between illusion and reality in figure 1.58. Using the textures of stones, stairs, and smoke, he created a wall-sized trompe l'oeil painting that actually appears to expand architectural space.

Combining Physical and Visual Texture

Each material has a distinctive physical texture, and each drawing method creates a distinctive visual texture. By combining physical and visual textures, we can unify a composition and add another layer of conceptual and compositional energy.

Blended graphite, pastel, or charcoal creates the smooth surface often favored for highly representational images. Claudio Bravo developed the visual

textures in *Package* (1.59) using pastel and charcoal. By carefully drawing every fold, he created a convincing simulation of a three-dimensional object.

Cross-hatching creates a more active visual texture. Dugald Stermer's portrait of mathematician Bertrand Russell (1.60) is constructed from a network of vigorous lines. The bumpy texture of the paper adds more energy to this lively drawing.

Physical and visual textures are combined in *Wayland's Song (with Wing)* (1.61). In this myth, a metalsmith named Wayland is captured by the King of Sweden, then crippled and forced to create treasures on demand. In revenge, he murders the king's sons and makes drinking cups from their skulls. He then flees, using wings fashioned from metal sheets. By adding straw and a lead wing to the photographic base image, Anselm Kiefer was able to combine the illusionistic qualities of painting with the physical immediacy of sculpture.

Marks and Meanings

Every textural mark we make can add to or subtract from the composition as a whole. When the texture is random or inappropriate, the composition becomes cluttered and confused. On the other hand, deliberate use of texture can enhance the illusion of space and increase compositional unity.

For example, each brushstroke in Benjamin Marra's *Self-Portrait* (1.62) describes a different facet of the face. Just as a sculptor carves out a portrait in plaster, so Marra used bold brushstrokes to carve out this portrait in paint. There are no random marks. Using both visual and physical texture, Marra increased the painting's immediacy and dimensionality.

Chuck Close's *Self-Portrait* (1.63) offers a very different interpretation of the head. Working from a photograph, Close methodically reduced the face to a series of squares within a grid. He then painted circles, diamonds, and other simple shapes inside each square. The grid provides structure, while the loosely painted interior shapes create an unexpected invented texture.

In Van Gogh's *The Starry Night* (1.64), the texture of oil paint serves three distinct purposes. First, it creates a physical texture, suggesting the actual texture of the trees in the foreground. Second, it brings great energy to every painted shape: we feel the wind; we become mesmerized by the glowing

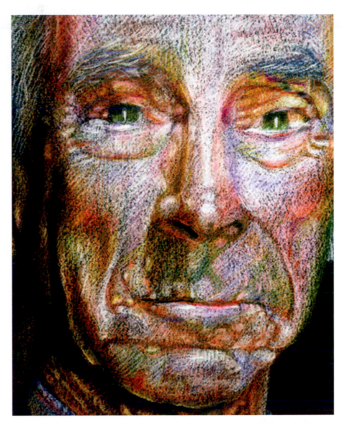

1.60 Dugald Stermer, Detail of Portrait of *Bertrand Russell, for the New York Times Book Review*, 2002. Colored pencil.

1.61 Anselm Kiefer, *Wayland's Song (with Wing)*, 1982. Oil, emulsion, straw, and photograph with lead wing, 110¼ × 149⅝ in. (280 × 380 cm).

1.62 Benjamin Marra, *Self-Portrait,* **1998.** Oil, 8½ × 11 in. (21.6 × 28 cm).

1.63 Chuck Close, *Self-Portrait,* **1997.** Oil on canvas, 8 ft 6 in. × 7 ft (2.59 × 2.13 m).

1.64 Vincent Van Gogh, *The Starry Night,* **1889.** Oil on canvas, 29 × 36½ in. (73.7 × 92.1 cm).

whirlpools of light. Finally, we become connected to the artist himself. Van Gogh's hand is clearly evident in every brushstroke he made.

VALUE

Value refers to the relative lightness or darkness of a surface. The word *relative* is significant. The lightness or darkness of a shape is largely determined by its surroundings. For example, on a white surface, a gray square seems stable and imposing (1.65A). The same gray square has less visual weight and seems luminous when it is surrounded by a black ground (1.65B). A **value scale** further demonstrates the importance of context (1.66). The solid gray line appears luminous when it is placed on a black background. As it crosses over the middle grays and into the white area, it seems to darken.

Contrast

Both communication and expression are affected by **value contrast,** or the amount of difference in values. High contrast tends to increase clarity and improve readability (1.67). Low contrast is often used for shapes of secondary importance or when the message is subtle. The same text can be dramatic or incoherent depending on the amount of contrast.

Photographers are especially aware of the importance of contrast. By using a filter, changing the print paper, or adjusting the image digitally, they can quickly modify contrast. High contrast gives the Timberland Ad (1.68) a gritty immediacy. Each word and shape is

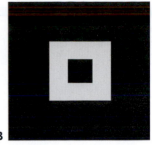

1.65A and B Relative value.

1.66 Value scale.

In Xanadu did Kubla Khan
A stately pleasure dome decree:
Where Alph, the sacred river, ran
Through caverns measureless to man
Down to a sunless sea

In Xanadu did Kubla Khan
A stately pleasure dome decree:
Where Alph, the sacred river, ran
Through caverns measureless to man
Down to a sunless sea

1.67 Contrast affects readability.

1.68 *Advertisement for Timberland Pro.* Winsper Inc.: Steve Bautista, Brian Fandetti, Kevin Cimo, Jim Erickson, Joanne DeCarlo, Caroline Bishop.

1.69 Alfred Stieglitz, *The Terminal,* c. 1892. Chloride print, 3½ × 4½ in. (8.8 × 11.3 cm).

clearly defined. The city in Alfred Stieglitz's photograph (1.69) is quieter and more atmospheric. This low-contrast photograph invites the viewer into a pre-industrial world of horses and carriages.

As demonstrated by Deborah Remington's *Capra* (1.70), value gradation can suggest a light source, create a sense of volume, or enhance the illusion of space. Composed from just five dominant shapes, this gradated painting seems to glow.

Value Distribution

Value distribution refers to the proportion and arrangement of lights and darks in a composition. Careful use of value distribution can increase emotional impact. A composition that is 80 percent black simply has a different "feel" than a composition that is 80 percent white.

Darker values are often used to create a sense of mystery or increase dramatic tension. For example, Ray K. Metzker's *Philadelphia* (1.71) is dominated by dark values. Surrounded by somber buildings in a silent city, the commuters huddle together under the brightly lit bus shelter like actors in a play.

Lighter values tend to suggest openness, optimism, and clarity. For example, lighter values dominate the bottom and right edges of Conley Harris's landscape (1.72), creating an expansive effect. The darker values at the center of the composition then pull us inward.

Value and Volume

When a full range of values is used, a two-dimensional shape can seem three-dimensional, or **volumetric.** Figure 1.73 shows the transformation of a circle into a sphere. We begin with a simple outline, then add the **attached shadows,** or values that directly define the basic form. Addition of a **cast shadow** in the third image grounds the sphere. In the fourth drawing, the separation between the shadow and the sphere creates a floating effect.

1.70 Deborah Remington, *Capra,* 1974. Oil on canvas, 6 ft 4 in. × 5 ft 7 in. (1.93 × 1.7 m).

1.71 Ray K. Metzker, *Philadelphia,* **1963.** Gelatin silver print on paper, 6⅛ × 8¾ in. (15.4 × 22.3 cm).

1.72 Conley Harris, *Doubles/Triples, Italy.* Charcoal drawing, 23 × 30 in. (58.42 × 76.2 cm).

This transformation of shapes through value is so convincing that objects can appear to extend out from a two-dimensional surface. The earliest oil painters often used **grisaille,** or a gray underpainting, to create the illusion of three-dimensionality. Color was then added, using transparent glazes or layers of paint. A detail from Jan van Eyck's *Ghent Altarpiece* (1.74) shows both the grisaille painting and the full-color painting. The two statues in the center were painted using a range of grays, while color has been added to the kneeling figures on the right and left. Variations in value give all of the figures a remarkable dimensionality.

Value and Space

When combined in a composition, very dark, crisp shapes tend to advance spatially, while gray, blurry shapes tend to recede. For example, in Thomas Moran's *Noon-Day Rest in Marble Canyon* (1.75), the dark values in the foreground gradually fade until the cliffs in the background become gray and indistinct. This effect, called **atmospheric perspective,** is one of the simplest ways to create the illusion of space.

1.75 Thomas Moran, *Noon-Day Rest in Marble Canyon,* from *Exploration of the Colorado River of the West,* by J. W. Powell, **1875.** Wood engraving after an original sketch by Thomas Moran, 6½ × 4⅜ in. (16.5 × 11 cm).

1.73 From shape to volume through use of value.

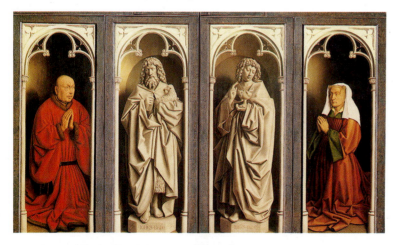

1.74 Jan van Eyck, *Ghent Altarpiece* (closed), completed **1432.** Oil on panel, approx. 11 ft 6 in. × 7 ft 7 in. (3.5 × 2.33 m).

Chiaroscuro (literally, "light-dark") is another way to create the illusion of space. A primary light source is used to create six or more values. A dark background is added to increase contrast. In *Judith and Her Maidservant with the Head of Holofernes* by Artemesia Gentileschi (1.76), the highlighted areas are clearly delineated, while darker areas seem to dissolve into the background. The resulting image is as dramatic as a theatrical stage.

Value and Lighting

Filmmakers and set designers are especially aware of the expressive uses of value. Working with a wide range of lights, including sharply defined spotlights and more diffused floodlights, they can increase or decrease the illusion of space, emphasize an object or an action, and influence our emotional response to a character.

Four common forms of lighting are shown in figure 1.77. As described by Herbert Zettl in *Sight, Sound, Motion: Applied Media Aesthetics*, a key light is the primary source of illumination. Placing this light at a 45-degree angle can enhance the illusion of space. Addition of a backlight separates the actor from the background and adds definition. When a fill light is added, the contrast between light and dark becomes less harsh, and the actor may appear less formidable. In theatrical performances, powerful side lighting is often used to increase drama while enhancing dimensionality.

1.76 Artemesia Gentileschi, *Judith and Her Maidservant with the Head of Holofernes,* **c. 1625.** Oil on canvas, 72½ × 54¾ in. (1.84 × 1.42 m).

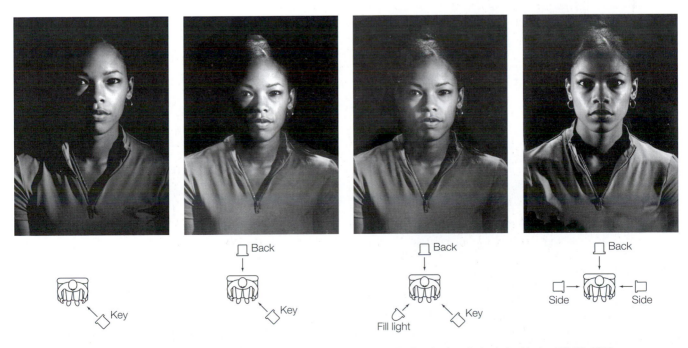

1.77 John Veltri, Lighting Techniques from *Sight, Sound, Motion: Applied Media Aesthetics*, 3rd ed., by Herbert Zettl, 1999.

1.78A

1.78B

1.78C

1.78D

All of these aspects of lighting are used expressively in the film *Casablanca*, directed by Michael Curtiz. The lighting is fairly dark when we first enter Rick's Café Américain, the saloon where most of the action occurs. In this dark and mysterious place, a man will be shot, a seduction will be thwarted, and a romance will be rekindled.

The piano player, Sam, and the audience members closest to the stage are brightly lit as he sings an optimistic song (1.78A). The two villains in the film, Major Strasser and Captain Renault, are often strongly side-lit (1.78B), which makes them appear more formidable and enhances the texture in their faces. By contrast, much softer light is used for the face of the heroine, Ilsa, who is emotionally and politically fragile.

Indeed, value and lighting is used to accentuate Ilsa's emotions throughout the film. When she tries to explain to Rick the reason she left him in Paris two years earlier, Ilsa wears a pure white dress and enters the darkened saloon like a virginal beam of light (1.78C). Later, when she visits Rick in his apartment, shadows cover her face, accentuating her conflicted emotions as she tries to decide whether to remain with her husband, Victor, whom she idealizes, or return to Rick, whom she loves. In the final scene at the airport, diffused lighting again emphasizes Ilsa's vulnerability (1.78D). She and Victor disappear into the foggy night, escaping from Casablanca, while Rick and a reformed Captain Renault stroll away together to join the Foreign Legion.

Key Questions

VALUE

- What is the advantage of a wide value range? What is the advantage of a narrow value range? Which works better in your design?

- What happens when you invert the values—that is, the black areas become white and the white areas become black?

- Would your design benefit from a stronger illusion of space? If so, how can value be used to accomplish this?

SUMMARY

- The elements of two-dimensional design are line, shape, texture, value, and color.

- Lines can contain, define, dissect, and connect. Line networks can be created using hatching, cross-hatching, and cross-contours.

- A shape is created whenever an area is enclosed. The figure is the primary shape, while the ground, or negative shape, provides the surrounding context.

- When figure and ground shapes are equally strong, figure/ground reversal can occur.

- There are many types of shapes, including rectilinear, curvilinear, geometric, organic, representational, nonrepresentational, and abstract. When gradated, shapes can appear three-dimensional.

- Texture is the visual or physical surface of a shape. Visual texture can be created through multiple marks, while actual variations in the surface create physical texture.

- Relative lightness or darkness in an artwork is called value. Value can be used to create the illusion of space, suggest volume, shift compositional balance, and heighten emotion.

KEY TERMS

abstract shape
actual line
atmospheric perspective
attached shadow
calligraphic line
cast shadow
chiaroscuro
closure
collage
continuity
contour line
cross-contour
cross-hatching
curvilinear shape

definition
direction
elements
engraving
figure/ground reversal
geometric shape
gesture drawing
gradation (shading)
grisaille
hatching
high-definition
implied lines
invented texture
line

low definition
medium
negative shape (ground)
nonobjective shape
nonrepresentational shape
organic shape
organizational line
orientation
physical texture
positive shape (figure)
pure form
rectilinear shape
representational shape

shape
stippling
texture
trompe l'oeil
value
value contrast
value distribution
value scale
visual texture
volume
volume summary
volumetric

STUDIO PROJECTS

To apply the concepts from this chapter in the studio, check out the Projects page in the Online Learning Center at www.mhhe.com/stewart4e. The following is a sample of the chapter-related assignments that are described in step-by-step detail.

LINE

Line Inventory. An introduction to the vocabulary and power of line.
Four Lines, Four Times. Sixteen linear compositions.
Line Dynamics. Combining line and balance.

SHAPE

Shape Inventory. Sixteen compositions using shape.
Concealing/Revealing #1. Figure/ground relationships.
Essence/Totality. Exploring abstraction.

TEXTURE

Texture Inventory. Sixteen texture studies.

VALUE

Concealing/Revealing #2. The impact of value on composition and communication.
The World Is a Stage. Light and its emotional impact.

Profile:
Phillia Yi, Printmaker

Energy and Expression Using
Woodcut on a Large Scale

Phillia Changhi Yi has revitalized the ancient process of woodcut through her large-scale prints. Drawing directly on luan plywood, Yi cuts away the negative shapes and inks the raised positive shapes to create abstract images that vigorously combine line, color, texture, and movement. Yi has over 20 solo shows and numerous international group shows to her credit. She lectures widely and has taught workshops at Manhattan Graphics Center, Women's Studio Workshop, and the Southern Graphics Council Conference.

MS: The energy in all of your images is impressive. What is its source?

PY: Conflict is my primary source, conceptually and compositionally. As a woman from Korea living in the United States, I find myself caught between cultures. This isolates me in an interesting way and gives me a unique perspective. My work reflects the day-to-day dilemmas and tension of my multicultural experience.

Crisis moments often trigger ideas, but historic events are never treated literally. I combine abstract imagery with representational elements in my prints. Both flat and illusory space is created, suggesting an altered sense of time and scale. Static forms are juxtaposed with fluid shapes, and both warm and cool colors are used in opaque and translucent layers. This activates the psychological space and creates a complex, highly charged composition.

MS: Many members of your family are doctors. How did you become an artist?

PY: Getting the right encouragement at the right time gave me the confidence to pursue art. All of my five siblings are talented, I think, but choosing an art career seemed too risky. My father encouraged me to study graphic design, but I found that printmaking was my real passion. My mentor, Professor Romas Viesulas at Tyler School of Art, said that I had the commitment and ability for a career in art. His confidence gave me confidence.

MS: How do you develop your images?

PY: I begin with a month of drawing, usually in charcoal, on 29″ × 41″ sheets of printmaking paper. In the drawings, I work out my images and ideas. Social and political themes dominate. For example, the beating of Rodney King by members of the Los Angeles Police Department and the subsequent burning of Koreatown inspired *Dance*.

The Other Side, shown here, deals with the power of women, who must prevail in a world dominated by men. The whole composition is based on the intersection between these two forces, near the center of the print. In a sense, the large black shape represents the unconscious, while the curving red shape suggests that which is conscious, palpable, and real. I am interested in the uneasy alliance or balance between complex life forces, rather than a simple battle between adversaries. Each corner is treated differently, adding more variety and energy to the print.

MS: The size of this piece is extraordinary. Using eight panels, you have created a print that is 12 feet long!

PY: When I was studying printmaking at SUNY–New Paltz, I was surrounded by printmakers. The size of the press, acid trays, rollers, and other equipment seemed to limit the size of the print. When I went to Tyler in Philadelphia, my roommate, who was a painter, introduced me to her friends. Some were completing a 5′ × 7′ painting a day! I realized that the small size and slow process of printmaking had historically given it a "second-class" status. I was determined to overcome this perception, so I developed a working method that is forceful, spontaneous, and direct. There is still a great deal of deliberation, but the cutting and printing processes are relatively fast.

MS: Some artists work very methodically over a long period of time, while others work in short, intensive bursts. What is your approach?

PY: I adapt my method to my situation. I have obligations as a teacher, a mother, and an administrator, so summer is my only solid block of work time. A regular schedule is best for me. At the beginning of the summer, I go to the studio for a few hours each day. I soon increase this to about 6 hours a day for drawing. When I am cutting the blocks and printing, I often work for 8 to 10 hours a day. I am very consistent.

MS: What is the best work method for your students?
PY: Success is primarily based on commitment.

I would say that art-making is about 5 percent talent and inspiration and 95 percent hard work. A professional or a serious student continues to work despite obstacles. It is important for students to explore ideas and make mistakes: that is the best way to learn.

MS: What is the purpose of your artwork?
PY: Art is expression, not explanation. Artists must be attentive, noticing every detail of experience. Art both reflects and influences society and culture. In that sense, I feel that artists have a responsibility to their generation, not just to create objects of beauty but to create objects of truth—whether they are beautiful or not. My ideas come from my daily life and my personal experience, both good and bad. The most important characteristic is my belief that art should be expressed in terms of human experience. My work is essentially optimistic: I embrace all that the world has to offer.

Phillia Changhi Yi, *The Other Side*, 1993. Color woodcut, 84 × 120 in. (213 × 305 cm).

The Element
of Color

Color immediately attracts attention. When presented with a collection of bottles filled with liquid in various colors, very young children will group the objects by color rather than by size or shape. Color has great emotional power, and designers carefully choose a color palette that supports the mood of each project. An interior designer may use rose-red walls in a restaurant to increase emotional warmth, while using light blue walls in a day-care center to encourage calm.

Selecting the right colors can make or break a design. To assist their clients in project planning, the Neenah Paper Company produced a witty and informative brochure describing the effects of color (2.1). Each color was given a personality as distinctive as an astrological sign. The colors were then organized in a booklet, creating an easy-to-use index of possibilities. While systems of this kind provide a shortcut to basic decision making, in this chapter we will see that color is a complex element that defies easy formulas. We will consider relationships between color and light, describe three major characteristics of color, explore harmony and disharmony, and analyze uses of color in various compositional contexts.

2.1 Neenah Papers and Partners design firm, brochure for Neenah Papers. Courtesy Neenah Papers and Partners Design. Color Attributes courtesy of Dewey Color System ®, deweycolorsystem.com.

COLOR PHYSICS

To use color fully, we must understand the major types of color, how they are created, and how they interact. **Color theory** is the art and science of color interaction and effects. In *The Art of Color,*[1] Johannes Itten lists the following approaches to color theory:

- The physicist studies electromagnetic wavelengths in order to measure and classify color.

- The chemist, working with the molecular structure of dyes and pigments, seeks to produce highly permanent colors and excellent paint consistency.

- The physiologist investigates the effects of color and light on our eyes and brain.

- The psychologist studies the expressive effects of color on our mind and spirit.

An artist combines all these areas of knowledge. Like the physicist, the artist uses color wavelengths to create visual effects. Like the chemist, the artist must be aware of the safety and permanence of dyes and pigments. When using color to create the illusion of space, the artist puts into practice theories developed by the physiologist. And both communication and expression are strongly affected by the psychological impact of color.

Additive and Subtractive Color

Two major color systems are used in art and design. **Additive color** is created using beams of light (2.2A). Red, green, and blue, the familiar RGB on a computer screen, are the primary colors in this system. Millions of colors can be mixed from these primaries. **Subtractive color** is created when white light is reflected off a pigmented or dyed surface (2.2B). The subtractive primaries are blue, red, and yellow.

2.2A Light primaries and their additive mixtures.

2.2B Pigment primaries and their subtractive mixtures.

2.3 Color printing detail of *Wheel of Fortune*, showing dot pattern used in CMYK printing.

A Yellow **B** Magenta **C** Yellow and magenta **D** Cyan **E** Yellow, magenta, and cyan **F** Black **G** Full color printing

2.4A–G Color separation in CMYK printing. Dots of yellow, magenta, cyan, and black are layered to create a full-color image.

This book was printed using cyan blue, magenta red, and yellow, the transparent primaries (or **process colors**) commonly used in mass production. Figure 2.3 provides an example of process printing. As viewers, we optically combine thousands of cyan, magenta, and yellow dots to create a coherent image. Black (abbreviated as *K* in the CMYK printing system) was then added to enhance detail and increase contrast (2.4A–G).

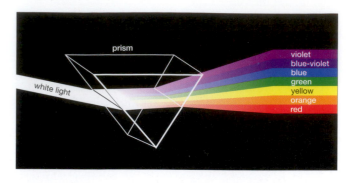

2.5 When white light passes through a prism, the spectrum becomes visible.

Color and Light

These two systems exist because of the inseparable connection between color and light. When white light passes through a prism, it is refracted, or bent. This creates a wide spectrum of hues, which is dominated by red, orange, yellow, green, blue, blue-violet, and violet (2.5). Each hue, or separate color, is defined by a specific electromagnetic wavelength, with red the longest and violet the shortest. When white light hits a colored surface, some wavelengths are reflected, while other wavelengths are absorbed. As shown in figure 2.6A, a red surface reflects the red wavelengths while absorbing the blue and green wavelengths. Similarly, a green surface reflects the green wavelengths while absorbing the red and blue (2.6B). All wavelengths are reflected off a white surface (2.6C); all wavelengths are absorbed by a black surface (2.6D). Color reflection and absorption are rarely total. As a result, we can often see hints of various colors within a dominant color.

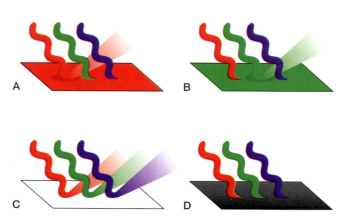

2.6A–D We see color when the primaries of light are reflected off a colored surface. A red surface absorbs the green and blue wavelengths, while reflecting the red. All wavelengths are reflected by a white surface. All wavelengths are absorbed by a black surface.

Using Additive Color

Lighting designers, videographers, and Web site artists use additive color extensively. Beams of red, green, and blue light are used to create a full-color video projection. The mixture of adjacent beams creates cyan, magenta, and yellow, which are the secondary colors in the additive system. When all three beams are combined, white light results.

We can quickly and easily create variations in additive color on a computer. In figure 2.7, the current color choice is shown in the center. Variations are shown in the eight surrounding squares. Even a 10 percent increase in a given color produces a very different result.

Our perception of additive color is influenced by

- The intensity (or wattage) of the projected light.
- The light source, from incandescent light and fluorescent light to daylight.
- The surface quality of the illuminated object. Projected light behaves very differently on transparent, translucent, and textured surfaces.
- The ambient (overall amount of) light in the environment.

Using Subtractive Color

Painters, printmakers, and illustrators use subtractive color in various forms, including acrylics, oils, pastels, and inks. Each pigment or dye used in the manufacture of such materials is chemically unique. Quinacridone red and pthalocyanide blue are

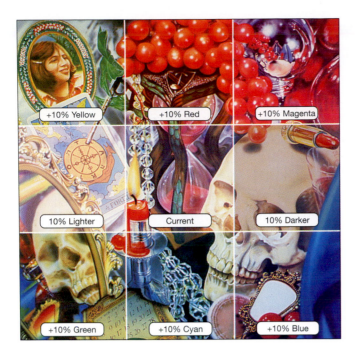

2.7 Color variations using a computer.

+10% Yellow | +10% Red | +10% Magenta
10% Lighter | Current | 10% Darker
+10% Green | +10% Cyan | +10% Blue

transparent and intense. The cadmiums and earth colors are generally opaque. **Color overtones** complicate matters further. Color theorist David Hornung defines an overtone as "a secondary hue bias in a primary color." For example, alizarin crimson is a red with violet overtones, while scarlet is a red with orange overtones. To create a wider range of mixtures, artists and designers often use a six-hue palette, including two reds, two yellows, and two blues, plus **achromatic** black and white, which have no hue. Since many foundation color projects are done using paint, ink, or colored paper, the remainder of this chapter will focus on subtractive color.

Color Interaction

Color interaction refers to the way colors influence one another. Colors are never seen in isolation. The blue sheets of paper we examine in an art supply store may remind us of the blue of the sky, the ocean, or the fabrics in a clothing store. Lighting also affects our perceptions. Incandescent light creates a warm orange glow, while standard fluorescent lights produce a bluish ambiance. And, when our blue paper is added to a design, it is profoundly affected by the surrounding colors.

The way a color changes when paired with another color is called **simultaneous contrast.** Three principles of simultaneous contrast are shown in figure 2.8A–C. Light/dark contrast is shown in the first pair of images. A blue-green square appears much lighter when it is placed on a black background. A complementary reaction is shown in the second pair. The same blue-green square appears to glow when it is surrounded by red rather than a neutral gray. In the third pair, the same blue-green square appears almost green when it is surrounded by solid blue, yet it appears almost blue when surrounded by green.

The **Bezold effect** demonstrates the profound influence of color interaction. Color theorist Wilhelm

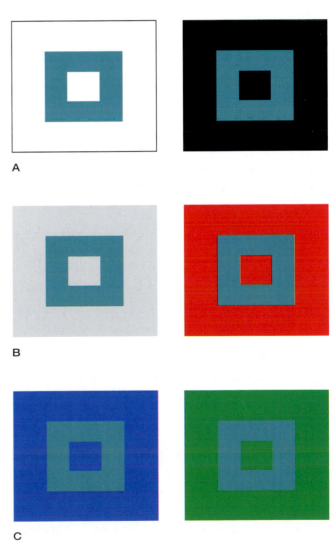

2.8A–C Examples of simultaneous contrast. Light/dark contrast is shown in A, a complementary reaction is shown in B, and subtle variations are shown in C. The blue-green square is the same color in all examples but appears different due to the surrounding colors.

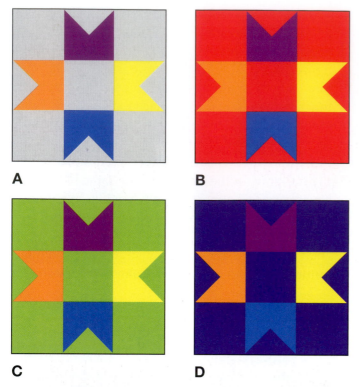

A

B

C

D

2.9A–D The Bezold effect. Changing a single color alters the entire design.

2.10 Pat Steir, *Inner Lhamo Waterfall*, **1992.** Oil on canvas, 114 × 90¼ in. (289.6 × 229.2 cm).

Bezold (1837–1907) realized that change in a single color can substantially alter our perception of an entire pattern. In figure 2.9A–D, changing the background color from gray to red adds an electric energy to the design. A light green background accentuates the darker shapes while diminishing the brightness of the orange shape. A dark violet background creates a strong contrast in value and pushes the orange and yellow shapes forward. The compositional impact can be substantial, even when only one color is changed.

Color interaction becomes especially dramatic when complementary colors, such as red-orange and blue-green, are used in a composition. In the human eye, two types of cells, known as rods and cones, are arranged in layers on the retina. These cells serve as photoreceptors. The rods record lightness and darkness, while the cones distinguish the hues, such as red and blue. According to **opponent theory,** the cones can register only one color in a complementary pair at a time. Constant shifting between the opposing colors creates a visual overload at the edges of the shapes, resulting in an electric glow. In *Inner Lhamo Waterfall* (2.10), Pat Steir used this effect to suggest the majesty and mystery of the falling water.

A similar characteristic of human vision can be used to create an **afterimage.** If we stare at a red square for 20 seconds (2.11) and then stare at a white sheet of paper, a blue or green shape will seem to appear. This is due to fatigue in the cones, the color sensors in our eyes. Overloaded by the intense red, our eyes revert to the blue and green cones, creating the afterimage.

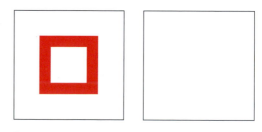

2.11 Afterimage exercise.

DEFINING COLOR

Hue

The **hue,** or name of a color, is determined by its wavelength. Red, blue, green, yellow, and so forth are all hues.

Physicists, painters, and philosophers have devised numerous systems to organize hues. Johannes Itten's 12-step color wheel (2.12) is a clear and simple example. Red, blue, and yellow **primary colors** are in the center. These colors can be mixed to produce many other colors. The **secondary colors** of green, orange, and violet follow. These colors are mixed from adjacent primaries. A circular spectrum of **tertiary colors** completes the wheel. The mixture of a secondary color and the adjacent primary color creates a tertiary color.

The Munsell color wheel (2.13) more accurately identifies cyan blue, magenta red, and yellow as the subtractive primaries, while the three-dimensional Munsell color tree (2.14) provides examples of changes in color value and intensity as well as hue.

Artists often use a wide range of hues to capture the richness of reality. In *Wheel of Fortune* (2.15), Audrey Flack used a full spectrum of hues to define a collection of symbolic objects in meticulous detail. The makeup and mirrors symbolize vanity; the candles, hourglass, and skull suggest the passage of time; the grapes suggest passion. Reds, blues, and yellows dominate the painting. Hints of orange, violet, and green complete the spectrum.

As demonstrated by Pat Steir's *Waterfall* (2.10, page 42), a limited range of hues can be equally effective. In this painting, interaction between just two hues creates an electric visual impact.

2.12 The 12-step Itten color wheel.

2.13 The 10-step Munsell color wheel.

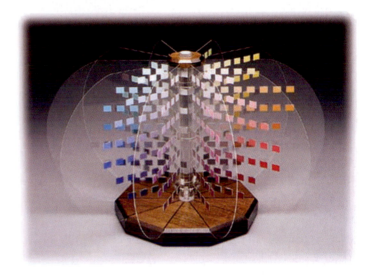

2.14 Munsell color tree, 1972. Clear plastic chart, 10½ × 12 in. (26.7 × 30.5 cm); base size 12 in. (30.5 cm) diameter; center pole size 12⅝ in. (32.1 cm) high; chip size ¾ × 1⅜ in. (1.9 × 3.5 cm).

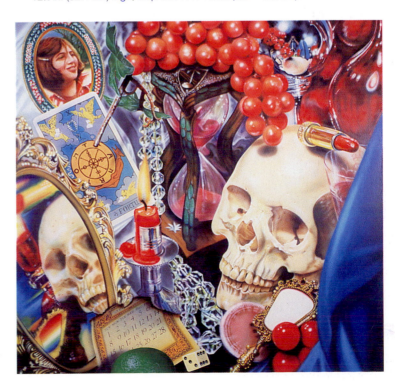

2.15 Audrey Flack, *Wheel of Fortune,* **1977–78.** Oil over acrylic on canvas, 8 × 8 ft. (2.44 × 2.44 m).

2.16 Separation of the color wheel by temperature.

Temperature is an especially important aspect of hue. **Temperature** refers to the heat a color generates, both physically and psychologically. Try laying six colored squares of equal value on fresh snow on a sunny day. By the end of the day, the warm-colored oranges, reds, and violets will sink into the melting snow, while the blue and green squares will remain closer to the surface. Figure 2.16 shows a simple division of the color wheel by temperature.

Color temperature can help create the illusion of space. Under most circumstances, warm colors advance, while cool colors recede. This effect is demonstrated very clearly in Kenneth Noland's *A Warm Sound in a Gray Field* (2.17). The red ring with its light yellow halo pushes toward us, while the blue-black circle pulls us inward. The small red dot in the center of the composition further activates the void by creating another advancing shape. Temperature can also be used to create a strong emotional effect. In figure 2.18, the glowing oranges and reds create a radiant representation of Christ.

2.18 **Page from the** *Book of Kells*, **Chi-Rho monogram, late 8th century.** Illuminated manuscript.

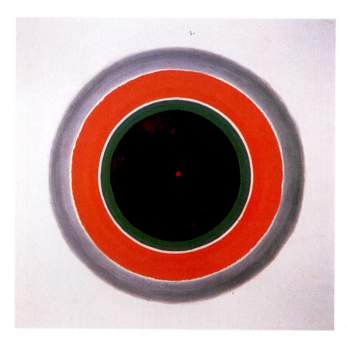

2.17 **Kenneth Noland,** *A Warm Sound in a Gray Field*, **1961.** 6 ft 10½ in. × 6 ft 9 in. (2.1 × 2.06 m).

Value

Value refers to the relative lightness or darkness of a color. By removing hue from the equation, we can create a simple value scale (2.19A) that shifts from white to black through a series of grays. As shown in figure 2.19B, hues such as violet, blue, and green are inherently darker in value than pure yellow or orange. Translation of color into value is shown in figure 2.19C; despite the wide variety of hues, all the colors have nearly the same value.

Three basic variations in value are shown in figure 2.20. When white is added to a hue, the resulting **tint** will be lighter in value. The addition of gray produces a **tone**. The addition of black creates a darker **shade**. One of the simplest ways to unify a design is to limit the colors used to the tints, tones, and shades of a single hue.

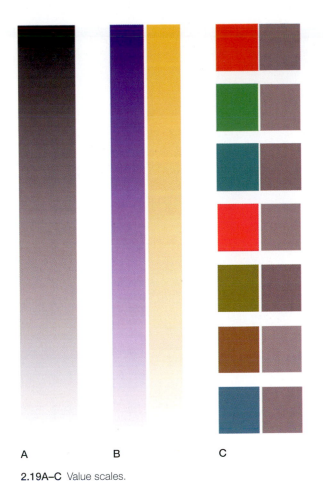

A B C

2.19A–C Value scales.

Using a full range of values, we can create a very convincing representation of reality. In *Vision* (2.21), Nicora Gangi transformed a simple still life into a dramatic drawing. A bright light in the background pushes the dark foreground vessels toward us. The limited value range in David Hockney's *Mist* (2.22) is equally effective. The gray-green palm trees dissolve into the peach-colored fog as quietly as a whisper.

By making a black-and-white photocopy, we can easily check the range of values in a design. The photocopied image will be quite readable when the value range is broad. When a very narrow range of values is used, the photocopy will produce a solid gray image.

Value is the dominant force in some paintings, while hue is a dominant force in others. Each approach has a distinctive emotional effect. Romaine Brooks's *Self-Portrait* (2.23) is essentially a value painting. Blacks, whites, and grays dominate the image. The woman's eyes are concealed by the brim of her hat and the shadow it casts. Patches of red on her lips and coat add just a touch of color. She

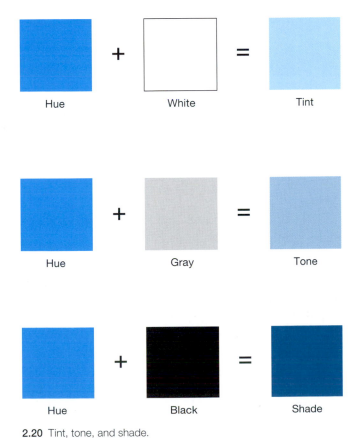

Hue	+	White	=	Tint
Hue	+	Gray	=	Tone
Hue	+	Black	=	Shade

2.20 Tint, tone, and shade.

2.21 Nicora Gangi, *Vision*, 1994. Pastel, 10 × 14 in. (25 × 36 cm).

2.22 David Hockney, *Mist,* From The Weather Series, 1973. Lithograph in 5 colors, edition 98, 37 × 32 in. (93.9 × 81.2 cm).

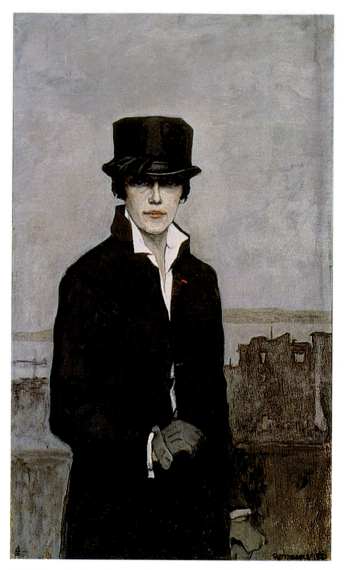

2.23 Romaine Brooks, *Self-Portrait,* 1923. Oil on canvas, 46¼ × 26⅞ in. (117.5 × 68.3 cm).

is wary and reserved. Value, rather than hue, is the appropriate choice for this image.

In contrast, hue dominates Henri Matisse's *Green Stripe* (2.24). Surrounded by large blocks of red, green, and violet, the woman seems bold and self-confident. The avocado-green dividing line separates blocks of pink on the right and lime-green on the left half of her face, suggesting warmer and cooler aspects of her personality. Even her eyes and hair are painted in blue-black, adding yet more color to this expressive portrait.

Intensity

Intensity, saturation, and **chroma** all refer to the purity of a color. The primary colors are the most intense. This intensity generally diminishes when colors are mixed.

Figure 2.25A–C presents three intensity scales. Column A shows the most intense primary, secondary, and tertiary colors. Column B demonstrates the loss of intensity when black is added to a single color. In column C, two complementary colors are

mixed, producing a range of elegant, low-intensity colors.

High-intensity colors are often used to maximize impact. Grace Hartigan's *City Life* (2.26) explodes with energy, as a full palette of blues, reds, and yellows dances across the canvas. In the background, a blue and orange striped awning vibrates with complementary color. Dark blocks of violet in the lower-left corner and blue in the lower-right compress the warm reds, oranges, and yellows at the center of the composition, adding yet more energy. The entire scene is highly abstracted. Our understanding of both space and movement is based on the use of color rather than on photographic representation.

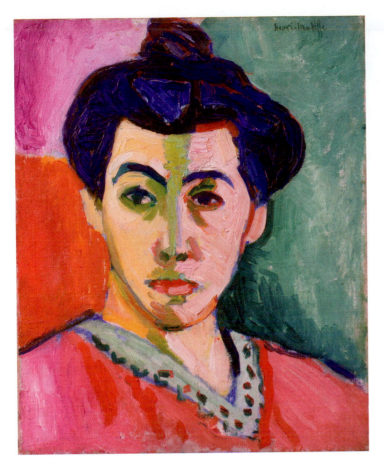

2.24 Henri Matisse, *Green Stripe (Madame Matisse),* 1905. Oil on canvas, 16 × 12¾ in. (40.6 × 32.4 cm).

A combination of high- and low-intensity colors can be equally effective. Arshile Gorky used primary hues and subtle earth colors in *The Liver Is the Cock's Comb* (2.27). Grays, tans, and browns cover more than half of the surface. Surrounded by these low-intensity colors, the brilliant yellow and red shapes seem to pulsate with energy. Like variations in volume and tempo in an interesting piece of music, the interplay between subdued and intense colors adds complexity to the composition.

Gorky's masterful understanding of how the eye reads and responds to color gives his paintings their unusual vibrancy and sense of animation. There is a wider range in his application of muted color than in Hartigan's work, but the impact is comparable. In both cases, the viewer is drawn into and moves throughout the painting because of the use of color.

2.25A–C Intensity scales. The most intense primaries, secondaries, and tertiaries are shown in A. The addition of black reduces the intensity of the color red in B. Mixing the complements yellow and violet creates low-intensity colors in C.

A   B   C

Key Questions
DEFINING COLOR

- Which will work better in your design, a limited or a wide range of hues?
- What proportion of warm and cool colors best communicates your idea?
- What happens when you combine low-intensity colors with high-intensity colors?

2.26 Grace Hartigan, *City Life,* 1956. Oil on canvas, 81 × 98½ in. (205.7 × 250.2 cm).

2.27 Arshile Gorky, *The Liver Is the Cock's Comb,* 1944. Oil on canvas, 72 × 98 in. (1.86 × 2.49 cm).

HARMONY AND DISHARMONY

Relationships among colors are critical to the success or failure of a design, and many theories of **color harmony** have been developed to help artists, architects, and designers make good choices. A basic color wheel can help illustrate five common approaches.

Monochromatic Color Schemes

Variations on a single hue are used in a **monochromatic** color scheme (2.28). The advantage of this system is a high level of unity: all the colors are strongly related. Boredom, due to the lack of variety, is a potential disadvantage. In *Tracers—Side Order* (2.29), Guy Goodwin used various textures, patterns, and words to add interest to the monochromatic image.

Analogous Color Schemes

Adjacent colors on the color wheel are used in an **analogous** color scheme (2.30). As with monochromatic harmony, a high degree of unity is ensured, but the wider range of hues offers greater variety and can increase interest. Blues and a surprising variety of greens activate the *Chromatics Place Settings*, shown in figure 2.31.

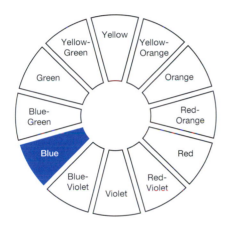

2.28 Monochromatic color system.

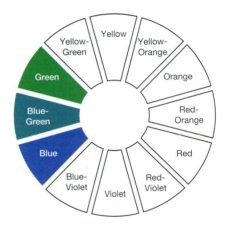

2.30 Analogous color system.

2.29 Guy Goodwin, *Tracers—Side Order,* **1999.** Resin, polyurethane, ink on polycarbonate, 51 × 54 × 4 in. (130 × 137 × 10 cm).

2.31 *Chromatics Place Settings,* **1970.** Gerald Gulotta, shape designer; Jack Prince, pattern designer. Porcelain, linen, and stainless steel.

2.32 Complementary color system.

2.33 Francis Bacon, *Four Studies for a Self-Portrait*, 1967. Oil on canvas, 36 × 13 in. (91.5 × 33 cm).

Complementary Color Schemes

The palette dramatically expands in a **complementary** color scheme (2.32). Complementary colors are opposites on the traditional color wheel. When mixed together, they can lower intensity and produce a wide range of browns. When paired in a composition, complementary colors can become powerful partners. Each increases the impact of the other.

Francis Bacon's *Four Studies for a Self-Portrait* (2.33) is dominated by the complements red and green. The design is unified by browns, including the reddish brown filling the background. Vigorous slashes of pure green and red add visual energy and create the illusion of movement.

In *Brilliant Scape* (2.34), Tetsurō Sawada used variations on blue and orange to create a subtle abstract landscape. Horizontal bands of blue-violets in the bottom half visually extend the composition to the left and right, while the gradated block of light blue at the top creates a soaring sky. Activated by just three

2.34 Tetsurō Sawada, *Brilliant Scape (Blue)*, 1985. Silkscreen, 22⅞ × 15¾ in. (58 × 40 cm).

2.35 Split complementary system.

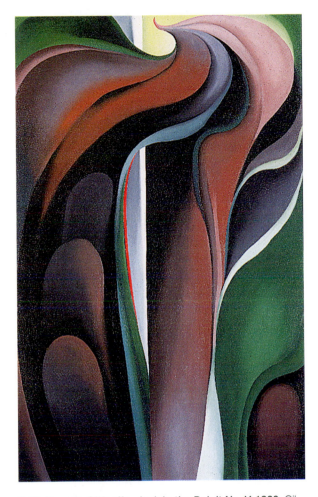

2.36 Georgia O'Keeffe, *Jack in the Pulpit No. V*, 1930. Oil on canvas, 48 × 30 in. (122 × 76 cm).

yellow-orange bands and one broken orange line, the overall composition is both energetic and serene.

Each complementary pair has its own distinctive strengths. Violet and yellow provide the widest value range, while orange and blue provide the widest range of variation in temperature. Red and green are closest in value and create extreme agitation when placed side by side. By mixing two complements plus black and white, we can create a range of colors that begins to suggest the power of a full spectrum.

Split Complementary Color Schemes

An even wider range of possibilities is offered by the **split complementary** color scheme (2.35). Rather than pair colors that are in opposite positions on the color wheel, the artist completes the scheme using the two colors on either side of one of the complements. Georgia O'Keeffe's *Jack in the Pulpit No. V* (2.36) is dominated by rich greens and violets, with accents of yellow at the top of the composition and a vertical line of red just to the left of the center.

Triadic Color Schemes

The **triadic** color scheme pushes the choices even farther apart, so that they are now located in a triangular position, equally spaced around the wheel (2.37). This scheme is often used when variety and a strong impact are essential. In a brochure for the *UCLA* extension open house (2.38), variations

2.37 Triadic system.

2.38 Tin Yen Studios, *UCLA Extension Open House.*

on yellow-green, red-orange, and blue-violet bring energy to the design, while the white areas provide openness.

Chromatic Grays and Earth Colors

While the basic color wheel can help us identify many kinds of relationships, two important types of colors are not included: chromatic grays and earth colors. A **chromatic gray** is made from a mixture of various hues, rather than a simple blend of black and white. The result is both subtle and vibrant. In *The Magpie* (2.39), the grays vary widely, from the purples and blue-grays in the shadows to the golden-gray light in the foreground and the silvery grays for the snow-covered trees. This is not a dark, sullen winter day. Through the use of chromatic grays, Claude Monet made the warm light and transparent shadows sparkle in the crisp air.

Earth colors, including raw and burnt sienna, raw and burnt umber, and yellow ochre, are made

2.39 Claude Monet, *The Magpie*, 1869. Oil on canvas, 35 × 51 in. (89 × 130 cm).

generally from pigments found in soil. Often warm in temperature, when used together they create a type of analogous harmony. For example, browns, oranges, and tans accentuate the gestural energy and organic shapes in *Bush Cabbage Dreaming at Ngarlu* (2.40), by Australian artists Cookie Stewart Japaljarri, Alma Nungarrayi Granites, and Robin Japanangka Granites. This acrylic painting was inspired by traditional aboriginal artworks,

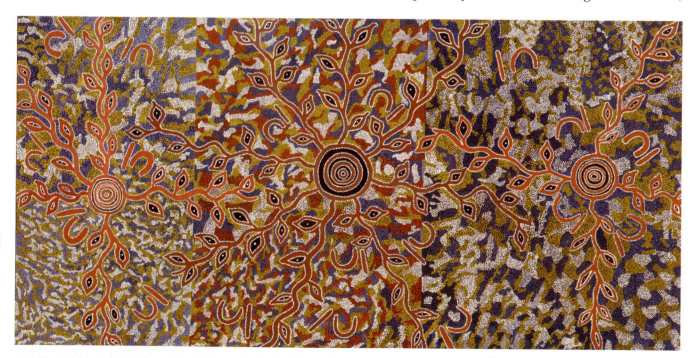

2.40 Paddy Japaljarri Stewart, *Bush Cabbage Dreaming at Ngarlu;* Yuendumn, Central Australia, 1986. Acrylic on canvas, 47½ × 93½ in. (120.5 × 237.5 cm).

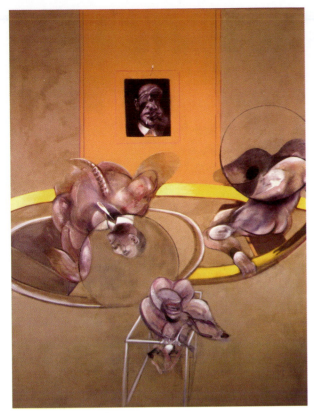

2.41 Francis Bacon, *Three Figures and Portrait*, 1975. Oil and pastel on canvas, 78 × 58 in. (198 × 147.5 cm).

2.42 Steve Quinn, *A Christmas Memory*, 1991. Photoshop, 11 × 17 in. (27.94 × 43.18 cm).

which are literally made from earth colors. When used alone, earth colors can unify even the most agitated composition. When used in combination with high-intensity colors, they can provide an elegant balance between subdued and louder, more overt colors.

Using Disharmony

Selecting the right colors can make the difference between a visual disaster and a visual delight. As a result, color harmony is the subject of endless books offering advice to artists, architects, and surface pattern designers. Monochromatic, analogous, complementary, split complementary, and triadic systems are traditional forms of color harmony.

However, cultural definitions of harmony are as changeable as popular music. In a search for eye-catching images, designers in all fields invent new color combinations each year. For example, the pink, gray, and black prized by designers in one year may seem passé in the next. Consequently, definitions and uses of color harmony are actually quite fluid.

Furthermore, when skillfully used, color **disharmony** can be as effective as color harmony. Disharmony is often used when the subject matter is disturbing or when an unusual visual approach is needed. In figure 2.41, Francis Bacon used tans, grays, pinks, orange, and blacks to produce a painting that is as disturbing as it is beautiful. The colors in the body suggest disease, while the areas of black, yellow, and gray create a room that is agitated and disorienting. Using similar pinks, gray, black, and yellow-orange, Steve Quinn created a gentle evocation of memory in his Christmas poster (2.42). Here, the words and images shift back and forth in space, as fluid as a dream.

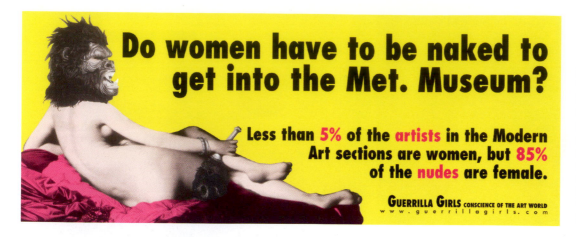

2.43 Guerrilla Girls, "Do women have to be naked to get into the Met. Museum? Less than 5% of the artists in the Modern Art sections are women, but 85% of the nudes are female," 1989. Poster, 11 × 28 in. (27.9 × 71.1 cm).

A third example is shown in figure 2.43. Bright yellow and hot pink add pizzazz to an eye-catching poster. Designed to call attention to a disparity in the number of exhibitions granted to male and female artists, this poster had to compete with other information displayed on walls around New York City. A witty image combined with jarring colors was just right in this case.

As these examples demonstrate, the degree and type of harmony used must depend on the ideas behind the image and on the visual context in which an image will appear.

COMPOSING WITH COLOR

Composition may be defined as the combination of multiple parts into a harmonious whole. The effect of color on composition is profound. Color can shift visual balance, create a focal point, influence our emotions, and expand communication. In this section, we will consider four major compositional uses of color.

Creating the Illusion of Space

Pictorial space is like a balloon. When we "push" on one side, the other side appears to bulge outward. Through our color choices, we can cause various areas in a composition to expand or contract visually. In most cases, cool, low-intensity colors tend to recede, while warm, high-intensity colors tend to advance. In Wolf Kahn's *The Yellow Square* (2.44), the greens and violets defining the exterior of the barn gently pull the viewer into the painting, while the blazing yellow window inside the barn pushes out as forcefully as the beacon in a lighthouse.

This effect can play an even more important role in nonobjective paintings. As described by painter Hans Hofmann, the "push and pull" of color can be a major source of energy in a nonobjective composition. For example, a large block of intense red dominates Hofmann's *Magnum Opus* (2.45). The blue rectangle at the left side pulls us inward, while the crisp yellow shape on the right pushes outward.

Weight and Balance

The effect of color on visual weight and balance is equally dramatic. In *Icarus* (2.46), Henri Matisse

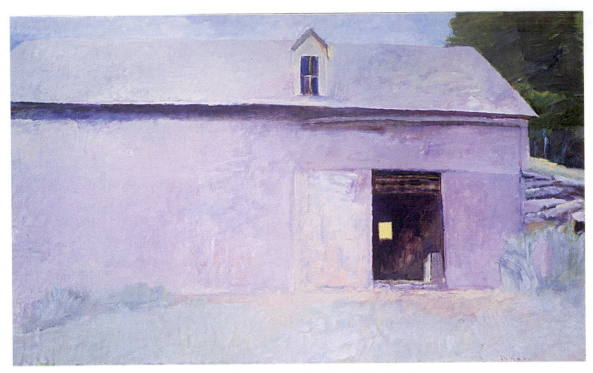

2.44 Wolf Kahn, *The Yellow Square,* **1981.** Oil on canvas, 44 × 72 in. (112 × 183 cm).

2.45 Hans Hofmann, *Magnum Opus,* **1962.** Oil on canvas, 84⅛ × 78⅛ in. (213 × 198 cm).

2.46 Henri Matisse, *Icarus,* from *Jazz* series, **1947.** Stencil print, 17⅛ × 13⅜ in. (43.6 × 34 cm).

2.47 Nancy Crow, *Double Mexican Wedding Rings 1*, 1988. Hand quilted by Marie Moore. 72 × 72 in. (183 × 183 cm).

2.48 Willem de Kooning, *Door to the River*, 1960. Oil on canvas, 80 × 70 in. (203.2 × 177.8 cm).

visually tells the story of the boy who flew too close to the sun, melting his wax wings and plunging into the ocean. The heavy black body "falls" into the blue background, while a vibrant red heart seems to pull the figure upward, away from death. Six bursts of yellow surround the figure. Equally suggestive of the stars above the boy and of light shimmering on the water below, these simple shapes add energy to the composition and meaning to the myth.

Distribution and Proportion

Through careful distribution, even the most disharmonious colors can work together beautifully. Four rectilinear gray shapes dominate Nancy Crow's *Double Mexican Wedding Rings 1* (2.47). Gradated values extend outward, creating a subtle glow. Four small multi-colored squares accentuate the edges of the four large squares, and eight colorful rectangles frame up the composition as a whole. In most compositions, the earth colors, chromatic grays, and high-intensity reds, blues, and yellows would clash. In this composition, an even distribution of colors creates a unified composition.

Proportional variation is another way to harmonize seemingly incompatible colors. Willem de Kooning's *Door to the River* (2.48) is dominated by a large mass of brilliant yellow. Five patches of blue-gray provide a subordinate **accent color.** Vigorous strokes of olive and grays create essential connections between major compositional shapes, adding both energy and unity to the design.

Color as Emphasis

Graphic designers often use color to emphasize critical information in a composition. The subway map in figure 2.49 provides a good example. Cooler areas of gray, green, and blue, placed on a black background, provide basic structural information. The bright yellow lines show the path through the subway. Red, which is used at only one point in the diagram, clearly locates the viewer on the map. A single color can make

2.49 PATH Station Maps, Louis Nelson Associates, Inc., NY. Graphic designer: Jennifer Stoller.

an equally powerful statement. In figure 2.50, a large block of yellow combined with the word *not* attracts our attention to the message in the lower-left corner.

Color can also be used to create a focal point. A small red astronomical observatory dominates Vernon Fisher's *Objects in a Field* (2.51). Located just above the center of the painting, it commands our attention while echoing the curved shape of the white parachute in the foreground.

2.50 Mark Schwartz, Greg Oznowich, and Teresa Snow, Annual Report for the Eaton Corporation.

Key Questions

COMPOSING WITH COLOR

- How much space is needed in your composition, and how can color increase the illusion of space?
- How "heavy" is each of your colors? How does weight affect balance?
- Can color proportion or distribution shift, enhance, or unify your overall composition?
- Can color add emphasis to your design?

2.51 Vernon Fisher, *Objects in a Field*, 1986. Acrylic on canvas, 8 × 8 ft (2.4 × 2.4 m).

2.52 **Andrew Wyeth,** *Wind from the Sea,* **1947.** Tempera on hardboard, 18½ × 27½ in. (47 × 69.9 cm).

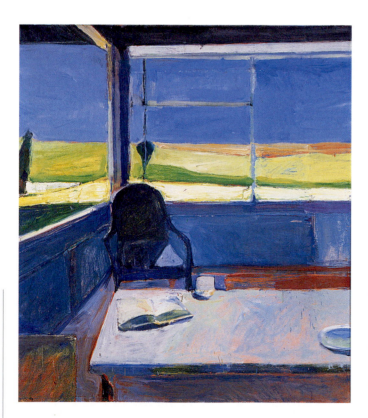

2.53 **Richard Diebenkorn,** *Interior with Book,* **1959.** Oil on canvas, 70 × 64 in. (178 × 163 cm).

EMOTION AND EXPRESSION

Colors are never emotionally neutral. The subtle browns and greens in Andrew Wyeth's *Wind from the Sea* (2.52) suggest the sepia color of a nineteenth-century photograph and evoke the slow pace and serenity of a countryside at rest. Richard Diebenkorn's *Interior with Book* (2.53), painted just 12 years later, provides a very different interpretation of a similar interior scene. The intense yellows and oranges in the background push toward us, while the solid blocks of blue pull inward, flattening the image. The tension and power thus generated create a California landscape that is a world apart from Wyeth's New England. The color in Sandy Skoglund's *Radioactive Cats* (2.54) creates yet another interpretation of an interior space. The gray walls, furniture, and clothing suggest a world that is lifeless and coated in ash. In contrast, the lime-green cats glow with an inquisitive energy that may be toxic!

Color Keys

A dominant color, or **color key,** can heighten psychological as well as compositional impact. The blues that dominate Joseph Spadaford's *Illustrated Man* (2.55) suggest both magic and melancholy. Based on a book by Ray Bradbury, Spadaford had to suggest the torment of a man whose tattoos come to life at night. At the other extreme, in Egon Schiele's *Portrait of Paris von Gütersloh* (2.56), the flaming orange around and within the figure places the anxious man in an emotional electric chair. Designers also use color keys. Blood red dominates Chaz Maviyane-Davis's *Our Fear Is Their Best Weapon* (2.57). The soldier's face is tightly cropped, highlighting his fierce red eyes.

2.54 Sandy Skoglund, *Radioactive Cats,* **1980.** Cibachrome print, 30 × 40 in. (76.2 × 101.6 cm). © 1980 Sandy Skoglund.

The powerful slogan, presented in faded black letters, is almost consumed by the red background. As

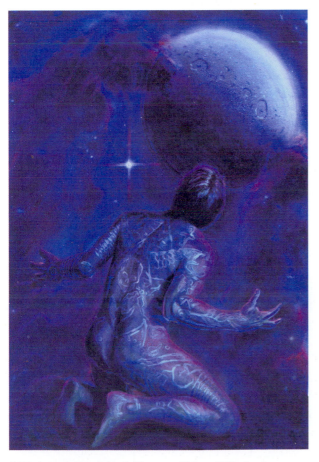

2.55 Joseph Spadaford, *Illustrated Man,* **1998.** Acrylic.

2.56 Egon Schiele, *Portrait of Paris von Gütersloh,* **1918.** Oil on canvas, 55¼ × 43¼ in. (140.3 × 109.8 cm).

2.57 Chaz Maviyane-Davis, *Our Fear Is Their Best Weapon,* 2002. Offset poster.

the text says, the voice of the people will be lost if fear is allowed to prevail. When color surrounds the viewer as in Hiroshi Senju's installations (2.58), the emotional impact can be profound. When immersed in color, we enter an alternate world. In each case, color was used to heighten emotion rather than represent reality.

Symbolic Color

Colors are often assigned symbolic meaning. These meanings may vary widely from culture to culture. In *The Primary Colors,* Alexander Theroux writes:

[Blue] is the symbol of baby boys in America, mourning in Borneo, tribulation to the American Indian and the direction South in Tibet. Blue indicates mercy in the Kabbalah and carbon monoxide in gas canisters. Chinese emperors wore blue to worship the sky. To Egyptians it represented virtue, faith, and truth. The color was worn by slaves in Gaul. It was the color of the sixth level of the Temple of Nebuchadnezzar II, devoted to the planet Mercury. In Jerusalem a blue hand painted on a door gives protection . . . and in East Africa, blue beads represent fertility.[2]

2.58 Hiroshi Senju, *New Light from Afar,* exhibition at Sundaram Tagore Gallery, 2008. Fluorescent pigment on rice paper on board.

2.59 Butterfly Maiden, Hopi Kachina. Carved cottonwood, 13½ in. (35 cm).

2.60 Jasper Johns, *Flag*, 1968. Lithograph, printed in color, composition: 34⅝ × 25⅞ in. (87.9 × 65.7 cm).

In Hopi culture, colors symbolize spatial location and geographic direction. The Kachina doll in figure 2.59 represents Butterfly Maiden, a benevolent spirit. Red represents a southerly direction; white, the east or northeast; blue or green, the west.

Symbolic color also plays a major role in *Flag* (2.60) by Jasper Johns. Part of a series of images based on the American flag, this print presents a reversal of the usual colors at the top. If we stare at this flag and then shift our attention to a white sheet of paper, we will see the familiar red, white, and blue. In this painting, an afterimage was used to suggest the contradictory nature of patriotism.

The Power of Color

Color and value each have unique strengths. A group of self-portraits by Käthe Kollwitz demonstrates three possibilities. The black-and-white value study on cream-colored paper (2.61) has a simple eloquence, while a more developed value drawing (2.62) adds drama and definition to the figure. The last portrait (2.63) places the warm figure against the cool background and makes her seem more accessible.

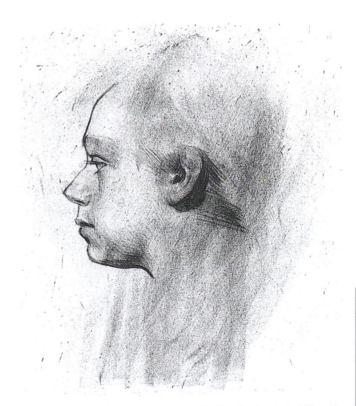

2.61 Käthe Kollwitz, *Self-Portrait in Profile, Facing Left, I (detail)*, 1889. Lithograph, 5⅞ × 5⅞ in. (15 × 15 cm).

Color can increase the power of a given shape, shift compositional weight, and create a focal point. It can enhance the illusion of space, suggest volume, and heighten emotion. Well used, color is one of the most expressive elements of art and design.

Key Questions

EMOTION AND EXPRESSION

- Will deeper space strengthen your composition? If so, what colors might you choose?
- Will a shift in coloristic balance improve your design?
- Will a dominant color key increase the emotional impact of your design?
- Considering the ideas you want to express, which is more effective: an even distribution of color or focused use, as a way to emphasize a particular shape or word?

2.62 Käthe Kollwitz, *Selbstbildnis und Aktstudien (Self-Portrait and Nude Studies)* (detail), 1900. Pencil, dark gray ink wash, with white and yellowish highlights, on heavy brown paper, 11 × 17½ in. (27.8 × 44.5 cm).

2.63 Käthe Kollwitz, *Selbstbildnis im Profil Nach Rechts,* c. 1900. Pastel on laid paper, 19 × 14⅜ in. (46.8 × 36.5 cm).

SUMMARY

- Color immediately attracts attention. Its emotional and physiological impact strengthens communication and heightens expression.

- Red, green, and blue are the additive color primaries. Blue, red, and yellow are the subtractive color primaries.

- The three basic qualities of color are hue (the name of the color), value (its lightness or darkness), and intensity (its purity).

- Using a monochromatic, analogous, complementary, split complementary, or triadic color scheme can increase harmony in your design.

- The level of color harmony must match the expressive intent. In the right context, disharmony can be more expressive than harmony.

- In a composition, color can enhance the illusion of space, shift visual weight and balance, and help emphasize compositional details.

- Distribution and proportion can help unify disharmonious colors.

- Colors are never emotionally neutral. A dominant color key can heighten psychological impact, while a symbolic color provides a cultural reference.

KEY TERMS

accent color	color interaction	intensity	split complementary
achromatic	color key	monochromatic	subtractive color
additive color	color overtones	opponent theory	temperature
afterimage	color theory	primary colors	tertiary colors
analogous	complementary	process colors	tint
Bezold effect	composition	saturation	tone
chroma	disharmony	secondary colors	triadic
chromatic gray	earth colors	shade	value
color harmony	hue	simultaneous contrast	

STUDIO PROJECTS

To apply the concepts from this chapter in the studio, check out the Projects page in the Online Learning Center at www.mhhe.com/stewart4e. The following is a sample of the chapter-related assignments that are described in step-by-step detail.

Concealing/Revealing #3. Color and communication. *Expressive Color.* Exploring meaning through color. *Sun and Substance.* Exploring shape and color as metaphors.

Profile:
Ann Baddeley Keister, Fiber Artist

Color, Construction, and Communication: Designing a Tapestry

Ann Baddeley Keister is a nationally renowned fiber artist. Her work has been exhibited both nationally and internationally and is in many private and corporate collections, including The Vanguard Group, The Discovery Channel, and the Indianapolis Museum of Art.

MS: When I look at your work, I am impressed by the very deliberate use of design in these complex narrative tapestries. These images could be painted or done on a computer so much more quickly. What is the advantage of weaving? What attracted you to fiber arts?

AK: My undergraduate degree actually was a general degree in design, which allowed me to explore a number of different craft and fine art media, including textiles. The University of Kansas has a great fiber facility, and since I had learned how to knit and sew at the age of seven, the materials of textile art just felt natural and familiar to me. I love making the structure through the repetitive action of weaving. And I'm attracted to the pliability of the material. For me, metals are too unforgiving, clay is too messy—fiber, as a material, just feels "right" to me. I feel that there is a strong symbiosis between the images that I am interested in making and the material from which those images are constructed. One seems to feed off of the other.

MS: Designer Paul Rand said, "Art is an idea that has found its perfect form. Design is the means by which this is realized." And it is often said that art is about expression, while design is about communication. Is your work both art and design?

AK: Yes, and it is also craft and decoration. Contemporary fiber arts is such a diverse field. I love pure pattern AND I love storytelling. I love looking at beautiful colors, and want to offer the viewer a visual feast through my work!

MS: What is your usual work process?

AK: Many of my projects begin with a commission.

I determine the client's requirements and puzzle over possible solutions. With *Memory*, during a walk along the Grand River, I saw a historical marker describing the late-nineteenth-century flood. I began to think about this terrible storm that washed away bridges and created piles of logs careening through the city. I immediately realized that this event could provide my image.

I made a number of pencil sketches, exploring compositional possibilities. I then developed these sketches in color, using Adobe Illustrator. I have an extensive knowledge of color theory and this actually gives me the freedom to choose my colors very intuitively. I am using a lot of blue in this piece, since it is one of the school's colors, and I have a lot of discordant colors, which seem appropriate for such a devastating event.

A full-size, 6' × 10' computer print comes next. I match colors from my collection of approximately 200 colors of wool yarns. One strand on the loom is made up of six strands of yarn. I use a lot of optical mixing to create very subtle gradations. Finally, I weave the piece. The most useful thing I learned from my teachers is this: DO YOUR WORK! There is no substitute for action. Weaving is slow and simply has to be done consistently. During my summer work time, I am in the studio from about 9 to 6 an average of five or six days a week. Since weaving is an activity that makes demands on the body and the concentration, I do take breaks in my daily work with forays into the garden or other household chores. This is one reason that I find working at home so satisfying. My domestic interests in cooking, the garden, and my home often find their way into the imagery in my work as well.

MS: What are your criteria for excellence?

AK: I seek unity between concept and composition. Each of the formal elements: line, shape, texture, and color — is essential. There is almost always a dynamic sense of space in my work, which makes the tapestry read well in an architectural setting. I seek an inseparable connection between imagery, technique, and material.

MS: Do you have any advice for my students?

AK: Take this time to be inventive. Try out many possibilities. If you don't like an image, don't do it! Invent another way to solve the problem. The joy you bring to the creative process will be apparent in the final design.

Ann Baddeley Keister, *Memory,* 2000. Wool tapestry, 6 × 10 ft (1.83 × 3.1 m).

Principles of Two-Dimensional Design

Imagine yourself practicing jump shots on a deserted basketball court. By focusing all of your attention on the basket, you can master the sequence of moves needed to score. Now imagine yourself playing in a high-paced game. You are now surrounded by skillful and cooperative teammates. The skills you practiced alone become heightened as you take passes and make shots. The complexities increase and the stakes rise when 10 players fill the court.

Developing a rich complex composition can be equally exhilarating. **Composition** can be defined as the combination of multiple parts into a unified whole. In a well-composed design, line, shape, texture, value, and color work together, as a team. As one element becomes dominant, the other elements must adjust. A dialogue is created between positive and negative shapes, and multiple visual forces increase vitality rather than creating confusion.

We begin this chapter with a discussion of unity and variety, the basis on which all design is built. We then define and discuss balance, scale, proportion, rhythm, and emphasis. Connections between concept and composition are emphasized throughout.

UNITY AND VARIETY

Unity can be defined as similarity, oneness, togetherness, or cohesion. **Variety** can be defined as difference. Unity and variety are the cornerstones of composition. When they are combined effectively, we can create compositions that are both cohesive and lively.

Mark Riedy used three major strategies to unify figure 3.1. First, all of the major shapes are organized diagonally, from the lower left to the upper right. A series of parallel lines in the sand and sea emphasizes this diagonal structure. The cast shadows then create another diagonal pattern, running from the upper left to the lower right. Second, the top third of the painting is filled with the blue water, while the beach fills the bottom two-thirds. This proportional relationship has been used since antiquity to create a dynamic form of balance. Third, one shape is repeated 19 times, creating the graceful collection of umbrellas. Repetition in any form tends to increase unity.

A sailboat, 9 groups of bathers, and especially the single red umbrella add variety. The red umbrella breaks the pattern set by the 18 white umbrellas. The resulting focal point attracts our attention to a particular spot on the

3.1 Mark Riedy, *Day at the Beach,* 1988. Acrylic airbrush.

3.2 Vija Celmins, *Untitled (Ocean),* 1969. Graphite on acrylic ground on paper, 14 × 18 in. (35.6 × 45.7 cm).

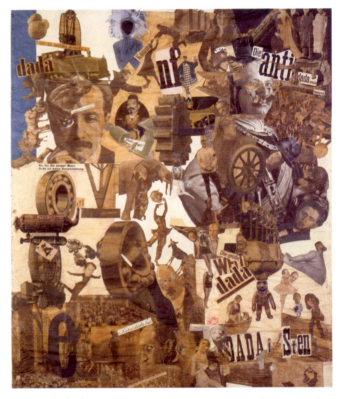

3.3 Hannah Höch, *Cut with a Kitchen Knife,* 1919. Collage, 44⅞ × 35½ in. (114 × 90 cm).

beach. As we begin to notice the number of people clustered around this umbrella, we are pulled into the painting and the miniature world it represents. One small red circle dramatically changes our visual and emotional response to the entire painting.

We face a new compositional challenge with each design we make. There are no simple formulas: each idea has its own expressive requirements. For example, in figure 3.2, Vija Celmins used a highly unified drawing to create a quiet, contemplative image. The size and shape of the waves are the only variations. At the other extreme, Hannah Höch's *Cut with a Kitchen Knife* (3.3) is crowded with conflicting images and fragmentary words. Created shortly after the end of World War I, this collage reflects the tumultuous economic and political conditions in postwar Germany. Celmins used a highly unified pattern of waves to suggest the ocean's hypnotic power, while Hoch used a collection of conflicting images to suggest chaos. Using very different approaches, each artist created an appropriate composition for the concept she wished to convey.

Excessive unity can be monotonous, while excessive variety can be chaotic. In the following section, we explore ways to create an effective partnership between the two.

Gestalt: Theory and Application

Artists and designers use many strategies to create compelling compositions. **Gestalt psychology** offers a fascinating analysis of these strategies. According to this theory, visual information is understood holistically before it is examined separately. We first scan the entire puzzle, then analyze the specific parts. An image composed of units that are unrelated in size, style, orientation, and color appears chaotic and unresolved. The implications of Gestalt are complex, and many books have been written on the subject. In this brief introduction, we will focus on six essential aspects.

Grouping

When presented with a collection of separate visual units, we immediately try to create order and make connections. **Grouping** is one of the first steps in this process. We generally group visual units by location, orientation, shape, and color. For example, the units in figure 3.4A form two distinct groups despite their dissimilarity in shape. Orientation creates group cohesion in figure 3.4B. The diagonal placement of

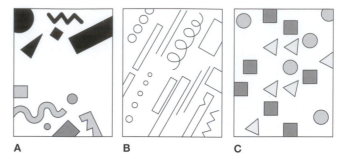

3.4A–C Examples of grouping by location, orientation, and shape.

the various elements creates unity despite the variations in shape. Grouping by shape is shown in figure 3.4C. We mentally organize this set of units by shape in spite of their similarity in size and value.

Rama and Lakshmana Bound by Arrow-Snakes (3.5) demonstrates the compositional and conceptual power of grouping. We first see the complete composition. Multiple groups of humans and animals fill the long, horizontal rectangle. Next, we may notice that the composition is divided into three sections, each dominated by a distinctive background color. Blue and gray dominate the section on the left; red and orange dominate the section on the right.

3.5 Sahibdin and workshop, *Rama and Lakshmana Bound by Arrow-Snakes,* **from the** *Ramayana,* **Mewar, c. 1650–52.** Opaque watercolor on paper, 9 × 15⅛ in. (22.86 × 38.42 cm).

A yellow background fills the center. Within these major groups, we can discern further subdivisions, including the two clusters of monkeys on the left, the four compositional boxes on the right, and the throng of horsemen in the center.

Like a graphic novel, this painting tells a complex story of prophecy, magical transformation, imprisonment, and escape. It begins in the rose-colored box on the right, as Indrajit devises a defense against Rama and Lakshmana, who are about to attack the palace. On the left, Indrajit's arrows turn into writhing snakes, binding the attackers. Indrajit's triumphal march dominates the center of the composition. By grouping the various events, the artist was able to present complex visual information effectively.

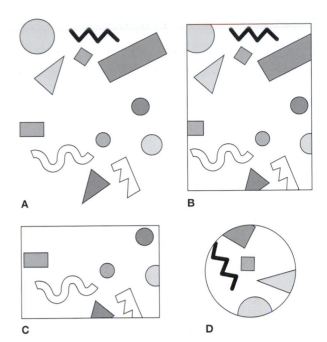

3.6A–D A container of any kind helps unify disparate visual units.

Containment

As we can see from figure 3.5, groups are most easily created when visual units are placed inside a container. **Containment** is a unifying force created by the outer edge of a composition or by a boundary within a composition. A container encourages us to seek connections among visual units and adds definition to the negative space around each positive shape. The random collection of shapes in figure 3.6A becomes more unified when a simple boundary is added (3.6B). Any shift in the location of this boundary creates a new set of relationships. A vertical rectangle is often used when a rising or sinking movement is needed, while a horizontal format can create an expansive effect (3.6C). The circular container in figure 3.6D draws our attention both to the center and to the outer edges of the composition.

Larry Moore's illustration in figure 3.7 uses containment in an especially inventive way. Three containers are used in this composition. The edge of the drawing provides the first container, the curtains provide the second, and the face itself provides the third. A wide variety of corporate logos cover the face. Logos must attract the viewer's attention, regardless of the context in which they are placed, and each of these logos was originally designed as a distinct visual unit. In this composition, however, the individualistic logos become a cooperative team. The connections created by the three levels of containment are stronger than the separations created by the individualistic logos.

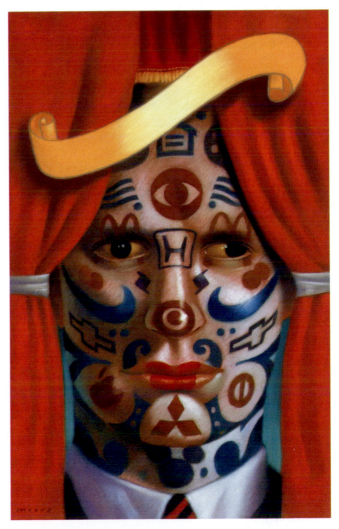

3.7 Larry Moore, *Tattoo Face Man.* Pastel on paper, 10 × 15 in. (25.4 × 38.1 cm).

Repetition

Repetition occurs when we use the same visual element or effect over and over. By leafing through Chapter One, we can find many examples of unity through repetition. Kandinsky's *Several Circles* (page 17) is unified by shape. The repeated circles create a cohesive design despite the wide range of colors used. Repeated textures unify many works, including the Villon portrait on page 7, the Dürer engraving on page 23, and the Moran landscape on page 32.

In Aaron Macsai's *Panels of Movement* (3.8), similar lines, shapes, textures, and colors were used in each of the 10 panels from which the bracelet was constructed. A spiral shape, an undulating line, a sphere, and at least one triangular shape appear in each of the panels. Despite their variations in size, texture, and location, these repeated shapes create a strong connection from panel to panel.

3.8 Aaron Macsai, *Panels of Movement.* Bracelet, 18K gold, sterling, copper, ⅞ × 7 in. (2 × 18 cm).

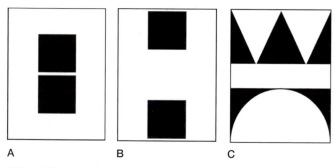

A   B   C

3.9 A–C Variations in proximity.

3.10 Michelangelo, *Creation of Adam* (detail), c. 1510. Sistine Chapel, Rome.

Proximity

In design, the distance between visual elements is called **proximity.** As shown in figure 3.9A, close proximity helps increase unity. More distant shapes read as separate events (3.9B). **Fusion** occurs when shapes or volumes are placed so close together that they share common edges. When shapes of similar color and texture fuse, new negative shapes can be created as the surrounding area becomes more clearly defined (3.9C).

Careful use of proximity can create visual tension, adding energy to the design. A detail from Michelangelo's *Creation of Adam* (3.10) demonstrates the expressive power of visual tension. Jehovah's hand, on the right, nearly touches Adam's hand, on the left. As we gaze at the ceiling of the Sistine Chapel, less than 6 inches of space separates the two. In this cosmology, all of human history begins when the spark of life jumps this gap. If the hands had been placed too far apart or too close together, the spark that animates both the man and the painting would have been lost.

Continuity

Continuity may be defined as a fluid connection among compositional parts. This connection can be actual or implied. With actual continuity, each shape touches an adjoining shape. With implied continuity, we mentally make the connections.

Skillful use of continuity can add visual movement to a design. **Movement** creates deliberate visual pathways and helps direct the viewer's attention to areas of particular interest. In Frank Stella's *Lac Laronge IV* (3.11), curving lines and shapes flow from one circle to the next, creating actual continuity. Color distribution creates implied continuity, which enhances this visual flow. The upward curve of blue in the upper-left corner is echoed by a quarter turn of blue in the lower-right corner. The downward curve of reds in the lower-left corner is echoed by a quarter turn of scarlet in the upper-right corner. The hints of olive and brown add a further spin to the wheel.

Movement can play an equally important role in a representational design. In Théodore Géricault's *Raft of the Medusa* (3.12A), a pattern of diagonal lines (3.12B) directs our attention to a single **focal point,** or primary point of interest. The arms and legs of the sailors, the floorboards of the raft, and even the angle of the sail all lead us toward the rescue ship in the upper-right corner. This dramatic use of movement greatly increases the emotional power of this historical painting. One hundred forty-nine survivors from a sinking ship began a desperate journey on the raft. When rescued two weeks later, only 15 had survived. The pattern of bodies and extended arms pulls us irresistibly toward the sailor at the front of the raft, whose very life depends on the attention he can attract.

Closure

Closure refers to the mind's inclination to connect fragmentary information to produce a completed form. In figure 3.13, thousands of spools of thread have been connected to form blocks of color. Using closure, we then read these blocks of color as a man's face.

Closure makes it possible to communicate using implication. Freed of the necessity to provide every detail, the artist or designer can convey an idea through suggestion, rather than description. When the viewer completes the image in his or her mind, it is often more memorable than an image that leaves no room for participation.

Combining Gestalt Principles

Artists and designers often combine all of the principles of Gestalt in a single composition. In figure 3.14, closure makes it possible for us to turn hundreds of dots into a face and fifteen letters in different fonts into words. The repeated dots in the face and the larger yellow and pink dots in the bottom section help unify the design. Both the pink face at the top and

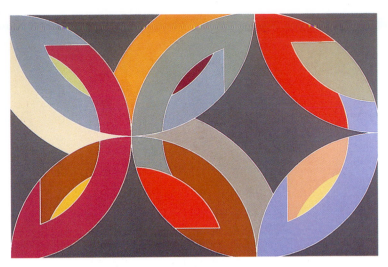

3.11 Frank Stella, *Lac Laronge IV,* **1969.** Acrylic polymer on canvas, 9 ft ⅛ in. × 13 ft 6 in. (2.75 × 3.11 m).

3.12A Théodore Géricault, *Raft of the Medusa,* **1818–19.** Oil on canvas, 16 ft 1 in. × 23 ft 6 in. (4.9 × 7.2 m).

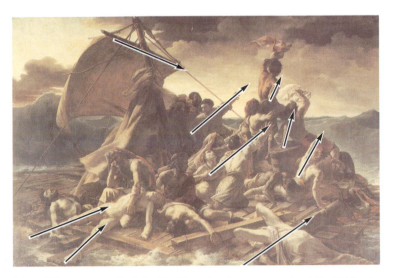

3.12B Diagram of *Raft of the Medusa,* **showing eye movement toward focal point.**

3.13 Devorah Sperber, *After van Eyck*, 2006. 5024 spools of thread, stainless steel ball chain and hanging apparatus, clear acrylic sphere on metal stand, 120 ×100 in. (305 × 254 cm).

the black-and-white face in the lower left lean to the left, increasing unity through orientation. Tightly contained within the rectangular format, a wide variety of visual components create an exuberant composition.

Patterns and Grids

A **pattern** is created when any visual element is systematically repeated over an extended area. Many patterns are based on a module, or basic visual unit. In a sly reference to the mass production of culture, Andy Warhol used the *Mona Lisa* as a module in figure 3.15. A **grid** is created through a series of intersecting lines in figure 3.16A–C. Both patterns and grids increase compositional unity by creating containment, suggesting continuity, strengthening proximity, and encouraging closure.

Patterns are often used to decorate walls, books, or fabrics. In his *Canterbury Tales* (3.17), designer William Morris used complex floral patterns to create multiple

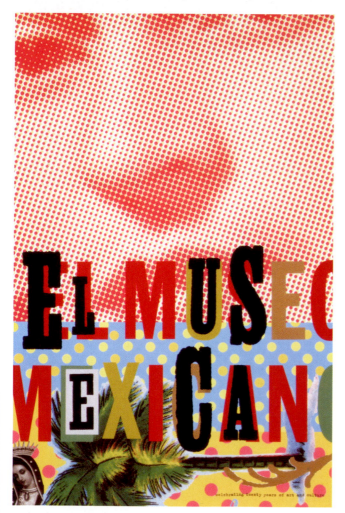

3.14 Morla Design, The Mexican Museum twentieth-anniversary poster, 1997.

3.15 Andy Warhol, *30 Are Better Than One,* 1963. Silkscreen ink and synthetic polymer paint on canvas, 110 × 82 in. (279.4 × 208.3 cm).

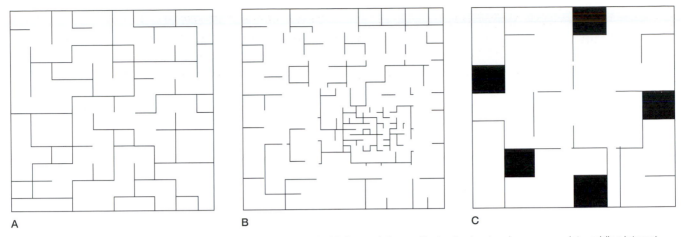

3.16A–C Grid variations. A simple checkerboard is a highly unified grid. Any variation on the basic structure increases variety, adding interest.

A   B   C

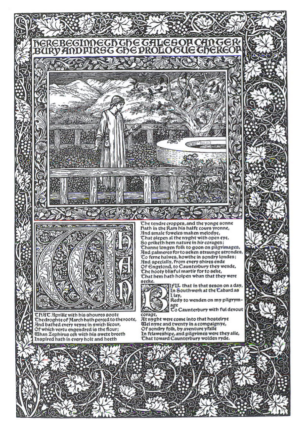

3.17 William Morris, designer; Edward Burne-Jones, illustrator. Illustrated page from *The Canterbury Tales*, 1896.

3.18 Faith Ringgold, *Tar Beach*, 1988. Acrylic on canvas, fabric border, 74 × 69 in. (187.96 × 175.26 cm).

borders and backgrounds. Curvilinear patterns of grapevines, flowers, and oak leaves fill the borders. The flowing text at the top of the page echoes these curving shapes and creates an additional pattern. There are even more patterns in the main drawing. The standing man is surrounded by two distinct leaf patterns, and a linear pattern suggests wood grain.

Multiple fragments of visual information can also be unified through pattern. In *Tar Beach* (3.18), Faith Ringgold used a pattern of repeating squares to organize blocks of printed fabric into a distinctive border. Based on Ringgold's own memories of sleeping on an apartment roof during hot weather, this pattern refers to the quilt depicted in the painting and to the magical expanse of buildings and lights visible from the rooftop.

Compositional grids are most commonly created using vertical and horizontal lines. The unifying power of a grid is so great that even the most disparate information gains cohesion when a grid is used.

A

B

3.19A and B
Kevin Sprague,
double-page spread
from Muse project.
Photographic collage,
8½ × 22 in. (21.6 ×
55.9 cm).

In Kevin Sprague's photographic collage (3.19A), the placement of a woman's face within a landscape immediately attracts attention. Lines of text descend like a staircase from the left to the right, helping to connect the seemingly unrelated photographs. Shown in figure 3.19B, a loose grid created by the vertical trees and the horizontal text adds just the right amount of unity to this poignant meditation on nature.

Key Questions

UNITY AND VARIETY

- What strategies have you used to unify your composition?
- What gives your composition variety?
- Is the balance between unity and variety appropriate for the ideas you want to express?
- What would happen if your composition were constructed using a pattern or grid?
- What happens when some areas in a pattern are disrupted?
- What happens when some areas in a grid compress while others expand?

BALANCE

In design, **balance** refers to the distribution of weight or force within a composition. Negative and positive shapes can work together to create an equilibrium among compositional units, regardless of variations in their size, weight, or shape.

Weight and Gravity

Visual weight can be defined in two ways. First, *weight* refers to the inclination of shapes to float or sink. Second, *weight* can refer to the relative importance of a visual element within a design.

The compositional forces that most influence visual weight are size, value, type of shape, texture, location, and orientation. The context in which a visual unit is placed strongly affects each of these forces. For example, when a shape is placed on a neutral white ground, darker values and vigorous textures generally increase its visual weight. As noted in Chapter One, circles tend to stand out when placed in a rectangular format, while squares fit together easily. Location within the format also affects visual weight. Shapes that appear to extend beyond the upper edge tend to rise, while shapes that appear to extend below the bottom tend to sink.

The vertical, horizontal, or diagonal orientation of the compositional frame also affects visual weight. Try this simple experiment. Which is the most dynamic and which is the most stable position for the box in figure 3.20? Most viewers find positions A and B the most stable. In these positions, the box is at rest, with the vertical and horizontal edges reconfirming the stability we experience when objects are at rest in the real world. By contrast, position C and position D place the box in a dynamic position, halfway between standing and falling. A composition that is dominated by diagonals tends to be visually dynamic, while a composition that is dominated by horizontals tends to be more stable, or static.

Bernice Abbott's photograph of New York skyscrapers (3.21) demonstrates the power of orientation. Using dramatic vertical shapes within a tall vertical

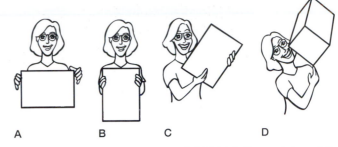

A   B   C   D

3.20A–D Which box is the most static? Which is the most dynamic?

format, she captured the soaring energy of Wall Street within a small image.

The compositional dynamics change dramatically when a square format is used. In *Radical Acts* (3.22), Kathryn Frund combined the stability of a square with the dynamism of the diagonal lines that dissect

3.21 Bernice Abbott,
Exchange Place, New York,
1934. Photograph.

3.22 Kathryn Frund, *Radical Acts,* **2008.** Mixed mediums with found objects and paper mounted on aluminum, 48 × 48 in. (121.9 × 121.9 cm).

3.23 Ansel Adams, *Moonrise, Hernandez, New Mexico*, **1941.** Silver print, 18½ × 23 in. (47 × 58.4 cm).

the painting from upper left to lower right. Integrating flat painting and actual objects, she presents us with a puzzle. Why construct an image using actual journal pages, a plumb-bob weight, a tiny ladder, and large, dramatic blocks of color? Frund challenges viewers to reconcile these seemingly contradictory visual forces in order to create a wide range of possible meanings.

Visual weight can also refer to the relative importance of a visual element within a design. In *Moonrise, Hernandez, New Mexico, 1941* (3.23), Ansel Adams combined balance, gravity, and movement to create an image that is both tranquil and dramatic. A squarish format dominated by horizontal lines provides stability. The quiet village sinks to the bottom of the design. The tiny moon, positioned just to the left of compositional center, pulls us into the velvety black sky at the top half of the image. As the focal point for the image, the tiny moon has the most visual weight in this photograph.

Symmetrical Balance

Symmetrical balance occurs when shapes are mirrored on either side of an axis, as in a composition that is vertically divided down the center (3.24A). A

shift in this axis (3.24B) creates symmetry between the top and bottom of the design.

A symmetrically balanced design can appeal to our desire for equilibrium and communicate calm and stability. The Taj Mahal (3.25) was built by a seventeenth-century Indian emperor as a tomb for his beloved wife. The three white marble domes and the four flanking towers create architectural symmetry. In the reflecting pool, a mirror image appears, increasing visual symmetry. The building is both graceful and serene.

Approximate symmetry is created when similar imagery appears on either side of a central axis. For example, in Richard Estes's *Miami Rug Company* (3.26), actual and reflected light poles divide the space as decisively as a gate. Radiating from the center of the composition, a network of diagonal lines pulls us into the painting. At the same time, the large pane of glass on the left side pushes toward us, shimmering with darkened reflections of the buildings on the right side. The overall effect is unnerving. The seemingly symmetrical shapes are actually quite different, and the resulting image is disorienting rather than serene.

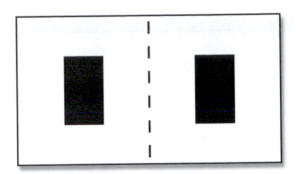

A

B

3.24A and B Examples of symmetrical balance.

3.25 Taj Mahal, Agra, India, 1630–48.

3.26 Richard Estes, *Miami Rug Company,* 1974. Oil on canvas, 40 × 54 in. (101.6 × 137.16 cm).

Radial Symmetry

With **radial symmetry,** lines and shapes are mirrored both vertically and horizontally, with the center of the composition acting as a focal point (3.27). An expanded approach to radial symmetry is shown in Judy Chicago's *Rejection Quintet: Female Rejection Drawing* (3.28). Because the format is now divided diagonally as well as vertically and horizontally, the entire design radiates from the center. Glowing and gradated colors accentuate the effect.

A variant on radial balance is the spiral. A spiral can increase energy within a circular format or add movement to a rectangular composition. In Rubens's *Tiger Hunt* (3.29), the spiral pulls the tiger and the hunters together in the center of the painting. It then spins outward, breaking apart near the edges. The resulting composition harnesses the compressive power of centripetal force and the expansive power of centrifugal force.

3.28 Judy Chicago, *Rejection Quintet: Female Rejection Drawing,* **1974.** Prismacolor and graphite on rag board, 39⅝ × 29⅝ in. (101 × 75 cm).

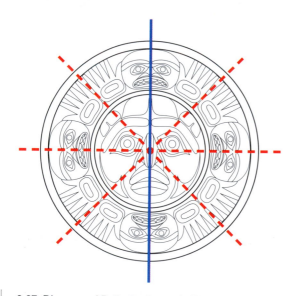

3.27 Diagram of Bella Coola mask. The central face is symmetrically balanced. The outer ring is an example of radial symmetry.

3.29 Workshop of Peter Paul Rubens, *Tiger Hunt,* **c. 1616.** Oil on canvas, 38⅞ × 49¼ in. (98.8 × 125 cm).

Asymmetrical Balance

Asymmetrical balance creates equilibrium among visual elements that do *not* mirror each other on either side of an axis. Depending on the degree of asymmetry, the resulting design may be quite stable, very dynamic, or nearly chaotic.

Many strategies can be used to create asymmetrical balance:

- A large shape is placed close to the fulcrum, while a small shape is placed farther away. Just as a child at the end of a seesaw can balance an adult near the center, so large and small shapes can be balanced in a design (3.30A).

- Multiple small squares, acting together, can balance a large square (3.30B).

- A small, solid square can balance a large, open circle. The solidity and stability of the square give it additional weight (3.30C).

- A textured shape placed near the fulcrum can be balanced by a distant open shape (3.30D).

Asymmetrical balance becomes even more interesting when a boundary is added. Because the negative space is just as important as each positive shape, more complex compositions can now be created:

- A small shape placed near the bottom of the format balances a large shape placed along the top. Especially within a tall rectangle, shapes placed near the top tend to rise, while shapes placed near the bottom tend to sink (3.31A).

- When the small square intersects the bottom edge and the large square moves away from the edge, the differences in weight become even more pronounced (3.31B).

- The top shape now gains energy through its diagonal orientation. Three bottom shapes are needed to create balance (3.31C).

- Finally, a small, aggressive triangle can balance a large, passive rectangle (3.31D).

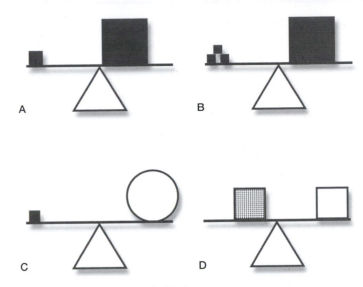

3.30A–D Creating asymmetrical balance.

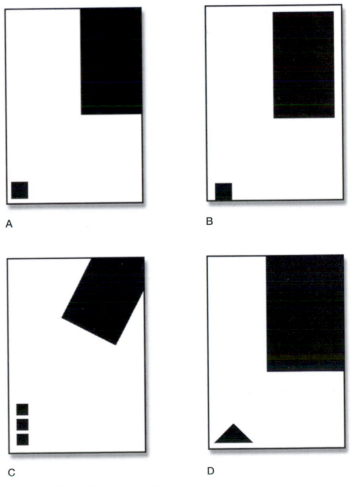

3.31A–D Examples of asymmetrical balance.

3.32 Piet Mondrian, *Composition with Blue and Yellow,* **1935.** Oil on canvas, 28¾ × 27¼ in. (73 × 69.2 cm).

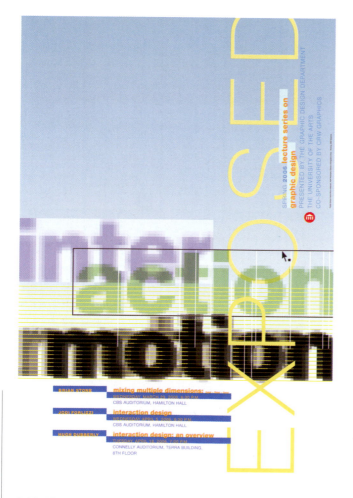

3.33 Alleman Almquistt Jones, Promotional Poster for the Graphic Design Department, University of the Arts. Digital image.

Balance in a composition shifts each time a visual element is added or subtracted. A crisp network of negative and positive lines and shapes creates the balance in Piet Mondrian's *Composition with Blue and Yellow* (3.32). The large yellow square positioned along the top edge is easily balanced by the small blue rectangle, which sinks to the bottom. As shown by the small vertical line positioned near the center-left edge, even very minor changes can shift compositional balance.

In figure 3.33, multiple layers of text have been balanced within a vertical rectangle. Returning to our earlier discussion of Gestalt, let's deconstruct this image step by step. A light-blue shape fills the top half of the image, then dissolves into the white shape at the bottom. A horizontal block of text is positioned slightly below the center, while along the right edge a vertical block of text pulls our eyes upward. A fine line encloses and emphasizes the word *action*. Five lines of red text connect the horizontal and vertical axes, with three near the bottom and two running parallel to the right edge. The small circular logo positioned nearby creates a visual exclamation point.

Expressive Uses of Balance

Each type of balance has its advantages. The approximate symmetry Frida Kahlo used for her double self-portrait (3.34) is symbolically appropriate and compositionally effective. Painted in response to her divorce from painter Diego Rivera, it presents the beloved Frida in a native costume on the right and the rejected Frida in European dress on the left. A linear vein connects the women's hearts. In figure 3.28 (page 78), Judy Chicago used radial symmetry to pull the viewer into the composition. And in figure 3.1 (see page 67), Mark Riedy used asymmetrical balance to animate his beach scene and accentuate the red umbrella.

There are even some cases in which a degree of **imbalance** is necessary. Eric Fischl used distortion to create imbalance in *Barbeque* (3.35). The table in the foreground is tilted, and the bowl of fish seems impossibly large. Pulled by the diagonal lines leading to the house, the pool also seems tilted, while the tiny women are more like dolls than people. Manning the grill, the father looks on approvingly as his son engages in a little recreational fire-breathing. Spatial distortion combined with a bizarre collection of objects and events turns a family picnic into a suburban nightmare.

Key Questions

BALANCE

- Which is the "heaviest" shape in your design? Does its weight match its importance?

- How does the outer shape of your design affect its compositional balance?

- In your composition, how does negative space affect overall balance?

- Various forms of balance were described in this section. Which is most effective for the ideas and emotions you want to express?

3.34 Frida Kahlo, *Las Dos Fridas,* 1939. Oil on canvas, 69⅛ × 69⅛ in. (176 × 176 cm).

3.35 Eric Fischl, *Barbeque,* 1982. Oil on canvas. 5 ft 5 in. × 8 ft 4 in. (165 × 254 cm).

SCALE AND PROPORTION

Scale and proportion create two types of size relationships. Both strongly affect compositional balance and emotional impact. **Proportion** refers to the relative size of visual elements *within* an image. When we compare the width of the head with its height or divide a composition into thirds, we are establishing a proportional relationship (3.36). **Scale** commonly refers to the size of a form when compared with our own human size. Thus, a 50-foot-long painting is a large-scale artwork, while a 10-square-inch square painting is an example of small scale.

Most designs distribute information fairly evenly within the format, with only modest size variation among the parts. Exaggerating these proportions can be eye-catching, because the image immediately stands out from the norm. In *Save Our City,* by Michael Bierut (3.37), a heavy black rectangle at the top presses down on the white shape below, covering the top part of the word *Save.* Meanwhile, the small vertical lines of white text suggest a city skyline and help pull the white section of the poster upward. Finally, a rectangle of tiny red text appears in the lower-left corner. This tension between the upper and lower sections of the design perfectly matches the urgency of the message.

Likewise, various expressive possibilities occur when scale is exaggerated. *Intermission* (see page 109) presented many challenges to painter Ken Stout. The 50-foot-long format had to become an asset, rather than a liability. We visually enter the theater through the pink doorway at the far left. Cool blue light bathes the restless audience. Two men in the balcony add to the action, as one aims a peashooter

and another launches a paper airplane. On the stage, a tiny actor creates a transition between the audience and the stage crew. The painting ends in a final burst of red, at the far right side. Taking advantage of each square inch, Stout created a swirling panorama of figures engaged in a wide variety of activities onstage, backstage, and in the audience.

3.37 Michael Bierut, *Save Our City.* Design Firm: Pentagram, NYC.

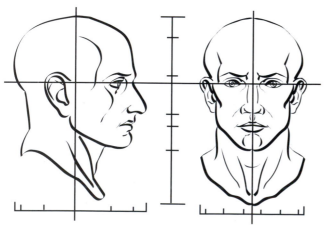

3.36 Proportion is an essential part of figure drawing.

Key Questions
SCALE AND PROPORTION

- Which is the largest shape in your design? Which is the smallest? Do their sizes match their significance?
- How can you make a small shape the most powerful compositional component?
- Can extremes in scale or proportion increase visual impact in your design?

RHYTHM

Rhythm is a sense of movement that is created by repetition of multiple units in a deliberate pattern. Visual rhythm is similar to musical rhythm. In music, rhythm is created through the organization of sound in time. Meter (the basic pattern of sound and silence), accents (which emphasize specific notes), and tempo (the speed at which the music is played) can be combined to create a dazzling array of compositional possibilities.

As with music, the rhythm in a visual composition can take many forms. In Bridget Riley's *Drift No. 2* (3.38), a simple line has been repeated to create an undulating rhythm similar to the waves on water. Vibrant words create a spatial rhythm in figure 3.39. Warm and cool colors in various values and intensities cause some words to advance while others recede.

Sue Benner used a looser and more layered approach to rhythm in *Sink or Swim #33* (3.40). Leaf shapes appear to move across the center (from the lower left to the upper right), while small circular shapes fill the upper-left and lower-right corners. Wavy lines in the background add additional movement, and variations in hue and value cause the entire design to undulate in and out.

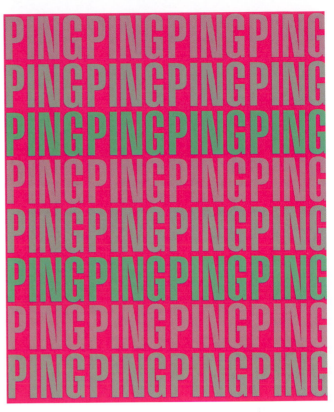

3.39 A repeated word becomes a rhythmic design through color choices.

3.40 Sue Benner, *Sink or Swim #33,* **2000.** Dye and paint on silk, fused, machine quilted. 40 × 60 in. (101.6 × 152.4 cm).

Visual rhythm can be as regular as a waltz or as syncopated as jazz. Multiplication, fragmentation, and superimposition propel the nude descending Marcel Duchamp's staircase (3.41). The jerking rhythm demonstrates the alternating stability and instability of human locomotion, rather than physical grace. When walking, we continually fall forward, then catch ourselves as we take the next step.

3.38 Bridget Riley, *Drift No. 2,* **1966.** Acrylic on canvas, 7 ft 7½ in. × 7 ft 5½ in. (2.32 × 2.27 m).

3.41 Marcel Duchamp, *Nude Descending a Staircase, No. 2*, 1912. Oil on canvas, 58 × 35 in. (147.3 × 88.9 cm).

Key Questions

RHYTHM

- What visual elements repeat in your design?
- Through deliberate use of repetition, can they create a more powerful and unified design?
- Is a consistent rhythm best for your idea, or is more variety needed?

EMPHASIS

Each player in a basketball game has a particular role to play. The guards primarily focus on defense, the forwards on offense. The point guard plays a dominant role, calling plays and controlling the action. Likewise, the various visual elements in a composition must work together as a team. In most cases, a few carefully selected visual elements dominate, or stand out, while others are more subordinate, or supportive.

Emphasis gives prominence to part of a design. A focal point is a compositional device used to create emphasis. Both emphasis and focal point are used to attract attention and increase visual and conceptual impact.

Emphasis by Isolation

Any **anomaly,** or break from the norm, tends to stand out. Because we seek to connect the verbal and visual information we are given, a mismatched word or an isolated shape immediately attracts our attention. In figure 3.42, the word *design* is emphasized through its separation from the word *magazine*. Its placement right at the bottom edge makes this shape even more eye-catching.

Just as a pattern tends to increase connection among visual elements, so any break in the pattern emphasizes isolation. In figure 3.1 (page 67), 18 white umbrellas establish the pattern that is so beautifully broken by the single red umbrella. In *I Never Liked Musical Chairs* (3.43), metalsmith Joana Kao created a pattern using 7 tiny chairs connected by a silver chain. The figure at the end of the chain breaks the pattern. This break conveys the isolation felt by a child ejected from the game.

Emphasis by Placement

Every square inch of a composition has a distinctive power. As a result, placement alone can increase the importance of a selected shape.

The compositional center is especially potent. In *The Power of the Center*, psychologist Rudolph Arnheim discusses **centricity** (compressive compositional force) and **eccentricity** (expansive compositional force). Both centricity and eccentricity activate *Flash Point*, shown on page 14. The central white square pulls us into the middle of the painting, while the explosive red rectangle pushes toward the outer edge.

This effect is even more pronounced in figure 3.44. Any representation of another human attracts our attention, and faces are of particular interest. Four major lines and a series of concentric circles direct us inward, toward the man's left eye. Fragments of text

3.42 Pentagram Design, Magazine. Publisher: Art Center College of Design, Pasadena, CA.

3.43 Joana Kao, *I Never Liked Musical Chairs.* Bracelet, sterling, 24K, 2¾ × 1¾ in. (7 × 4 cm). In this example of emphasis by isolation, the figure at the end of the chain represents a child ejected from a game.

extend outward, beyond the edge of the composition. Continually compressing and expanding, the seemingly simple image pulls the viewer inward while simultaneously appearing to extend outward, beyond the boundary.

Emphasis Through Contrast

Contrast is created when two or more forces operate in opposition. By reviewing the elements and principles of design discussed in this section, we can quickly create a long list of potential adversaries, including static/dynamic (3.45A), small/large (3.45B), solid/textured (3.45C), and curvilinear/rectilinear (3.45D).

When the balance is just right, powerful compositions can be created from any of these combinations. Devoting about 80 percent of the compositional space to one force and about 20 percent to the other is especially effective. The larger force sets the standard, while the smaller force creates the exception. Just as a single basketball player wearing a blue uniform will stand out if the other four players wear yellow, so a smaller force can dominate a design. Consider these examples:

3.44 Jacey, *Untitled.* Computer graphics. Example of centricity and eccentricity.

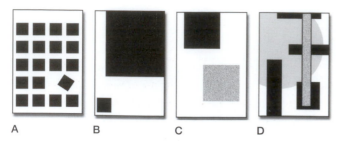

A   B   C   D

3.45A–D Examples of contrast: static/dynamic, small/large, solid/textured, curvilinear/rectilinear.

- *Contrast in scale.* In figure 3.46, the small airplane and the moon become charged with meaning when combined with the image of the sleeping child. Dreams take flight.

- *Contrast in shape.* Zurbarán's *Saint Serapion* (3.47) provides a brilliant example of contrast by shape as well as emphasis by separation. The small note pinned at the right edge of the canvas gains so much power that it easily balances the large figure filling the rest of the frame.

- *Contrast in color.* One of the most compelling uses of emphasis by color occurs in *Schindler's List*, by Steven Spielberg (3.48). Midway through the black-and-white film, a small girl in a red coat is shown walking toward her death. She breaks away from the line and runs back to hide under a bed in a nearby house. This is the only use of color in the main body of the film. When her red coat appears again, her body is being transported to a bonfire. This simple use of color creates one of the most emotional moments in a remarkable film.

3.47 Francisco de Zurbarán, *Saint Serapion,* 1628. Oil on canvas, 47½ × 41 in. (120.7 × 103.5 cm).

3.48 Still from *Schindler's List,* by Steven Spielberg.

3.46 Robert Crawford, *Jamie Sleeping,* 1988. Acrylic on canvas, 20 × 14 in. (50.8 × 35.5 cm).

Key Questions

EMPHASIS

- What would happen conceptually if you dramatically changed the scale, shape, or color of a crucial visual unit?

- Is there a dominant shape in your composition? If so, is it the shape you most *want* to emphasize?

- Is there a focal point in your composition? If not, should there be?

- Contrast tends to add interest. Can a shift in contrast strengthen your composition?

SUMMARY

- Using composition, we can organize multiple parts into a harmonious whole. In a well-composed design, visual elements work together as a team.

- Gestalt psychology describes six unifying strategies: grouping, containment, repetition, proximity, continuity, and closure.

- Effective design requires a dialogue between unity and variety. Too much unity can lead to boredom, while too much variety can lead to chaos.

- Any similarity between visual elements tends to increase unity; any difference between visual elements tends to increase variety.

- Symmetry, radial symmetry, and asymmetry are three common forms of balance. Visual balance creates equilibrium among compositional units, regardless of variations in their size, weight, or shape.

- Scale and proportion are two types of size relationships. Proportion refers to the size relationships within an image, while scale involves a size comparison to our physical reality.

- Emphasis is most commonly created through isolation, placement, or contrast. A focal point can strengthen emphasis.

KEY TERMS

anomaly	continuity	grouping	rhythm
approximate symmetry	contrast	imbalance	scale
asymmetrical balance	eccentricity	movement	symmetrical balance
balance	emphasis	pattern	unity
centricity	focal point	proportion	variety
closure	fusion	proximity	visual weight
composition	Gestalt psychology	radial symmetry	
containment	grid	repetition	

STUDIO PROJECTS

To apply the concepts from this chapter in the studio, check out the Projects page in the Online Learning Center at www.mhhe.com/stewart4e. The following is a sample of the chapter-related assignments that are described in step-by-step detail.

The Parts and the Puzzle. Exploring unity and variety through line and shape.
Dualities. Integrating line, shape, texture, and color in a special kind of self-portrait.
Pushing Proportion. How proportion affects meaning.

Profile:
Bob Dacey, Illustrator

Tell Me a Story: Illustrating *Miriam's Cup*

Bob Dacey is an internationally renowned artist whose drawings and paintings have been published as limited- and multiple-edition prints, as well as in a wide range of books and periodicals, including *McCall's,* Ballantine Books, Book-of-the-Month Club, *Playboy,* and Scholastic Publications. His commercial clients include The White House, ABC, CBS, NBC, PBS, Mobil Oil, Sony, the U.S. Post Office, Air Japan, and many others. Dacey received a Silver Medal from the Society of Illustrators in New York for one of the 16 paintings he produced for Scholastic Publications illustrating *Miriam's Cup,* which is themed on the Exodus of the Israelites from Egypt. Dacey collected an extensive library of books on Egypt and spent almost a year on research. From costumes to musical instruments, Dacey insisted on getting all the details just right.

MS: Give me a bit of background on *Miriam's Cup.* What was the significance of this project, and what aspects of the story did you want to emphasize in the illustrations?

BD: *Miriam's Cup* gave me a chance to expand on my single-image work. I've always approached each illustration as a moment in time, as if it had a "before" and an "after." This book gave me a chance to push that much further. I started every painting by focusing on the emotion in the moment being depicted. I always ask myself: "What is the essence of this moment?" The composition follows. Shapes and values serve the emotional content, while movement is used to unify the composition.

MS: You have said that 75 percent of your work on this project was devoted to research. Can you describe your research and tell me why it was so important?

BD: For *Miriam's Cup,* I had to understand the culture of Egypt and the Jewish culture of the time. Fortunately, I've always had an extensive interest in both. My personal library contains more books on Egypt than the local library system. Research helped open new ideas, leading in some unexpected directions. Those bulrushes are one example. I looked up the word in three dictionaries and two encyclopedias. One of these sources mentioned that the bulrushes of ancient Egypt are papyrus, those beautiful fan-shaped reeds that can be fashioned into a kind of paper. Without that knowledge, the image I arrived at would have been impossible.

MS: I understand that you have a seven-step process by which you refine and expand your ideas. Can you describe this process as it applies to the cover image for *Miriam's Cup*?

BD: I first consider the intent of each painting: what must this piece communicate? In this painting, I focused on Miriam's exuberance as she celebrates her escape from Egypt. Second, the composition must support my intent. The circular movement of the tambourine and flowers dominates this painting. The movement from the raised hand holding the tambourine, to Miriam's hair, to her face, and on to her cupped hand provides a secondary pattern. And that cupped hand repeats the curve of the flowers. Third, the shapes depend on both the intent and the composition. If I am painting a very stoic character, I use a lot of verticals. Diagonals are used when the character or event is very dynamic. Value is fourth on my checklist. I assign value according to the mood of the painting. Lighter values are used for celebratory images, like this one; darker values dominate when the mood is somber. A mix of light and dark value is best. I base my compositions on the Golden Section [a classic use of proportion], and I often use a 60/40 proportion between light and dark values. Texture, step five, often results from the placement of shape and value—but it really deserves a place of its own, due to its importance as a constructive or destructive factor. When everything else works but the image still suffers, textural discord is usually the culprit! Color comes next. I really have to have the other questions resolved first. Color without composition, value, or intent just doesn't cut it. This painting is dominated by rich pastel colors, which help convey the exuberant emotion.

All of this contributes to the overall image, the final step. If all of the preceding factors serve my intent, the image can emerge naturally and effectively.

MS: In addition to the extensive research you did for *Miriam's Cup,* it seems that you have a very wide range of interests in general.

BD: Well, everything feeds into my work—and I've always been interested in everything! My undergraduate majors included theater and anthropology before I settled on ad design as the field in which I finally got my degree. Now, my readings range from archaeology to philosophy to psychology to paleontology, and more. I'm also developing my interest in writing and plan to pursue a master's in writing in order to increase my understanding of narrative.

MS: One of the questions my students often have is this: how do I get from where I am as a student to where you are as a professional?

BD: Focus on your goals and research the field. Talk to professionals you admire. Set high standards for yourself and be realistic about the level of professionalism and quality required.

MS: Any final bits of advice?

BD: Don't limit yourself. We all have great potential that serves the higher purpose of society. Pursue your goals with the knowledge that you can succeed. And remain flexible and open-minded, so that you can redirect your efforts as opportunities present themselves. Read everything! Draw everything!

Bob Dacey, Cover of *Miriam's Cup,* by Fran Manushkin, 1988. Scholastic Press.

Bob Dacey, *In the Bulrushes* compositional study.

Bob Dacey, *Miriam's Celebration* compositional study.

Bob Dacey, *Plague of Frogs* compositional study.

Preliminary drawings Bob Dacey developed for *Miriam's Cup*.

Bob Dacey, *Washing Hands* compositional study.

Illusion of Space, Illusion of Motion

An event that shaped human history was the Battle of Issus, fought by Alexander the Great of Macedonia and Darius III of Persia on November 5, 333 BCE. Control of all of Asia Minor (present-day Turkey and the Near Middle East) was at stake. At age 47, Darius III ruled the greatest empire of its time, stretching across Asia Minor. At age 23, Alexander was king of the small mountainous empire north of modern-day Greece. Alexander began the battle on a rocky hillside and seemed doomed to fail. When Darius moved in for the kill, additional Macedonian troops swept in from the side, cut the Persian forces in half, and routed the larger army. This battle launched Alexander's 10-year campaign to extend his empire from Greece to India, thereby changing the course of human history.

In his *Battle of Issus* (4.1), Albrecht Altdorfer created an apocalyptic vision, combining the dramatic landscape and swirling armies with a crescent moon (representing Darius) and a blazing sun (representing Alexander). Commissioned by the Duke of Bavaria in anticipation of his own battle against Turkish forces, the painting was a clarion call to the Bavarian people. The illusion of space provided the setting for the desperate battle, while the illusion of motion captured both the movement of men and the shimmering sky.

As noted in Chapter Three, each image and idea presents unique challenges. Jasper Johns's *Target with Plaster Casts* (figure 1.50, page 22) demanded a confrontational approach, and reaffirming the flat surface of an actual canvas was the best solution. Altdorfer, on the other hand, needed deep space for his epic battle. How can you best meet the challenges presented by your own ideas? In this chapter, we explore ways to create the illusion of space and of motion and consider the conceptual implications of each.

4.1 Albrecht Altdorfer, *Battle of Issus,* **1529.**
Limewood, 47¼ × 62¼ in. (120 × 158 cm).

CREATING THE ILLUSION OF SPACE

Linear Perspective

Linear perspective is a mathematical system for projecting the apparent dimensions of a three-dimensional object onto a flat surface. This surface, called the **picture plane,** is comparable to a window overlooking a city street. By tracing the outlines of the buildings on the pane of glass, you can make a simple perspective drawing.

Developed during the Renaissance, perspective offered a methodical approach to depicting the rational reality perceived by artists in the fifteenth century. It soon gained wide acceptance as a means of systematically diminishing the size of objects as they recede in space. Raphael's *School of Athens* (figure 4.2) is one example. A broad arch in the foreground frames the compositional stage. Three additional arches diminish in size, pulling us into the painting. The diagonal lines in the buildings and floor converge at a point in the center. The viewer is invited to enter into an illusory world.

Even though many recent philosophical and aesthetic theories challenge this conception of reality, perspective remains the most pervasive Western system for suggesting three-dimensionality on the two-dimensional surface. Linear perspective is based on five basic concepts, shown in figures 4.3 and 4.4:

1. Objects appear to diminish in size as they recede into the distance. Perspective is possible because the rate at which objects appear to diminish is regular and consistent.

2. The point at which objects disappear entirely is called a **vanishing point.** Sets of parallel lines (such as train tracks) converge at a vanishing point as they go into the distance, creating an illusion of space.

3. In basic one- and two-point perspective, all vanishing points are positioned on the **eye level,** or **horizon line,** which is level with the artist's eyes.

4. Because all proportional relationships shift with each change in position, a fixed viewing position is an essential characteristic of linear perspective.

5. Only a limited area is clearly visible from a fixed position. To accommodate a larger viewing area, you must move farther away from the object to be drawn. This expands the **cone of vision** and increases the area being viewed.

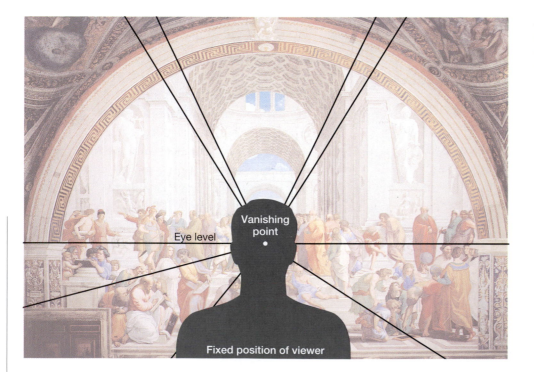

4.2 Perspective used in Raphael's *School of Athens* (for the full painting, see figure 7.3 on page 145).

Eye level

Vanishing point

Fixed position of viewer

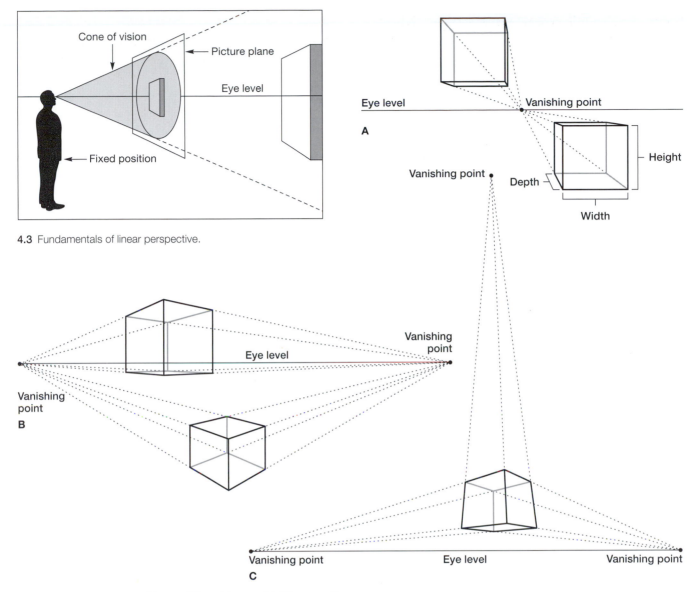

4.3 Fundamentals of linear perspective.

4.4A–C Examples of one- (A), two- (B), and three-point (C) perspective.

One-point perspective is used to represent a straight frontal view of a scene. In this type of perspective, the top and bottom lines of a cube (representing width) are horizontal — that is, they are parallel to the horizon line or eye level (4.4A). The lines representing depth are angled to converge on a single point at eye level, and the lines representing height are perpendicular to the horizon line. One-point perspective is relatively simple to master and can pull the viewer into the image with a single dramatic focal point (4.5).

Two-point perspective is effective for representing an object that is angled in space. A cube drawn in two-point perspective will not have any lines positioned parallel to the horizon line. Instead, the

4.5 Jan Vredeman de Vries, *Perspective Study,* from *Perspective,* Leiden, 1604.

4.6 Frank Lloyd Wright, Detail from Drawing for *Fallingwater*, Kaufmann House, Bear Run, Pennsylvania, 1936. 15⅜ × 27¼ in. (39 × 69 cm).

lines representing depth and width are angled to converge on two vanishing points (4.4B). Because two-point perspective is effective in showing both the front and sides of a structure, it is often used for diagrams and architectural drawings (4.6).

In one- and two-point perspective, the lines representing height are perpendicular to the horizon line. In **three-point perspective** (4.4C), these lines are tilted so that they converge on a third vanishing point, high above or below eye level. The lines representing depth and width converge on two points at eye level, as in two-point perspective. Three-point perspective is used to exaggerate the sense of space and to present a unique "bird's-eye" or "worm's-eye" view, as illustrated by Charles Sheeler's *Delmonico Building* (4.7).

Other Ways to Create the Illusion of Space

- *Overlap.* Overlap is the simplest way to suggest space, and it can be especially effective when combined with size variation. In *Deposition* (4.8), Rogier van der Weyden used overlap combined with value to create a convincing drama within a crowded compositional space.

- *Size variation.* Because the diminishing size of distant objects is a basic characteristic of human vision, any systematic variation in size can enhance the illusion of space. This effect is demonstrated most clearly when the distance is great. In Ansel Adams's *Monolith, The Face of Half Dome* (see page 17), the imposing cliff in the foreground rapidly diminishes in size as it moves back in space.

4.7 Charles Sheeler, *Delmonico Building*, 1926. Lithograph, 9¾ × 6⅞ in. (24.7 × 17.4 cm).

- *Definition.* Sharply focused shapes also tend to advance, while blurred shapes tend to recede. When we look at a landscape, dust and water droplets in the air blur outlines and add a blue-gray color to distant shapes. This effect is known as **atmospheric perspective.** In *The Rocky Mountains, Lander's Peak* (4.9), Albert Bierstadt combined dramatic lighting with atmospheric perspective to increase the illusion of space.

- *Location.* Visual elements placed near the top of the page tend to recede, while shapes placed at the bottom tend to advance. In *A Thousand Peaks and Myriad Ravines* (4.10) on page 96, the mountains at the top of the scroll appear more distant, despite their large size.

- *Color.* Contrast in hue, value, or color temperature can enhance the illusion of space.

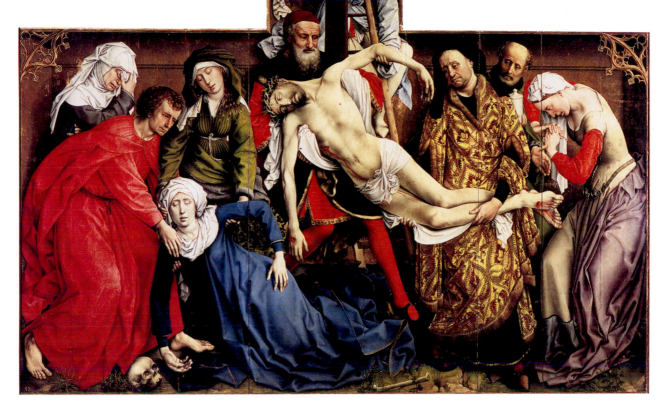

4.8 Rogier van der Weyden, *Deposition*, from an altarpiece commissioned by the Crossbowman's Guild, Louvain, Brabant, Belgium, c. 1435. Oil on panel, 7 ft 2⅝ in. × 8 ft 7⅛ in. (2.2 × 2.6 m).

4.9 Albert Bierstadt, *The Rocky Mountains, Lander's Peak,* 1863. Oil on canvas, 6 ft 1¼ in. × 10 ft ¾ in. (186.7 × 306.7 cm).

4.10 Wang Hui, *A Thousand Peaks and Myriad Ravines,* **Qing dynasty, 1693.** Hanging scroll, ink on paper, 8 ft 2½ in. × 3 ft 4½ in. (2.54 × 1.03 m).

Using the Illusion of Space

Through the illusion of space, artists invite viewers to enter into an imaginary world. Expression can be heightened when this world is particularly intriguing or when the illusion is especially dramatic.

Amplified perspective can be defined as the exaggerated use of linear perspective to achieve a dramatic and engaging presentation of the subject. Amplified perspective is often created using an unusual viewing position, such as a bird's-eye view, accelerated spatial convergence, or distortion.

In Salvador Dalí's *Christ of St. John of the Cross* (4.11), amplified perspective changes our interpretation of the crucifixion of Jesus. Dramatic three-point perspective emphasizes the importance of the note pinned at the top of the cross. As we look down, the vulnerability of Jesus emphasizes his humanity, while the hovering position of the figure suggests his divinity.

Fractured space can be created when multiple viewpoints are combined in a single image. In his portrait of sculptor Henry Moore (4.12), David Hockney used multiple photographs to manipulate space and suggest the passage of time. The repeated hands gesture to us as we visually converse with the old master.

Layered space can be created when the foreground, middle ground, and background are clearly defined. Layered space is used extensively in the film *Citizen Kane.* In figure 4.13, young Charlie Kane plays in the background, while his mother in the foreground signs over his care to a lawyer. His father, who opposes this action, occupies the middle ground, caught between the mother and the child. The tensions in the family, the determination of the mother, and the innocence of the child are heightened when Charlie shouts, "The Union forever!" as part of his game. When the lawyer takes charge of Charlie, the family will be split apart forever. These three compositional layers communicate complex emotions while telling a story.

4.11 Salvador Dalí, *Christ of St. John of the Cross,* **1951.** Oil on canvas, 80⅞ × 45⅝ in. (204.8 × 115.9 cm).

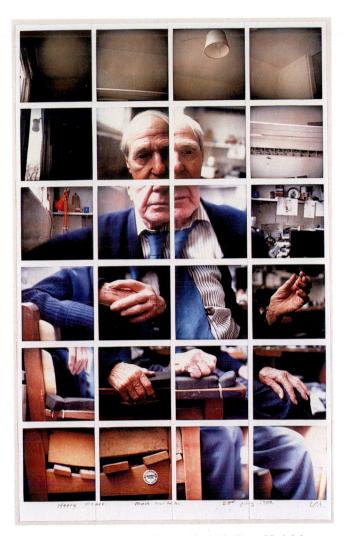

4.12 David Hockney, *Henry Moore Much Hadham 23rd July 1982.* Composite Polaroid, 21 × 14 in. (53 × 36 cm).

Key Questions

ILLUSION OF SPACE

- Which is more appropriate for your idea: a flat design or a spatial design?

- How can spatial depth be increased or decreased in your composition?

- If a spatial illusion is used, where will you place the viewer relative to the setting you create?

4.13 Scene from *Citizen Kane.* Three layers of space divide this shot from *Citizen Kane:* the mother in the foreground, the father in the middle ground, and the child in the background.

Spatial Dynamics

A Compositional Setting

The illusion of space creates a setting in which action can occur. Objects can move within this illusory world, or the setting itself can begin to shift. Both create **dynamic space,** space that embodies movement. In *Inside Running Animals/Reindeer Way,* Robert Stackhouse combined diagonal lines with definition and size variation to pull us into a mysterious tunnel (4.14). Ann Strassman's *Humphrey I* (4.15) comes charging out of the picture plane, ready to lick us or attack us. Cropping (the cutting away of part of the image) combined with vigorous brushstrokes helps push the dog forward. In Mark Messersmith's *Edge of Town* (4.16), a logging truck rushing into the background pulls the viewer into the painting, while the dead animals atop the hunter's car are thrust forward. However, the tree in the foreground traps this apocalyptic action, forcing the space to swirl around a central compositional pole. As we look down into the flaming car and up toward the white birds, we become even more disoriented. The space seems to bulge, twist, and rotate in the madness and mystery of the night.

4.14 Robert Stackhouse, *Inside Running Animals/Reindeer Way,* **1977.** Mixed mediums, 64 × 43¾ × 2 in. (162.6 × 111 × 5.1 cm).

Key Questions
SPATIAL DYNAMICS

- Viewed as a setting in which action can occur, is your composition more dynamic (suggesting movement) or more static (suggesting stability)? What is the advantage of each?

- What is the advantage of shifting the viewpoint within a spatial setting?

- How can deliberate manipulation of spatial dynamics strengthen the idea or emotion you want to get across?

4.15 Ann Strassman, *Humphrey I,* **2004.** Acrylic on cardboard, 70 × 65 in. (177.8 × 165.1 cm).

4.16 Mark Messersmith, *Edge of Town,* 2005. Oil on canvas and mixed mediums.

Constructing *Mulan*

Animators use the illusion of space with great inventiveness. Freed from the restrictions of reality, they can invent and explore a rich variety of dynamic spaces. Every type of space discussed in this chapter was used beautifully in Walt Disney's *Mulan*. From the opening shots to the grand finale, the illusion of space is of critical importance to the visual and conceptual power of the film.

4.17B

- *Overlap.* After a brief battle with the invader Shan-Yu and his men, a Chinese soldier lights a signal fire to warn of the invasion. With Shan-Yu filling the foreground, we see six towers, with signal fires gradually blazing forth from each one (4.17A). Here, overlap and size variation enhance the illusion of space.

- *Angle of vision.* As the general approaches the throne, the angle of vision shifts to an aerial view. Three-point perspective is now used to emphasize the insignificance of the figures within this great hall (4.17C). We look down on the standing emperor and the prostrate soldiers.

4.17A Cells from Disney's Mulan. © Disney Enterprises, Inc.

4.17C

- *Linear perspective.* Linear perspective is used in the next sequence, when General Li enters the imperial palace to inform the emperor of the invasion. One-point perspective is used to create the large, majestic hall (4.17B). Because our eye level is that of a child, the hall seems even more intimidating and imposing. Positioned just above the vanishing point and framed by three hanging scrolls, the emperor epitomizes power.

- *Atmospheric perspective.* Atmospheric perspective is often used as the troops travel through the mountains. After learning of the death of his father in battle, Captain Shang walks to the edge of a cliff. Like the massive mountains in the background, his seemingly invincible father has dissolved in the mist. A small man within a vast landscape, Captain Shang remains sharply focused, dignified, and powerful, even as he grieves (4.17D).

4.17D

4.17F

Camera angle orients the viewer and can help determine the amount and type of space in each shot. An aerial view can provide the sweeping panorama needed to convey the enormity of a battle, while a low camera angle can provide an expansive view of the sky.

The major battle scene in *Mulan* beautifully demonstrates the critical role camera angle can play in a film. The enormity of the enemy army is shown in figure 4.17E. A low camera angle positions the Mongols along a ridge, above the small company of Chinese soldiers.

4.17E

As the Mongols pour over the ridge and gallop toward Mulan, the camera angle shifts to a slanted, oblique view (4.17F).

A complete aerial view is used in the next shot (4.17G). The riders now pour across the screen.

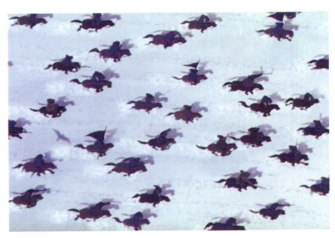

4.17G

The shifting perspectives give us a more comprehensive view of the extent of the battle and emphasize the hopelessness of the emperor's warriors, who are confronted with an apparently invincible enemy. When Mulan grabs the one remaining cannon and races forward to create an avalanche, an aerial view is again used to show her vulnerability against the advancing enemy. Throughout the battle, shifts in camera angle provide the emotional and compositional power needed to create a dramatic battle sequence using the fewest number of shots.

4.18 Robert Longo, *Untitled*, 1980. From the *Men in Cities* series. Crayon and graphite on paper, 40½ × 28 in. (102.9 × 71.1 cm).

THE ILLUSION OF MOTION

Mulan is constructed from thousands of tiny frames. When run through a film projector, they create the fluid movement that is a hallmark of Disney animation. Animation is possible because we have the perceptual ability to integrate the sequential images into a continuous flow.

Substantial audience involvement is also required to create the illusion of motion within a static drawing or sculpture. When presented with multiple images on a single surface, we must feel the movement, complete the action, or anticipate the next event. Based on our day-to-day experience in an ever-changing world, we use our imagination to connect static images to create the illusion of motion.

The Kinesthetic Response

Kinesthetics is the science of movement. Through the very process of walking, we consistently engage in a complex balancing act as we fall forward, then catch ourselves with the next step. When we are confronted by a life-sized figure, such as the man from Robert Longo's *Men in Cities* series (4.18), the lurching movement of the model resonates on a physical level: we feel as well as see the gesture. Capturing the gesture at the right moment is critical. In Myron's *Discus Thrower* (4.19), the athlete is caught at the moment *before* the whirling vortex of energy explodes, releasing the disc. By capturing this moment rather than the moment of release, the sculptor has trapped within the marble the implied energy of the throw.

4.19 Myron, *Discus Thrower (Diskobolos).* Roman copy after the original bronze of c. 450 BCE. Marble, height 5 ft 1 in. (1.54 m).

4.20 Henri Cartier-Bresson, *Valencia*, 1933. Photograph, 7¹¹⁄₁₆ × 11½ in. (19.6 × 29.2 cm).

The Decisive Moment

Photographer Henri Cartier-Bresson used his understanding of impending change to formulate a theory of photography he called "the decisive moment." A pioneer in the use of the 35-mm camera, he specialized in capturing the most telling

UNDER THE RUG

Two weeks passed and it happened again.

4.21 Chris Van Allsburg, "Under the Rug" from *The Mysteries of Harris Burdick*, Houghton-Mifflin, 1984.

moment in time. The space, emotions, and events he recorded in *Valencia* (4.20) are both fascinating and disturbing. Sharply focused and framed by the window, the policeman's fierce face dominates the foreground. Squeezed between the target shapes and the wall on the left, a boy turns toward us apprehensively. A dissected target shape is balanced by the man's monocle on the right and the boy's face on the left. The resulting interplay of shapes creates a complex dialogue between childhood fears and adult authority.

Before and After

The kinesthetic response and the perception of a decisive moment are both based on our past experience and our ability to relate this experience to the images we see. Based on our physical experience, we can feel the awkward and unbalanced position of the Longo figure. Likewise, through our emotional experience, when we look at the Cartier-Bresson photograph, we realize that we are seeing a single moment in a more extensive story.

To create a story through a single image, many illustrators deliberately plan the moment that takes place *before* and the moment that takes place *after* an actual event. An example of this is illustrated in Chris Van Allsburg's book *The Mysteries of Harris Burdick* (4.21). Each drawing in the book is accompanied by a title and a short piece of text. Based on the clues in the title, text, and image, we can invent all sorts of stories.

Fragmentation

As an object moves, it sequentially occupies various positions in space. Visual fragmentation can be used to simulate this effect in art. For example, the superimposed figures in Thomas Eakins's *Double Jump* (4.22) record the multiple positions the man occupies during an athletic event. Even when figures are simply repeated, as in Edgar Degas's *Frieze of Dancers* (4.23), movement is strongly suggested.

What attracted these two painters to explore the illusion of motion? Thomas Eakins was one of

4.22 Thomas Eakins, *Double Jump,* **1885.** Modern print from a dry-plate negative, 4 × 5 in. (10.2 × 12.7 cm).

4.23 Edgar Degas, *Frieze of Dancers,* **c. 1895.** Oil on canvas, 27.6 × 79 in. (70 × 200.5 cm).

the first artists in America to use photography as a tool in the art-making process. His *Double Jump* was taken in the early days of photography when artists became fascinated by the study of movement and the possibility that they could capture an action through photography. Even though it is a still image, the viewer clearly understands that figure 4.22 shows one body captured at different stages in an action.

Although Edgar Degas was primarily a painter, he also became a talented photographer later in his career. He had always been fascinated by both human and animal locomotion, and photography expanded his ability to observe and record the nuances of movement. *Frieze of Dancers* is a painting of four different dancers, yet it can also be perceived as a study of a single dancer in multiple poses.

For Eakins, Degas, Longo, and Van Allsburg, the illusion of motion expanded both the conceptual and the emotional possibilities in an image. Always searching for more effective means of visual expression, any artist or designer can gain from the use of this powerful tool.

4.24 Paul Jenkins and Jae Lee, from *Inhumans:* "First Contact." Volume 2, Issue 5, March 1999. Comic book.
© 2010 Marvel Characters, Inc.

Multiplication

Multiplication can also play a role in visual storytelling. In this page from *Inhumans* (4.24), by Paul Jenkins and Jae Lee, a dialogue between an alien child and a human politician unfolds over five panels. Notice how "time" moves faster in the four smaller panels, and how a close-up is used when the child delivers his ultimatum. Multiplication creates a very different effect in George Tooker's *Government Bureau* (4.25). Repeated images of the central male figure combined with endless bureaucratic faces create a scene from a nightmare. No matter where the man goes in this hall of mirrors, he always returns to the beginning.

4.25 George Tooker, *Government Bureau*, 1956. Egg tempera on gesso panel, 19⅝ × 29⅝ in. (50 × 75 cm).

SUMMARY

- The illusion of space can be created through linear perspective, overlap, size variation, location, definition, atmospheric perspective, and use of color.

- Linear perspective is based on five fundamental concepts, listed on page 92.

- Three common types of linear perspective are one-point, two-point, and three-point perspective.

- Overlap, size variation, definition, location, and color can also create the illusion of space.

- The illusion of motion is often created by selecting the most decisive moment in an event, through fragmentation, or through various types of multiplication.

KEY TERMS

amplified perspective	dynamic space	layered space	three-point perspective
atmospheric perspective	eye level (horizon line)	linear perspective	two-point perspective
camera angle	fractured space	one-point perspective	vanishing point
cone of vision	kinesthetics	picture plane	

STUDIO PROJECTS

To apply the concepts from this chapter in the studio, check out the Projects page in the Online Learning Center at www.mhhe.com/stewart4e. The following is a sample of the chapter-related assignments that are described in step-by-step detail.

Architectural Abstraction. An introduction to perspective.
Homage to Hockney. An exploration of space and movement.
Strata. Increasing complexity through layers of space.

Profile:
Ken Stout, Painter
Immediacy and Energy in Large Scale

Ken Stout is an internationally renowned figurative painter. He has shown his work widely, including group shows at the Nelson-Atkins Museum of Art in Kansas City and the Butler Museum of American Art, as well as solo shows at the Goldstrom Gallery in New York City and the Cité Internationale des Arts in Paris. *Intermission* was commissioned by the Walton Arts Center in Fayetteville, Arkansas, funded by Saatchi and Saatchi in 1992, and permanently installed in 1994.

MS: How did *Intermission* begin?

KS: I began work in 1989. During visits to Paris and Madrid, I was bowled over by a Toulouse-Lautrec mural I saw at the Orsay Museum and by a mural by Delacroix at St. Sulpice. Both were vibrant with energy. The strident reds and greens in the Delacroix sent the viewer's eyes hurtling around and through the composition. I was interested in a mural project because it gave me an opportunity to combine the immediacy of drawing with the richness of painting.

MS: Why show the intermission, not the play?

KS: It is a moment that is highly charged. The mural depicts a cross section of the theater, from backstage to stage and from audience to lobby. The performer onstage is like a toggle switch, connecting the audience to the action backstage. As he bows through the closing curtain, the audience begins to break apart, dissolving into its own private plays. Applause fills the theater, children begin to awaken, and neighbors discuss the performance. I wanted to pull the viewer into a scene bursting with energy, as if all things were in orbit, pushing, pulling, and flowing. The whole painting is a gesture, an embodiment of bodies in motion, with both the volumes and voids ignited with energy.

MS: Your preliminary research on this project was extensive. What did you learn from the masters?

KS: Mostly, I learned ways to increase compositional complexity without sacrificing gestural energy. These compositional lessons helped me sustain a vigorous visual pace for all 50 feet of the painting.

Technically, though, my work method was more exploratory and direct than is the usual practice.

First, the 300 preliminary drawings and paintings I did stand as autonomous images in themselves. I learned from all of them—but didn't copy any when I painted the mural. I confronted the painting directly, rather than replicating ideas I had worked out beforehand.

Second, I didn't graph out, project, or otherwise draw the outlines on the canvas. I just drew blue lines to divide the canvas into halves, quarters, and eighths, then drew freehand, using a brush attached to a 3-foot-long bamboo pole, starting with light washes in earth colors.

Finally, every figure was painted from life, using over 50 community members as models. They were amazingly generous and patient, considering it wasn't putting a penny in their pockets. This process increased the connection between the audience and the artwork, and we had a great party for everyone when the painting was installed.

MS: So it sounds like you didn't really know what would happen when you began to paint each day.

KS: Each model, each pose, and each prop provided variations and surprises. I actually used at least two models for each figure in the painting, which basically means that there is another 50-foot-long painting underneath the one that you see!

MS: What advice do you have for my students?

KS: Take risks. Without daring—indeed, without great daring—there is no beauty. We must go beyond ourselves if we are ever to fulfill our real potential.

Ken Stout, *Intermission,* 1994. Oil on canvas, 9 × 50 ft (2.74 × 15.24 m).

Georgiana Nehl and David Browne, *Solstice Greetings,* **1998.** Color photograph of constructed assemblage, 5 × 5 in. (12.7 × 12.7 cm).

Concepts and Critical Thinking

In *A Kick in the Seat of the Pants,* Roger Von Oech identifies four distinct roles in the creative process.

First, the *explorer* learns as much as possible about the problem. Research is crucial. Ignorance may result in a compositional or conceptual cliché.

Second, the *artist* experiments with a wide variety of solutions, using all sorts of combinations, proportions, and materials. By creating 10 answers to each question, the artist can select the best solution rather than accepting the only solution.

Third, the *judge* assesses the work in progress and determines what revisions are required. Innovative ideas are never fully developed when first presented; most need extensive revision and expansion. Rather than discard an underdeveloped idea, the judge identifies its potential and determines ways to increase its strength.

Finally, the *warrior* implements the idea. When obstacles appear, the warrior assesses the situation, determines the best course of action, and then moves ahead decisively.

We will explore each of these roles in the next four chapters. Chapter Five deals with concept development and visual problem solving. Strategies for cultivating creativity and improving time management are discussed in Chapter Six. Chapter Seven is devoted to critical thinking and provides specific ways to improve any design. In Chapter Eight, we expand our discussion of visual communication and consider ways to create more meaningful artworks.

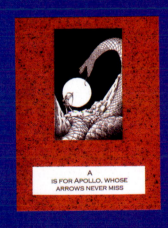

A
IS FOR APOLLO, WHOSE
ARROWS NEVER MISS

U
IS FOR URANIA THE MUSE OF
CELESTIAL FORCES IS SHE

Problem Seeking
and Problem Solving

By mastering the basic elements and principles of design, you can increase the visual power of your work. Composition, however, is only part of the puzzle. With the increasing emphasis on visual communication, the ideas being expressed by artists and designers have become more varied and complex. Conceptual invention is just as important as compositional strength.

New ideas invite development of new types of artwork. When the concept is fresh and the composition is compelling, expression and communication expand. In this chapter, we consider ways in which artists and designers define problems and explore various problem-solving strategies.

PROBLEM SEEKING

The Design Process

In its most basic form, the design process can be distilled down to four basic steps. When beginning a project, the designer asks

1. What do we need?

2. What existing designs are similar to the design we need?

3. What is the difference between the existing designs and the new design?

4. How can we transform, combine, or expand these existing designs?

By studying the classic Eames chair, we can see this process clearly. Charles and Ray Eames were two of the most innovative and influential designers of the postwar era. Charles, trained as an architect, was a master of engineering and had a gift for design integration. Ray, trained as a painter, contributed a love of visual structure, a sense of adventure, and an understanding of marketing. Combining their strengths, this husband-and-wife team designed furniture, toys, exhibitions, and architecture and directed over 80 experimental films.

Their first breakthrough in furniture design came in 1940, when they entered a chair competition sponsored by the Museum of Modern Art in New York City. Many architects had designed furniture, and the Eameses were eager to explore this field.

Many similar products existed. The most common was the overstuffed chair, which continues to dominate American living rooms. Extensive padding on a boxy framework supported the sitter. Another popular design was the

5.1 Marcel Breuer, *Armchair*, 1925. Tubular steel, canvas, 28¹¹⁄₁₆ × 30⁵⁄₁₆ × 26¾ in. (72.8 × 77 × 68 cm).

5.2 Alvar Aalto, *Paimio Lounge Chair*, 1931–33. Laminated birch, molded plywood, lacquered, 26 × 23¾ × 34⅞ in. (66 × 60.5 × 88.5 cm).

Adirondack chair, made from a series of flat wooden planes. Of greatest interest, however, were designs by architects such as Marcel Breuer (5.1) and Alvar Aalto (5.2). These designs used modern materials and clearly displayed their structure.

By comparing existing chairs with the chair they wanted, Charles and Ray could identify qualities they needed to retain and qualities that needed to be changed. The familiar overstuffed chair (5.3) was bulky and awkward, but it was comfortable. The Adirondack chair (5.4) was easy to mass-produce but too large for interior use. The modern chairs were elegant and inventive but were expensive to produce and often uncomfortable. The Eameses wanted to create a modern chair that was comfortable, elegant, and inexpensive.

During World War II, the Eames team had designed and manufactured molded plywood splints, which were used by doctors in the U.S. Navy. After extensive research and experimentation, they had mastered the process of steaming and reshaping the sheets of plywood into complex curves. In developing their competition entry, they combined their knowledge of splints, love of modern chairs, understanding of anatomy, and mastery of architecture. Their plywood chair, designed in collaboration with architect Eero Saarinen, won the first prize.

5.3 Overstuffed chair.

5.4 Adirondack chair.

5.5 Charles and Ray Eames, *Side Chair, Model DCM,* **1946.**
Molded ash plywood, steel rod, and rubber shockmounts,
28¾ × 19½ × 20 in. (73 × 49.5 × 50.8 cm).

5.6 Frank Gehry, *Cross Check Armchair,* **1992.** Maple,
33⅜ × 28½ × 28½ in. (85.3 × 72.4 × 72.4 cm).

A series of Eames designs followed, including a metal and plywood version in 1946 (5.5) and numerous cast plastic versions. To create the plastic chairs, the Eames team invented a new manufacturing process. This led to a breakthrough in the field of furniture design.

By addressing a need, researching existing designs, making comparisons, and combining the best characteristics of existing chairs, the Eames team produced a new kind of chair and thus firmly established themselves as leaders in the design field.

The Fine Art Process

For a designer, the problem-solving process begins when a client requests help or the designer identifies a societal need. With the Eames chair, the museum competition provided the impetus for an experiment that reshaped an industry.

By contrast, contemporary sculptors, filmmakers, painters, and other fine artists generally invent their own aesthetic problems. Ideas often arise from personal experience and from the cultural context. Combining self-awareness with empathy for others,

many artists have transformed a specific event into a universal statement. For example, Picasso's *Guernica* (see figure 8.24, page 168), painted in response to the 1937 bombing of a specific Spanish village, is now seen as a universal statement about the horrors of war. Working more independently and with fewer deadlines, artists can explore ideas and issues of personal interest. Adam Kallish's interview at the end of this chapter emphasizes the design process, while interviews with Suzanne Stryk, Kendall Buster, and Roger Shimomura emphasize the fine art process.

Sources of Ideas

Regardless of the initial motivation for their work, both artists and designers constantly scan their surroundings in an omnivorous search for images and ideas. As demonstrated by the profiles that appear throughout this book, the most improbable object or idea may provide inspiration. Memories of growing up in small-town America provide the stimulus for *Storefront Stories,* by Nancy Callahan and Diane Gallo. Biological systems and architecture inspire sculptor Kendall Buster. Ordinary vegetables and African vessels influence ceramicist David MacDonald. If you are at a loss for an idea, take a fresh look at your surroundings. Here are three strategies.

Transform a Common Object

Architect Frank Gehry based the exuberant armchair in figure 5.6 on the wood-strip bushel basket used by farmers (5.7). If you consider all the ideas that can be generated by a set of car keys, a pair of scissors, or a compass, you will have more than enough to get a project started.

Study Nature

Ceramicist Ray Rogers is inspired by many natural forms, including mushrooms, stones, and aquatic life. His spherical pots (5.8) often suggest the colors, textures, and economy of nature. In figure 5.9, Vera Lisková used the fluidity and transparency of glass to create a humorous version of a prosaic porcupine. Through an inventive use of materials, both artists have reinterpreted nature.

Visit a Museum

Artists and designers frequently visit all kinds of museums. Carefully observed, the history and physical objects produced by any culture can be both instructive and inspirational. Looking at non-Western artwork is especially valuable. Unfamiliar concepts and compositions can stimulate creativity. Beau Dick's *Mugamtl Mask* (5.10) is one example. First developed by a man who had revived from a

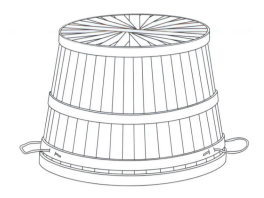

5.7 Wood-strip bushel basket.

5.8 Ray Rogers, *Vessel*, New Zealand, 1984. Large, pit-fired (porous and nonfunctional) with "fungoid" decorative treatment in relief. Diameter approximately 21⅝ in. (55 cm).

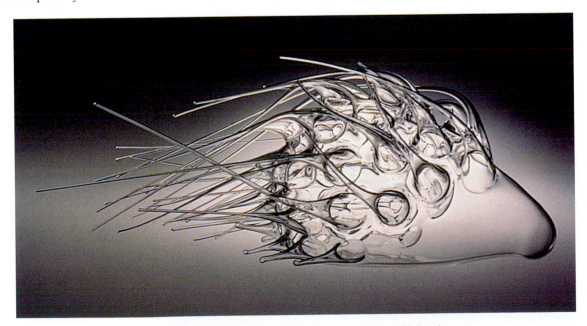

5.9 Vera Lisková, *Porcupine*, 1972–80. Flame-worked glass, 4¼ × 11 in. (10.8 × 28.2 cm).

deadly illness, it depicts the supernatural abilities (including flight) that he gained during his experience. His descendants now have the right to construct and wear this special mask. By understanding the story and studying this mask, you can more readily design a mask based on your own experiences.

Historical examples such as Albrecht Dürer's *The Knight, Death and the Devil* (5.11) can be equally inspiring. Two hundred years before this print was made, the Black Plague killed nearly half the population of Europe. This horrific disease remained a threat in Dürer's time. As a result, Renaissance conceptions of life and death were very different from our contemporary viewpoint. This difference can spark a new way of thinking and lead you to a fresh idea.

Characteristics of a Good Problem

Regardless of its source, the problem at hand must fully engage either the artist or the designer. Whether it is assigned or invented, a good problem generally includes the following characteristics.

Significant

When substantial amounts of time, effort, and money are being spent, it is wise to prioritize problems and focus on those of greatest consequence. Identifying your major goals can help you determine the significance of a job.

5.10 Beau Dick, *Mugamtl Mask (Crooked Beak)*, **1993.** Red cedar, cedar bark, paint, 24 × 26 × 16 in. (61 × 66 × 40.6 cm).

5.11 Albrecht Dürer, Detail of *The Knight, Death and the Devil*, 1513. Engraving, 11 × 14 in. (28 × 36 cm).

described. For the professional artist or designer, there are no "bad" problems, only bad solutions. However, when limited to a narrow range of possible solutions, even the most inventive person will become frustrated. If you find yourself in a straitjacket, rethink the problem and try a new approach.

Authentic

Regardless of the source, every person approaches each problem on his or her own terms. Each of us has a unique perspective, and the connections we make will vary. As a student, you will learn more when you really embrace each assignment and make it your own. Ask questions, so that you can understand the conceptual implications of each project. When you reframe the *question* in your own terms, the creative possibilities will expand and your imagination will soar.

Socially Responsible

With the human population approaching 7 billion, it is unwise to pursue a project that squanders natural resources. What resources will be required for a major project, and how will you dispose of resulting waste? Increasingly, artists and designers consider the environmental as well as the economic implications of each project.

Comprehensible

It is impossible to solve a problem you don't fully understand. Ask questions if the assignment specifications and objectives are unclear to you.

Open to Experimentation

It is important to distinguish between clear definition and restrictive limitations. Consider the following two assignment descriptions:

1. Organize at least 20 photocopies in such a way that they convey an idea or emotion.
2. Organize 20 photographs by American Civil War photographer Mathew Brady in order to tell a story about the life of Abraham Lincoln.

In the first case, the requirements of the project are clearly stated, but the solution remains open. In the second case, the *solution* as well as the *problem* is

CONVERGENT AND DIVERGENT THINKING

To see how it all works, let's work our way through an actual assignment, using two different problem-solving strategies.

> *Problem:* Organize up to 20 photocopies from library sources so that they tell a story. Use any size and type of format. Any image can be enlarged, reduced, cropped, or repeated.

Using Convergent Thinking

Convergent thinking involves the pursuit of a predetermined goal, usually in a linear progression and through a highly focused problem-solving technique. The word *prose* can help you remember the basic steps:

1. Define the *problem*.
2. Do *research*.
3. Determine your *objective*.
4. Devise a *strategy*.
5. *Execute* the strategy.
6. *Evaluate* the results.

In convergent thinking, the end determines the means. You know what you are seeking before you begin. For this reason, clear definition of the problem is essential: the most brilliant idea is useless if it doesn't solve the problem.

Convergent thinking is familiar to most of us in the scientific method, which follows the same basic procedure. It is orderly, logical, and empirical; there are clear boundaries and specific guidelines. Clearly focused on the final result, convergent thinking is a good way to achieve a goal and meet a deadline. Let's analyze each step.

Define the Problem

Determine all of the physical and technical requirements of the assignment and ask whether there are any stylistic limitations. Be sure that you understand the preliminary steps as well as the final due date.

Next, assess your strengths and weaknesses relative to the problem assigned, and determine your best work strategy. Let's consider the approaches taken by two hypothetical students, Jeremy (as a convergent thinker) and Angela (as a divergent thinker).

Using a dictionary, Jeremy begins by analyzing the words *story* and *images*. He finds that a *story* is shorter than a novel, that it may be true or fictitious, that a series of connected events is needed, and that it may take many forms, including a memoir, a play, or a newspaper article. Next, he determines that an *image* is a representation of a person or thing, a visual impression produced by reflection in a mirror, or a mental picture of something—an idea or impression. This means that photographs from books or magazines and reproductions of paintings are fair game. Jeremy realizes that he can even include a mirror in the project, to reflect the viewer's own image.

He spends the first hour of class on brainstorming, then decides to develop a story about Irish immigration to America in the 1890s.

Do Research

Creativity is highly dependent on seeking connections and making new combinations. The more information you have, the more connections you can make. Through research, you can collect and assess technical, visual, and conceptual possibilities.

For this assignment, Jeremy reads extensively, then develops a plausible story based on immigrant diaries. He begins to collect images of ships, cities, and people.

Determine Your Objective

Jeremy now has the raw material needed to solve the problem. However, many questions remain unanswered, including

- What happens in this story? Is it fiction or nonfiction?

- Who is the storyteller? A 12-year-old boy will tell a very different story than a 20-year-old woman.

- What is the best format to use? A dozen letters sent between fictitious brothers in Dublin and Boston? A Web site describing actual families? A photo album?

At this point, Jeremy pauses to rethink his strategy. What does he really want to communicate? He considers:

- *Does it solve the problem?* He reviews the assignment parameters.

- *Is the solution conceptually inventive?* Is it really intriguing, or is it something we've all seen before, a cliché?

- *Is the planned solution visually compelling?*

- *Can this solution be completed by the due date?* To meet the due date, it may be necessary to distill a complex problem down to an essential statement. In this case, Jeremy decides to simplify his project by focusing on one main character.

Devise a Strategy

While some assignments can be done in an afternoon, three-dimensional projects and multiple-image works tend to take longer. Jeremy determines the supplies he needs and considers the best time and place to work on the project.

Execute the Strategy

Now, Jeremy just digs in and works. He has found it best to work with great concentration and determination at this point, rather than second-guessing himself.

Evaluate the Results

At the end of each work session, Jeremy considers the strengths and weaknesses of the work in progress. What areas in each composition seem cluttered or confusing? How can those areas be strengthened? He finally presents the project for a class critique.

Convergent Thinking Applications

Convergent thinking is most effective when

- The problem can be defined clearly.
- The problem can be solved rationally.
- The problem must be solved sequentially.
- Firm deadlines must be met.

Because many problems in science and industry fit these criteria, convergent thinking is favored by scientists, businesspeople, and graphic designers.

Using Divergent Thinking

The advantages of convergent thinking are clarity, control, focus, and a strong sense of direction. For many tasks, convergent thinking is ideal. In some cases, however, convergent thinking can offer *too* much clarity and not enough chaos. Inspiration is elusive. Over-the-edge creativity is often messy and rarely occurs in an orderly progression. If you want to find something completely new, you will have to leave the beaten path.

In **divergent thinking,** the means determines the end. The process is more open-ended; specific results are hard to predict. Divergent thinking is a great way to generate completely new ideas.

There are two major differences between convergent and divergent thinking. First, in divergent thinking, the problem is defined much more broadly, with less attention to "what the client wants." Research is more expansive and less tightly focused. Second, because the convergent thinker discards weak ideas in the thumbnail stage, the final image is more pre-planned and predictable. The divergent thinker, on the other hand, generates many variables, is less methodical, and may have to produce multiple drafts of a composition in order to get a polished result.

While convergent thinking is usually more efficient, divergent thinking is often more inventive. It opens up unfamiliar lines of inquiry and can lead to a creative breakthrough. Divergent thinking is a high-risk/high-gain approach. By breaking traditional rules, the artist can explore unexpected connections and create new possibilities.

Let's try the same assignment again, now using Angela's divergent thinking.

> *Problem:* Organize up to 20 photocopies from library sources so that they tell a story. Use any size and type of format. Any image can be enlarged, reduced, cropped, or repeated.

Realizing that the strength of the source images is critical, Angela immediately heads for the section of the library devoted to photography. By leafing through a dozen books, she finds 40 great photographs, ranging from images of train stations to trapeze artists. She photocopies the photographs, enlarging and reducing pictures to provide more options. Laying them out on a table, she begins to move the images around, considering various stories that might be generated. Twenty of the images are soon discarded; they are unrelated to the circus story she decides to develop. She then finds five more images to flesh out her idea.

At this point, her process becomes similar to the final steps described in the preceding section. Like Jeremy, she must clarify her objective, develop characters, decide on a format, and construct the final piece. However, because she started with such a disparate collection of images, her final story is more likely to be nonlinear. Like a dream, her images may *evoke* feelings rather than *describe* specific events.

Divergent Thinking Applications

Divergent thinking is most effective when

- The problem definition is elusive or evolving.
- A rational solution is not required.
- A methodical approach is unnecessary.
- Deadlines are flexible.

Many creative people have used divergent thinking to explore the subconscious and reveal unexpected new patterns of thought. Surrealism, an art movement that flourished in Europe between the world wars, provides many notable examples of divergent thinking in art and literature. More interested in the essential substance of ideas and objects than in surface appearances, painter Yves

5.12 Yves Tanguy, *Multiplication of the Arcs*, 1954. Oil on canvas, 40 × 60 in. (101.6 × 152.4 cm).

5.13 Giorgio de Chirico, *The Mystery and Melancholy of a Street*, 1914. Oil on canvas, 24¼ × 28½ in. (62 × 72 cm).

Tanguy constructed *Multiplication of the Arcs* (5.12) from evocative abstract shapes. In *The Mystery and Melancholy of a Street* (5.13), Giorgio de Chirico used distorted perspective and threatening cast shadows to create a feeling of anxiety. More interested in stimulating the viewer's own response than in imposing a specific vision, the surrealists rejected rational thought.

Which is better—convergent or divergent thinking? A good problem-solving strategy is one that works. If five people are working on a Website design, a clear sense of direction, agreement on style, an understanding of individual responsibilities, and adherence to deadlines are essential. On the other hand, when an artist is working independently, the open-ended divergent approach can lead to a major breakthrough. As noted in the Adam Kallish interview at the end of this chapter, combining convergent and divergent thinking is ideal. When you need to expand an idea through open-ended exploration, use divergent thinking. When focus or distillation is needed, shift to convergent thinking.

BRAINSTORMING

Brainstorming plays an important role in both convergent and divergent thinking. It is a great way to expand ideas, see connections, and explore implications. Following are four common strategies.

Make a List

Let's say that the assignment involves visualizing an emotion. Start by listing every emotion you can, regardless of your interest in any specific area. Getting into the practice of opening up and actively exploring possibilities is crucial—just pour out ideas!

> **joy   sorrow   anger   passion   jealousy   sympathy   horror   exaltation**

From the list of emotions, circle one that looks promising. To move from the intangible name of the emotion to a visual solution, develop a list of the *kinds, causes,* and *effects* of the emotion. Following is one example, using *anger* as a starting point.

KINDS	CAUSES	EFFECTS
annoyance	wrong number phone call at 5 A.M.	slammed down phone
smoldering rage	friend gets award you want	argument with friend
desperate anger	fired from job	shouted at your child
anger at self	poor performance on test	major studying

By investigating specific kinds of anger and determining the causes and the effects, you now have some specific images to develop, rather than struggling with a vague, intangible emotion.

Use a Thesaurus

Another way to explore the potential of an idea is to use a thesaurus. Be sure to get a thesaurus that lists words conceptually rather than alphabetically. Use the index in the back to look up the specific word you need. For example, *The Concise Roget's International Thesaurus* has a section titled "Feelings," including everything from *acrimony* to *zeal.* Here is a listing of synonyms from the section on resentment and anger: *anger, wrath, ire, indignation, heat, more heat than light, dudgeon, fit of anger, tantrum, outburst, explosion, storm, scene, passion, fury, burn, vehemence, violence, vent one's anger, seethe, simmer,* and *sizzle!* Thinking about a wide range of implications and connections to other emotions can give you a new approach to a familiar word.

Explore Connections

By drawing a conceptual diagram, you can create your own thesaurus. Start with a central word. Then, branch out in all directions, pursuing connections and word associations as widely as possible. In a sense, this approach lets you visualize your thinking, as the branches show the patterns and connections that occurred as you explored the idea (5.14).

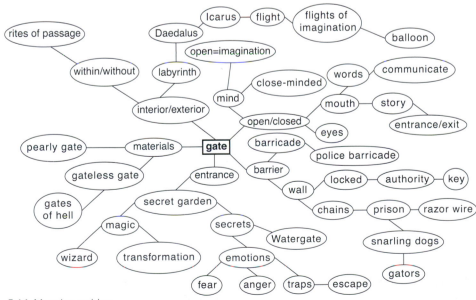

5.14 Mapping an idea.

If I am going to make drawings or photographs which include a bicycle, I might go for a bike ride, but more importantly I would fantasize about a bike. I would picture a bike in my mind. The most obvious depiction is the side view because this is the significant profile. I would then imagine a standing bicycle with no rider, looking from above, directly down on the bike, or from behind or in front of the standing bike with my eye-level midway between the ground and the handlebars. In these three positions the bicycle is seen from the least significant profile. It is a thin vertical line with horizontal protrusions of the pedals, seat and handlebars. The area viewed is so minimal that the bicycle almost disappears.

Before long in examining a bike I would become involved with circles. Looking at the tires, I think about the suspension of the rim and the tire, indeed, the entire vehicle and rider, by the thin spokes. It amazes me that everything is floating in space, connected only by thin lines. I imagine riding the bike through puddles and the trace of the linear journey from the congruent and diverging water marks left by the tread on the pavement. I might think about two friends together and separated. Symbolism.

I think about cycles of being with friends and apart. And again I would think literally of cycles, circles and tires.

I would think of the full moon as a circle and how in its cycle it turns into a line. I would see the tires from the significant profile and in my mind I would turn it in space and it would become an ellipse.

If I turned it further, until it was on an axis 90 degrees from the significant profile, it would no longer be a circle or an ellipse, but it would be a line. So again, line comes into my thoughts.

A circle is a line.

A circle is a straight line.[1]

5.15 Keith Smith. Brainstorming.

In *Structure of the Visual Book,* Keith Smith demonstrates the value of verbal connections. Smith seeks immersion in his subject. He wants to know it so well that he can pursue his images intuitively, with all the power and grace of a skilled cyclist. Try to follow the steps in figure 5.15, as he explores the word *bicycle.* Using a single object, he explores movement, friendship, and geometry.

Keep a Journal

Keeping a journal or a sketchbook is an ideal way to record your ideas and create connections. In it, you can

- Classify, arrange, and record information
- Develop new ideas
- Examine your current beliefs and analyze the beliefs of others
- Record your responses to critiques
- Make connections among your various classes

Recording your ideas at the end of each class and reviewing them at the beginning of the next can help you construct your own learning process. Anything that expands your thinking is fair game, including

- Plans for projects, such as thumbnail sketches and rough drafts
- Comments on how your work can be improved
- Notes from textbook readings and clippings from magazines
- Notes on visiting artists or gallery visits
- Technical notes or information on materials used in class
- Questions you want to pose in the next class meeting

Your record keeping can take many forms, including

- Drawings and diagrams
- Written ideas, descriptions, and lists
- Poetry and song lyrics

Periodically ask yourself the following questions:

- What was the most compelling image I saw today? What made it compelling?
- What similarities and differences were there among my studio classes this week?
- What connections were there between my lecture classes and my studio classes?
- What do I need to know in order to push my ideas further?

Viewing the journal as a record of your creative process is liberating. A random idea today can help you solve a visual problem tomorrow. Indeed, it is wise to review the journal as you move into upper-level classes. Many ideas that were too ambitious for a first-year class are perfectly suited to further development later on.

Collaborative Creativity

Designers generally use group brainstorming. This helps them explore a wider range of possibilities and better meet client needs. In *The Art of Innovation*, IDEO general manager Tom Kelley lists seven characteristics of effective group brainstorming. The following list is based on a chapter titled "The Perfect Brainstorm."

1. Sharpen your focus. A good brainstormer will generate a lot of ideas. When these ideas all address the same problem, many viable solutions result. On the other hand, when participants don't understand the problem, chaos can result.

2. Use playful rules, such as "write it down" and "think bigger." A visual and verbal record of your ideas is helpful. Premature criticism is not.

3. Number your ideas. Numbers ("Let's aim for 50 ideas in the next hour") can create quantitative targets and provide a record of the order in which ideas occurred.

4. Build and jump. As the momentum builds, more and more ideas burst forth. A thoughtful question can then help the group leap to the next level, rather than getting stuck on a plateau.

5. The space remembers. Fill your brainstorming space with 22 × 30 in. Post-it notes covered with ideas the group has developed. By seeing the information, you can more easily spot bridges and build connections.

6. Warm up. If you are working with a completely new group, it may be necessary to provide an icebreaker to build trust. This is especially true if the participants are unfamiliar with brainstorming. I often ask each participant to present one succinct question or to draw a quick cartoon of the problem as they see it. It may be an enraged elephant, a tangle of thorns, or a whirling chain saw. Both the questions and the cartoons can reveal participant insights without demanding too much too soon.

7. Get physical. A wide range of simple materials opens up possibilities, especially if you are brainstorming a three-dimensional design problem. Cardboard, plasticine, and canvas all behave very differently. Playing with various materials can lead to a wider range of possibilities.

VISUAL RESEARCH

Thumbnail Sketches

Now let's practice turning ideas into images.

Return to your original list of emotions you developed in the brainstorming exercise. Circle the most promising words or phrases you have generated and look for connections between them. Start working on thumbnail sketches, about 1.5 × 2 in. in size (5.16). Be sure to draw a clear boundary for the sketches. The

5.16 Examples of thumbnail sketches.

5.17A Peter Forbes, Models for *Shelter/Surveillance Sculpture,* **1994.** Mixed mediums, 10½ × 9½ × 9 in. (27 × 24 × 23 cm).

size of the sculpture relative to the viewer and developed a construction strategy. As a result, when he constructed the final, 11-foot-tall sculpture (5.17B), Forbes was able to proceed with confidence. A **model** is a technical experiment. A **prototype** can be quite refined, such as the fully functional test cars developed by automobile companies. In addition to the aesthetic benefit of these preliminary studies, they often are needed to help solve technical problems at this stage. Is the cardboard you are using heavy enough to stand vertically, or does it bow? Is your adhesive strong enough? If there are moving parts, is the action fluid and easy, or does the mechanism constantly get stuck?

By completing these preliminary studies, you can refine the idea, strengthen the composition, and improve the craft of the final piece. As with a well-rehearsed performance, the work you bring to the critique now is really ready for discussion.

5.17B Peter Forbes, *Shelter/Surveillance Sculpture,* **1994.** Mixed mediums, 11 ft 2 in. × 10 ft 4 in. × 10 ft (3.4 × 3.2 × 3 m).

edge of the frame is like an electric fence; by using the edge wisely, you can generate a lot of power!

As with the verbal brainstorming, move fast and stay loose at this point. It is better to generate 10 to 20 possibilities than to refine any single idea. You may find yourself producing very different solutions, or you may make a series of multiple solutions to the same idea. Either approach is fine—just keep moving!

Model Making

When working two-dimensionally, it is often necessary to make one or more full-sized rough drafts to see how the design looks when enlarged. Refinements made at this stage can mean the difference between an adequate solution and an inspired solution.

Prototypes, models, and maquettes serve a similar purpose when you are working three-dimensionally. A **maquette** is a well-developed three-dimensional sketch. Figure 5.17A shows Peter Forbes's maquette for *Shelter/Surveillance Sculpture.* In this chipboard "sketch," Forbes determined the

AN OPEN MIND

The very best artists and designers are often accomplished in more than one field. For example, Michelangelo was acclaimed as a painter, sculptor, and poet, while Leonardo da Vinci was a master of art, biology, and engineering. The study of philosophy has had a major impact on videographer Bill Viola and on installation artist Robert Irwin. Performer Laurie Anderson is equally an artist and a musician and derives many of her ideas from literature. Whenever the base of knowledge expands, the range of potential connections increases. When the islands of knowledge are widely scattered, as with interdisciplinary work, the imaginative leap is especially great.

The message is clear: the more you know, the more you can say. Read a book. Attend a lecture. Take a course in astronomy, archaeology, psychology, or poetry. Use ideas from academic courses to expand your studio work. Art and design require conceptual development as well as perceptual and technical skill. By engaging your heart, your eye, your hand, and your mind, you can fully use your emotional, perceptual, technical, and conceptual resources to create your very best work.

SUMMARY

- Concept and composition are equally important aspects of art and design.
- Designers usually solve problems presented by clients. Artists usually invent aesthetic problems for themselves.
- Ideas come from many sources, including common objects, nature, mythology, and history.
- Good problems are significant, socially responsible, comprehensible, and authentic. They provide basic parameters without inhibiting exploration.
- Convergent thinking is highly linear. The word *prose* can help you remember the steps.

- Divergent thinking is nonlinear and more open-ended than convergent thinking. It is less predictable and may lead to a creative breakthrough.
- Any idea can be expanded or enriched using brainstorming. Making lists, using a thesaurus, making a conceptual diagram, and creating connections are all common strategies.
- Visual and verbal research can provide the background information needed to create a truly inventive solution.
- The best artists and designers have a wide range of interests and approach new challenges with an open mind.

KEY TERMS

| brainstorming | divergent thinking | model | prototype |
| convergent thinking | maquette | | |

STUDIO PROJECTS

To apply the concepts from this chapter in the studio, check out the Projects page in the Online Learning Center at www.mhhe.com/stewart4e. The following is a sample of the chapter-related assignments that are described in step-by-step detail.

Poster Design. Discovering the importance of research to creating an effective ad.
Limited/Unlimited. Using the limitations of a design problem as a springboard to solutions.
Superhero Mask/Headgear Design. Exploring a variety of strategies for developing a three-dimensional design.

Profile:
Adam Kallish, Designer/Consultant

Creativity by Design

Adam Kallish has dedicated his career to brand design with underpinnings in business consulting and collaborative deployment of innovation teams for large corporations. His interests range from traditional graphic design and brand strategy to organizational design. These areas are integrated through multidisciplinary teams and program management, linking vision (desire) to requirements (specifications) to results (benefits).

MS: You are an advocate of "Design Methods," which is a particular approach to solving problems. Why?

AK: Designers are often invited into a project after many crucial decisions have been made. They are then urged to "be creative." While developing a great composition is important, the outcome may miss the mark because the designer is entering too late in the game. Design Methods presents a disciplined approach to creativity from the very start.

MS: Please give me some historical background.

AK: Design Methods was developed by John Chris Jones and others in reaction to the scientific reductivism of the post–World War II world. It recognized a new way to solve the world's problems by striking a balance between intuition (imagination, experience, and beliefs) and logic (objectivity, phenomenology, and repeatability).

The convergent and divergent strategies described in Chapter Five are a part of Design Methods. In fact, they are interdependent. Rather than simply solve a problem as presented, through Design Methods, we redefine the problem itself, which often leads to a creative breakthrough. From the outset Design Methods combines rationality, proof, and definitions with experience, feelings, and precedent.

MS: Why seek a balance between intuition and logic?

AK: Intuition is based on established patterns derived from our personal experiences. We use it every day, especially when making quick decisions. Yet, a purely intuitive response can only illuminate what has been experienced, not what *can* be experienced.

Thus, intuition provides a narrow doorway into the future. Rationality is based upon logical patterns that many people can understand. But a purely rational approach tends to oversimplify problems and the results are often mediocre.

Innovation acts as a bridge between the two by exploring three key areas: what is desirable, what is possible, and what is viable. Innovation is difficult to achieve because it requires us to move from desirability to viability.

MS: It sounds pretty daunting!

AK: In the beginning, it can feel counterintuitive. But with practice, Design Methods leads to a deeper understanding of both problem seeking and problem solving.

MS: You are really talking about ways to invent the future. What are the essential questions that apply to *all* change processes?

AK: The act of designing is difficult because we tend to seek future solutions using past and current information. For example, the solutions to global warming we develop today will work only if our predictions of the future are correct.

For simple problems involving incremental change, the future is pretty easy to understand. The redesign of an existing object like a poster or a coffee cup has many constraints that are fairly obvious, and a single designer can solve these problems. However, for highly complex problems involving many designers, many interdependencies, and many unknowns, the act of designing can easily fall apart. These four key questions can guide us when discussing the future. What should we stop doing; what should we start doing; what should we continue doing; and how can we become more effective in what we do?

MS: What is the typical Design Methods sequence?

AK: Step one is Divergence (sometimes called Analysis or Discovery). This stage is about generating doubts, posing insightful questions, exploring what is critical to the stakeholders, including the client and the users.

Step two is Transformation (sometimes called Genesis or Development). This stage is about creating appropriate boundaries and prioritizing information. The criteria and specifications that begin to emerge help the design team agree on a specific course of action.

Step three is Convergence. This stage is about focusing on an emerging solution and narrowing as many variables as possible in implementing a designed result.

With complex problems (such as systems or technological change), this sequence may need to be repeated several times before reaching a final result.

MS: It seems that Design Methods is best used in collaborative situations.

AK: It actually *requires* collaboration among various stakeholders, including clients, marketing personnel, manufacturing, users, and the designers themselves. While individualism seems easier, each of us has too many blind spots and prejudices to create a balanced future. Collaboration provides us with multiple lenses. Through these lenses, we can see our problem more fully. Even though they are harder to manage, teams bring the critical mass of skills and ideas we need when creating the best future for the greatest number of people.

MS: Let's see Design Methods in action.

AK: We can use a project from one of my classes as an example. The Nehring Center, a nonprofit art center in DeKalb, Illinois, needed to expand membership and increase attendance. Working with center director Jessica Witte, we began with an overview of the organization, discussing its goals and objectives, and noting areas for possible improvement. We interviewed a wide range of stakeholders, reviewed activities offered at the Center, analyzed its program content, and considered its affiliations to other institutions. Students began to delve deeply into its operational, marketing, and philanthropic activities and created a prioritized list of challenges.

Students then divided into two teams, one of which focused on issues of identity and the other on fundraising, which were seen as interdependent. Using convergent thinking, the teams redefined their topics and recommended specific actions. Finally, the students presented their findings to Ms. Witte, to a board member, and to School of Art faculty members. After the final presentation, she wrote:

"Design Methods sketches out a plan for the gallery's future and its current needs. I am really thankful that the presentation did not just put a Band-Aid of a logo together for me. Addressing the issue of the gallery in a greater scope . . . is really valuable."

MS: Essentially, it sounds like you took the long way around, and arrived at a more interesting end point.

AK: Yes. Despite its initial difficulty, the full process provoked the students to intensify their investigation. Their conceptual tool kit then allowed them to dig deeper and wrestle with a much more expansive problem space.

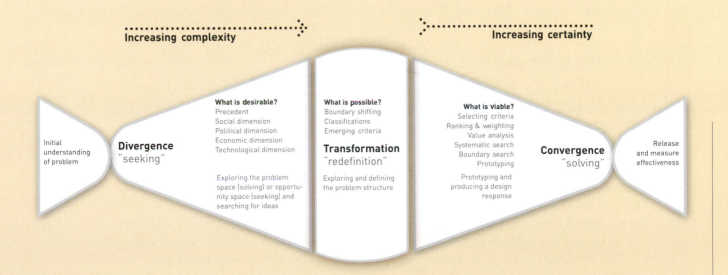

Increasing complexity

Increasing certainty

Initial understanding of problem

Divergence "seeking"

What is desirable?
Precedent
Social dimension
Political dimension
Economic dimension
Technological dimension

Exploring the problem space (solving) or opportunity space (seeking) and searching for ideas

Transformation "redefinition"

What is possible?
Boundary shifting
Classifications
Emerging criteria

Exploring and defining the problem structure

Convergence "solving"

What is viable?
Selecting criteria
Ranking & weighting
Value analysis
Systematic search
Boundary search
Prototyping

Prototyping and producing a design response

Release and measure effectiveness

Cultivating Creativity

"The heart of all new ideas lies in the borrowing, adding, combining or modifying of old ones. Do it by accident and people call you lucky. Do it by design and they'll call you creative."

Michael LeBoeuf, in *Imagineering*

The problem-seeking and problem-solving processes described in Chapter Five seem methodical and deliberate. The creative challenges we actually confront in the studio are often much messier. This chapter is designed to help you bridge the gap between the ideal situation and your actual experience. In it we consider characteristics of creative people, discuss goal setting, list time-management strategies, and explore habits of mind and habits of work that can increase success.

SEVEN CHARACTERISTICS OF CREATIVE THINKING

"Conditions for creativity are to be puzzled, to concentrate, to accept conflict and tension, to be born every day, to feel a sense of self."

Erich Fromm, in *Creativity and Its Cultivation*

Creativity is inherently unpredictable. Through creative thinking, old habits are broken and familiar patterns of thought are transformed. Anything can happen. Predicting the future based on past experience becomes inadequate when a creative breakthrough occurs. Like a shimmering drop of mercury, creativity eludes capture.

We can actively encourage creative thinking, however. Rather than waiting for inspiration, we can set up the conditions favorable to creativity. Based on observation and on interviews, various researchers have noted the following characteristics in many creative people.

Receptivity

Creative people are open to new ideas and welcome new experiences. Never complacent, they question the status quo and embrace alternative solutions to existing problems. Listening more and talking less is helpful. As journalist Larry King says, "I never learn anything new when I'm the one talking!"

Curiosity

A good designer brings an insatiable curiosity to each project. Researching unfamiliar topics and analyzing unusual systems is a source of delight for most creative people. "How does it work?" and "How can it work better?" are frequently asked questions.

Wide Range of Interests

With a broad knowledge base, a creative person can make a wider range of connections. Consider the number of words you can create from the letters in the word *image*:

age, game, gem, am, aim, a, I, me

Try the same game with the word *imagination*:

gin, nation, gnat, ton, tan, not, man, again, gain, oat, got, tag, am, aim, ant, no, on, tin, gamin, inn, ingot, main, a, I

With more components, the number of combinations increases. Likewise, an artist who has a background in literature, geology, archery, music, and history can make more connections than can a narrow-minded specialist.

Attentiveness

Realizing that every experience is valuable, creative people pay attention to seemingly minor details. Scientists often develop major theories by observing small events, which they then organize into complex patterns. Artists can often see past superficial visual chaos to discern an underlying order. Playwrights develop dramatic works by looking past the surface of human behavior to explore the substance of the human condition. By looking carefully, creative people see possibilities that others miss.

Connection Seeking

Seeing the similarity among seemingly disparate parts has often sparked a creative breakthrough. For example, Egyptian hieroglyphs became readable when a young French scholar realized that they carried the same message as an adjacent Greek inscription on a slab of stone. By comparing the two and cracking the Rosetta Stone code, Jean-François

Champollion opened the door for all subsequent students of ancient Egyptian culture.

Conviction

Creative people value existing knowledge. Since new ideas are often derived from old ideas, it is foolish to ignore or dismiss the past. However, creative people also love change. Never satisfied with routine answers to familiar questions, they constantly consider new possibilities and often challenge the status quo.

Complexity

In lecture classes, we must take notes, memorize facts, and collect and analyze data. We are encouraged to think rationally, write clearly, and present our ideas in a linear progression. In studio classes, exploration, experimentation, and intuition are encouraged, especially during brainstorming sessions. Synthesis, intuition, visualization, spatial perception, and non-linear thinking are highly valued.

To be fully effective, a creative person needs to combine the rational with the intuitive. While intuition may be used to generate a new idea, logic and analysis are often needed for its realization. As a result, the actions of creative people are often complex or even contradictory. As noted by psychologist Mihaly Csikszentmihalyi,[1] creative people often combine

- Physical energy with a respect for rest. They work long hours with great concentration, then rest and relax, fully recharging their batteries. They view balance between work and play as essential.

- Savvy with innocence. Creative people tend to view the world and themselves with a sense of wonder, rather than cling to preconceptions or stereotypes. They use common sense as well as intellect in completing their work.

- Responsibility with playfulness. When the situation requires serious attention, creative people are remarkably diligent and determined. They realize that there is no substitute for hard work and drive themselves relentlessly when nearing completion of a major project. On the other hand, when the situation permits, a playful, devil-may-care attitude may prevail, providing a release from the previous period of work.

- Risk-taking with safe-keeping. Creativity expert George Prince has noted two behavioral extremes in people.[2] Safe-keepers look before they leap, avoid surprises, punish mistakes, follow the rules, and watch the clock. A safe-keeper is most comfortable when there is only one right answer to memorize or one solution to produce. Risk-takers are just the opposite. They break the rules, leap before they look, like surprises, are impetuous, and may lose track of time. A risk-taker enjoys inventing multiple answers to every question.

  An imbalance in either direction limits creativity. Fear inhibits the safe-keeper, while irresponsibility may inhibit the risk-taker. Creative thinking requires a mix of risk-taking and safe-keeping. When brainstorming new ideas, open-ended exploration is used. But, when implementing new ideas, deadlines, budgets, and feasibility become major concerns. The risk-taker gets the job started; the safe-keeper gets the job done.

- Extroversion with introversion. When starting a new project, creative people are often talkative and gregarious, eager to share insights and explore ideas. When a clear sense of direction develops, however, they often withdraw, seeking solitude and quiet work time. This capacity for solitude is crucial. Several studies have shown that talented teenagers who cannot stand solitude rarely develop their creative skills.

- Passion with objectivity. Mature artists tend to plunge into new projects, convinced of the significance of the work and confident of their skills. Any attempt to distract or dissuade them at this point is futile. However, when the model or rough study is done, many will pause to assess their progress. This analysis and judgment may occur in a group setting or may be done by the artist alone. In either case, the emotional attachment required while creating is now replaced by a dispassionate objectivity. Work that does not pass this review is redone or discarded, regardless of the hours spent in its development. In major projects, this alternating process of creation and analysis may be repeated many times.

- Disregard for time with attention to deadlines. Time often dissolves when studio work begins. An artist or a designer can become engrossed in a project: when the work is going well, 6 hours can feel like 20 minutes. On the other hand, an acute attention to deadlines is necessary when preparing an exhibition or working for a client.

- Modesty with pride. As they mature, creative people often become increasingly aware of the contributions to their success made by teachers, family, and colleagues. Rather than brag about past accomplishments, they tend to focus on current projects. On the other hand, as creative people become aware of their significance within a field, they gain a powerful sense of purpose. Distractions are deleted from the schedule, and increasingly ambitious goals are set.

When the balance is right, all of these complex characteristics fuel even greater achievement.

GOAL SETTING

Human behavior is strongly goal-directed. Every action occurs for a reason. When we focus our attention on a specific task, we can channel our energy and better manage our time. When we reach our goals, our self-esteem increases, which then helps us overcome obstacles. And, with each goal met, our knowledge increases. Michael LeBoeuf has diagrammed this effect clearly (6.1).

A Goal-Setting Strategy

Self-knowledge is essential. No matter how hard we try, we can never really fulfill our potential when pursuing goals set by others. The following exercise can help you clarify your personal interests.

1. Get a package of Post-it notes. Working spontaneously, write one of your characteristics on each note, such as "I am creative," "I love music," "I write well." Identify as many attributes as possible.

2. When you finish, lay out the notes on a table and look at them for a while. Consider the type of person they describe. What are this person's strengths? What additional interests might this person need to develop?

3. On a fresh stack of notes, write a new set of responses, this time dealing with the question

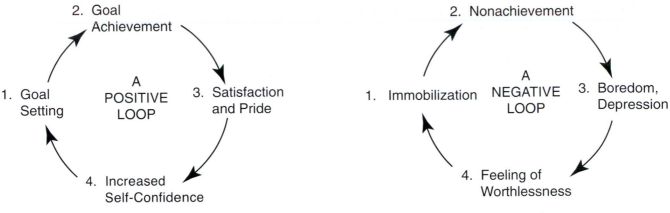

6.1 Michael LeBoeuf, *Imagineering*, 1980. Achievement feeds self-confidence, while nonachievement induces inertia.

"Why not?" as an expansion of your interests. Why not travel to Tibet? Why not learn Spanish? Why not master canoeing? Add these to the grid.

4. Then take a break. Let your subconscious mind play with the possibilities suggested by your notes.

5. Next, organize the notes into four general categories: intellectual goals, personal-relationship goals, spiritual or emotional goals, physical fitness goals. If you are an extreme safe-keeper, add a category called "Adventure." If you are an extreme risk-taker, consider adding a category called "Organization." Since a mix of activities helps feed the psyche, working with each of these categories is helpful.

6. Choose one goal from each category and develop an implementation strategy. Be specific! "I want to become a better artist" is too vague. Consider specific actions you can take to improve your artwork. "I need to improve my drawing" is better. "I want to learn anatomy" is better still. To learn anatomy, you can take a class, study an anatomy book, or draw from a skeleton. These are tangible actions—you now know what to do.

7. Prioritize your goals and develop a rough timetable, listing weekly goals, semester goals, and one-year goals. It is not necessary to list career goals just yet. Most of us explore many ideas during our first year of college, and formalizing career goals prematurely is counterproductive.

8. At least once a month, review your chart and add or delete information as necessary. If you realize that you are overextended this term, shift one of your minor goals to next semester. This system is intended to provide clear targets, not to create a straitjacket.

9. If you achieve all your goals, congratulate yourself — then set more ambitious goals next term. If you achieve half of your goals, congratulate yourself — then prioritize more carefully next term. You may have taken on too many tasks. Because there is always a gap between intention and outcome, a 70 to 80 percent completion rate is fine.

Characteristics of Good Goals

Ambitious yet Achievable

Too modest a goal will provide no sense of accomplishment. Too ambitious a goal will reduce, rather than increase, motivation. No one wants to fight a losing battle! Knowing your strengths and weaknesses will help you set realistic goals.

Compatible

Training for the Boston Marathon while simultaneously trying to gain 20 pounds is unwise, since you will burn off every calorie you consume. Trying to save a thousand dollars while touring Europe is unrealistic, since travel always costs more than you expect. On the other hand, by taking a dance class or joining a hiking club, you may be able to combine a fitness goal with a social goal.

Self-Directed

Avoid goals that are primarily dependent on someone else's actions or opinions. "I want to earn an A in drawing" is a common example. Since the grade is determined by a teacher, your control in this area is limited. Instead, focus on improving your drawing as much as possible. This will increase your receptivity to learning and focus your attention on actions you can control. When you do your best work, good grades generally follow.

Temporary

Set clear target dates, get the job done, and move on to the next project. Each completed task increases your self-confidence and adds momentum. By contrast, unfinished work can drain energy and decrease momentum. If you are overloaded, delete secondary goals so that you can complete primary goals.

TIME MANAGEMENT

Time management can help you achieve your goals. Working smarter is usually more effective than simply working harder. In a world bursting with opportunity, using your work time well can increase the time available for travel, volunteer work, or socializing. The following time-management strategies have been used by many artists and designers.

Set the Stage

Choosing when and where to work can significantly increase your output. If you are a lark, bursting with energy and enthusiasm early in the morning, tackle major projects before noon. If you are an owl, equipped with night vision and able to hunt after dark, work on major projects after dinner. If you are distracted by clutter, clean your desk before beginning your workday, and tidy up your desk before you leave. These seemingly minor actions can substantially increase your productivity.

Prioritize

Note which tasks are most *urgent* and which tasks are most *important*. Timing can be crucial. When you pay your phone bill on time, you easily complete an urgent but unimportant task. When your phone bill is overdue and the service is cut off, this unimportant task becomes a major headache. Dispense with urgent tasks quickly so that you can focus on more important issues.

See the Big Picture

Use monthly calendar pages to record your major projects and obligations. A calendar that is organized by months can help you see which weeks will be packed with deadlines and which weeks will be relatively quiet. To avoid all-nighters, distribute large, important tasks over several weeks. To avoid missing a pivotal lecture or critique, schedule out-of-town trips during "slow" weeks.

Work Sequentially

Many activities are best done in a specific sequence. If you are writing a 20-page paper, it is best to start with research, make an outline, complete a rough draft, make corrections, then write the final draft. If you are designing a poster, it is best to start with research, make thumbnail sketches, assess the results, make a full-size rough layout, consult the client, and *then* complete the poster. Trying to cut out the intermediate steps and move directly to the final draft is rarely effective. With most large projects, you learn more, save time, and do better work by following the right sequence of tasks.

Use Parts to Create the Whole

Seen as a whole, a major project can become overwhelming. In an extreme case, creative paralysis sets in, resulting in a condition similar to writer's block. Breaking down big jobs into smaller parts helps enormously. In *Bird by Bird*, Anne Lamott gives a wonderful description of this process:

> Thirty years ago my other brother, who was ten years old at the time, was trying to get a report on birds written that he'd had three months to write. [It] was due the next day. . . . He was at the kitchen table close to tears, surrounded by binder paper and pencils and unopened books on birds, immobilized by the hugeness of the task ahead. Then my father sat down beside him, put his arm around my brother's shoulder, and said, "Bird by bird, buddy. Just take it bird by bird."[3]

By doing the job incrementally, you are likely to learn more and procrastinate less.

Make the Most of Class Time

Psychologists tell us that beginnings and endings of events are especially memorable. An experienced teacher knows that the first 10 minutes of class set the tone for the rest of the session and that a summary at the end can help students remember the lesson. Similarly, the wise student arrives 5 minutes early for class and maintains attention to the end of class.

Be an active learner. You can use that 5 minutes before class to review your notes from the previous session and organize your supplies. This helps create a bridge between what you know and the new information to be presented. Try to end the class on a high note, either by completing a project or by clearly determining the strengths and weaknesses of the work in progress. By analyzing your progress, you can organize your thinking and provide a solid beginning point for the next work session.

When in Doubt, Crank It Out

Fear is one of the greatest obstacles to creative thinking. When we are afraid, we tend to avoid action and consequently miss opportunities.

Both habit and perfectionism feed fear. If you consistently repeat the same activities and limit yourself to familiar friendships, you will become more and more fearful of new experiences. Perfectionism is especially destructive during brainstorming, which requires a loose, open approach.

Creativity takes courage. As IBM founder Thomas Watson noted, "If you are not satisfied with your rate of success, try failing more." Baseball player Reggie Jackson is renowned for his 563 home runs—but he also struck out 2,597 times. Thomas Edison's research team tried over 6,000 materials before finding the carbon-fiber filament used in lightbulbs.

"When in doubt, don't!" is the safe-keeper's motto. "When in doubt, do!" is the risk-taker's motto. By starting each project with a sense of adventure, you increase your level of both learning and creativity.

Work Together

Many areas of art and design, including filmmaking, industrial design, and advertising design, are often done collaboratively. Working together, artists and designers can complete projects that are too complex or time-consuming to be done solo. Collaborative thinking helps us break familiar patterns and teaches us to listen to alternative or opposing ideas.

Here is one example. Gather 20 people. Start with a copied fragment from an existing image, such as *Metamophosis II,* an 8 × 160 in. banner by M. C. Escher (6.2). In this case, design students were provided with a 1-inch strip of the banner to create a beginning point and another 1-inch strip of the banner to create the ending point (6.3A). Each person invented an 8½ × 11 in. connection between the two strips. Buildings, plants, chess pieces, and other images were used to bridge the gap between the strips at the beginning and the end. The images were then connected end to end, like cars in a train. When combined, they created a collaborative banner 20 feet long. One piece of the banner is shown in figure 6.3B. Students had to negotiate with the person ahead of them in the line and with the person behind them in order to make a continuous image with graceful transitions. In effect, all 20 participants became members of a creative team. Finally, each 8½ × 11 in. section was photocopied and traded, providing each person with the completed artwork. In a collaboration of this kind, everyone gains, both in the learning process and in the sharing of the final product.

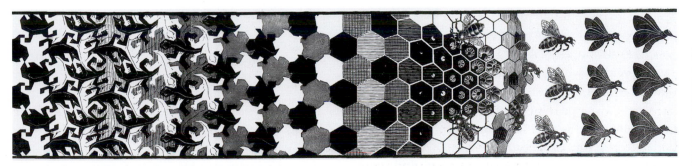

6.2 M. C. Escher, Part of *Metamorphosis II,* 1939–40. Woodcut in black, green, and brown, printed from 20 blocks on three combined sheets, 7½ × 153⅜ in. (19 × 390 cm).

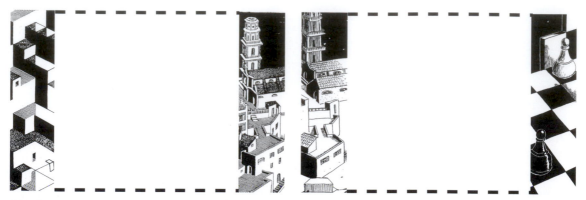

6.3A Examples of Escher Starter Images.

6.3B Mary Stewart and Jesse Wummer, **Expanded Escher Collaboration.** Student work.

VARIATIONS ON A THEME

When we work creatively, the idea develops right along with the image. As the project evolves, we see other implications that go beyond our initial intention. By courageously pursuing these implications, we can exceed our original expectations. Just as the landscape appears to expand when we climb a mountain, so an image can expand when our conceptual understanding increases.

One way to get a lot of mileage out of an idea is through variations on a theme. Professional artists rarely do just one painting or sculpture of a given idea—most do many variations before moving to a new subject. *Thirty-Six Views of Mount Fuji* is one example. Printmaker Katsushika

6.4A Katsushika Hokusai, *Thirty-Six Views of Mount Fuji: Under the Mannen Bridge at Fukagawa*, Edo Period, c. 1830. Color woodblock print, 10 1/16 × 14 1/16 in. (25.7 × 37.5 cm).

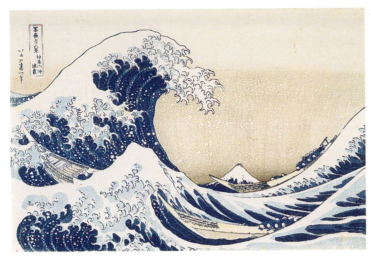

6.4B Katsushika Hokusai, *Thirty-Six Views of Mount Fuji: The Great Wave off Kanagawa*, Edo Period, c. 1830. Color woodblock print, 10³⁄₁₆ × 14¹⁵⁄₁₆ in. (25.9 × 37.5 cm).

6.4C Katsushika Hokusai, *Thirty-Six Views of Mount Fuji: Near Umezawa in Sagami Province*, Edo Period, c. 1830. Color woodblock print, 10¹⁄₁₆ × 14⅞ in. (25.6 × 37.8 cm).

Hokusai was 70 years old when he began this series. The revered and beautiful Mount Fuji appeared in each of the designs in some way. Variations in the time of year and size of the mountain helped Hokusai produce very different images while retaining the same basic theme (6.4A–C).

Variations on the standard chess set are shown in the next three figures. Completed by industrial design students in response to a design competition, each set offers a unique approach to an ancient game. Eddie Chui's *Let's Dance* (6.5) retains the familiar forms of the various pieces but adds a curved bottom. Rather than sitting stoically in place, the knights, pawns, and other pieces tend to dance back and forth, while magnets connect them to the board. Deborah Tan used a very different approach. Her set (6.6) is designed for blind players. To help them distinguish each piece, Tan created a collection of very distinctive forms. Depressions in the board help secure each piece in place. Finally, Sergio Silva provided a carrying case along with his set of geometric forms (6.7). Created from square and rectangular forms, the set is crisp and highly unified.

Many variations on a cube are shown in figure 6.8. Submitted by beginning architecture students at Auburn University, they demonstrate one advantage of studying art and design in a classroom setting: you get to see variations on a theme every time an assignment is due.

6.5 Eddie Chui, *Let's Dance*, 2005. Maple, magnets, and silicon.

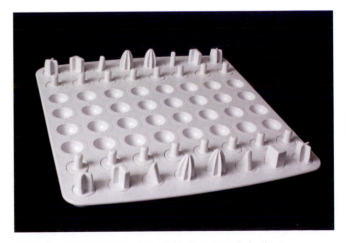

6.6 Deborah Tan, *Chess Set*, 2005. Plaster and plastic.

6.7 Sergio Silva, *Chess Set*, 2005. Anodized aluminum and wood.

6.8 Cubes from above, study models from Auburn University School of Architecture.

HABITS OF MIND AND WORK

Habits of Mind

Dr. Arthur L. Costa and Dr. Bena Kallick have identified 16 "habits of mind" essential to success. Here their list has been distilled down to four attributes that characterize the most effective art and design students, with commentary added.

Flexibility

Convergent, divergent, and collaborative problem-solving strategies present distinct advantages and disadvantages. Limiting yourself to just one approach reduces your ability to solve a wide range of problems. Flexibility, on the other hand, gives you the ability to question existing assumptions, adopt new ideas, and shift strategies as needed.

Analytical Thinking

In general, designers are hired to solve a client's problem. Limitations imposed by time, materials, and budget complicate matters. An analytical mindset helps the designer solve the real problem rather than wasting time on an imagined problem.

Capacity for Synthesis

Synthesis may be defined as the capacity to combine separate parts to create a coherent whole. Two aspects of synthesis are particularly important for artists and designers. First, they must be able to combine lines, shapes, textures, and so on to create a compositional whole. Second, they must be able to apply past knowledge to new situations. By retaining your understanding of each problem solved, you accumulate a vast storehouse of knowledge and experience.

Responsible Risk Taking

Risk-takers are willing to risk failure in order to achieve success. They view setbacks as opportunities for growth rather than occasions for despair. Irresponsible risk-takers leap before they look. Responsible risk-takers weigh benefits and hazards, gather their energy, and then leap.

Habits of Work

To provide beginning designers with a realistic checklist, Professor Rusty Smith and his colleagues in the School of Architecture at Auburn University have developed the following list of "habits of work" for architects.

Self-Reliance

Essentially, self-reliance creates an active approach to work. Rather than waiting for directions or blaming others for delays, each architecture student actively generates possibilities, weighs benefits, and makes choices. To a substantial degree, self-reliant students drive their own learning process.

Organized Persistence

Beating your head against a brick wall is an example of mindless persistence. It is impressive but ineffective. Chiseling away at the mortar between the bricks until the wall falls apart is an example of organized persistence. It may take weeks, but eventually organized persistence results in a solution. It gives us the ability to prevail, even when we are faced with the most daunting task.

Daily Practice

Momentum is extremely powerful when you are working on a difficult problem. Daily practice helps maintain momentum. For example, when learning a new computer program, practicing for a couple of hours each night is better than working on it one full day a month.

Appropriate Speed

Some tasks are best completed quickly, with brisk decision making and decisive action. Slowing down to reframe a question and weigh alternative solutions is necessary in other cases. Knowing when to speed up and when to slow down is one mark of a "master learner."

Valuing Alternative Viewpoints

Listening to others, understanding diverse points of view, and considering alternatives expand our capacity to solve a wide variety of problems. Even when the advice is off-base, we can often use the idea as a springboard to a fresh approach.

Incremental Excellence

Most art and design problems are best developed in a series of stages. Ideas evolve, skills improve, compositions are distilled. Rather than trying for the "perfect solution" on the first day of work, it is better to start with a "funky junky" draft.

Direct Engagement

Talk is cheap. Work is hard. The only way to solve most art and design problems is to get involved. You will never win a race when you are standing on the sidelines!

SUMMARY

- Creativity and design both require new combinations of old ideas.
- Creative people are receptive to new ideas, are curious, have a wide range of interests, are attentive, seek connections, and work with great conviction.
- A combination of rational and intuitive thinking feeds creativity. While intuition may be used to generate a new idea, logic and analysis are often needed for its completion. As a result, the actions of creative people are often complex or even contradictory.
- Goals you set are goals you get. Establishing priorities and setting appropriate goals will help you achieve your potential. Good goals are ambitious but achievable, compatible, self-directed, and temporary. Deadlines encourage completion of complex projects.

- Completing tasks in an appropriate sequence, making the most of each work period, maintaining momentum, and reducing stress are major aspects of time management.
- Collaborative work can help you expand your ideas, explore new fields, and pursue projects that are too complex or time-consuming to do alone.
- Ideas can be explored more fully using variations on a theme.
- Flexibility, analytical ability, the capacity for synthesis, and responsible risk taking are effective habits of mind.
- Self-reliance, organized persistence, daily practice, appropriate speed, valuing alternative viewpoints, incremental excellence, and direct engagement are effective habits of work.

STUDIO PROJECTS

To apply the concepts from this chapter in the studio, check out the Projects page in the Online Learning Center at www.mhhe.com/stewart4e. The following is a sample of the chapter-related assignments that are described in step-by-step detail.

Collaborative Compositions. Digitally creating a collaborative collage.
Expanding Escher. Working within the boundaries of a partner's design.
Audio Assemblage. Building a musical instrument from found objects as a team.

Profile:
Suzanne Stryk, Painter
An Art of Observation

Suzanne Stryk's artwork has appeared in over 60 group shows, and in solo exhibitions at the National Academy of Sciences, the Morris Museum of Art, the Eleanor B. Wilson Museum, and the William King Museum (an affiliate of the Virginia Museum of Fine Arts). Among the collections that own her work are the Tennessee State Museum, Bank of America's Southeastern Collection, the Taubman Museum of Art, and the Smithsonian Institution.

MS: You initially studied fine art and biology and then shifted to major in art history. Why?

SS: When I began my studies, I didn't really fit into the abstract expressionist and pop art approaches that were prevalent at the time. I was fascinated—and still am—with the depiction of nature in the art of different cultures. My papers explored topics such as animals in Egyptian tomb painting and nature marginalia drawn into medieval manuscripts. This "detour" into art history turned out to be invaluable to me as an artist.

MS: You then developed a career as a scientific illustrator. What kinds of jobs did you do, and what did you learn from these jobs?

SS: Seeking to merge my interest in nature and art, I studied scientific illustration in the early eighties. I then worked in a university biology department, drawing graphs and charts, along with the fun stuff—plant specimens and animals. The job required discipline and patience, which remains with me to this day, along with the arrows, labels, measurements, and grids that fill my images.

MS: When and why did you shift toward more self-directed studio work?

SS: Scientific illustration stimulated more and more questions. I wondered, "What does my precise drawing really say about an animal? Doesn't it say more about us as a species of observers?" In the mid-eighties, I discovered Russian icons, which often use a grid format to depict events in a saint's life. I decided to put a cicada's life cycle in a similar grid. This inspired a whole series called *Life Cycles*. Then, a couple of these paintings were selected for my first major exhibition in Chicago. You know, if

you're doing work that makes you think, "Either this is the stupidest thing in the world or really profound," then you might be onto something! It was the turning point in my discovery of personal voice.

MS: What are the greatest challenges in your work?

SS: Well, it's always a great challenge to make the concept and the visual idea seamless. Right now, I'm constructing life-sized birds from printouts of their genomic sequences. The finished birds will perch or hang around my paintings. I've done very little three-dimensional work and must therefore become fluent in a new "language."

MS: Your sketchbooks are numbered and lined up on a shelf in your studio, thirty in a row. Why are they so well organized, and what do they contribute to your studio practice?

SS: My sketchbooks are the primary source for my finished images. They include drawings of creatures surrounded by my notes, dates, measurements, and names, like a field naturalist's journal. But you'll also find interpretive notes about my personal response to the animal. As an illustrator, I focus on observation. As an artist, I must turn my observations into meaning.

MS: You look up the specific species of beetle or other subject. Why is specificity important?

SS: Knowing the species leads me to learn more about the animal, about its special features or behaviors. For example, I may discover a plump green caterpillar with tiny bristles and reddish dots. When I identify it as a Luna moth larva, I learn to feed it walnut leaves. I can then witness it pupate and, if lucky, watch it emerge as a huge milky-green adult. This is no small thing for me, for my whole worldview—as reflected in my art—centers on the awareness of other lives.

MS: You emphasize the importance of intuition. Please describe intuition and give us an example.

SS: It may sound like a contradiction, but a lot of intuition is learned. For instance, in my *Genomes and Daily Observations* series, I invent microorganisms or insect parts from the accidental stains and drips on the paper. I recognize that it just "feels right." These examples of intuition may take years of painting and familiarity with biological forms to do convincingly. Louis Pasteur got it right when he said, "Chance favors the prepared mind."

I can also be very analytical. While working on a drawing, I may use a high-powered magnifier to help me meticulously paint tiny bristles on a beetle's leg. But isn't the analytical—knowing where and when to use it—informed by the intuitive? For me, the analytical and the intuitive are partners.

MS: Do you purposely seek subjects for your work?

SS: Not with the *Daily Observations* series. When my path crosses with, say, a salamander, then it's a salamander painting that day. This series is simultaneous with the other art projects I do—it keeps me grounded with actual living things.

MS: You show your work in a wide variety of settings, from galleries and museums to science centers. What do you most want to communicate?

SS: Art humanizes science. It suggests nature is not just something "out there" or in the realm of laboratories, but part of our own story. I'm humbled when my work hangs next to the armature of a dinosaur or a display of beetles in a natural history museum. Evolution is, in the end, the greatest artist of all.

Recently I painted a blue finch on what looks like a torn piece of paper floating in a suggestive landscape. I'd like viewers to ask questions, such as, "Is this image about our partial understanding of the natural world? About the fragmentation of nature? Our own fragmentation? Is it a memory? A personal dream?" But a viewer said, "Oh, I love the blue of that bird against the white!" So you see, the first communication begins as a purely visual experience. The conceptual sneaks in there after the eye is seduced.

MS: Do you have any advice for my students?

SS: Find your own voice. Ask yourself, "What sight makes me want to make an image? Soldiers on a battlefield? Graffiti? The patterned wing of a moth?" The answer should help point you in a personal direction. Probe what it is that attracts you, visually and conceptually. As artists, we must embrace a life that is fully engaged, connected to the experience of being alive. I think of a life in art as analogous to evolution: it winds around, mutates, some creations live, others fail, and along the way surprising and even marvelous things are made.

Suzanne Stryk, *Genomes and Daily Observations Series,* 2005. Mixed media on paper, 10 × 14 in. (25.4 × 35.6 cm).

Developing Critical Thinking

chapter seven

Critical thinking combines

- Evaluation of all available information
- Analysis of visual relationships
- Exploration of alternative solutions

Never complacent, the best artists and designers continually seek to improve each image and expand each idea. Critical thinking is used to determine compositional strengths, develop concepts, and improve visual communication. Knowing what to keep and what to change is crucial. By enhancing the best aspects of a design and deleting the weak areas, we can dramatically strengthen both communication and expression.

ESTABLISHING CRITERIA

Establishing the criteria on which judgments will be made is the first step. For example, if technical skills are being emphasized in an assignment, craftsmanship will be highly valued. Likewise, if the assignment must be done in analogous colors, a black-and-white painting will not meet the criteria, no matter how well it is composed. By determining the major questions being raised in each problem, we can understand the basis on which judgments will be reached. Consider the following questions:

- What is the purpose of the assignment? Does your teacher want you to learn any specific skills? What compositional and conceptual variables will you need to explore?
- What are the basic assignment parameters? Are there limitations in the size, style, or materials?
- When is the assignment due and in what form must it be presented?

It is important to distinguish between understanding assignment criteria and seeking the "right answer." In the first case, by determining the boundaries, you can fully focus your energy when you begin to work. Just as a magnifying glass can be used to focus sunlight into a powerful beam, so assignment parameters can help you focus creative energy. On the other hand, students who try to determine the right answer to a problem often simply want to know the teacher's solution. Such knowledge is rarely helpful. The assignment simply sets a learning process in motion: you learn through your work!

FORM, SUBJECT, CONTENT

Form may be defined as the physical manifestation of an idea or emotion. Two-dimensional forms are created using line, shape, texture, value, and color. The building blocks of three-dimensional forms are line, plane, volume, mass, space, texture, and color. Duration, tempo, intensity, scope, setting, and chronology are combined to create time-based art forms. For example, film is the form in which *Star Wars* was first presented.

The **subject,** or topic, of an artwork is most apparent when a person, an object, an event, or a setting is clearly represented. For example, the conflict between the rebels and the Empire provides the subject for *Star Wars.*

The emotional or intellectual message of an artwork provides its **content,** or underlying theme. The theme of *Star Wars* is the journey into the self. Luke Skywalker's gradual understanding of himself and acceptance of Darth Vader as his father provide an essential emotional undercurrent to the entire series.

STOP, LOOK, LISTEN, LEARN

Any of these three aspects of design can be discussed critically. A **critique** is the most common structure used. During the critique, your peers or professors analyze your work. Many solutions are presented, demonstrating a wide range of possibilities. The strengths and weaknesses in each design are identified, and areas needing revision are revealed. These insights can be used to improve the current design or to generate possibilities for the next assignment.

Critiques can be extremely helpful, extremely destructive, or just plain boring, depending largely on the amount and type of student involvement. Specific recommendations are most helpful. Be sure to substantiate each judgment so that your rationale is clear.

Whether you are giving or receiving advice, come with your mind open, rather than with your fists closed. A critique is not a combat zone! Listen carefully to any explanations offered and generously offer your insights to others. Likewise, receive suggestions gracefully rather than defensively. You will make the final decision on any further actions needed to strengthen your design; if someone gives you bad advice, quietly discard it. A substantial and supportive critique is the best way to determine the effect your design has on an audience, so speak thoughtfully and weigh seriously every suggestion you receive.

When beginning a critique, it is useful to distinguish between objective and subjective criticism. **Objective criticism** is used to assess how well a work of art or design utilizes the elements and principles of design. Discussion generally focuses on basic compositional concerns, such as

- The type of balance used in the composition and how it was created
- The spatial depth of a design and its compositional effect
- The degree of unity in a design and how it was achieved

Objective criticism is based on direct observation and a shared understanding of assignment parameters. Discussion is usually clear and straightforward. Alternative compositional solutions may be discussed in depth.

Subjective criticism is used to describe the personal impact of an image, the narrative implications of an idea, or the cultural ramifications of an action. Discussion generally focuses on the subject and content of the design, including

- The meaning of the artwork
- The feelings it evokes
- Its relationship to other cultural events
- The artist's intent

Because subjective criticism is not based on simple observation, it is more difficult for most groups to remain focused on the artwork itself or to reach any clear conclusions regarding possible improvements. The discussion may become more general and wide-ranging as political or social questions raised by the works of art and design are analyzed. Because of the potential lack of clarity, subjective criticism may be used sparingly during the foundation year.

TYPES OF CRITIQUES

Description

The first step is to look carefully and report clearly. Without evaluating, telling stories, drawing conclusions, or making recommendations, simply describe the visual organization of the work presented. A **descriptive critique** can help you see details and heighten your understanding of the design. The student whose work you describe learns which aspects of the design are most eye-catching and which areas are muddled and need work.

This is a particularly useful exercise when analyzing a complex piece, such as figure 7.1A. In an art history class, you might write:

Place de l'Europe on a Rainy Day is a rectangular painting depicting a street in Paris. A vertical lamppost and its shadow extend from the top edge to the bottom edge, neatly dividing the painting in half. A horizon line, extending from the left side and three-quarters of the way to the right, further divides the painting, creating four major quadrants. Because this horizon line is positioned just above center, the bottom half of the composition is slightly larger than the top half. A dozen pedestrians with umbrellas occupy the bottom half of the painting. At the right edge, a man strides into the painting, while next to him a couple moves out of the painting, toward the viewer. To the left of the lamppost, most of the movement is horizontal, as people cross the cobblestone streets.

When using description in a spoken critique in a studio class, it is useful to note essential compositional characteristics:

- What is the shape of the overall composition? A circle or sphere presents a very different compositional playing field than does a square or a cube.

- What range of colors has been used? A black-and-white design is very different from a full-color design.

- What is the size of the project? Extremes are especially notable. A sculpture that is 10 feet tall or a painting that is 1 inch square will immediately attract attention.

- Is the visual information tightly packed, creating a very dense design, or is the design

7.1A Gustave Caillebotte, *Place de l'Europe on a Rainy Day,* 1877. Oil on canvas, 83½ × 108¾ in. (212.2 × 276.2 cm).

more spacious, with a lot of space between shapes or volumes?

The Key Questions that appear throughout this book can provide a springboard into a critique.

Cause and Effect

A descriptive critique helps us analyze the compositional choices made by the artist. A **cause-and-effect critique** (also known as a **formal analysis**) builds on this description. In a simple description, you might say that the design is primarily composed of diagonals. Using cause and effect, you might conclude that, *because* of the many diagonals, the design is very dynamic. In a cause-and-effect critique, you discuss consequences as well as choices. Analyzing the same painting, you might write:

> *Place de l'Europe on a Rainy Day* depicts a city street in Paris near the end of the nineteenth century. A lamppost, positioned near the center, vertically dissects the painting in half. The horizon line

creates a second major division, with 45 percent of the space above and 55 percent below this line.

A dozen pedestrians in dark clothing cross the cobblestone streets from left to right, creating a flowing movement. To the right of the post, the pedestrians move in and out of the painting, from background to foreground. Both types of movement add compositional energy. Two men and one woman are the most prominent figures. The man at the far right edge pulls us into the painting, while the couple to his immediate left moves toward us, pushing out of their world and into our world. The movement that dominates each side of the painting is arrested by the lamppost. It is almost as if we are getting two paintings on one canvas.

As shown in figure 7.1B, a visual diagram can be used to support your written comments.

While a written formal analysis is used more often in art history classes than in studio classes, artists often mentally assess their own work using the same strategy. Sculptor Rodger Mack described *The Oracle's Tears* (7.2) as follows:

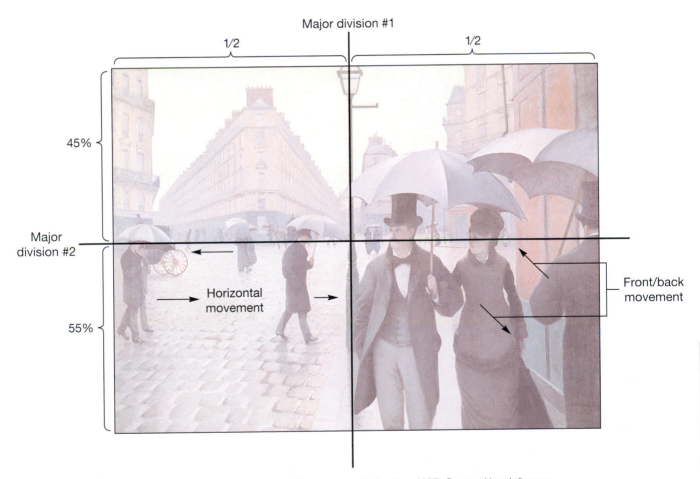

7.1B Gustave Caillebotte, *Place de l'Europe on a Rainy Day*, 1877. Compositional diagram.

This sculpture is made from five major parts. The column dominates, structurally and conceptually. Just above it, I have placed a form that has reappeared in my work for 30 years, the Oracle. It is like an image on a tarot card, the hanging man, perhaps. A smaller piece, based on a shape I found in a market in Athens, connects the oracle and the column. The tears are created using three descending lines. The base is the final element. It provides a stable support and adds a sense of completion.

A description of technical aspects of the project can enhance the viewers' understanding of the artwork. Professor Mack wrote:

I used a combination of fabrication and casting. The oracle form was made by cutting shapes from a sheet of ⅛-inch bronze and welding them together. The tears and the column were cast in sections, then welded. A potassium dichloride patina, applied using a blowtorch, gives the piece its golden color.

Professor Mack then concluded his commentary with a subjective discussion of his intentions:

I've always been drawn to ancient cities and architectural forms and have been working with mythological themes for the past six years. I've completed a series of maidens, a minotaur, a Trojan horse, and several oracles so far. When I visit these ancient civilizations, it saddens me that they are gone, destroyed to make way for new civilizations.

Because written descriptions of this kind are often required in fellowship applications and grant proposals, developing your analytical skills and your writing ability can really pay off professionally.

7.2 Rodger Mack, *The Oracle's Tears*, 1999. Cast and welded bronze, 17 × 6 × 4 ft (5.18 × 1.83 × 1.22 m).

Compare and Contrast

In a **compare/contrast critique,** similarities and differences between two images are noted. Let's return to the Caillebotte painting one more time, now comparing the perspective used with the perspective in Raphael's *The School of Athens* (7.3).

> The city streets depicted in *The School of Athens* and *Place de l'Europe* demonstrate many differences between Renaissance and Impressionist perspective.
>
> The one-point perspective used in Raphael's painting leads our eyes to Plato and Aristotle, positioned just below the center of the composition. The other figures in the painting are massed in a horizontal band from the far right to the far left side and in two lower groups, to the right and left of the central figures. Our eyes are led back to the philosophers by a man sprawled on the steps to the right and by the scribes' tables on the left. Like a proscenium arch in a theater, a broad arch in the foreground frames the scene. Overlapping arches add to the depth of the painting. This composition combines the stability of one-point perspective with a powerful illusion of space.
>
> In the Caillebotte painting, a lamppost occupies center stage, rather than a philosopher. The perspective in the cobblestone street and in the buildings on the right is complicated by the perspective used for a large background building on the left. This unusual illusion of space, combined with the movement of the pedestrians, creates a feeling of instability.

Compare and contrast essays are often used in art history classes. This form of analysis helps demonstrate differences in historical periods or artistic styles. The same approach, however, may be used in the studio, for either spoken or written critiques. The following, written by two students in a basic design class, is an example. The assignment was to complete an 18 × 24 in. design, transforming the music building (Crouse College) into a labyrinth.

7.3 Raphael, *The School of Athens,* **1509–11.** Fresco, 26 × 18 ft (7.92 × 5.49 m). Stanza della Segnatura, Vatican, Rome.

7.4 Cally Iden, *Transforming Crouse College into a Labyrinth.* Student work, 18 × 24 in. (45.7 × 61 cm).

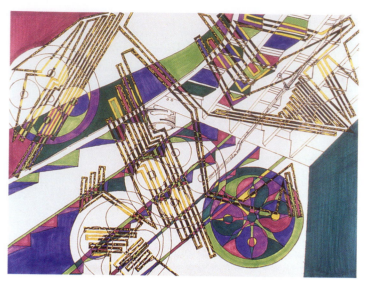

7.5 Tricia Tripp, *Transforming Crouse College into a Labyrinth.* Student work, 24 × 18 in. (61 × 45.7 cm).

Looking at Cally's design (7.4), Trish wrote:

Cally's piece uses strong black-and-white contrast, with both negative and positive space clearly defined. In contrast, my design is brightly colored, representing a kaleidoscope based on the stained glass windows in the building.

We both use the staircase as a major element. Cally's stair leads you in and around the building, creating a way to explore the space. My stair becomes part of the overall pattern.

I thought of the labyrinth as an abstract puzzle, a design you could draw your pencil through to find the ending. I wanted my design to be playful. Cally's design focuses on the psychological, creating an entry into the human mind. Cally's design is mysterious. Her staircases lead nowhere.

We both use lines very deliberately. Where one line ends, another begins. Without lines in a labyrinth, it wouldn't be as puzzling or mysterious. It would just be another design, rather than a puzzle to solve or a fun house to explore.

Looking at Trish's design (7.5), Cally wrote:

My labyrinth uses black and white to form a high-contrast composition, whereas Trish uses color to transform the building into a complex pattern. My vertical format helps suggest the height of the building, which is dominated by two amazing staircases. Trish's horizontal format contains a design that is as abstract as a computer circuit board.

Next, I notice conceptual differences between our solutions. My drawing is representational, depicting a psychological labyrinth, whereas Trish's turns the labyrinth into a puzzle. The space is generally flat in her design: color is used to create a balanced composition rather than being used to create any illusion of space. On the other hand, because my design is representational, I used size variation to create a convincing interior space.

One similarity between our drawings is in the inclusion of the staircase. Trish used the stairs as a background shape that adds dynamism to the composition. I used the stair as a primary motif, a means by which people using the building can explore their own minds.

For me, Trish's design creates a sense of alienation. There is no evidence of human experience here—it is a purely visual world, made up of complex shapes. It is as beautiful as an image in a kaleidoscope.

On the other hand, there are hints of "the human" in my composition, but it is lost within the maze of repetitive stairs: only traces remain. I want to convey the feeling of being caught in a labyrinth, solving mysteries, and finding one's self.

Both critiques are honest without being abusive and offer a discussion of both concept and composition. While the critiques are very different, each student clearly respects the approach taken by the other.

Greatest Strength/ Unrealized Potential

Many projects have one notable strength and one glaring weakness. To create a positive atmosphere, start by pointing out the strength in the work. Begin by looking for

- The level of unity in the design and how it was achieved

- The amount of variety in the design and how much energy it generates

- The type of balance used and its emotional effect

- The attention to detail. This could include craftsmanship, conceptual nuance, or compositional economy.

- A conceptual spark. We all love to see an unexpected solution that redefines the imaginative potential of a project.

Using figure 7.6A as an example, you could say:

The primary strength of this project is unity. The use of black marker throughout gives the design a simple, clean, and consistent look. The repetition of the arches helps tie it all together. Vertical and horizontal lines dominate, creating a type of grid.

Next, consider ways to improve the project. Mentally arm yourself with a magic wand. If you could instantly transform the design, what single aspect would you change? How can the potential of the project be more fully realized? Here are some basic questions:

- Is it big enough? Is it small enough?

- Is it bold enough? Is it subtle enough?

- How rich is the concept? Can it be expanded?

- How can the concept be communicated more clearly? How can the concept be communicated more fully?

The assignment was to create a labyrinth. Figure 7.6A is spatially shallow. To strengthen the composition, you might suggest:

When I think about a labyrinth, I think of it as a mysterious place that I can enter and explore. As it

7.6A Initial design.   **7.6B** Design variation.

now stands, this design is spatially flat: it gives me no place to go. You might try increasing the illusion of space. Greater size variation in the arches, with larger ones in the front and smaller ones in the back, could help. Overlapping some of the arches could increase the space and add rhythm to the work. And have you considered using gray marker for the background shapes? This would reduce the contrast and push those shapes back in space.

The resulting design (7.6B) is more spatially complex.

DEVELOPING A LONG-TERM PROJECT

Critical thinking is useful at many points in a project, not just at the end. When working on a project for 10 hours or more, it is useful to assess progress at the beginning or the end of each work period. This may be done in a large-group critique, in small teams, in discussion with your teacher, or on your own. Several effective strategies follow.

Week One Assessment

Determine Essential Concept

As a project begins to evolve from brainstorming to thumbnails to rough drafts, the concept may also evolve. Your initial idea may expand or shift during the translation from the mind to the hand to the page. Stopping to reconsider your central concept and refine your image can bring great clarity and purpose to the work. What is the design *really* about? You can speak more forcefully when you know what you want to say.

Explore Polarities

Sometimes, the best way to strengthen an idea is to present the exact opposite. For example, if you want to show the *joy* a political prisoner feels on being released from jail, you may need to show the *despair* she felt before her release. To increase the *dynamism* in a design, add some emphatically *static* elements. The contrast created by polarities can heighten communication.

Move from General to Specific

"Be specific!" demands your writing teacher. Just as vague generalities weaken your writing, so vague generalities can weaken your designs. Details are important. "A bird watched people walk down the street" is far less compelling than "Two vultures hovered over University Avenue, hungrily watching the two hapless students stagger from bar to bar." Specifying the kind of bird, type of people, and exact location makes the image come alive.

Move from Personal to Universal

Autobiography is an especially rich source of images and ideas. The authenticity of personal experience is extremely powerful. However, if you focus too tightly on your own family, friends, and experiences, the viewer must know you personally in order to appreciate your design. Try expanding your field of vision. Use a story about your high school graduation to say something about *all* rites of passage from childhood to adulthood.

Week Two Assessment

A well-developed rough draft or a full-scale model may be presented at this stage. The purpose of this critique is to help the artist or designer determine ways to increase the visual and conceptual impact of an existing idea. Following are three major strategies.

Develop Alternatives

By helping someone else solve a problem, we can often solve our own problem. Organize a team of four or five classmates. Working individually, design 5 to 10 possible solutions to a visual problem using 2 × 3 in. thumbnail sketches. Then have one person present his or her ideas verbally and visually. Each team member must then propose an alternative way to solve the problem. This can be done verbally; however, once you get going, it is more effective and stimulating if everyone (including the artist) draws alternative solutions. This process helps the artist see the unrealized potential in his or her idea. And, because of the number of alternatives presented, the artist rarely adopts any single suggestion. Instead, the exercise simply becomes a means of demonstrating ways to clarify, expand, and strengthen intentions already formed.

Edit Out Nonessentials

Have you ever found it difficult to determine the real point of a lengthy lecture and thus lost interest? In our zeal to communicate, teachers sometimes provide so many examples and side issues that students get lost. Likewise, if your design is overloaded with peripheral detail or if a secondary visual element is given the starring role, the result will be cluttered and impact will be lost. Look carefully at your design, focusing on visual relationships. Are there any shapes or volumes that can be deleted?

Amplify Essentials

Just as it is necessary to delete extraneous information, it is equally important to strengthen the essential information. Review the section on emphasis in Chapter Three and consider ways to increase your compositional power. Try "going too far," wildly exaggerating the size, color, or texture of an important visual element. The only way to get an extraordinary image is to make extraordinary compositional choices.

Developing a Self-Assignment

On pages 149 and 150, Jason Chin describes the development of a month-long self-assignment he completed near the end of his freshman year. The original project proposal is given at the top of the first page. The rest of the text is devoted to Jason's analysis of his actual work process. This type of personal assessment can bring an extended project to a memorable conclusion.

Self-Assignment:
Jason Chin

The Mythological Alphabet

Original Proposal

Description: I plan to make an illustrated alphabet book with 32 pages and a cover. The theme of the book will be myths and heroes. I am interested in illustrating the essence of each hero's story. Specifically, how can I visually communicate the story of a tragic hero versus a triumphant one? Further concerns with the book will be making it work as a whole. That means keeping it balanced and making it flow: I don't want the images to become disjointed.

Primary Concerns

1. How do I communicate the individual nature of the characters?
2. How do I connect each hero to all the others?
3. How will the book affect the reader? I want to get the reader fully involved in the book.
4. How can I best use the unique characteristics of the book format?

Time Management

Week 1: Research myths and heroes. Identify possible characters for the book.

Week 2: Bring at least 20 thumbnail sketches to the first team meeting.

Week 3: Bring finalized design/layout for book. Each page must have a final design in the form of thumbnails.

Week 4: Complete half of the pages.

Week 5: Finish remaining pages and present at the critique.

Commentary

The independent project was both a blessing and a curse. Given the freedom to do what I chose was liberating, but the burden of what to do with that freedom was great. Ultimately, it became one of the best learning experiences of my freshman year.

I had decided to pursue illustration as my major, because of my interest in storytelling. This interest in stories led me to choose to make a book for my project. The next step was to find a story to tell. To limit my workload, I looked for a story that had already been told, one that I could reinterpret, as opposed to writing my own story. At this point, I came across two books, one of Greek myths, and an alphabet book illustrated by Norman Rockwell, and my initial concept was born.

Once the idea was initiated, I set to work researching Greek myths. The idea was to find one character for each letter of the alphabet. It proved more difficult than I had first thought. I found about 20 names with no problem, but I soon realized that several letters in our alphabet did not exist in the Greek alphabet. To overcome this hurdle, I took some liberties on the original problem and did not limit myself strictly to characters from myths (for example, I included the White Island for the letter W). Once the subject of each illustration was chosen, I set about the task of doing the images and designing the format of the book.

Doing the illustrations and designing the format of the book all came together at about the same time.

As I was working out the drawings I made several key decisions that heavily influenced the outcome of the project. First, I decided that each picture would have to be black and white if I was going to pull this whole thing off. Second, I knew that they would have to be relatively small. Through my art history class, I gained a strong interest in Japanese woodblock prints and was especially attracted to their strong compositional sensibility. This became the focus of my attention while working out the illustrations. Finally, the decision to make the illustrations small helped determine the way I used text in the book, because it all but eliminated the possibility of overlaying text on image.

I designed each image in my sketchbook, doing thumbnails and comp sketches of all sizes and shapes, until I found the image that I felt best represented the character. For example, Zeus has the biggest and busiest frame in the book because he is the king of the gods, while the image of the White Island is quite serene because it is a burial ground.

When I had each individual image worked out, I redrew them in order in the pages of my sketch book as if they were in the real book. I could now see how each image would work as a double-page spread, as well as how well the book could flow visually. With this mockup of the book in front of me it was very easy to see obvious mistakes and correct them before going to final art.

I did the final illustrations in pen and ink, on illustration board, and when they were finished, it was time to drop in the text. My first concept for the text was to be very minimal; each page would read, "A is for," "B is for," and so on. However,

I soon realized that making each page rhyme would drastically increase the reader's interest in the book. So I wrote a more extensive text and put the rhyming parts on opposite pages in order to give the reader one more incentive to turn the page.

The final touch for the book was putting the colored paper down. The decision to do this came when I went to place the type. The only means I had to get good type was to print it out on the computer, but I had no way to print it on the illustration board. So I had to put it on printer paper and cut and paste it. No matter how carefully I cut the paper and pasted it on, it just didn't look right. I came up with two solutions: one, print the words on colored paper and paste it on, or two, cut frames of colored paper to cover over the entire page except for the image and the text. I chose the latter and was pleased to discover that the local art store had a vast selection of handmade and colored papers.

Today I look back on this project as a pivotal experience in my art education, because I had free range to pursue storytelling, something that has since become an essential aspect of my art. In the professional world, bookmaking is rarely an individual process. It is a collaborative process, involving editors, artists, and writers, so for me to be able to pursue it on my own was in fact a blessing. I got to make a book the way that I thought it should be done, and pursue my own personal vision of what a Mythological Alphabet should be. By making this book, I discovered something that I love to do, and want to make a career of doing, and to me the vision that I have gained from this experience is invaluable.

Jason Chin, *A Is for Apollo* (left) and *U Is for Urania* (right). Student work.

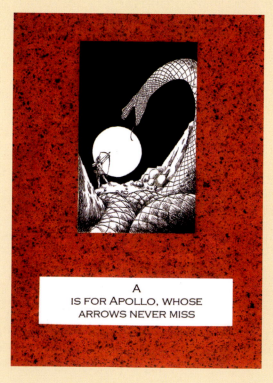

A
IS FOR APOLLO, WHOSE
ARROWS NEVER MISS

U
IS FOR URANIA THE MUSE OF
CELESTIAL FORCES IS SHE

7.7A Linear design.

7.8A Visual clutter.

7.9A Completed labyrinth design.

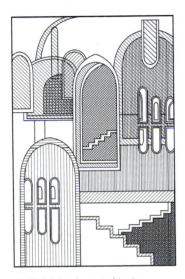

7.7B Adding invented texture.

7.8B Visual clarity.

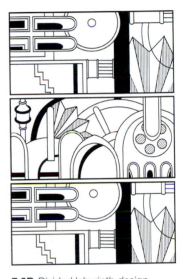

7.9B Divided labyrinth design.

TURN UP THE HEAT: PUSHING YOUR PROJECT'S POTENTIAL

Some compositions are so bold that they seem to explode off the page. Other compositions have all the right ingredients but never really take off. By asking the following questions, you can more fully realize the potential of any assignment.

Basic Arithmetic

1. Should anything be *added* to the design? If your composition lacks energy, consider adding another layer of information or increasing the illusion of space. Notice how texture changes the composition in figures 7.7A and 7.7B.

2. Should anything be *subtracted*? If the composition is cluttered, try discarding 25 percent of the visual information. Then use the remaining shapes more deliberately (7.8A and B). Get as much as possible from every visual element. Economy is a virtue.

3. What happens when any component is *multiplied*? As shown in figures 7.6A and 7.6B, repetition can unify a design, add rhythm, and increase the illusion of space.

4. Can the design be *divided* into two or more separate compositions? When a design is too complicated, it may become impossible to resolve. Packing 20 ideas into a single design can diminish rather than improve communication. In figures 7.9A and 7.9B, a complicated source image has been separated into several different designs, creating a series of stronger images.

7.10 Claes Oldenburg and Coosje van Bruggen, *Shuttlecocks,* 1994. South facade of the Nelson-Atkins Museum of Art and the Kansas City Sculpture Park. Aluminum, fiberglass-reinforced plastic, and paint. 230⁹⁄₁₆ × 191⅞ in. (585.63 × 487.36 cm).

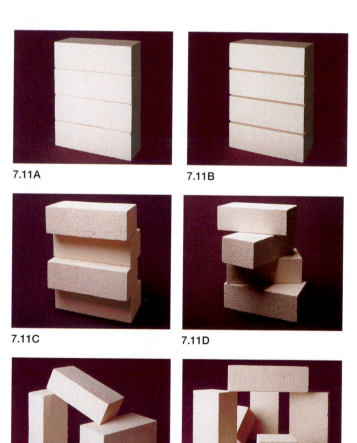

7.11A

7.11B

7.11C

7.11D

7.11E

7.11F

Transformation

Works of art and design present ideas in physical form. Each composition is strongly influenced by the materials used, the relationships created, and the viewing context chosen. Consider the following alternatives:

1. What happens when the material is changed? Even when the shapes stay the same, a silver teapot is very different from a glass, steel, or ceramic teapot. Sculptors Claes Oldenburg and Coosje van Bruggen used transformations in material extensively, often changing hard, reflective materials into soft vinyl. This form of transformation is especially effective when the new material brings structural qualities and conceptual connotations that challenge our expectations.

2. What is the relationship of the piece to the viewer? What is the relationship between the artwork and its surroundings? What happens when a chair is reduced to the size of a salt shaker? Or when a 19-foot-tall badminton shuttlecock is placed in front of a museum (7.10)? How does any image change, both visually and conceptually, when size is dramatically reduced or increased?

3. Can a change in position increase impact? Working with the same four blocks, a seemingly endless number of solutions can be created (7.11A–F).

4. Is a physical object compelling from all points of view? Does the composition of the artwork encourage the viewer to view it from other angles?

5. Will a change in viewing context increase meaning? For example, a side of beef has a very different meaning when it is hung in a gallery rather than staying in a slaughterhouse. Likewise, pop artists, such as Andy Warhol and Roy Lichtenstein, brought new meaning to soup cans and comic books by using them as subject matter in their paintings.

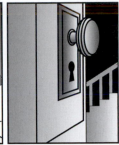

7.12

7.13

7.14

Reorganization

Time-based work, such as visual books, comic books, film, and video, is generally constructed from multiple images. Changing the organization of the parts of the puzzle can completely alter the meaning of the piece. For example, Angela contemplates entering the building in the sequence shown in figure 7.12. Using a different organization of the same three images, Angela now wonders what will happen when she opens the door at the top of the stairs (7.13). By repeating the image of Angela, we can present a dilemma: she is now in a labyrinth—which route should she take (7.14)?

7.15 Robert Rauschenberg, *Monogram*, 1955–59. Freestanding combine, 42 × 63¼ × 64½ in. (106.7 × 160.7 × 163.8 cm).

7.16 Robert Rauschenberg, *Monogram, 1st State*, c. 1955.
Combine painting: oil, paper, fabric, wood on canvas, plus stuffed Angora goat and three electric light fixtures, approx. 75 × 46 × 12 in. (190.5 × 114.3 × 30.5 cm). No longer in existence.

7.17 Robert Rauschenberg, *Monogram, 2nd State*, c. 1956.
Combine: oil, paper, fabric, wood, plus rubber tire and stuffed Angora goat on wood, 115 × 32 × 44 in. (292 × 81.3 × 111.8 cm).

CONCEPTUAL VARIATIONS

Any compositional change affects the conceptual impact of an artwork. Henry M. Sayre provides a striking example in *A World of Art*.[1] A distilled version of his ideas follows.

Robert Rauschenberg's *Monogram* (7.15) is constructed from a stuffed goat, an automobile tire, and a painted plywood base. Seeking to combine painting and sculpture, Rauschenberg created three different versions of this piece. In the first version (7.16), he placed the goat on a shelf that extended from the center of a 6-foot-tall painting. This created a connection between the painting and the goat but diminished its sculptural impact. In the second

version (7.17), Rauschenberg placed a tire around the goat's midsection and moved the animal in front of the painting. This enhanced the artwork's three-dimensionality but created too much of a separation between the animal and the painting. He finally hit on the right combination when he placed the painting on the floor and positioned the goat in the center. The painting retained its integrity as a two-dimensional surface, the goat retained its physical presence, and a highly unified combination of the two elements was achieved. The addition of the tire enhanced the goat's sculptural form and gave the artwork a humorous twist.

ACCEPTING RESPONSIBILITY

We have explored only a few of the many approaches to critical thinking in this chapter. Every assignment presents new possibilities for critiques, and each teacher invents his or her own way to address the needs of a specific class.

Regardless of the specifics, however, two facts are inescapable. First, you will learn only what you want to learn. If you reject out-of-hand the alternatives suggested, or if you avoid responsibility for your conceptual and compositional choices, you will gain nothing from the critique, no matter what strategy is used. Second, there are no free rides. Everyone in the class is responsible for the success of the session. It is often difficult to sustain your attention or honestly assess your work or the work of others. When you get a superficial response to a project, insisting on further clarification is not easy. Every critique demands sincere and sustained attention from each participant. And, when the responses are supportive and substantial, remarkable improvements in works of art and design can be made.

SUMMARY

- Critical thinking helps us identify strengths and weaknesses in a project and determine the improvements that need to be made.

- Understanding the criteria on which a project will be judged helps focus critical thinking.

- Many artworks can be analyzed in terms of three basic aspects: form, subject, and content.

- Objective critiques focus on observable facts. Subjective critiques focus on feelings, intentions, and implications.

- Four common critique methods are description, cause and effect, compare and contrast, and greatest strength/unrealized potential.

- Many critique methods may be used when you are working on a long-term project. In all cases, there are three primary objectives: explore alternatives, delete nonessentials, and strengthen essentials.

- Basic arithmetic, transformation, and reorganization can be used to increase compositional impact.

- An open mind combined with a willingness to share ideas can strengthen any critique.

KEY TERMS

cause-and-effect critique
(formal analysis)
compare/contrast critique

content
critique
descriptive critique

form
objective criticism
subject

subjective criticism

STUDIO PROJECTS

To apply the concepts from this chapter in the studio, check out the Projects page in the Online Learning Center at www.mhhe.com/stewart4e. The following is a sample of the chapter-related assignments that are described in step-by-step detail.

Capstone Project. Expanding creativity through in-depth exploration.

Profile:
Kendall Buster, Sculptor
Biological Architecture

Kendall Buster's large-scale "biological architecture" projects have been exhibited at Artist's Space and the American Academy of Arts and Letters in New York City; the Hirshhorn Museum and the Kreeger Museum in Washington, DC; the Kemper Museum in Kansas City; Suyama Space in Seattle; the Nevada Museum of Art in Reno; and the KZNSA Gallery in South Africa. Buster has created commissioned sculptures for the Washington, DC, Convention Center; Massey Cancer Center in Richmond, VA; and the Agave Library in Phoenix. Current projects include commissions for the new chemistry building at Princeton University, Johns Hopkins University, and the Indianapolis Museum of Art.

MS: Microbiology was your initial academic passion, and you worked in this field for twelve years. What attracted you to microbiology, and what did you learn from it?

KB: Peering into a microscope gave me access to an intricate and beautiful world that was beyond ordinary perception. As I learned more, I became increasingly interested in the architecture of natural forms—the way cells are constructed to maximize efficiency or the permeability of a particular cell wall. The sculptures I now create begin with an internal skeleton that I wrap in a fabric or plastic skin. And, I am still fascinated by shifts in perception, from very small scale to very large scale. For me, art and science are simply aspects of the same impulse.

MS: How do you translate your ideas into large-scale objects? Most of your recent projects could fill an entire gymnasium!

KB: Ideas often occur just as I am waking up. At this point, they are more intuitive than intentional. I begin to record possibilities through pencil drawings. Drawing is crucial—it is the first step in getting the idea out of my head and into the world. I then move to what I see as three-dimensional sketching, using carved Styrofoam, wire, or various types of board.

Further work is done with an entire team of collaborators. Computer-aided design helps us explore variations further and analyze the structural requirements and possibilities of the forms. With my studio team, I create physical models of the building in which the artwork will be placed in order to study

the ways in which the sculpture converses with the site. I have a project coordinator who communicates with the client on the architectural particulars of the site and a rigger who is an installation specialist.

MS: How are the pieces actually constructed?

KB: My large-scale sculptures are made with many interlocked parts, and so creating patterns for the parts is critical. These patterns, both computer generated and hand drawn on the studio floor, are used for shaping and welding the steel frames or cutting planar material. The frames are professionally powder-coated, and when the frames are covered in cloth I might work with as many as ten to twenty helpers in a marathon "screening party."

MS: Please talk us through *New Growth*, installed in the Boise Art Museum.

KB: *New Growth* is an inventory of architectural models that function like biological systems. In this imagined city, old forms generate new forms through processes that suggest germination, budding, merging, hybridization, or absorption. The model city is conceived as a single organism constructed from many interdependent parts. Some structures are connected by passageways that suggest either umbilical cords or parasitic invasions. Contiguous membranes create distinct regions in the city, and the transparency of these membranes allows inner layers to be visible through the outer shell.

Architectural structures form and re-form the fabric of cities over time. To evoke this process, I wanted to build a structure that seems to be based on a precise blueprint, while at the same time contradict this idea by creating a structure that seems dynamic, continually changing. I am also interested in exploring the tension between what is revealed and what is concealed; how windows link interior space with exterior place to create shifting sight lines; how narrow entryways or low passages act in direct confrontation with the body; how space is compressed and movement directed; how one is at times hidden, and at times exposed.

New Growth is also a response to the particulars of the Boise Art Museum site. On my first visit I visualized a kind of floating cityscape made up of forms that behaved both as individual structures and as a continuous membrane. The sculpture that I finally built connected to the exhibition site in unexpected ways. Curved rooftops in my architectural models seemed to echo the arched beams in the ceiling, and the ever-changing light penetrating through the floor-to-ceiling windows created subtle shades of white and gray on the transparent layers of fabric.

Scale shifts between the viewer's initial "panoramic" overview and the more closely observed details were also important. At one moment, the viewer is dwarfed by the artwork; at another, the artwork reads as a model that the viewer can command. As a result, the viewer is enveloped, embraced, and engaged—all at the same time.

MS: What advice do you have for beginning students?
KB: I have three bits of advice. First, realize that each of us has our own work process and embrace the process that is right for you. Second, find the right balance between conceptual breadth (lateral thinking) and conceptual depth (vertical thinking). Too much lateral thinking can result in superficiality, while too much vertical thinking can narrow your possibilities. Finally, embrace the idea of an ongoing and preferably daily studio practice. Complex ideas and structures don't happen overnight!

Kendall Buster, *New Growth,* 2007. Dimensions variable, as installed in Boise Art Museum.

chapter eight

Constructing Meaning

Seeking and solving visual problems, cultivating creativity, and developing critical judgment all require hours of hard work. Why are these skills so highly valued by artists and designers and so strongly emphasized by college teachers?

The answer is simple. At a professional level, art and graphic design projects are done in order to communicate ideas and express emotions. Turning elusive concepts into effective communication is not easy. Clay, ink, metal, fabric, and other physical materials must somehow stimulate an audience to see, understand, and respond. In this chapter, we explore the essentials of visual communication and identify some of the strategies artists and designers use to construct meaning. The interviews at the end of each chapter provide an insider's view of this process.

BUILDING BRIDGES

Shared Language

A shared language is the basis on which all communication is built. For example, if you are fluent in English and I am effective as a writer, the ideas I want to communicate in this chapter should make sense to you. On the other hand, if English is your second language, some of the vocabulary may be unfamiliar. In that case, you may have to strengthen the bridge between us by looking up words in a dictionary.

Figure 8.1 demonstrates the importance of shared language. For a reader of Chinese, the flowing brushstrokes form characters that communicate

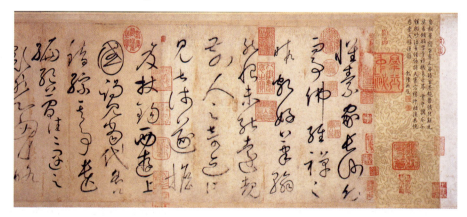

8.1 Huai-su, Detail of Autobiography, Tang dynasty, 7th–10th centuries. Ink on paper.

specific ideas. For those of us who know no Chinese, the calligraphy is visually enticing but conveys no specific message. We cannot understand the characters.

Historical and cultural "literacy" can create another type of bridge. As an American, I live within a framework that is driven by a capitalist economic structure, a two-party political system, and social systems based on Judeo-Christian values. South African William Kentridge brings a very different frame of reference to his artwork. Born in 1951, he experienced apartheid firsthand as the son of white civil rights lawyers and has extensive knowledge of the history of many African genocides. In *Black Box/Chambre Noir* (8.2), he uses a miniature theater to tell the story of one such genocide, which nearly wiped out the Herero people. Powered by the type of mechanism used in ink-jet printers, six automatons enter and exit the stage. Projections of historical documents, combined with fragments of music from Mozart's opera *The Magic Flute* and Namibian songs, expand the tragic story. While viewers are immediately drawn to the fascinating structure, we cannot fully understand the meaning without expanding our knowledge of African history.

Iconography

Many artworks depend on cultural and historical references to build meaning. **Iconography** (literally, "describing images") is the study of such symbolic visual systems.

Deborah Haylor-McDowell's *The Serpent Didn't Lie* (8.3) is loaded with references. An anatomical diagram copied from Leonardo da Vinci's notebooks appears in the upper-left corner, while the nude couple near the center is based on *The Kiss*, a sculpture by Auguste Rodin. Einstein's computations for the theory of relativity appear in the upper-right corner, and in the foreground a baby takes his first steps. A snakeskin border surrounds the image. What does it all mean? Haylor-McDowell says:

> Ignorance may spare us the pain of difficult decisions. However, the price we pay is high. Can humankind's greatest gifts, emotion and intellect, mature in a world that is free of suffering? In the absence of adversity, will our humanness be lost?

8.2 View of William Kentridge's *Black Box/Chambre Noire*, 2005. Miniature theater with mechanized objects, projections and sound, dimensions variable.

8.3 Deborah Haylor-McDowell, *The Serpent Didn't Lie*, 1997. Etching, 15 × 23 in. (38.1 × 58.42 cm).

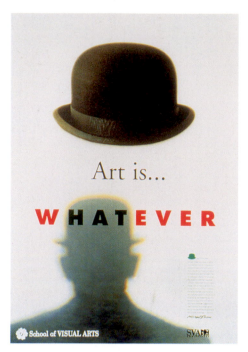

8.4 Milton Glaser, *Art is . . .* , 1996. Poster.

8.5 René Magritte, *Golconde*, 1953. Oil on canvas, 31¾ × 38⅝ in. (80.65 × 98.11 cm).

The Serpent Didn't Lie is based on a biblical text dealing with good and evil in the Garden of Eden. What is the price we pay for knowledge? The images I used in the composition deal with the complexities and responsibilities of our pursuit of knowledge.

Through a sophisticated use of iconography, the artist created a puzzle that is filled with ideas for us to unravel and explore. For those who understand the cultural references, this print presents a survey of types of knowledge in a compelling visual form. For those who do not understand the references, the print is simply a beautifully crafted collection of architectural and figurative fragments.

Graphic designers are especially aware of the importance of iconography. On a purely visual level, Milton Glaser's 1996 poster for the School of Visual Arts (8.4) is intriguing and evocative in itself. The hovering hat, shadowy figure, and curious text raise all sorts of questions. When we compare the poster with surrealist René Magritte's *Golconde* (8.5), the ideas expand much further. In this and other paintings by Magritte, the man in the bowler hat represents anyone who is courageously navigating through the chaos of contemporary life. When we make the connection between Glaser and Magritte,

the School of Visual Arts poster becomes poignant as well as provocative. Like the man in the bowler hat, each art student must find a path through the complexities of contemporary life in order to develop a meaningful approach to art and design.

Audience

Just as films are targeted and rated for specific audiences, so many forms of visual communication are designed for specific viewers. George Balanchine was a master choreographer renowned for his love of classical ballet as well as his modern sensibility and commitment to endless invention. A powerful yet restrained poster was needed to publicize a performance of his work (8.6). The dancers in blue are carefully balanced by simple text on a blue background. By contrast, in *Dancing Downtown 2003* (8.7), the soloist wears a loose dress that accentuates her physicality. She dances with wild abandon. Both shows attracted diverse audiences, but the Balanchine poster was targeted at those seeking more traditional ballet, while *Dancing Downtown 2003* was targeted at those seeking a more exuberant and contemporary approach.

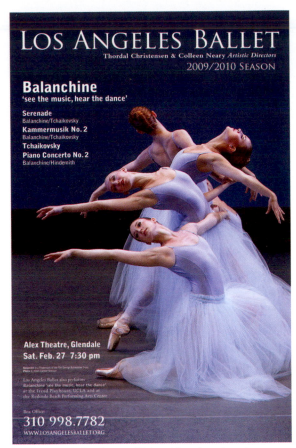

8.6 *Serenade* by George Balanchine, Los Angeles Ballet. Poster. Design by Catherine Kanner, photo by Reed Hutchinson.

8.7 *Dancing Downtown*, 2003. Poster. Designed by Noon.

Immediacy

When the bridge between the image and the audience is explicit, communication can occur almost instantaneously. When the iconography is elusive or complex, communication takes longer and is more varied. Each approach can be effective in the right time and place. When we are driving a car, our lives depend on the immediate message we receive when a traffic light turns red. The "Stop!" is clear and concise. When visiting a museum, we often seek greater complexity and emotional resonance.

Graphic designers generally aim for a combination of immediacy, clarity, and resonance. For them, an effective poster or billboard can be understood at a glance. Figure 8.8 is an excellent example. The bold, white hanged man immediately attracts attention, and the book title itself is simple and direct. The position of the figure's head adds another layer of meaning to this critique of capital punishment.

By contrast, *Some Words* (8.9) by Markus Schaller requires extended viewer involvement. Created

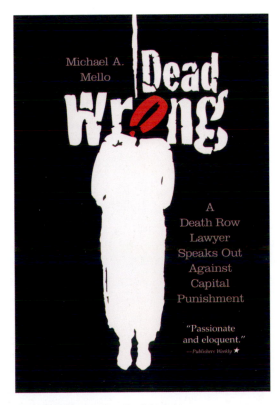

8.8 Mark Maccaulay. Book jacket.

8.9 Markus Schaller, *Some Words*, 2007. Steel, dimensions variable.

Stereotypes

A **stereotype** is a fixed generalization based on a preconception. On a benign level, when we use a stereotype, we ignore individual characteristics and emphasize group characteristics. For example, the broken wine glass in figure 8.10 is widely used on shipping crates to communicate fragility. Glass is actually a very versatile material that can be cast as bricks, spun into fiber-optic cables, and polished to create lenses. However, we are most familiar with fragile wine glasses and bottles. Relying on this *general* perception, the shipping label designer used a stereotype to communicate fragility.

Racial stereotyping, which is never benign, tends to exaggerate negative generalizations. Even when a positive assumption is made (such as "Asian Americans are brainy overachievers"), the overall effect is demeaning. Rather than learning about an individual person, we make judgments based on our preconceptions.

Stereotypes are often used to create the bridge on which communication depends. Because they are based on preconceptions, stereotypes require little thought. The viewer responds automatically. In some situations, an automatic response is ideal. Four airport pictograms are shown in figure 8.11. Can you determine the meaning of each? If the designer is successful, even an exhausted traveler from New Zealand will be able to determine at a glance where to find a baggage locker, an elevator, or a toilet. Especially notice the use of the male and female stereotypes for the toilet pictograms. Despite the wide range of clothing worn by female travelers, the designers used a dress to create a stereotypical female.

from a sequence of stream-of-consciousness texts inscribed onto 70 iron panels, this installation was designed as a meditation on the very process of thinking. Viewers entering this visual labyrinth had to be willing to puzzle over the words presented and explore their own cognitive response. The message here is neither explicit nor immediate. As with Haylor-McDowell's work (figure 8.3), the viewer must piece together a complex set of clues, then reach his or her own conclusions about the nature of knowledge and the development of literacy.

8.10 "Fragile" pictogram.

Baggage lockers	Elevator	Toilets, men	Toilets, women

8.11 Roger Cook and Don Shanosky, images from a poster introducing the signage symbol system developed for the U.S. Department of Transportation, 1974.

Clichés

A **cliché** is an overused expression or a predictable treatment of an idea. Phrases such as "Let's level the playing field" and "Think outside the box" are powerful the first time we hear them. However, when we hear them repeatedly, they lose their impact and become clichés. Visual clichés are equally predictable. Skulls representing death and seagulls representing tranquility may be effective at first but tend to become worn out when used repeatedly.

Surprise

A shift in a stereotype or cliché upsets our expectations and challenges our assumptions. The resulting shock can surprise or delight an audience, making the message more memorable. Originally based on the cowboy stereotype, the Marlboro Man has been reinterpreted in figure 8.12. This ad, which begins like an ordinary cigarette commercial, quickly shifts from the heroic cowboy to a man with a hacking cough. At this point, the narrator suggests that "cowboys are a dying breed" because of the cancer caused by smoking. By breaking the stereotype, the designers attract the viewers' attention, challenge the conventional cigarette ad, and strengthen their nonsmoking message.

Na Zha Cradle (8.13) is equally surprising. Cradles are "supposed" to be soft, safe, and comforting. This cradle is metallic, threatening, and dangerous. Metaphorically commenting on the aggressive capitalism that has driven the Chinese economy in recent years, Shi Jinsong suggests that there is a price to be paid when society progresses too quickly.

Key Questions

BUILDING BRIDGES

- Are there any symbolic or cultural meanings embedded in your composition? Are these meanings consistent with the message you want to convey?
- Have you used a stereotype or a cliché? Does this strengthen or weaken your message?
- What audience do you want to reach? Are the form and content of your design appropriate for that audience?

NARRATOR: No wonder cowboys are a dying breed. If

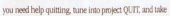
you need help quitting, tune into project QUIT, and take

control of your life.

8.12 Agency: Ruhr/Paragon, Minneapolis. Production: Lotter, Minneapolis. Details: TV, 30 seconds, color. First appearance: February 1988. Account Supervisor: Anne Bologna. Creative Director/Art Director: Doug Lew. Associate Creative Director/Copywriter: Bill Johnson. Agency Producer: Arleen Kulis. Production Company Director: Jim Lotter.

8.13 Shi Jinsong, *Na Zha Cradle*, 2005. Stainless steel, 24 × 31.9 × 24.3 in. (61.4 × 81.7 × 62.2 cm).

PURPOSE AND INTENT

Any number of approaches to visual communication can be effective. We simply choose the style, iconography, and composition best suited to our purpose.

Let's consider four very different uses of human anatomy. *Arterial Fibrillation* (8.14) was developed for the cover of a medical journal. With equal training in art and science, medical illustrator Kim Martens combined anatomical accuracy with artistic imagination to create this design. Intent on sales, the art director for the magazine requested an image that was both physically correct and visually enticing.

Designed as an anatomical roadmap, *Understanding Healthcare* (8.15) had to present complex information in a clear and concise way. To make the text accessible to a general audience, the designers used a loose grid dominated by vertical columns at the top and a strong horizontal band at the bottom. Arrows and other visual cues help the reader navigate from page to page.

Booster (8.16) is dominated by a series of X-rays of the artist's body. In this unconventional self-portrait, Robert Rauschenberg combined a collection of personal X-rays with various examples of technological notation, including an astronomer's

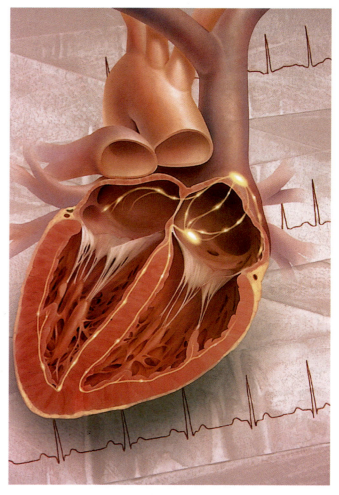

8.14 Kim Martens, *Arterial Fibrillation*, 2000. Photoshop.

chart, diagrams analyzing the movement of drills and arrows, graphs, and an empty chair. The title adds further meaning, suggesting a connection to booster shots, booster rockets, and booster seats, which increase the height of an ordinary chair so that young children can sit at a table comfortably. Reduced to an X-ray image and surrounded by fragments of technological information, the artist becomes a cog in the machinery of mass culture. By contrast, the woman in Kiki Smith's *Virgin Mary* (8.17) seems both vulnerable and graceful. She displays her flayed body unapologetically, extending her open hands in a type of blessing.

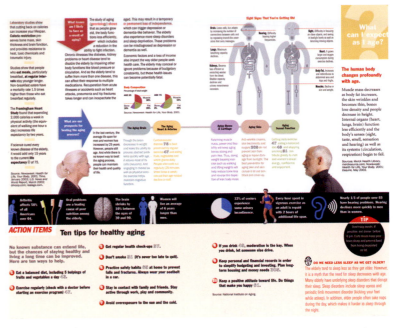

8.15 **United Healthcare Brochure.** Design Firm: Pentagram, NY. Courtesy of Richard Saul Wurman.

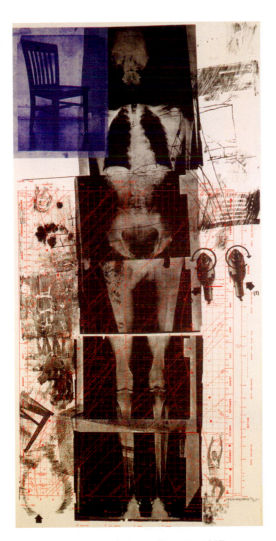

8.16 **Robert Rauschenberg,** *Booster,* **1967.** Lithograph and serigraph, printed in color, composition 71⁹⁄₁₆ × 35⅛ in. (181.7 × 89.1 cm).

8.17 **Kiki Smith,** *Virgin Mary,* **1992.** Beeswax, microcrystalline wax, cheesecloth, and wood on steel base, 67½ × 26 × 14½ in. (171.5 × 66 × 36.8 cm).

8.18 Margaret Bourke-White, *At the Time of the Louisville Flood,* 1937. Gelatin silver print.

8.19 Alfred Eisenstadt, *Winston Churchill, Liverpool,* 1957. Gelatin silver print.

CONTEXT

The compositional context in which any image appears profoundly influences meaning. In figure 8.18, the juxtaposition of a quiet line of flood survivors with a propagandistic billboard makes us rethink the phrase "There's no way like the American way."

The social context in which an image appears is equally important. In figure 8.19, Winston Churchill, the prime minister most responsible for British victory during World War II, extends two fingers to create the "V for victory" gesture he used throughout the war. If we are familiar with Churchill and know about the desperate struggle of the British people during the war, we immediately make the correct connection. In figure 8.20, the same gesture communicates a very different idea. As part of the signage for the Minnesota Children's Museum, the extended fingers now communicate the number two. Realizing that many young visitors to the museum may not be able to read, the designers used both a number and a gesture to communicate location. Finally, in Sean O'Meallie's *Out-Boxed Finger Puppets Perform the Numbers 1 Through 5 in No Particular Order* (8.21), the same gesture becomes a playful piece of sculpture as well as an indication of the number two. We now see the extended fingers in the context of a series of whimsical forms. In each of these three cases, the meaning of the two fingers depends on the context.

8.20 Minnesota Children's Museum, Pentagram design, New York, NY. Tracy Cameron and Michael Bierut, Designers.

8.21 Sean O'Meallie, *Out-Boxed Finger Puppets Perform the Numbers 1 Through 5 in No Particular Order,* 1999. Polychromed wood, 17.5 × 42 × 11 in.

CONNECTIONS

Analogies, similes, and metaphors are figures of speech that link one thing to another. An **analogy** creates a general connection between unrelated objects or ideas, while a **simile** creates the connection using the word *as* or *like*, as in "She has a heart as big as Texas." A **metaphor** is more explicit: Speaking metaphorically, we would say "Her heart *is* Texas." As you can see, a substantial shift in meaning occurs when metaphor is used.

In all cases, the original word is given the qualities of the linked word. For example, when Robert Burns wrote the simile "My love is like a red red rose," he gave the abstract concept of "love" the attributes of a glorious, colorful, fragrant, thorny, and transient rose.

Metaphorical thinking can be used to connect an image and an idea. Take the phrase "I have butterflies in my stomach." This phrase is widely used to describe nervousness. Substitute other insects for butterflies, such as bees or wasps. How does this change the meaning? To push it even further, start with the phrase "My mind was full of clouds." What happens when "clouds" is replaced by mice on treadmills, rats in mazes, shadowy staircases, beating drums, screaming children—or even butterflies? When my mind is full of butterflies, I am happy, but butterflies in my stomach indicate fear. In addition to expanding ideas, metaphors can help provide specific images for elusive emotions.

Metaphorical thinking and symbolism have always been used by artists and designers to strengthen communication. Exaggerated metaphors are especially common in advertising design. The massive wave that threatens the computer user in figure 8.22 is a metaphor for the destructive power of the Y2K computer bug that once seemed likely to create massive computer failures on January 1, 2000. Editorial cartoons also rely on metaphors. In figure 8.23, a congressional hand puppet vows independence from the very lobbyist who is controlling his vote.

8.22 Iomega Corporation, "Y2K's coming. Don't just sit there."

8.23 Jimmy Margulies, Editorial Cartoon, 2006.

8.24 Pablo Picasso, *Guernica,* 1937. Oil on canvas, 11 ft 5½ in. × 25 ft 5¼ in. (3.5 × 7.8 m).

Picasso's *Guernica* (8.24) is also loaded with metaphors. In *A World of Art*, Henry Sayre offers the following description:

> The horse, at the center left, speared and dying in anguish, represents the fate of the dreamer's creativity. The entire scene is surveyed by a bull, which represents at once Spain itself, the simultaneous heroism and tragedy of the bullfight, and the Minotaur, the bull-man who for the Surrealists stood for the irrational forces of the human psyche. The significance of the electric light bulb at the top center of the painting, and the oil lamp, held by the woman reaching out the window, has been much debated, but they represent, at least, old and new ways of seeing.[1]

Rather than showing exploding bombs or collapsing buildings, Picasso filled his painting with abstracted animals, screaming humans, and various sources of light. In so doing, he focused on the meaning and emotion of the event, rather than its appearance.

AESTHETICS

Definitions

In *Design in the Visual Arts*, Roy Behrens noted the difference between the words *anesthetic* and *aesthetic*. An **anesthetic** is used to induce insensitivity or unconsciousness. In an anesthetic state, we are numbed and disoriented. We may not be able to determine the size or location of objects or the sequence of events. On the other hand, **aesthetics** is the study of human responses to beauty. In an aesthetic experience, our feelings are enhanced and our understanding expands. As a result, an aesthetic experience tends to heighten meaning, while an anesthetic experience tends to dull meaning. Dentists use anesthetics; artists and designers use aesthetics.

Aesthetic theories reflect community values, and thus vary greatly from culture to culture. For example, an exalted conception of Christianity dominated civic life during the Middle Ages in Europe. To express their faith, architects developed ingenious building strategies to create the soaring Gothic cathedrals we associate with that period (8.25). By contrast, intimacy and a sense of community were highly valued by the Unitarian congregation that commissioned Frank Lloyd Wright's

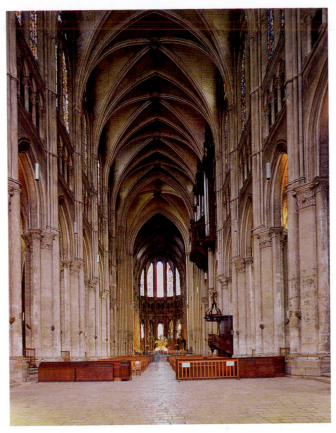

8.25 Notre-Dame Cathedral nave vaults, Chartres, 1194–1230.

8.26 Frank Lloyd Wright, Unity Temple interior, 1906. Oak Park, Illinois.

Unity Temple (8.26). The sanctuary is essentially a cube, with rows of seats facing inward from three sides. Congregants face each other while at the same time maintaining close contact with the minister. The Pompidou Center (8.27), by Renzo Piano and Richard Rogers, offers a third approach to public architecture. From the outside, it looks more like a roller coaster than a major art museum. To emphasize the importance of technology in contemporary life, the blue ventilation ducts, red elevators, and green water pipes are highlighted rather than being

hidden. Because cultural values are so variable, before we conclude our discussion of meaningful design, we must delve into contemporary aesthetics.

Postmodernism

Contemporary art and design are widely categorized as **postmodernism.** This emphasizes the extent to which today's artists and designers seek solutions that challenge or exceed modernism. Thus, to understand contemporary aesthetics, we must first examine the basic characteristics of the previous aesthetic period.

In the arts, **modernism** is a general term that encompasses a wide range of individual movements. Beginning in Europe in the latter part of the nineteenth century, modernism became the dominant force in art and design from around 1915 to 1975.

In a sense, modernism rose from the ashes of World War I. After this devastating conflict, traditional attitudes and images seemed inadequate and out of date. Architects began to strip away traditional ornamentation to reveal the underlying structures and spaces in their buildings. Designers such as Marcel Breuer, Raymond Lowry, and Charles and Ray Eames used plastic, metals, and glass to mass-produce objects and images for an expanding consumer market. Artists such as Wassily Kandinsky, Naum Gabo, and Piet Mondrian valued abstraction over traditional representation. The international art world became a hotbed of experimentation.

Many modernists shared four fundamental beliefs. First, they were fascinated by **form,** which may be defined as the physical manifestation of an idea. "Less is more" became a mantra for designers, while "the form is the content" became a catchphrase for many painters. Second, modernists readily embraced new materials and methods of production. Especially in architecture, traditional materials such as wood, brick, and stone began to be replaced by concrete, plastic, and glass. Third, the early modernists strongly believed in the social significance of the arts. They wanted to bring art and design to the general population, rather than working for an elite. Finally, many modernists sought to understand and express universal truths. No longer satisfied with a conventional representation of reality, they began to develop a new visual language based on distillation and abstraction.

8.27 Renzo Piano and Richard Rogers, Pompidou Center, Paris, 1976.

These four fundamental beliefs stimulated innovation in all areas of art, architecture, and design, and an enormous amount of brilliant work was produced. Over time, however, many modernists became trapped by their own success. Constructed from hard, reflective materials and dominated by right angles, modernist buildings often seemed cold and monolithic. Based on an underlying grid and typographical conventions, modernist posters often seemed predictable. Reduced to the most essential forms, modernist painting and sculpture became detached from the chaos and complexity of contemporary life. It seemed that all the questions of modernism had been answered. Something had to change.

The 1966 publication of *Complexity and Contradiction in Architecture* set the stage for postmodern architecture. In it, architect Robert Venturi extolled the energy and ambiguities of renaissance architecture:

> I like elements which are hybrid rather than "pure," compromising rather than "clean," distorted rather than "articulated," perverse as well as impersonal, boring as well as "interesting," conventional rather than "designed," accommodating rather than excluding, redundant rather than simple, vestigial as well as innovating, inconsistent and equivocal rather than direct and clear. I am for messy vitality over obvious unity.

At the same time, philosophers Jean-Louis Lyotard, Jacques Derrida, Michael Foucault, and Roland Barthes began to expand our understanding of the process of communication. They argued that both knowledge and communication are impermanent and conditional: there *are* no universal truths. The audience rather than the artist ultimately creates the meaning of an artwork; thus, meaning changes constantly. Furthermore, they tended to see knowledge as cyclical rather than progressive. They argued that we are pursuing a complex path with multiple branches rather than a grand journey that will culminate in human perfection.

Influenced by these theorists and seeking fresh ideas and approaches, many contemporary artists and designers reject the central tenets of modernism. For the postmodernist, context and content are as important as pure form. Postmodern use of materials tends to be omnivorous and irreverent. An exhibition may be constructed from trash, and fiberglass may be manipulated to mimic metal.

Distinctions between "high art" (such as painting and sculpture) and "low art" (such as advertising and crafts) are considered artificial. And, since all aspects of visual culture are intertwined, the postmodernist may recycle images and ideas with impunity, "appropriating" them for use in a new context. Finally, for the postmodernist there are multiple rather than universal truths, and all truths are continually changing. As a result, where late modernism tended to be stable and reductive, postmodernism tends to be expansive and dynamic. As Venturi suggested, complexity and contradiction can be seen as strengths.

For the past 30 years, the collision between modernism and postmodernism has released an enormous amount of energy. Taboos have been broken repeatedly, and the criteria for excellence continue to evolve.

Visual Strategies

Five common characteristics of postmodern art and design follow.

Appropriation (the reuse of an existing artwork) is often used to create a connection between past and present cultural values. In *We Don't Need Another Hero* (8.28), Barbara Kruger borrowed a Norman Rockwell illustration in which a young girl admires her male counterpart's muscles. The emphatic text shifts the meaning from the original gender stereotype to a contemporary feminist statement.

Recontextualization is another postmodern strategy. Constructed from steel pins and placed in a gallery, Mona Hatoum's *Doormat* (8.29) forces us to rethink a commonplace object. As part of a series on racism, this artwork suggests that the opportunities

8.28 Barbara Kruger, *Untitled (We Don't Need Another Hero)*, 1987. Photographic silksreen, vinyl lettering on Plexiglas, 109 × 210 in. (276.9 × 533.4 cm).

8.29 **Mona Hatoum**, *Doormat II*, **2000–01.** Steel and rubber, 1 × 28 × 16 in. (2.5 × 71 × 40.6 cm).

offered by civil rights legislation may be as ironic as a welcome mat made of pins.

Layering is often used to create complex or even contradictory meanings. In *The Red Mean: Self-Portrait* (8.30), Jaune Quick-to-See Smith reinterprets Leonardo da Vinci's famous drawing of ideal human proportions (8.31). As a Renaissance man, Leonardo was fascinated by both perfection and the grotesque. In this drawing, he mapped out an idealized figure radiating out from the navel in the center.

Despite its superficial similarity, the aesthetic basis for Smith's self-portrait is entirely different. Her circular outline simultaneously suggests a target, negation, and the four directions emphasized in Native American spiritual practices. A sign proclaiming "Made in the USA" combined with the artist's tribal identification number covers the chest of the figure, and tribal newspapers fill the background. While the da Vinci drawing is simple and elegant, Smith's self-portrait provides a rich commentary on the complexities of her life as a Native American.

All of these examples demonstrate a fourth postmodern characteristic: words and images are often integrated in order to expand emotional impact or to create conflict. For the postmodernist, contradiction and complexity are celebrated as facts of life and sources of inspiration.

Finally, **hybridity** may be defined as the creation of artworks using disparate media and meanings to create a unified conceptual statement. In *I Wish I Could Help You* (8.32), Daniel Sutherland combined abstract painted shapes with a tiny, highly detailed figure and surrounded the entire image with a three-dimensional frame made of wood and hardware. For Sutherland, the deep frame is suggestive of both a shipping crate and a contemporary reliquary. Kathryn Frund combined government

8.30 Jaune Quick-to-See Smith, *The Red Mean: Self-Portrait*, 1992. Mixed medium.

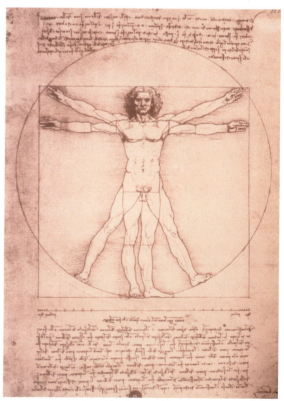

8.31 **Leonardo da Vinci**, *Proportions of the Human Figure* (after Vitruvius), **c. 1485–90.** Pen and ink, 13½ × 9¾ in. (34.3 × 24.8 cm).

8.32 Daniel Sutherland, *I Wish I Could Help You*, 1994. Oil on canvas on wood with hardware, 75 × 84 in. (190.5 × 213.4 cm).

documents and a carpenter's plumb bob with paint on aluminum to create *Radical Acts* (see figure 3.22, page 75). Jaune Quick-to-See Smith's *Self-Portrait* (8.30) is constructed from newspapers, posters, and identity cards as well as paint. And, as we will see in the interview at the end of this chapter, Roger Shimomura added Mickey Mouse ears to a pair of paintings dealing with racial stereotypes. For the postmodernist, visual impact and conceptual meaning are more important than technical purity.

DRAMA

Regardless of the medium used or the message conveyed, all communication can be strengthened through dramatic delivery. Even Martin Luther King Jr.'s "I Have a Dream" speech loses much of its power when delivered in a flat, monotonous tone of voice. Just as a playwright sets the stage for the story he or she seeks to tell, so an artist can set the stage for visual communication.

All of the elements and principles of design described in this book can be used to increase *compositional* drama. To increase *conceptual* drama, we can:

- *Personify the idea.* When we identify with a character in a play, we become more empathetic and involved in the story. Likewise, when we identify with a character in a painting or a poster, we are much more likely to remember the idea or emotion being conveyed.

- *Focus on essentials.* It has often been said that theater is "life with the boring parts left out." To be meaningful to an audience, the characters and events in a play must have a strong relationship to direct experience. However, a playwright rarely shows a character flossing his or her teeth. Too much detail clutters the composition, confuses the audience, and muddles the message. Including the right amount of information in just the right way can add drama to even the simplest idea.

- *Seek significance.* Any event, character, or time period can be used to create an effective play. Likewise, any object, event, or idea can be used in our quest for visual communication. A unique approach to a familiar subject or an insightful interpretation of personal and political events can add significance and increase impact.

SUMMARY

- A shared language is the basis on which all communication is built.

- Iconography (the study of symbolic visual systems) provides us with a way to analyze the meaning of images and objects.

- Just as films are targeted for specific audiences, so many forms of visual communication are designed for specific viewers.

- Immediacy is often highly valued in graphic design. By comparison, many paintings require extended viewer involvement and longer viewing time.

- A stereotype is a fixed generalization based on a preconception. Stereotypes can easily create a bridge between the image and the audience.

- A cliché is an overused expression or predictable treatment of an idea. Even the most interesting image will lose its power if overused.

- A shift in a stereotype or cliché challenges our assumptions and can increase impact.

- Artists and designers choose the style, iconography, and composition best suited to their purpose. A mismatch between the type of image and its purpose creates confusion.

- The visual and social context in which an image appears will profoundly affect its meaning.

- Analogies, similes, and metaphors are figures of speech that link one thing to another. Metaphors are especially widely used in visual communication.

- Appropriation, recontextualization, layering, word/image integration, and hybridity are five common strategies used to create postmodern meaning.

- Dramatic delivery of a message enhances meaning.

KEY TERMS

aesthetics	cliché	layering	postmodernism
analogy	form	metaphor	recontextualization
anesthetic	hybridity	metaphorical thinking	simile
appropriation	iconography	modernism	stereotype

STUDIO PROJECTS

To apply the concepts from this chapter in the studio, check out the Projects page in the Online Learning Center at www.mhhe.com/stewart4e. The following is a sample of chapter-related assignments that are described in step-by-step detail.

Benign to Sublime. Transforming a benign still life into a compelling vehicle for the communication of an idea.

Build a Concept Generator. A basic cube turns into a conceptual toy.

Word/Image Synergy. Using Photoshop or photocopies to combine one or more images with a single word to create an unexpected message.

Detail of William Kentridge's *Black Box/Chambre Noire*, **2005.** Miniature theater with mechanized objects, projections and sound, dimensions variable.

Profile:
Roger Shimomura, Artist
Exploring Identity

Roger Shimomura's paintings, prints, and theater pieces address sociopolitical issues of Asian Americans and have often been inspired by 56 years of diaries kept by his late immigrant grandmother. He has had over a hundred solo exhibitions of his paintings and prints and has presented his experimental theater pieces nationally. Shimomura taught as a Distinguished Professor at The University of Kansas for 35 years and has been a visiting artist at over two hundred universities, art schools, and museums across the country. His work is found in nearly a thousand museums and private collections, including the Whitney Museum of American Art, Chicago Art Institute, Smithsonian, and Philadelphia Museum of Art.

MS: How do you define stereotyping, and why is it the focus of your artwork?

RS: Racial stereotyping is an oversimplified opinion or mental snapshot of members of that race. It's the focus of my artwork because it has caused harm to not only Asian Americans, but also every marginalized group in this country. This harm ranges from personal pain to larger legal actions that affect the entire community.

MS: What are the sources of your images?

RS: My sources range from old *Marvel* comic books to films by Kurosawa, from an image of Minnie Mouse to a geisha in an Utamaro print. Anything I see can generate an idea or become part of a composition.

Collecting objects and images that stereotype Japanese people is my current obsession. This includes Jap hunting licenses, slap-a-Jap club cards, postcards, ads, and movie posters featuring the buck-toothed, slant-eyed, yellow-skinned depictions of Asian people.

My collection of experiences is even more important. Following the Japanese attack on Pearl Harbor, my family was forcibly moved to Minidoka, a concentration camp in the southern Idaho desert. We were released two years later, when I was five years old. All through grade school and junior high, our favorite neighborhood game was not "Cowboys and Indians" but "Kill the Japs,"

bringing to life the values from the comics that I collected at that time. We reluctantly took turns being the "Jap," though we all preferred to be John Wayne, the most prolific Jap killer of the time. As a soldier during the Korean War, I was nicknamed "Pop-Up" because my fellow white officers thought I resembled the pop-up targets we used for target practice. All of these experiences feed into my exploration of stereotypes and racism.

MS: *Florence, South Carolina* is part of your "Stereotypes and Admonitions" series. Each painting in this series describes a single racist incident in a very straightforward, almost deadpan way. What is the advantage of this approach?

RS: It is the most direct and simplest way to tell a story of injustice. A verbal story accompanies the painting, making the content completely accessible. Hopefully, the work will resonate beyond the viewing, leading viewers to continue the conversation long after they leave.

MS: *Yellow Rat Bastard, Or How to Tell the Difference Between the Japanese and the Chinese* is much more complex. Can you talk us through this piece? What is the source and what do the various elements mean?

RS: *Yellow Rat Bastard* is a mixed media comparison between Roger (right panel) who is Japanese American, surrounded by his current family, with his friend, Norman Gee, who is a Chinese American painter.

It seems pretty simple. Each artist holds his respective country's chopsticks with either a short- or long-grained rice kernel, and is surrounded by appropriate cultural references. It gets complex when we look more carefully. Roger is married to a blonde-haired, blue-eyed Caucasian, has a daughter-in-law who is Filipina, and a grandchild that is half Filipino and half Japanese. Norman is married to a Japanese American (who studies Chinese Tai Chi). His children are half Chinese and half Japanese, as referenced by his daughter, who holds a bao (Chinese bun) in one hand and Makizushi (sushi roll) in the other.

Racist reminders are referenced by the WWII clichéd depiction of a *Yellow Peril Jap* looming behind Roger's portrait, while Fu Manchu peers out behind Norman's head. Both portraits are surrounded by contemporary pop icons from China and Japan.

Separating the two canvases is a shopping bag with the emblazoned words "Yellow Rat Bastard."

While this term was popularly used to describe the Japanese during WWII, it has been revived today, as the name of a trendy men's clothing store in New York City. Acting as a gesture to defuse the deadly yellow rat, the ears of a benign Mickey Mouse protrude out of the top of the bag. While non–Asian Americans continue to have difficulty distinguishing between the Japanese and Chinese, the unfortunate fact is that many still view Asians as a generically alien race in this country.

MS: You are renowned as a teacher as well as an artist. What advice can you offer to beginning students?

RS: When my students came up to me and said that they didn't know what to paint, I would tell them to take a hard look at themselves first. It is important to consider whether there is significant value in sharing what you are experiencing in life. Sometimes the simplest approach to making art ends up being the most poignant.

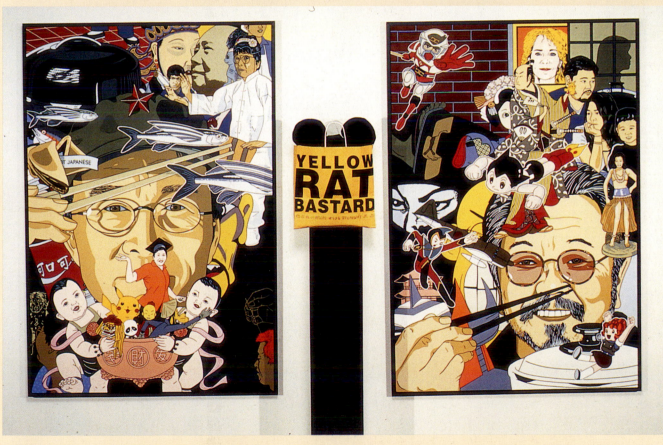

Roger Shimomura, *Yellow Rat Bastard,* **2006.** Oil on canvas, 72 × 126 in. (182.9 × 320 cm).

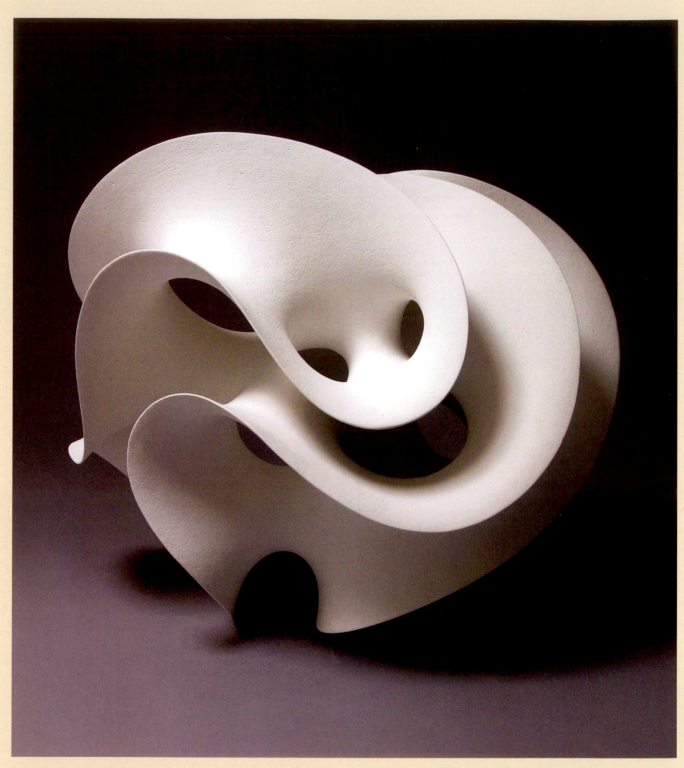

Eva Hild, *Lamella*, 2008. Stoneware, 26 × 23 × 22 in. (66 × 58 × 55 cm).

Three-Dimensional Design

As we begin our investigation of three-dimensional design, it is useful to consider both the similarities and differences between flat compositions and physical constructions. In both cases, the basic principles of design are used to create artworks that offer an effective balance between unity and variety. And, in both two- and three-dimensional design, concept development and critical thinking are complementary aspects of the creative process.

However, in two-dimensional design, we use our technical, perceptual, and conceptual skills to create flat visual patterns and convincing illusions. It is the viewer's *mental* response that gives the artwork meaning. In contrast, our experience in the three-dimensional world is more physical and direct. As we traverse an architectural space, we alter our perception with each step we take. When we circle a sculpture, we encounter new information on each side. The materials used in the construction of a three-dimensional object determine its aesthetic appeal as well as its structural strength.

This physical connection gives three-dimensional design inherent power. When we shift from an illusory world to a tangible world, a substantial shift in communication occurs. Confronted by the physical presence of a three-dimensional object, the viewer responds viscerally as well as mentally.

This section is devoted to the elements, organization, and implications of three-dimensional design. The basic building blocks are discussed in Chapter Nine. In Chapter Ten, the principles of three-dimensional design are described. The unique characteristics of various materials are considered in Chapter Eleven. Chapter Twelve is devoted to the ways in which artists have transformed their ideas into physical objects and to a discussion of differences between traditional and contemporary sculpture.

Part Three

Elements of Three-Dimensional Design

The chess pieces in Eddie Chui's *Let's Dance* (figure 6.5, page 135) rock back and forth on their curving bottoms. When the pieces are used in a game, their polished sides and hefty weight delight the players who hold them.

Beau Dick's *Mugamtl Mask* (*Crooked Beak*) (figure 5.10, page 116) embodies a powerful myth of deadly illness and glorious resurrection. When worn, it symbolically transforms an actor in costume into a man who can fly.

Xu Bing's *A Book from the Sky* (9.1) consists of printed volumes and scrolls containing thousands of "false" Chinese characters that he invented and then painstakingly hand-cut onto wooden printing blocks. Those who are not fluent in Chinese may admire the graceful characters and wonder at their meaning. Those who do know Chinese find that their familiar cultural references have turned into conceptual chaos. The 70-foot-long printed sheets of incomprehensible text mirror the books below and envelop the viewer in a world of mystery.

Our experience in the three-dimensional world is physical, cerebral, and emotional. While a painting or video can pull us into an imaginative world, a sculptural object offers a tangible presence that is powerful in itself. In the hands of a skillful artist or designer, this raw power is translated into insight and energy.

9.1 Xu Bing, *A Book from the Sky*, 1987–91. Hand printed books, ceiling and wall scrolls printed from wood letterpress type using false Chinese characters, dimensions variable.

Line, plane, volume, mass, space, texture, light, color, and time are the basic building blocks from which three-dimensional designs are made. In this chapter, we will consider the unique characteristics of each **element,** both individually and in combination with other elements.

FORM

As noted in Chapter Seven, **form** can be defined as the physical manifestation of an idea. **Content** refers to the idea itself, including the subject matter plus its emotional, intellectual, spiritual, and symbolic implications.

Form has an additional definition in three-dimensional design. In this context, *form* can refer to three-dimensionality itself. For example, a circle, a square, and a triangle are two-dimensional shapes, while a sphere, a cube, and a pyramid are three-dimensional forms.

Types of Form

- An empty three-dimensional form is generally defined as a **volume,** while a solid form is generally defined as a **mass.**

- An effective three-dimensional composition balances **positive forms** (areas of substance) with **negative space.**

- **Organic forms** (forms that visually suggest nature or natural forces) create a very different effect than do **geometric forms,** which typically are based on cubes, spheres, and other simple volumes. **Mechanical forms,** such as belts and gears, can suggest an industrial source.

- The degree of actual or implied movement in a form can expand our vocabulary even further. **Static forms** appear stable and unmoving. Designed to last forever, the Great Pyramids at Giza exemplify stability and repose. **Dynamic forms** imply movement. *The Dance* (9.2), by Jean-Baptiste Carpeaux, is a highly dynamic form. Dominated by rotating figures and curving lines, this sculpture swirls with energy. **Kinetic forms** actually move. In Jean Tinguely's *Chaos 1* (9.3), a bowling ball on a track trips a series of movements in a massive mechanism.

9.2 Jean-Baptiste Carpeaux, *The Dance* (after restoration), 1868–69. Marble, 7 ft 6½ in. (2.3 m).

9.3 Jean Tinguely, *Chaos 1*, 1973–74. Sculpture in Columbus Park. Metal construction with moving balls on tracks, electric motors, 30 × 28 × 15 ft (915 × 854 × 458 m).

Form and Function

Each artist seeks to express concepts and evoke emotions. Accordingly, a sculptor explores an idea, chooses materials, and develops a composition based on his or her aesthetic intention. Public art projects, such as Eero Saarinen's *Jefferson National Expansion Memorial* (9.4), and ritual objects, such as the Mugamtl mask, often commemorate historical events or express social values.

A designer uses the same mastery of concept, composition, and materials to create an object that is functional as well as beautiful. For example, when designing aquatic gear, designer Bob Evans carefully analyzes the needs of swimmers and then creates equipment to best meet those needs. The basic *Force Fin* (9.5A) provides the maneuverability needed for snorkeling. The *Multi Force Fin* (9.5B) was designed as a training device to strengthen a swimmer's legs, while the *Excellerating Force Fin* (9.5C) provides the extended power needed by scuba divers. For the designer, the form must fulfill a specific **function,** or purpose.

While an industrial designer has a different purpose than the sculptor, both use the same basic elements and principles of design. Both must organize line, plane, volume, mass, space, texture, and color into coherent form. The structural integrity of a sculpture is just as important as the structural integrity of a wheelchair, and a teapot that is both beautiful and functional is ideal.

Orthographic Projection

Height, width, and depth are the three dimensions in three-dimensional design. In computer-aided design, these three dimensions are defined using the *x*-, *y*-, and *z*-axes from geometry (9.6). Using the cube as a basic building block, we can create many variations on these basic dimensions. In figure 9.7A, the cube is modified through removal and displacement. In figure 9.7B and C, additional planes and unexpected intersections increase complexity.

There are many methods of depicting three-dimensional form on a two-dimensional surface. **Orthographic projection** is one of the most useful. Unlike perspective drawing, which relies on vanishing points to create the illusion of space,

9.4 Eero Saarinen, *Jefferson National Expansion Memorial (Gateway Arch)*, St. Louis, 1966.

A Force Fin

B Multi Force Fin

C Excellerating Force Fin

9.5A–C Bob Evans, *Force Fin Variations*, 1990–present. Molded polyurethane, size variable.

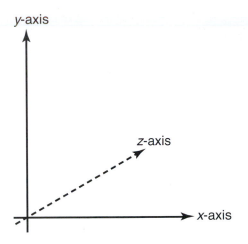

y-axis

z-axis

x-axis

9.6 The three dimensions are defined through height, width, and depth.

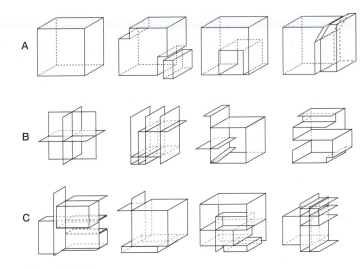

9.7A – C Variations on a cube.

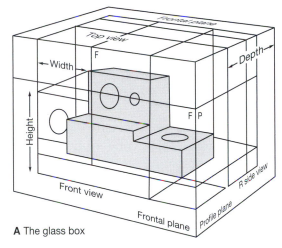

A The glass box

B Unfolding the glass box

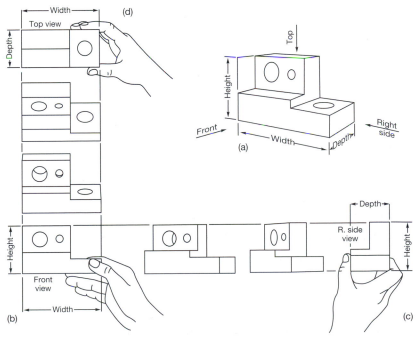

C Rotating the object in space

9.8A – C Orthographic projection can be used to define structural details.

orthographic projection uses parallel lines to define structural details. These details are essential to many types of construction.

An orthographic projection represents six views of a three-dimensional form. Imagine that your project is enclosed in a glass box (9.8A). As you look through the top, bottom, front, and back, then through the right and left sides, you can see six distinctive views. In effect, an orthographic drawing is created when you unfold and flatten this imaginary box (9.8B). Using orthographic projection, we can examine and record various surfaces of a three-dimensional object (9.8C).

9.9 Robert Longo, *Corporate Wars* (detail), 1982. Cast aluminum, lacquer on wood relief, 7 × 9 × 3 ft (2.1 × 2.7 × 0.9 m).

Degrees of Dimensionality

Relief

When working in **relief,** the artist uses a flat backing (such as a wall or ceiling) as a base for three-dimensional forms. For example, Robert Longo's *Corporate Wars* (9.9) is like a sculptural painting. Using the boundaries created by the supporting wall and the four outer edges, it presents a group of white-collar warriors engaged in hand-to-hand combat. The figures are trapped, bound both to the backing and by their struggle for money.

Three-Quarter Works

A **three-quarter work,** such as Jean-Baptiste Carpeaux's *The Dance* (see figure 9.2) is more three-dimensional. We can walk around this piece, examining the front and two sides. As a result, the dancing figures create a vortex of implied motion. Based on the information we see, we assume that the dance continues into the wall.

Freestanding Works

Freestanding works are designed to be seen from all sides. When we circle Auguste Rodin's *The Kiss* (9.10A and B), we capture every nuance in the movement of the two figures. Details (such as the man's stroking hand and the woman's raised heel) bring life to the inanimate stone.

Environmental Works

An **environmental work** (or **environment**) presents a space that can be physically entered. Installations (which are usually presented indoors) and earthworks (which are usually presented outdoors) are two major types of environments. Such works often require active audience participation and may present a series of images, ideas, and experiences that unfold over time.

Installations

Typically, an **installation** is an ensemble of images and objects that are presented within a three-dimensional environment. Surrounded by information, we become emotionally and physically involved. For example, on entering Antoni Muntadas's *The Board Room* (9.11), the viewer confronts 13 chairs facing a long table. In a reference to the Last Supper described in the Bible, these chairs are accompanied by photographs of religious leaders, from Ayatollah Khomeini to Billy Graham. Inserted in the mouth of each man, a small video monitor plays a film clip showing him in action. In this installation, religion becomes an extension of both business and politics.

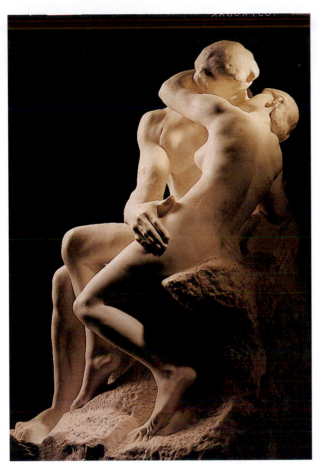

9.10A Auguste Rodin, *The Kiss,* 1886–98. Marble, over life size. Dramatic lighting accentuates form and can heighten emotion.

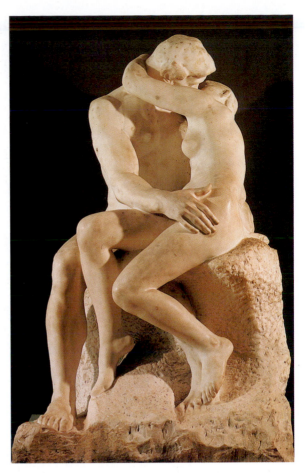

9.10B Auguste Rodin, *The Kiss,* 1886–98. Marble, over life size. A slight change in the viewer's position substantially changes the apparent orientation of the figures.

9.11 Antoni Muntadas, *The Board Room,* 1987. Installation at North Hall Gallery at Massachusetts College of Art, Boston. Thirteen chairs placed around a boardroom table. Behind each chair is a photo of a religious leader, in whose mouth a small video monitor shows the leader speaking. Subjects include Ayatollah Khomeini, Billy Graham, Sun Myung Moon, and Pope John Paul II.

The Board Room presents a series of clearly defined figures in a dark and dramatic setting. By contrast, Celotex panels covered with aluminum foil created a brightly lit and reflective space in Rudolf Stingel's installation (9.12). Visitors were invited to inscribe messages into the soft metal, creating overlapping layers of personal comments.

Earthworks

An **earthwork** is a large-scale outdoor installation. Often extending over great distances in time and space, earthworks may require substantial physical engagement by the artist, the audience, and inhabitants of the site. Robert Smithson's *Spiral Jetty* (9.13) is a classic example. This 1,500-foot-long coil of rock and earth extends from the shore into the water of the Great Salt Lake in Utah. For Smithson, the spiral created "a dot in the vast infinity of universes, an imperceptible point in a cosmic immensity, a speck in an impenetrable nowhere."[1] Remote and mysterious, this artwork evokes a cosmic connection that extends far beyond the walls of a museum or gallery.

9.12 Rudolf Stingel, *Untitled,* **2007.** Chandelier and graffitied Celotex installation boards at the Whitney Museum of American Art.

9.13 Robert Smithson, *Spiral Jetty,* **Great Salt Lake, Utah, 1970.** Rock, salt crystals, earth, algae, coil, 1,500 ft (457 m).

9.14 Todd Slaughter, *Mano y Bola* (details), 1997. Aluminum and steel, hand 27 × 40 × 4 ft (8.2 × 12.2 × 1.2 m), ball 20 ft (6 m) diameter. Overlooking the Strait of Gibraltar.

Site-Specific Artwork

A **site-specific** artwork is designed for and installed in a particular place. Commissioned by the port city of Algeciras in Spain, *Mano y Bola* (9.14) rests on a bluff overlooking the Strait of Gibraltar. The 40-foot-long hand may be catching or throwing the 20-foot-tall ball positioned roughly 50 feet away. This artwork metaphorically alludes to the historical exchange of religion, power, and conflict between Europe and Africa. To heighten the metaphor, the hand has been designed to disappear when the wind blows. One thousand movable panels were covered with a photographic image of a hand. A brisk wind shifts the panels to a horizontal position, causing the image to dissolve visually into the surrounding sky.

Key Questions

FORM

- Experiment with organic, geometric, and mechanical forms. Which is best suited to the idea you wish to express?
- What proportion of static and dynamic forms is most appropriate for your artwork?
- Will the addition of a kinetic component add to or detract from the overall effect?
- When you are creating a freestanding artwork, how much similarity and how much contrast are needed on each side? What does the viewer gain by walking around the artwork?

LINE

In three-dimensional design, **line** can be created through the following:

- *A series of adjacent points.* The cars that make up Ant Farm's *Cadillac Ranch* (9.15) are distinct objects in themselves as well as the points that create a line of cars. Commissioned by a rancher in Texas, this sculpture has been described as a requiem for the gas-guzzling American automobile.[2]

- *A connection between points. Free Ride Home,* by Kenneth Snelson (9.16), was constructed using two types of line. The aluminum tubes provide a linear skeleton that becomes elevated when the connecting lines are attached. The resulting sculpture is compositionally dominated by diagonal lines that seem to defy gravity.

- *A point in motion.* A skater who wears the *Neon Skates* by Moira North and Rudi Stern (9.17) can literally create lines from a moving point of light. Because this artwork is dynamic, the simple skates become more dramatic.

9.15 **Ant Farm (Chip Lord, Hudson Marquez, Doug Michels),** *Cadillac Ranch,* **1974.** Ten Cadillacs, Amarillo, TX.

9.17 **Moira North and Rudi Stern,** *Neon Skates,* **1986.** Battery-operated neon skates for performance by The Ice Theater of New York, Moira North, director.

9.16 **Kenneth Snelson,** *Free Ride Home,* **1974.** Aluminum and stainless steel, 30 × 30 × 60 ft (9.1 × 9.1 × 18.2 m). Storm King Art Center, Mountainville, NY.

Line Quality

Each line has its own distinctive quality. This quality is determined largely by the line's orientation, direction, and degree of continuity, as well as the material used.

Orientation

Orientation refers to the horizontal, vertical, or diagonal position of a line. Based on our experience in the natural world, we tend to associate horizontal lines with stability and diagonal lines with movement. Vertical lines tend to accentuate height and can make an object or an interior appear more formidable and imposing.

All three types of line are used in Mark di Suvero's *Ik Ook Eindhoven* (9.18) and Peter Pierobon's *Ladderback Chair* (9.19). The di Suvero sculpture is dominated by two horizontal I beams suspended from a nearly vertical support. The diagonal lines that are connected to this primary structure emphasize the weight of the artwork and add visual movement. On the other hand, it is the tall vertical back that transforms Pierobon's chair into a whimsical sculpture. Its exaggerated height pulls our eyes upward and provides support for the nine jagged lines that create the rungs of the ladder.

Curved lines can carve out complex patterns in space and may encompass an object to create a harmonious whole. For David Mach's *Eckow* (9.20), a full-size head was constructed from a collection of coat hangers. The undulating lines simultaneously define the form and create a vortex of energy.

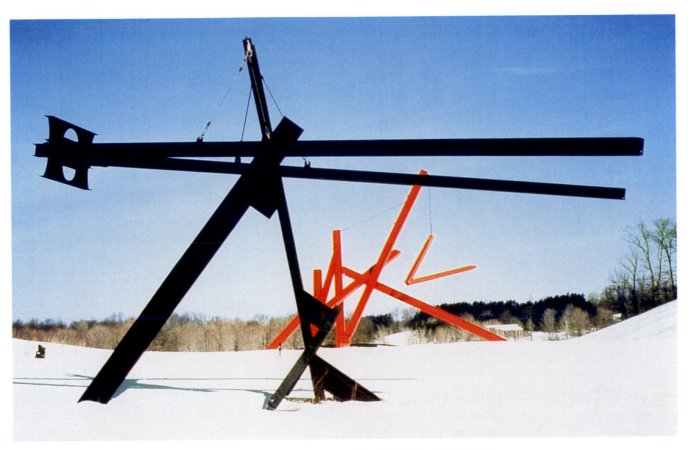

9.18 Mark di Suvero, *Ik Ook Eindhoven,* **1971–72.** Painted steel, 24 × 24 × 33 ft (7.3 × 7.3 × 10 m).
In the background: *Are Years What?* **(for Marianne Moore), 1967.** Painted steel, 40 × 40 × 30 ft (12.2 × 12.2 × 9.1 m).

9.19 Peter Pierobon, *Ladderback Chair.* Firm & Manufacturer: Snyderman Gallery.

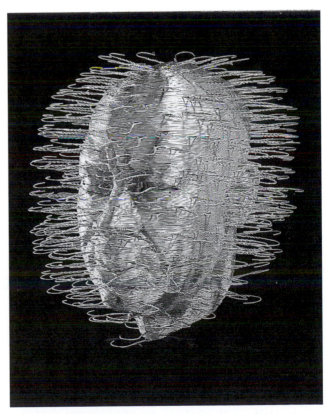

9.20 David Mach, *Eckow,* **1997.** Coat hangers, 2 ft 2¼ in. × 1 ft 11½ in. × 2 ft 5½ in. (67 × 60 × 75 cm).

9.21 Chris Burden, *Medusa's Head*, 1989–92. Cement, wood, stone, train tracks, 16 ft (4.8 m) diameter, 5 tons.

Direction

Direction refers to the implied movement of a line. A line of consistent width tends to suggest equal movement in both directions. Varying line width can create a more specific sense of direction. For example, in *Jefferson National Expansion Memorial* (see figure 9.4, page 182), the massive lines at the bottom drive downward into the earth, while the tapered arch at the top lifts our eyes skyward.

Continuity

Continuity, or linear flow, can increase movement and accentuate form. In David Mach's *Eckow* (9.20), the smooth metal is both elegant and energetic. Continuity plays a very different role in Chris Burden's *Medusa's Head* (9.21). Here, a mad tangle of toy train tracks flows around and through the mass of stone, plywood, and cement. Representing the snakes that crowned the head of a mythical monster, these writhing lines accentuate the spherical mass and give us a fresh interpretation of an ancient Greek myth.

Actual Lines

Through their physical presence, **actual lines** can connect, define, or divide a design. *Laocoön and His Two Sons* (9.22) depicts a scene from the Trojan War. When the Greeks offer a large, hollow wooden horse to the Trojans, Laocoön warns against accepting the gift. The Greek goddess Athena then sends two serpents to attack and kill the seer, thereby gaining entry into Troy for the soldiers hidden in the horse. The writhing serpent compositionally connects the terrified men while adding emotional intensity to this depiction of Athena's wrath.

Implied Lines

Implied lines are created through mental rather than physical connections. *The Rape of the Sabine Women,* by Giovanni da Bologna (9.23), relies on a series of implied lines for its impact. Starting at the bottom and exploding upward, the repeated diagonals in the sculpture create a visual vortex as powerful as a tornado. At the bottom is the husband of the captured

9.22 Laocoön and His Two Sons. Marble, 7 ft (2.13 m).

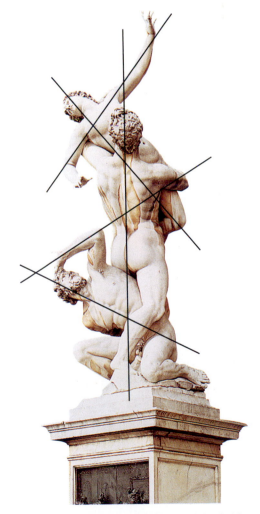

9.23 Giovanni da Bologna, *The Rape of the Sabine Women*, completed 1583. Marble, 13 ft 6 in. (4.1 m).

9.24 Nancy Holt, *Sun Tunnels*, 1973–76. Great Basin Desert, UT. Four tunnels, each 18 ft long × 9 ft 4 in. diameter (5.5 × 2.8 m), each axis 86 ft long (26.2 m). Aligned with sunrises and sunsets on the solstices.

9.25 Steve McAllister, *Fencing Mask.* Photograph.

woman. In the center, a standing Roman soldier is intent on stealing a wife for himself. The agitated movement culminates at the top with the extended arm of the embattled woman.

A **sight line** activates Nancy Holt's *Sun Tunnels* (9.24). At first glance, the four 22-ton concrete tunnels seem static. Upon entering each tunnel, the viewer discovers a series of holes that duplicate the size and position of the stars in four major constellations. The light pouring in through these holes shifts as the sun rises and travels across the sky. During the winter and summer solstices, the sculpture is further transformed as light from the rising and setting sun is framed by an alignment of the circular tunnels. Like a telescope, the massive cylinders are more important for the visions they create than as objects in themselves.

Line Networks

Both artists and designers use linear networks in many different ways. In figure 9.25, interlocking metal lines form the woven mesh on a fencer's mask. Due to its linear construction, it is light in weight and protects the athlete's face without blocking vision. As shown in Claire Zeisler's *Red Forest* (9.26), most fiber works are created through the organization of multiple lines of thread, yarn, or other materials. Single lines can bring a simple eloquence to a design, while multiple lines can be used to create strong, complex, and versatile forms.

Key Questions

LINE

- Vertical, horizontal, diagonal, and curving lines all have unique strengths. What can each type contribute to your design?
- What can line continuity or discontinuity contribute to your composition?
- What happens when you dramatically increase or decrease the number of lines?
- Can intersecting lines strengthen your design, both structurally and compositionally?

9.26 Claire Zeisler, *Red Forest*, 1968. Dyed jute, 8 ft 2 in. × 7 ft 4 in. × 2 ft (249 × 224 × 61 cm).

PLANE

A **plane** is a three-dimensional form that has length and width but minimal thickness. Depending on the material used, planes can be transparent or opaque, rigid or flexible, flat or curved. Complex surfaces and enclosures can be constructed using folded or bent planes, and when slotted together planes can be used to create a variety of sturdy forms (9.27). As demonstrated by Maya Lin's *Blue Lake Pass* (9.28), when modified incrementally and organized sequentially, planes can create forms that are as descriptive as a topographical map.

Alexander Calder was a master of planar construction. In his famous mobiles (9.29), he put simple planes in motion. Inspired by the delicate weights and balances he saw in the paintings of Piet Mondrian (see figure 3.32, page 80), Calder used these structures to represent the movement of heavenly bodies within the universe. Exquisitely balanced, the flat planes and curving lines can be activated by the slightest flow of air.

Finallly, intersecting planes can create large-scale structures that are remarkably strong. With outdoor sculptures, such as Alexander Calder's *La Grande Vitesse* (9.30), structural integrity is especially important. Located in a public plaza, the sculpture must withstand wind, rain, and snow while presenting minimal risk to pedestrians. Intersecting planes combined with a ribbed reinforcement at stress points create a durable structure.

9.27 *Scapes* cards. Artist: Darren Waterston. Designer: Ryan Burlinson. Art direction: Kurt Wolken. Client: Bellevue Art Museum. Wolken, Communica, Seattle, WA.

9.28 Maya Lin, *Blue Lake Pass* (detail), 2006. Duraflake particleboard, 20 blocks, approx. 5¾ × 17½ × 22½ ft (1.75 × 5.3 × 6.8 m).

9.29 Alexander Calder, *125,* also known as *Flight,* 1957. Painted aluminum and tempered steel, 300 in. × 540 in. × 204 in.

VOLUME AND MASS

Volume

In general terms, volume is the amount of space an object occupies. In three-dimensional design, **volume** refers to an enclosed area of three-dimensional space.

Cubes, cylinders, cones, and spheres are among the most prevalent volumes found in both nature and architecture. Fascinated by such "biological structures," Kendall Buster has created entire exhibitions using large-scale, translucent volumes (9.31). By contrast, Xiao Min created his *Secret Room* series from elegant and seemingly weightless organic volumes. Using a twelfth-century Chinese sex manual as a source, he constructed a series of life-sized

9.30 **Alexander Calder,** *La Grande Vitesse,* **1969.** Painted steel plate, 43 × 55 ft (13.1 × 16.8 m). Calder Plaza, Vandenberg Center, Grand Rapids, MI.

9.31 **Kendall Buster,** *New Growth,* **2007.** Steel frame, cable ties, greenhouse shadecloth. Installation at Boise Art Museum. Size variable.

9.32 **Xiao Min,** *Secret Room #3,* **2008.** Steel wire, 90 × 19 × 17 in. (127 × 48 × 43 cm).

couples embracing. Made from translucent sheets of steel wire, the suspended figures are both dream-like and erotic (9.32).

Designers often create functional objects using **polyhedra,** or multifaceted volumes (9.33). Such volumes can be surprisingly strong. In an assignment at The Ohio State University (9.34), students used a variety of polyhedra to construct lightweight bristol board helmets.

The specific amount of enclosed space is especially important when we create any kind of container, from architecture to glassware. *The Ginevra*

Carafe, by Ettore Sottsass (9.35), easily holds a liter of wine. The elegant cylinder requires little table space, and an extra disk of glass at the base increases its weight and stability. An additional glass cylinder at the top ensures that the lid will remain firmly in place.

Linear networks, folding, and slotting are a few of the strategies artists and designers use to create volume. Defining an enclosed space while maintaining structural integrity is essential. If the structure fails, the volume will collapse and the space will be lost.

Each strategy has its advantages. As demonstrated by the fencer's mask in figure 9.25 (page 190), woven structures can be elegant, lightweight, and remarkably strong. On the other hand, package designers generally create volume through folding. The heavy paper used for this purpose can be printed while flat, then scored, cut, and folded. The patterns used are mathematically specific and often structurally complex. And surprisingly strong volumes can be created using slotted planes. Slotted structures can be used to protect and separate fragile contents (such as wine bottles) and hold them in a specific position.

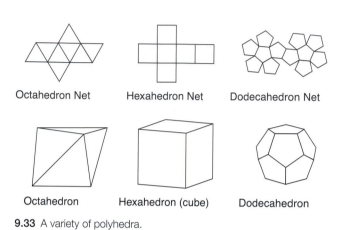

Octahedron Net   Hexahedron Net   Dodecahedron Net

Octahedron   Hexahedron (cube)   Dodecahedron

9.33 A variety of polyhedra.

9.34 Charles Wallschlaeger, professor emeritus, The Ohio State University, Department of Industrial, Interior, and Visual Communication Design. OSU students used a variety of polyhedra to construct bristol board helmets.

9.35 Ettore Sottsass, *Ginevra Carafe,* **1997.** Manufactured by Alessi, Crusinallo, Italy.

Mass

A **mass** is a solid three-dimensional form. A massive object can be as dense and heavy as a bar of gold or as light and porous as a sponge.

Massive sculptures are often carved from a solid block of plaster, clay, or stone or cast using bronze, glass, or other materials. Solid and imposing, they tend to dominate the environment in which they are placed.

Just as Alexander Calder took advantage of the buoyancy of a thin plane to create his mobiles, so did Henry Moore take advantage of the power of mass when he created *Locking Piece* (9.36A). In such structures, the **primary contours** (or outer edges) are complemented by the **secondary contours** created by internal edges (9.36B). As the viewer circles the form, these contours visually alternate as the primary contours become the secondary contours and the secondary contours become the primary contours.

Massive forms tend to suggest stability, power, and permanence. A series of colossal heads produced by the Olmec people of ancient Mexico combine the abstract power of a sphere with the specific power of a human head (9.37). Tom Friedman produced a very different type of mass in figure 9.38. He cut hundreds of pencils at various angles, and then reconstructed them to create an energetic maze.

A

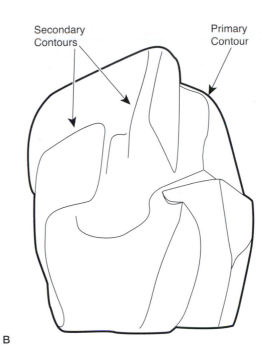

Secondary Contours

Primary Contour

B

9.36A and B Henry Moore, *Locking Piece,* 1963–64. Bronze, 115 × 110¼ × 90½ in. (292 × 280 × 230 cm).

9.37 *Colossal Head,* 1300–800 BCE. Stone, 11 × 9⅝ × 9⅝ ft (3.4 × 3 × 3 m). Olmec culture, Jalapa, Veracruz, Mexico.

Key Questions

VOLUME AND MASS

- How can planar source materials (such as bristol paper and cardboard) be used to create sturdy volumes?

- What are the advantages of transparent versus opaque volumes?

- An enclosed volume can be filled with space, sand, marbles, or other materials. Experiment!

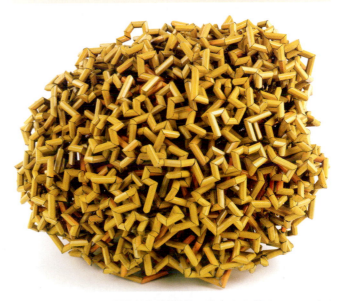

9.38 Tom Friedman, *Untitled,* 1995. Pencils cut at 45-degree angles and glued in a continuous loop, 11 × 14 × 11 in. (28 × 35 × 28 cm).

SPACE

In three-dimensional design, **space** is the area within or around an area of substance. A dialogue between a form and its surroundings is created as soon as an artist positions an object in space. Space is the partner to substance. Without it, line, plane, volume, and mass lose both visual impact and functional purpose.

The proportion of space to substance triggers an immediate response. The space in Alice Aycock's *Tree of Life Fantasy* (9.39) is defined by a filigree of delicate lines and planes. Inspired by the double-helix structure of DNA and by medieval illustrations showing people entering paradise through a spinning hole in the sky, Aycock combined a linear structure with a series of circular planes. The resulting sculpture is as open and playful as a roller coaster. By comparison, Burden's *Medusa's Head* (see figure 9.21, page 190) presents a relatively solid mass of tangled cement, wood, and metal. With sculptures of this kind, the *surrounding* space becomes more important than any enclosed space. Like a stone placed in a glass of water, the large, solid mass seems to displace the surrounding space, pushing it into the edges of the room.

Positive and Negative Space

The interrelationship between space and substance is demonstrated in every area of three-dimensional design. David Smith's *Cubi XXVII* (9.40) is dominated by a central void. The 10 gleaming geometric volumes are activated by the space they enclose. Space plays an equally important role in representational work. The open mouth in *Model of a Trophy Head* (9.41) really animates the mask. No facial expression, however extreme, would be as lively if this mouth were closed.

Negative space is especially noticeable in designs that are dominated by positive form. Karen Karnes's *Vessel* (9.42) is a functional pot, with its internal bottom placed just above the vertical slit. In effect, the lower half of the design serves as a pedestal for the functional container at the top. This narrow slit of negative space presents a strong contrast to the solidity of the cylindrical form and helps activate the entire form.

Compression and Expansion

Space is never passive or meaningless. It is just as important as the surrounding substance, and it can be manipulated very deliberately. The tangibility of space is especially apparent in the works of Richard

9.39 Alice Aycock, *Tree of Life Fantasy*, Synopsis of the Book of Questions Concerning the World Order and/or the Order of Worlds, 1990–92. Painted steel, fiberglass, and wood, 20 × 15 × 8 ft (6.1 × 4.6 × 2.4 m).

Serra and Walter de Maria. Using four enormous steel plates, Serra created a sense of spatial compression in figure 9.43. Upon entering the piece, the viewer immediately becomes aware of the weight of the tilted planes and of the support the compressed space seems to provide. The space in de Maria's *The Lightning Field* (9.44) is equally clearly defined yet is wonderfully expansive. Arranged in a grid over nearly 1 square mile of desert, 400 steel poles act as a collection of lightning rods. Impressive even in daylight, the site becomes awe-inspiring during a thunderstorm. Lightning jumps from pole to pole and from the sky to earth, creating a breathtaking pyrotechnic display.

Activated Space

The space in an artwork may be contemplative, agitated, or even threatening. For example, a Japanese Zen garden is usually made from an enclosure containing several large rocks surrounded by carefully raked white sand. A few simple objects

9.40 David Smith, *Cubi XXVII,* March 1965. Stainless steel, 111⅜ × 87¾ × 34 in. (282.9 × 222.9 × 86 cm).

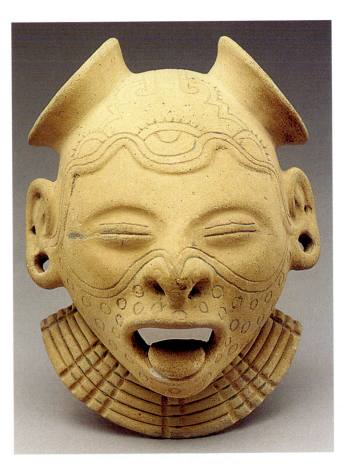

9.41 *Model of a Trophy Head,* Ecuador, La Tolita, 600 BCE–AD 400. Ceramic.

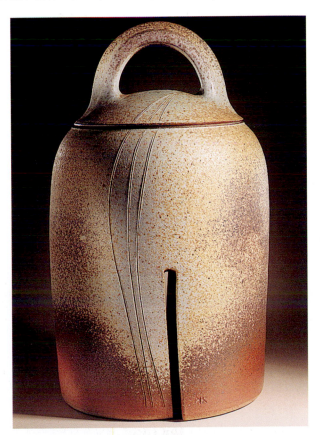

9.42 Karen Karnes, *Vessel,* 1987. Stoneware, wheel-thrown, glazed, and wood-fired, 16½ × 10½ in. (41.9 × 26.7 cm).

9.43 Richard Serra, *Betwixt the Torus and the Sphere,* 2001. Weatherproof steel, 142 × 450 × 319 in. (361 × 1,143 × 810 cm).

9.44 Walter de Maria, *The Lightning Field,* 1977. Stainless steel poles, average height 20 ft 7½ in. (6.1 m), overall 5,280 × 3,300 ft (1,609.34 × 1,005.84 m). Near Quemado, NM.

are used to create a contemplative space. By contrast, the space in Anish Kapoor's sculptures is often disorienting. Placed at the entrance to Millennium Park in Chicago, *Cloud Gate* reflects the surrounding buildings while the lower "gate" section visually pulls the viewer into a reflective interior chamber (9.45).

Entering Space

Some sculptures are designed to be entered physically. Lucas Samaras's *Mirrored Room* (9.46) multiplies and divides the reflection of each visitor who enters. Other sculptures can be entered only mentally. *Subway with Silver Girders* (9.47), by Donna Dennis, re-creates in great detail the architecture and lighting we find in a subway station. Constructed at two-thirds the scale of an actual station,

the sculpture presents a magical entry into a prosaic place. This subway station provides transportation for the mind rather than the body.

Key Questions

SPACE

- What relationships between substance and space have you built into your design?

- What would happen if you substantially increased or decreased the amount of space? For example, would 70 percent space and 30 percent mass strengthen or weaken your design?

- How might space play a stronger conceptual and compositional role in your design?

9.45 Anish Kapoor, *Cloud Gate,* Dedicated 2006. Millennium Park, Chicago. Stainless steel, 66 × 42 × 33 ft (20.12 × 12.8 × 10 m). Visitors and the surrounding city are reflected in the mirrorlike finish.

9.46 **Lucas Samaras,** *Mirrored Room,* **1966.** Mirrors on wooden frame, 8 × 8 × 10 ft (2.44 × 2.44 × 3 m).

9.47 **Donna Dennis,** *Subway with Silver Girders,* **1981–82.** Wood, masonite, acrylic, enamel, cellulose compound, glass, electrical fixtures, and metal, 12 × 12 × 13.5 ft (3.6 × 3.6 × 4.11 m).

TEXTURE

Texture refers to the visual or tactile quality of a form. The increased surface area of a three-dimensional form heightens the impact of texture. The surface shifts and turns, presenting numerous opportunities for textural elaboration.

Degrees of Texture

Variations in the suface of a volume may be subtle or pronounced. In *Blackware Storage Jar*, by Maria Montoya Martinez and Julian Martinez (9.48), a burnished, shiny surface was combined with a subtle matte surface. The visual effect is dramatic despite the minimal textural variation. Geometric patterns enhance the surface of the jar but never compete with the purity of the graceful globe. On the other hand, Walter Oltmann's *Pillow* (9.49) is abuzz with texture. Hundreds of fragments of metal wire have been organized into a wide variety of textural units to create the oversized insect. In this case, the smoother areas on the extended legs contrast beautifully with the more compact textures on the wings and in the surrounding border. The result is a technical tour de force and a conceptual puzzle: Why is there a fly on my pillow?

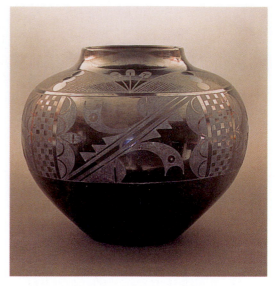

9.48 Maria Montoya Martinez and Julian Martinez, *Blackware Storage Jar*, 1942. Hopi, from San Ildefonso Pueblo, NM. Ceramic, 18¾ × 22½ in. (47.6 × 57.1 cm).

9.49 Walter Oltmann, *Pillow*, 2004. Aluminum wire, 40.9 × 39 × 9 in. (104 × 101 × 23 cm).

Characteristic and Contradictory Textures

Every material has its own inherent textural properties. Clay, glass, and metal can be poured, cast, or pressed to create a wide variety of textures. Gold, which may occur in nature as dust, in nuggets, or in veins, can be cast, hammered, enameled, and soldered. Despite the adaptability of most materials, however, we are accustomed to their being used in specific ways. The reflective surface of a steel teapot, the transparency of glass, and the earthy functionality of clay fulfill our expectations.

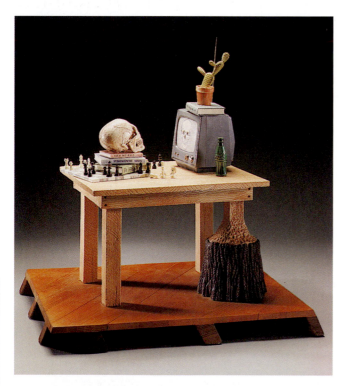

9.50 Richard Notkin, *Vain Imaginings*, 1978. White earthenware, glaze, brass, redwood, white cedarwood, 16 × 13½ × 16½ in. (40.6 × 34.3 × 41.9 cm).

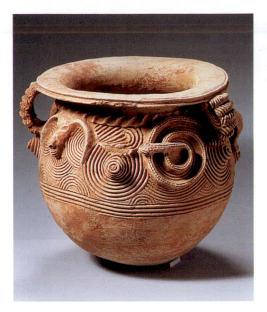

9.51 Globular vessel with inverted rim, tenth century, Igbo, Nigeria. Terra-cotta, 16 in. (40.6 cm).

9.52 Takako Araki, *Rock Bible*, 1995. Ceramic, silkscreen, 8¼ × 23⅝ × 16½ in. (21 × 60 × 42 cm).

When a material is used in an uncharacteristic way or when strange textures are added to familiar forms, we must reappraise both the material and the object it represents. Except for the wooden platform and brass screws, Richard Notkin's *Vain Imaginings* (9.50) is made of clay. The textures of wood, plastic, glass, and bone have been skillfully imitated. Clay is very unlike any of these materials, and a purist might argue that such mimicry violates its inherent nature. On closer examination, however, we can see a perfect match between the image and the idea. The table, which symbolizes the world, supports a chess set, which suggests risk, and a television set, which presents an illusion. The ceramic skull is placed on top of four books titled *The Shallow Life, Moth and Rust, Vain Imaginings*, and *By Bread Alone*. The image on the screen repeats the skull. The clay itself suggests impermanence (as in "he has feet of clay") and mortality (as in "earth to earth, dust to dust," which is often said during funerals). In this masterwork of metaphor, ceramicist Richard Notkin has created a "fake" sculpture for a false world.

The Implications of Texture

On a compositional level, texture can enhance or defy our understanding of a physical form. In figure 9.51, the lines carved into the surface of the vessel increase our awareness of its dimensionality. Concentric circles surrounding the knobs at the base of each handle create a series of visual targets that circle the globe, while additional grooves accentuate the surface of the sturdy handles. On a conceptual level, texture can add layers of meaning to art and design. In *Rock Bible* (9.52), Takako Araki used three kinds of texture to animate the artwork and expand its meaning. The words on the pages of the Bible provide one texture, the rough surface of the disintegrating book provides a second, and the inherent texture of the clay provides a third.

In summary, texture can increase the surface area of an object, add contrast, and enrich our understanding of the physical and conceptual qualities of any three-dimensional object.

Key Questions

TEXTURE

- How many textures can be created with the material you are using?
- What happens visually when a surface gradually shifts from a polished, smooth texture to a very rough texture?
- Can contradictory texture enhance or expand the idea you want to convey?

LIGHT

Light can enhance or obscure our understanding of form. It can entice us to enter a room, heighten our emotions, and create a mystery. It can even become a sculptural medium in its own right. Often overlooked, light is actually a pivotal aspect of three-dimensional design.

9.53 Daniel Chester French, *Head of Abraham Lincoln* (detail of seated figure), 1911–22. Full-size plaster model of head of marble statue, Lincoln Memorial, Washington, DC, 1917–18. Head 50½ in. (128.3 cm), total figure 19 ft (5.8 m) h.

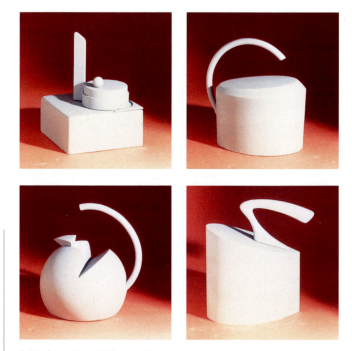

9.54 Stan Rickel, *Teapot Sketches*, 1991. Mixed mediums, 12 × 12 × 12 in. (30.5 × 30.5 × 30.5 cm).

Value and Volume

A gradated series of highlights and shadows is produced whenever light pours across a surface. These values, or variations in light and dark, are our primary means of perceiving space. As demonstrated by two views of Daniel Chester French's *Head of Abraham Lincoln* (9.53), a surface that appears flat when lit from the front can become spatially rich when lit from the top or sides. Product designers are equally aware of the importance of light. A badly lit form will lack definition and impact, while even the simplest form will attract attention when it is dramatically lit. In figure 9.54, highlights, gradations, and shadows give definition to each of Stan Rickel's *Teapot Sketches*.

Striking a Surface

Light is strongly affected by the substance it strikes. As demonstrated by the teapots, light creates a continuous series of values when it strikes an opaque surface. Light behaves very differently when it strikes a **transparent** surface, such as clear plastic or glass. It is often **refracted** (or bent), creating a complex network of luminous shapes. **Reflective** surfaces can bounce light back into space. As a result, objects that are made from polished steel, mirrors, and other reflective materials can appear to emit their own light. A **translucent** surface is partially transparent. Neither fully opaque nor fully transparent, translucent surfaces can be mysterious and evocative.

Each type of surface can be used expressively. *The Dance* (figure 9.2) is dominated by the movement of seven opaque figures in and out of space. Light and shadow accentuate the action of the exuberant dancers. The same composition would dissolve into visual chaos if it were cast in transparent glass. Cast shadows further expand expressive potential. In Ruth Asawa's sculptures (9.55), suspended organic forms seem to float through the silent space. Spotlights illuminate the sculptures and create mysterious cast shadows.

Translucent materials can create even more complex effects. Robert Irwin's *Part II: Excursus: Homage to the Square*[3] (9.56) was installed at the Dia Center for the Arts in New York in 1998–99. This structure consisted of nine cubic rooms, defined by delicate walls of translucent cloth. The translucency of the fabric varied depending on the amount and location of the light. Two vertical fluorescent lights illuminated each cube, creating subtle changes in color from room to room.

Entering the installation was both inviting and disorienting. From any point, all of the rooms were visible yet veiled. The layers of fabric and the variations in light made the most distant rooms appear to dissolve. The vertical fluorescent lights, which always remained visible, read first as individual, then as mirror, images, creating a hallucinatory experience similar to a carnival funhouse. All activity within the space was created by the visitors themselves, who entered, explored, and left the installation like ghostly silhouettes.

9.55 Ruth Asawa, *Exhibition at de Young Art Museum in San Francisco*, 2005.

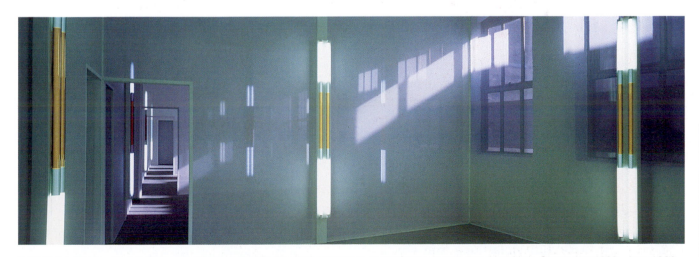

9.56 Robert Irwin, *Part II: Excursus: Homage to the Square³.* Installation at Dia Center for the Arts, New York, September 1998–June 1999.

Ambient and Directed Light

Ambient light encompasses an entire space or setting. For example, when we enter an open courtyard on a sunny summer afternoon, we are surrounded by warm ambient sunlight. Everything we see is colorful and brightly lit. **Directed light** is localized and focused, like a spotlight on a singer.

Exhibition designers are masters of light. They use directed light to focus the viewer's attention and increase visual drama. They use ambient light to create the underlying feeling. For example, the designers of a 1989 NASA exhibition used low ambient light to suggest the mystery of space travel. Bright pools of directed light were then used to emphasize individual displays (9.57).

Light as Sculpture

Many types of sculptural light are used by contemporary artists and designers. Some shape neon tubes into sculptural forms. Others use commercial lighting fixtures and illuminated signs to convey aesthetic meaning. Still others project light onto various shapes and surfaces, creating effects ranging from the humorous to the tragic to the bizarre.

Projection and containment are two common ways to create sculptural light. The neon tubes in Robert Irwin's *Excursus* emit light, while in Ruth Asawa's work light is projected to create expressive shadows. Stephen Knapp's light paintings (9.58) are created when light passes through shards of colored glass, creating a prismatic explosion. In all these cases, light is an essential component of the artwork.

The expressive possibilities increase when an image is projected onto a specific surface. On the anniversary of the bombing of Hiroshima, Krzysztof Wodiczko combined video interviews with a specific architectural structure—the A-Bomb monument, one of the few buildings that remained standing after the explosion (9.59). Standing near the epicenter, over 5,000 spectators heard the stories of Japanese and Korean survivors from World War II.

With the increasing use of new media, light has become an eloquent and versatile addition to the elements of three-dimensional design. Moving beyond its traditional role in accentuating form, it has become a sculptural medium in itself. For example, in *The Veiling* (9.60), Bill Viola hung thin sheets of translucent fabric on parallel lines across the center of a darkened room. An image of a man was projected from one end, while an image of a woman was projected from the opposite end. These projections became increasingly diffused as they passed through the multiple layers of cloth. Finally, the two figures merged on a central veil as pure presences of light.

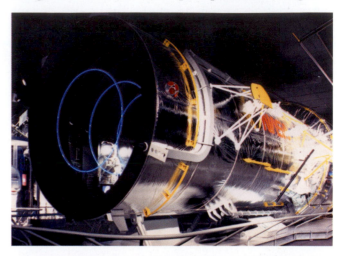

9.57 **NASA Exhibit at the 1989 Paris Air Show.** Designers: Bill Cannan, Tony Ortiz, H. Kurt Heinz. Design Firm: Bill Cannan & Co.

9.58 Stephen Knapp installing *First Symphony.*

Key Questions

LIGHT

- How can lighting direction diminish or accentuate the dimensionality of your artwork?

- Does your artwork require special illumination, such as an internal light source, fiber optics, or a video screen?

- How can light enhance the expressive content of your artwork?

- Can your project be redesigned to use light and shadow more effectively? If so, how?

9.59 Krzysztof Wodiczko, *Hiroshima Projection,* 1998. Public projection of video images at the A-Bomb Dome, Hiroshima, Japan.

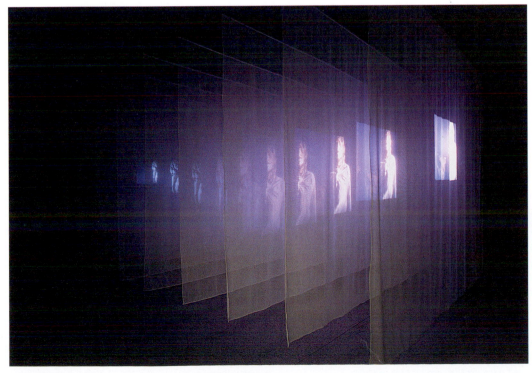

9.60 Bill Viola, *The Veiling,* 1995. Video/sound installation.

COLOR

Color definitions remain the same whether we are creating a three-dimensional or a two-dimensional composition. Each color has a specific **hue** (9.61A), which is determined by its wavelength. **Value** (9.61B), the lightness or darkness of a color, helps determine legibility. **Intensity,** or **saturation** (9.61C), refers to the purity of a color. **Temperature** (9.61D) refers to the psychological characteristics attributed to a color.

Degrees of Harmony

Selecting the right colors for a product and determining the degree of color **harmony** can make or break a design. The triadic harmony used in the Smartronics Learning System by Fisher-Price (9.62) creates an attractive educational toy for young children. The large red, yellow, and blue buttons are easy to push and invite even the most skeptical child to play. A very different type of harmony is offered in *Kita Collection*, by Toshiyuki Kita (9.63). These simple chairs with their removable seats can be color-customized to fit any interior. The buyer can create his or her own sense of harmony.

Analogous colors, such as green, blue, and violet, can be especially harmonious. In *Reflection* (9.64), Do Ho Suh used such colors to produce a mysterious mirrored image. The inverted gatelike form was combined with its reflected counterpart to create an installation that was both magical and meditative.

9.61A Hue.

9.61B Value.

9.61C Intensity.

9.61D Temperature.

Clashing colors can also be used effectively. In figure 9.65, Keith Edmier portrays his pregnant mother on the day President Kennedy was assassinated. She is wearing the same Chanel suit pattern that Jackie Kennedy wore, and she pensively rubs her glowing belly. The artist himself appears as a fetus in the womb. The orange-reds and purple-reds suggest traditional monochromatic harmony but seem skewed and off-key. While the surface of normalcy remained intact, the substance of American politics shifted after Kennedy's death. Likewise, while the artist's mother seems calm, the colors and materials used suggest an undercurrent of anxiety.

9.62 Smartronics Learning System by Fisher-Price.

9.63 Toshiyuki Kita, *Kita Collection* **of chairs with removable seats for Stendig International Inc.** Beechwood frame and upholstered seat.

9.64 Do Ho Suh, *Reflection*, 2004. Nylon and stainless steel tubing, dimensions variable.

Contrast

Artists and designers often use contrasting colors to accentuate the function of a product or to create a distinctive image. Contrasting colors and contrasting materials distinguish Michael Graves's *Alessi Coffee Set* (9.66). The fragile, transparent glass is protected by metallic armor. These metal bands emphasize the cylindrical forms, while the blue handles and bright red accents further animate the set.

Using natural materials in natural settings, Andy Goldsworthy often creates intense areas of red, green, or gold to alert the viewer to junctions, boundaries, or unusual configurations between objects in the landscape. These accents of color are especially powerful when the surrounding colors are subdued. In figure 9.67, scarlet leaves dramatically distinguish the central stone from its somber gray neighbors.

Color and Emotion

The emotional implications of color can be demonstrated by a visit to any car dealership. Bright red, black, or silver sports cars are often marketed as

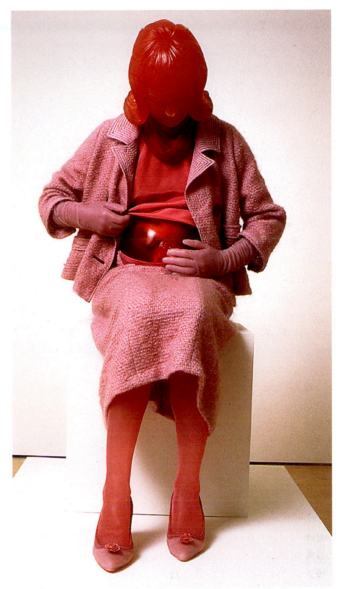

9.65 Keith Edmier, *Beverly Edmier, 1967*. Cast resin, silicone, acrylic paint, fabric.

9.66 Michael Graves, *Alessi Coffee Set*. Glass, silver, mock ivory, and Bakelite.

oversized toys for single drivers, while more subdued colors are often used for the minivans and station wagons favored by families. In figure 9.68, color is used to add a sporty look to quite a different vehicle. This children's wheelchair gives the user a psychological boost while encouraging the development of physical strength and dexterity. On the other hand, it is the absence of color that brings power to the life-size figures in George Segal's installations. Despite their proximity to the viewer and their large scale, the white figures in *Walk, Don't Walk* (9.69) are drained of color, alienated, and emotionally distant.

9.67 Andy Goldsworthy, Red Rock, 1989. Leaves and stones.

Symbolic Color

Symbolic color is culturally based. Because each culture is unique, color associations vary widely. For example, yellow signifies the direction north in Tibet but represents the qualities of light, life, truth, and immortality to Hindus.[4] Blue represents mourning in Borneo, while in New Mexico it is painted on window frames to block the entrance of evil spirits. Blue represented faith and truth to the Egyptians yet was the color worn by slaves in Gaul.[5]

The blue face that dominates the mask of the Aztec god Tlaloc in figure 9.70 is both symbolically and visually appropriate. Symbolically, the blue represents sky and the rain that Tlaloc calls forth to nourish crops. Visually, the contrast between the warm, reddish clay and the sky-blue paint enhances the impact of the ferocious face.

Key Questions

COLOR

- Which will better communicate your ideas—a limited range of hues or a wide range of hues?

- Are all the colors in your design similar in intensity? What would happen if you combined low-intensity colors with high-intensity colors?

- What is the proportion of warm and cool colors in your design—is it around 50/50? 70/30? 20/80? What would happen if these proportions were changed?

- What are the conceptual or symbolic implications of the colors you have chosen?

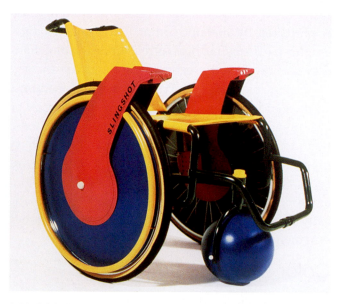

9.68 Adele Linarducci, *Slingshot Wheelchair,* 1989. Polystyrene, vinyl, PVC, and other materials. A nonworking model created while the artist was a student at Rochester Institute of Technology.

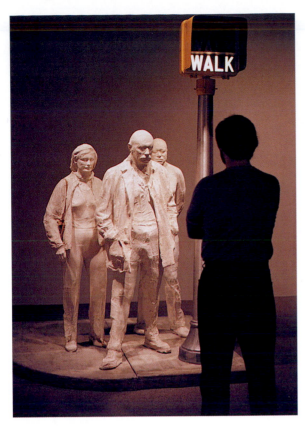

9.69 George Segal, *Walk, Don't Walk,* **1976.** Museum installation, with viewer. Plaster, cement, metal, painted wood, and electric light, 104 × 72 × 72 in. (264.2 × 182.9 × 182.9 cm).

9.70 **Ritual Vessel Depicting Mask of Tlaloc, Aztec, Mexico, Tenochtitlán, 1400–1521.** Ceramic, 13.8 × 13.8 × 12.4 in. (35 × 35 × 31.5 cm).

TIME

Every object occupies a position in time as well as space. In some cases, the specific temporal location is of minor importance. For example, *Locking Piece* (see figure 9.36A and B, page 197) is as meaningful now as it was when constructed in 1963. Formalist in approach, it makes no specific reference to social or political events. Constructed from durable bronze, it has effectively withstood the test of time. In other cases, temporal location gives the object its meaning. As noted on page 192, Nancy Holt's *Sun Tunnels* creates a kind of celestial observatory. Light pours through the holes in the curving walls, creating projections that mark the movement of the planets. Without the element of time, the concrete tunnels would have no more meaning than drainage pipes at a construction site.

Two aspects of time are particularly important to sculptors. **Actual time** refers to the location and duration of an actual temporal event. For example, it takes less than a minute for the bowling ball to roll down the ramps in Tinguely's *Chaos 1* (see figure 9.3, page 181). By contrast, **implied time** is the suggested location or duration of an event. The traffic light in Segal's *Walk, Don't Walk* changes, but the sculptural figures never move.

Actual motion and implied motion are equally important. In a brilliant use of actual time, actual motion, and natural forces, Ned Kahn constructed *Wind Veil* (9.71) from 80,000 aluminum panels. Activated by each breath of wind, the wall shimmers with both energy and light. By contrast, *Shuttlecocks* (9.72), by Claus Oldenburg and Coosje van Bruggen, seems to capture the oversize game pieces just as they begin to hit the ground. In this case, the artwork depends on implied time and motion for its impact. A final example combines time and motion with anticipation. Positioned alongside Michigan Avenue in Chicago's Millennium Park, Jaume Plensa's *Crown Fountain* (9.73) attracts thousands of visitors each summer day. Smiling images of everyday people from various city neighborhoods are projected on the multiple video screens contained within each five-story tower. Every 15 minutes, the projected face purses its lips and a stream of water

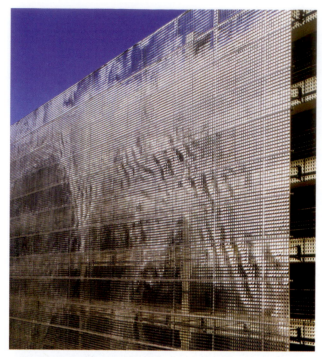

9.71 Ned Kahn, *Wind Veil,* **2000.** 80,000 aluminum panels, total length 260 ft (79.25 m). Installation in Charlotte, North Carolina.

9.72 Claes Oldenburg and Coosje van Bruggen, *Shuttlecocks,* **1994.** Aluminum, fiberglass-reinforced plastic, and paint. 230⁹⁄₁₆ × 191⅞ in. (585.63 × 487.36 cm).

9.73 Jaume Plensa, *Crown Fountain,* **2000–04.** Glass, stainless steel, LED screens, light, wood, granite, and water, two 52½-ft-high towers, total area 7,217 ft² (2,200 m²).

bursts forth, drenching the delighted children waiting below.

Viewing time is a final basic consideration. The multiple surfaces presented by any three-dimensional object require extended analysis. We walk around Rodin's *The Kiss* (figure 9.10A and B, page 185), noting every nuance in form and texture; we rotate a ceramic vessel in our hands, savoring every detail. *The Board Room* (see figure 9.11, page 185), *Part II: Excursus* (see figure 9.56, page 207), and other installations require even more viewing time. To understand the artwork, the viewer must enter and fully explore the site.

Key Questions

TIME

- Is a "timeless" or a "timely" artwork more appropriate for the idea you want to communicate?

- What compositional choices can you use to increase timelessness?

- How can actual, implied, or viewing time expand meaning in your design?

SUMMARY

- *Form* may be defined as the physical manifestation of an idea. *Content* refers to the idea itself, including the subject matter plus its emotional, intellectual, spiritual, and symbolic implications.

- In three-dimensional design, *form* also refers to dimensionality itself. Thus, a circle is a shape, while a sphere is a form.

- The first step in creating a design is to understand its purpose. A sculptor seeks to convey ideas and express emotions. A craftsperson or designer is equally concerned with the function and the beauty of an object.

- Height, width, and depth are the three dimensions in three-dimensional design. Orthographic projection provides a means of clearly drawing these dimensions.

- Artworks can vary in dimensionality from relief, which uses a flat backing to support dimensional forms, to environmental works that the viewer can enter and physically explore.

- A line can connect, define, or divide a design. It can be static or dynamic, increasing or decreasing the stability of the form.

- A plane is a three-dimensional form that has length and width but minimal thickness.

- In three-dimensional design, *volume* refers to an enclosed area of three-dimensional space.

- A mass is a solid three-dimensional form. A massive object can be as dense and heavy as a bar of gold or as light and porous as a sponge.

- Space is the area within or around an area of substance. Space is the partner to substance. Without it, line, plane, volume, and mass lose both visual impact and functional purpose.

- *Texture* refers to the visual or tactile quality of a form. The increased surface area of a three-dimensional form heightens the impact of texture.

- Light can enhance our perception of a three-dimensional form, attract an audience, or be used as a material in itself. Light behaves very differently when it hits a reflective or translucent surface.

- Hue, value, intensity, and temperature are the major characteristics of color.

- Every object occupies a position in time as well as space. Actual time, implied time, actual space, and implied space can be combined in various ways to create compelling objects of great complexity.

KEY TERMS

actual lines	work (or environment)	intensity	polyhedra	static forms
actual time	form	kinetic forms	positive forms	symbolic color
ambient light	freestanding works	line	primary contours	temperature
content	function	mass	reflective	texture
continuity	geometric forms	mechanical forms	refracted	three-quarter work
directed light	harmony	negative space	relief	translucent
direction	hue	organic forms	saturation	transparent
dynamic forms	implied lines	orientation	secondary contours	value
earthwork	implied time	orthographic projection	sight line	viewing time
elements	installation	plane	site-specific	volume
environmental			space	

STUDIO PROJECTS

To apply the concepts from this chapter in the studio, check out the Projects page in the Online Learning Center at www.mhhe.com/stewart4e. The following is a sample of the chapter-related assignments that are described in step-by-step detail.

Calderesque Self-Portrait. A linear project using wire.
Spheres of Influence #1 and #2. Planar construction problems.
Discovering Mass. Modeling an object using foam rubber and carving a form from a plaster block.
Dominant and Subordinate. Exploring hierarchical composition.

Profile:
Todd Slaughter, Sculptor
Materials and Metaphors

Todd Slaughter was born in Memphis, Tennessee, in 1942. After majoring in chemistry and then in mathematics, he transferred into the art program at the University of Texas, where he earned a BSA (Bachelor of Science in Art) degree. He subsequently earned a master's degree in industrial design at Pratt, in New York City, and is now a professor in the sculpture program at The Ohio State University. He has had solo shows at the Wexner Center for the Arts, PS 1, and the Chicago Cultural Center, and his major commissions include *Mano y Bola* near Algeciras, Spain.

MS: Abstract forms dominated your early work. For the past 15 years, you have shifted more toward representational and narrative work. What is the advantage of each approach?

TS: There is a simple beauty in formal relationships. Like music, lines, planes, volumes and spaces can be organized into wonderful and expressive visual patterns. However, as I have gotten older, I have become more attuned to human relationships and more interested in the power of metaphor. Representational imagery helps the viewer understand the metaphor in a specific way.

MS: Your use of materials is especially distinctive. Many of your works have been constructed using graphite, sulfur, salt, paprika, and turmeric. Why use these unusual materials?

TS: They carry meanings and references that I want my artwork to reflect. I am especially interested in transience. Nothing is permanent; even the most massive chunk of steel changes over time. When I cast a thousand pounds of salt to create a full-sized sofa and then place it in a steam room, or set two opposing graphite fists in motion grinding each other to a powder (figure 12.28, page 275), the rate of change becomes accelerated and highly visible.

MS: I'm fascinated by your use of everyday objects, such as hats and domestic objects such as sofas, chairs, and houses.

TS: I want to create the strongest, most personal connection possible between the audience and the artwork. Transforming known objects has become more effective for me than introducing forms that are outside of common experience. I am interested in exploring complex relationships within this world rather than in creating an escape into an alternative world.

MS: I'd like to highlight one of your most ambitious projects. Can you describe it to us?

TS: *Mano y Bola (Hand and Ball)* is a large-scale, permanent sculpture. It is installed on El Cabrito Ridge overlooking the Strait of Gibraltar and the coast of Morocco, Africa, seven miles from the Port of Algeciras, geographically the first Spanish port on the Mediterranean Sea. The sculpture was commissioned by the Port to mark its 200th anniversary, in conjunction with Galeria Magda Bellotti.

The hand is a double flat-sided structure, measuring 27 × 40 × 4 ft with a painted photographic image of an open hand on one side and its mirror image on the other. The surface of each side is made up of 1,116 movable panels that swing out horizontally when activated by a breeze. The ball is approximately 20 ft in diameter. It rotates very slowly, suggesting a line that is being drawn continuously.

MS: How did you develop the idea?

TS: In 1992 I was an artist in residence near the Strait of Gibraltar, in Manilva, Spain. The idea of a large artwork located within the landscape came to me as I was driving through southern Spain. To my surprise and delight at several locations, I came upon 30- to 40-ft-high, charging black bull silhouettes as I drove around a bend or over a rise. These were actually advertising signs with no text—the logo for a liquor company. While standing near the future site of my artwork and looking across the Strait at the city of Tangier, Morocco, my thought was to somehow create a temporary artwork addressing the historic and ongoing cultural, religious, and economic interaction of Europe and Africa in this region. The implied action of the hand—catching and throwing—metaphorically alludes to the history of exchange of religion, art, and power between the European and African continents.

MS: It seems remarkably dynamic for such a large sculpture.

TS: Yes, I hope so! During most day hours, the sculpture appears almost transparent and ephemeral due to its sky-blue color and the sky-revealing transformations of both hand and ball produced by variations in wind velocity. When backlit by the sun, the hand and ball become part of the silhouette of the ridge.

Todd Slaughter, *Mano y Bola* (details), 1997. Aluminum and steel, hand 27 × 40 × 4 ft (8.2 × 12.2 × 1.2 m), ball 20 ft (6 m) diameter. Overlooking the Strait of Gibraltar.

chapter ten

Principles of Three-Dimensional Design

Composition can be defined as the combination of multiple parts into a unified whole. In a well-composed design, all the elements work together as a team. A dialogue is created between positive and negative forms, and opposing forces add vitality rather than causing confusion. Each compositional part makes a positive contribution to the unified whole. Graceful metal lines have been combined with a series of contoured masses to create the elegant and utilitarian form of Niels Diffrient's *Freedom Chair* (10.1). In Alice Aycock's *Tree of Life Fantasy* (see figure 10.9, page 222), line, plane, and space have been combined to create an exuberant dance. Martin Puryear's *Seer* (10.2) consists of a closed volume at the top and an open volume at the bottom. The horn-shaped

10.1 Niels Diffrient, *Freedom Chair,* **1999.**
Die-cast aluminum frame with fused plastic coating; four-way stretch black fabric.

10.2 Martin Puryear, *Seer,* **1984.** Water-based paint on wood and wire, 78 × 52¼ × 45 in. (198.2 × 132.6 × 114.3 cm).

top piece is powerful and imposing, while the open construction at the bottom invites us to enter and visually explore the structure. A series of curving vertical "ribs" unifies the top and bottom sections, while the contrast between open and closed forms adds a touch of mystery. In all three cases, every element is both dependent on and supportive of each other element.

The elements of design are the building blocks from which compositions are made. The principles of design describe the ways these building blocks can be combined.

UNITY AND VARIETY

Unity can be defined as similarity, oneness, togetherness, or cohesion. **Variety** can be defined as difference. Unity and variety are the cornerstones of composition.

Increasing Unity

We tend to scan an entire composition, then analyze the individual parts. A composition composed of units that are unrelated tends to appear random and unresolved. Evidence of deliberation and order tends to increase unity. As we will see in this section, grouping, containment, proximity, continuity, repetition, and closure are six common strategies for increasing order.

Grouping

When presented with a collection of separate visual units, we immediately try to create order and make connections. **Grouping** is one of the first steps in this process. As noted in the discussion of Gestalt psychology in Chapter Three, we generally group visual units by location, orientation, shape, and color. *Towards the Corner* (10.3), by Juan Muñoz, clearly demonstrates grouping by location. We first see a complete composition, comprised of seven figures. It is roughly triangular in shape, starting with the single seated figure on the right and extending to the standing figure at the far left. The division between the two sets of bleachers creates two subgroups, comprised of two figures on the right and five figures on the left. We can further group the three figures seated on the top bleachers and the three figures seated on the bottom, with the single standing figure providing a visual exclamation point for the sculpture as a whole.

10.3 Juan Muñoz, *Many Times*, 2000. Seven figures, wood, resin, and mixed mediums, 6¾ × 12½ × 3¾ ft (2.1 × 3.79 × 1.13 m).

10.4 Roni Horn, *How Dickinson Stayed Home,* **1993.** Installation. Solid aluminum and plastic. 26 cubes, each 3 × 3 × 3 in. (7.6 × 7.6 × 7.6 cm).

10.5A Louise Nevelson, *Wedding Chapel IV,* **1960.** Painted wood, height approx. 9 ft (2.7 m).

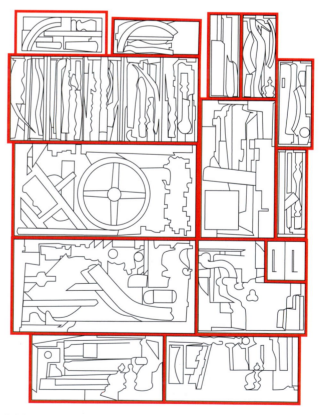

10.5B Line drawing of Figure 10.5A, showing containers in red and overall continuity in black.

10.6 Aaron Macsai, *Panels of Movement.* Bracelet, 18K gold, sterling, copper, ⅞ × 7 in. (2 × 18 cm).

Containment

Containment is a unifying force created by the outer edge of a composition or by a boundary within a composition. A container encourages us to seek connections among visual units and adds definition to the negative space around each positive form. The room itself provides the container for Roni Horn's *How Dickinson Stayed Home* (10.4). Letters from the alphabet are presented on 26 small cubes. Like Emily Dickinson's poetry, the installation is both economical and expansive. A minimal amount of information evokes a wide range of interpretations. Contained by the white walls and dark floor of the room itself, the blocks create a unified statement, despite their seemingly random distribution.

Proximity

In design, the distance between visual units is called **proximity.** Even the most disparate forms can become unified when they are placed in close proximity. For example, Louise Nevelson constructed *Wedding Chapel IV* (10.5A) from an improbable collection of wooden crates, staircase railings, dowels, chair legs, and other scrap. Organized into 14 rectilinear containers and placed in close proximity, the various pieces have become unified into a lively whole.

Continuity

Continuity can be defined as a fluid connection among compositional parts. When objects are placed in close proximity, continuity often happens naturally. As demonstrated by figure 10.5B, each form in *Wedding Chapel IV* touches several other forms. As a result, our eyes move easily from section to section, increasing the connections among the parts.

10.7 Zac Freeman, Detail of *Steve,* **2006.** Found objects on board, 60 × 48 in. (152 × 122 cm).

Repetition

Repetition occurs when we use the same visual element or effect any number of times within a composition. In Aaron Macsai's *Panels of Movement* (10.6), similar lines, shapes, textures, and colors were used in each of the 10 panels from which the bracelet was constructed. A spiral shape, a wavy line, a sphere, and at least one triangular shape appear repeatedly. Despite their variations in size, texture, and location, these repeated forms create a strong connection from panel to panel.

Closure

Closure is the mind's inclination to connect fragmentary information to produce a completed form. In Zac Freeman's *Steve* (10.7), we must visually connect hundreds of washers, screws, and other hardware to create a man's face. Closure makes it possible to communicate using implication. Freed of the necessity to provide every detail, the artist or designer can convey an idea through suggestion rather than description. When the viewer completes the image in his or her mind, it is often more memorable than an explicit image.

Combining Unifying Forces

James Ingo Freed used all of these unifying forces to create the *Tower of Photos* in the Holocaust Memorial Museum in Washington, DC (10.8). His design team wanted to demonstrate the number of lives lost in one Polish village while honoring the individuality of the inhabitants. They collected and framed thousands of photographs, including groups of schoolchildren, weddings, and family snapshots. Placed in close proximity, the photographs personalize the victims while emphasizing their connection to the lost community. Based on the chimneys used to burn the bodies of the dead, the tower itself provides the dominant framework for the exhibition, both structurally and emotionally.

Increasing Variety

Difference in any aspect of a design increases variety. By reviewing the elements of design described in Chapter Nine and the principles of design described in this chapter, you can quickly create a checklist of areas for variation, such as

- *Line variation.* Lines of different diameter were combined with double linear "train tracks" in Aycock's *Tree of Life Fantasy* (10.9).

- *Variation in texture.* Combining smooth and textured surfaces can add energy and interest to even the simplest form.

- *Variation in pattern.* The Pacific island mask shown in figure 10.10 is unified through symmetrical balance. This underlying order freed the artist to experiment with many colors and patterns.

Degrees of Unity

As noted in Chapter Eight, our compositional choices must support our conceptual intentions. Some designs require a high level of unity. For example, Eva Hesse's *Accession II* (10.11) consists of a single cube. Dramatic contrast between the methodical exterior and the fiercely textured interior is the only significant variation. Other designs require a high level of variety. The lines, shapes, volumes, and masses in Judy Pfaff's *3-D* (10.12) ricochet off the floor, walls, and ceiling with an almost chaotic energy.

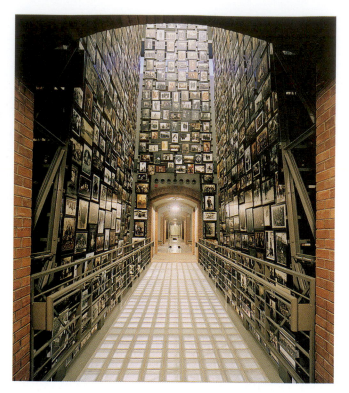

10.8 *Tower of Photos* **from Ejszyszki, completed in 1993.** United States Holocaust Memorial Museum, Washington, DC. James Ingo Freed, lead designer.

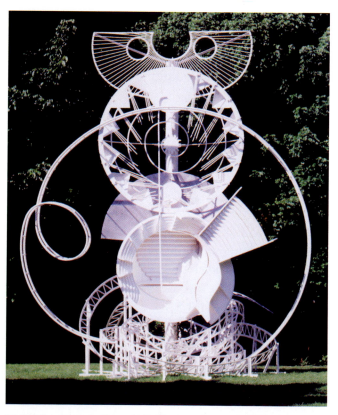

10.9 Alice Aycock, *Tree of Life Fantasy,* **Synopsis of the Book of Questions Concerning the World Order and/or the Order of Worlds, 1990–92.** Painted steel, fiberglass, and wood, 20 × 15 × 8 ft (6.1 × 4.6 × 2.4 m).

10.10 Mask (Wanis), New Ireland. 37 × 20⅞ × 19 in. (94 × 53 × 48.3 cm).

10.11 Eva Hesse, *Accession II,* 1967. Galvanized steel, rubber tubing, 30.5 × 30.5 × 30.5 in. (77 × 77 × 77 cm).

10.12 Judy Pfaff, *3-D,* 1983. Mixed mediums, installation in a 22 × 35 ft (6.71 × 10.67 m) room.

10.13 Leonardo Drew, *Number 56*, 1996. Rust, plastic, wood, 113 × 113 in. (287 × 287 cm).

Grid and Matrix

A **grid** is created through a series of intersecting lines. A **matrix** is a three-dimensional grid. Both can unify a design by creating containment, continuity, and proximity.

In *Number 56* (10.13), Leonardo Drew poured rust into hundreds of plastic bags, which were then connected to a wooden support. The rust and the methodically numbered plastic bags create a dialogue between the orderly grid and the decaying metal. This combination of order and disorder balances monotony with mystery.

Daniel Buren's *The Two Plateaus* (10.14) offers another variant on the grid. This public art project, located in the Palais Royal in Paris, covers a 1,000-square-foot plaza. The striped cylinders range in height from about 2 to 5 feet. Mimicking the columns in the building and organized on the pavement like players on a checkerboard, they bring both energy and humor to the site.

10.14 Daniel Buren, *The Two Plateaus*, 1985–86. 1,000-square-foot sculpture for the Cour d'Honneur, Palais Royal, Paris. Black marble, granite, iron, cement, electricity, water.

Key Questions

UNITY AND VARIETY

- What strategies have you used to unify your composition?
- What gives your composition variety?
- Is the balance between unity and variety appropriate for the ideas you want to express?
- What would happen if your composition were constructed using a grid or matrix?
- How can space be used to increase unity or increase variety?

BALANCE

Balance refers to the distribution of weight or force among visual units. Like physical balance, visual balance requires equilibrium in size, visual weight, and force. Visual balance can be created through the absence as well as the presence of form. And, as figure 10.15 demonstrates, balance and dynamism are interconnected.

There are three major types of balance. In **symmetrical balance,** forms are mirrored on either side of a central axis. The resulting form generally is physically and visually stable. The central face in figure 10.16A is an example of symmetrical balance.

With **radial symmetry,** design elements extend out from a central point, like the spokes of a wheel. Radiating in all directions while remaining anchored at the center, this type of balance tends to generate a great deal of energy while retaining a high level of unity. The outer ring in figure 10.16 is an example of radial balance. The diagram in figure 10.16B shows both of these forms of symmetry.

Asymmetrical balance creates equilibrium among visual elements that do *not* mirror each other on either side of an axis. Depending on the degree of asymmetry, the resulting design may be quite stable, very dynamic, or nearly chaotic.

10.16A Bella Coola Mask Representing the Sun, from British Columbia, before 1897. Wood, diameter 24¾ in. (63 cm).

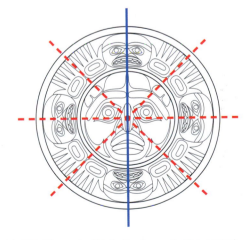

10.16B Diagram of Bella Coola mask. The central face is symmetrically balanced. The outer ring is an example of radial symmetry.

10.15 Claes Oldenburg and Coosje van Bruggen, *The Typewriter Eraser,* 1998–99. MGM Mirage, Las Vegas. Aluminum, fiberglass, urethane paint, size variable.

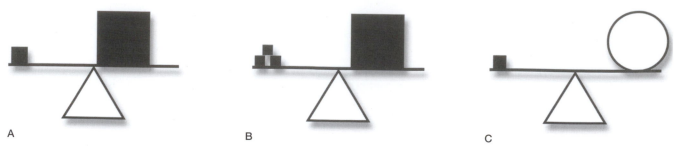

A   B   C

10.17A–C Examples of asymmetrical balance.

Many strategies can be used to create asymmetrical balance:

- A large form is placed close to the fulcrum, while a small form is placed farther away. Just as a child at the end of a seesaw can balance an adult near the center, so large and small forms can be balanced in a design (10.17A).

- Multiple small forms can balance a single large form (10.17B).

- A small, solid form can balance a large, open form. The solidity and stability of the square give it visual weight as well as physical weight (10.17C).

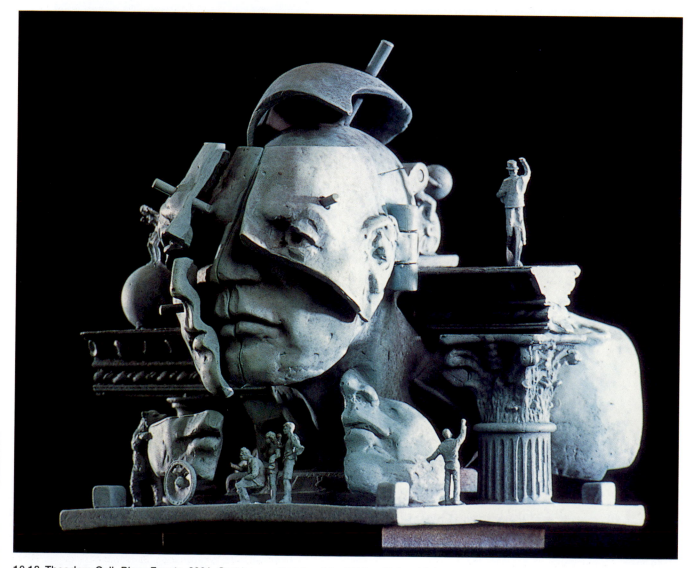

10.18 Theodore Gall, *Plaza Facets*, **2001.** Cast bronze, 6 × 6 × 6 in. (15.2 × 15.2 × 15.2 cm).

Most artworks are constructed from multiple parts. Size variations among the parts affect both the physical balance and the expressive impact. A **dominant,** or primary, form is often balanced by one or more **subordinate,** or secondary, forms. For example, in Theodore Gall's *Plaza Facets* (10.18), the large head on the left is balanced by the column and fragmentary heads on the right. The seven smaller figures create yet a third compositional level. Using these compositional hierarchies, artists and designers can create unified designs from distinctly individual parts.

Two contrasting interpretations of a single figure further demonstrate the expressive power of balance. St. Bruno, an eleventh-century Catholic saint, is shown in figures 10.19 and 10.20. His followers, known as the Carthusian Order, lived in caves and devoted their time to manuscript transcription, meditation, and prayer.

The first statue, completed by Michel-Ange Slodtz in 1744, dramatizes a pivotal moment in Bruno's life. Preferring his contemplative existence to the power and prestige of a more public life, Bruno rejects promotion to the office of bishop. Slodtz used asymmetrical balance to express this dramatic moment. The small bishop's hat, offered by the angel in the lower-right corner, is the focal point of the entire sculpture. The much larger figure of St. Bruno recoils when confronted by this symbol of authority. As a result, the small hat matches the saint in compositional weight.

A very different interpretation of the life of St. Bruno is given in the second sculpture. Completed by Jean-Antoine Houdon in 1766, it emphasizes the contemplative nature of the Carthusian Order and its founder. Using symmetrical balance, Houdon presents a dignified, introspective man. If we divide the figure in half from top to bottom, the two sides basically mirror each other. This saint is a philosopher, very much at peace with the choices he has made. Just as asymmetrical balance is appropriate for the dramatic moment represented by Slodtz, so symmetrical balance is ideal for the serenity shown by Houdon.

10.19 Michel-Ange Slodtz, *St. Bruno*, 1744. Marble.

10.20 Jean-Antoine Houdon, *St. Bruno of Cologne*, 1766. Stucco.

Exaggerated weight or buoyancy can shift the balance in an artwork and expand meaning. In Chuichi Fujii's *Untitled* (10.21), a cedar log seems to have been crushed by the weight of a second log. At the other extreme, Patricia A. Renick's *Life Boats/Boats About Life* (10.22) seems to float on air, as weightless as a dream. Dramatic lighting and cast shadows heighten the magical effect. This artwork derives its power from the denial of gravity, while figure 10.21 derives its power from exaggerated gravity.

10.21 Chuichi Fujii, *Untitled*, 1987. Japanese cedar, 10 ft 6 in. × 13 ft ½ in. × 11 ft 6 in. (320 × 400 × 350 m).

Key Questions

BALANCE

- Which form of balance is most appropriate to the ideas you want to express?

- Which is the dominant form in your composition? Is its dominance conceptually justified?

- What happens when an unexpected part of the design plays the dominant role?

- How does space affect compositional balance?

10.22 Patricia A. Renick, *Life Boats/Boats About Life*, 1979–80. 1 to 1½ ft high × 5 to 6½ ft long × 1 to 1½ ft deep (30.5 to 45.7 m high × 152.4 to 198.1 m long × 30.5 to 45.7 m deep).

SCALE AND PROPORTION

Scale

Scale commonly refers to the size of a form when compared with human size. Using our body as a constant, we can identify three major types of scale relationships. Small-scale objects can be **handheld,** while **human scale** refers to designs that are roughly our size. Very large objects and installations are **monumental** in scale.

Returning to Theodore Gall's sculpture (Figure 10.18, page 226), we can explore the implications of each scale type. The actual artwork is roughly 6 × 6 × 6 inches and can be handheld. At this scale, we are invited to enter and explore the artwork mentally rather than physically (10.23A). At triple this size (18 × 18 × 18 in.), the dominant head in the design would be about the size of our own head (10.23B). This would create a very different dialogue between the audience and the artwork. Expanded to monumental scale—say, 32 × 32 × 32 feet—the artwork would invite physical entry (10.23C). We could now stand beside the sculptural figures in the piece. Simply by changing the scale, the artist could create three very different responses to the same composition.

Proportion

Proportion refers to the relative size of visual elements *within* an image. When we compare the width of the head with its height, or divide a composition into thirds, we are establishing a proportional relationship.

In industrial design, changes in proportion can enhance or diminish function. The five gardening tools in figure 10.24 are all based on the same basic combination of handle, blades, and a simple pivot. Variations in proportion determine their use. The short-handled pruner in the lower-left corner is used to trim twigs and small branches from shrubs. It must fit comfortably in a single hand. The proportions of the lopper in the lower-right corner are much different. Its 20-inch-long handle provides the leverage needed to cut heavier branches from small trees. For the industrial designer, function often determines proportion.

In sculpture, variations in proportion can increase aesthetic impact. Three proportional variations on Constantin Brancusi's *Bird in Space* are shown in figures

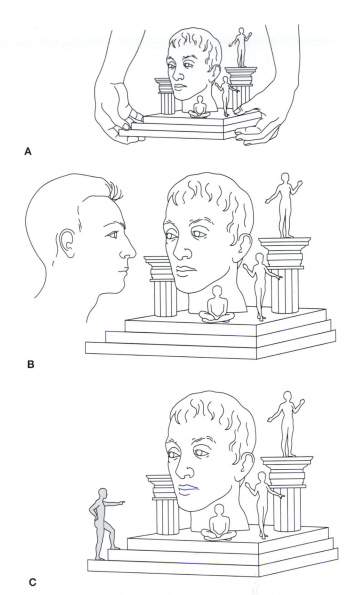

A

B

C

10.23A–C Scale variations, from handheld to monumental.

10.24 Home Pro garden tool line. Designers: James E. Grove, John Cook, Jim Holtorf, Fernando Pardo, Mike Botich. Design Firm: Designworks/USA.

10.25 Constantin Brancusi, *Maiastra,* **1912.** Polished brass, 29⅞ × 7¼ × 7½ in. (75.7 × 18.5 × 19 cm).

10.26 Constantin Brancusi, *Golden Bird,* **1919, Pedestal c. 1922.** Bronze, stone, and wood, 37¾ in. (95.9 cm), base 48 in. (121.9 cm).

10.27 Constantin Brancusi, *Bird in Space,* **1928.** Bronze (unique cast), 54 × 8½ × 6½ in. (137.2 × 21.6 × 16.5 cm).

10.25 through 10.27. In *Maiastra* (10.25), the abstract bird form is dominated by the egg-shaped torso, which tapers into the folded wings at the bottom and the raised head at the top. This bird is approximately 3 times taller than it is wide. Brancusi further abstracted *Golden Bird* (10.26) and elongated the body. The bird is now 7 times taller than it is wide, and an elaborate base adds even more height to the sculpture. With *Bird in Space* (10.27), Brancusi elongated the form even more and added an expanding "foot" below the folded wings. This bird is almost 10 times taller than it is wide. By lengthening the columnar structure in this final version and carefully tapering the sculpture near the base, Brancusi made this simple sculpture fly.

As with all design decisions, choosing the right scale and proportion greatly increases expressive power. Giovanni Bologna's *Apennine* (10.28) is scaled to overwhelm the viewer with a sense of the mountain spirit's presence. His human frame is monumental, and the surrounding trees and cliff appear to diminish by comparison.

Proportional extremes can be equally expressive. Less than 5 feet tall, Alberto Giacometti's *Chariot* (10.29) offers a somber analysis of the human condition. The solitary figure is delicately balanced on gigantic wheels, which rest on two small pedestals. The entire form is linear, as if distilled down to the barest essentials. Both the chariot and the life it transports are precariously balanced and seem fragile and vulnerable.

Key Questions

SCALE AND PROPORTION

- What would happen to your composition if you dramatically changed its scale?

- What would happen conceptually if you dramatically changed its proportions?

- Imagine that your design can be stretched or compressed in any direction. What are the advantages of a very tall, thin composition compared to a short, cubic composition?

- How does a change in proportion affect overall balance?

10.28 Giovanni Bologna, *Apennine*, 1580–82. Stone, bricks, mortar. Villa di Pratolino, Florence region, Italy.

10.29 Alberto Giacometti, *Chariot*, 1950. Bronze, 57 × 26 × 26⅛ in. (144.8 × 65.8 × 66.2 cm).

EMPHASIS

Emphasis gives particular prominence to part of a design. A **focal point** is a compositional device used to create emphasis. For example, the bishop's hat in Slodtz's version of St. Bruno (figure 10.19, page 227) is the focal point of the composition. Both emphasis and focal point are used to attract attention and increase visual and conceptual impact.

Emphasis by Isolation

Any **anomaly,** or break from the norm, tends to stand out. Because we seek to connect the verbal and visual information we are given, a mismatched word or an isolated object immediately attracts attention. In *I Never Liked Musical Chairs* (10.30), metalsmith Joana Kao established the norm through

10.30 Joana Kao, *I Never Liked Musical Chairs.* Bracelet, sterling, 24K, 2¾ × 1¾ in. (7 × 4 cm).

seven tiny chairs connected by a silver chain. The figure at the end of the chain breaks the pattern. This break conveys the isolation felt by a child who has been ejected from the game.

Emphasis Through Contrast

Contrast is created when two or more forces operate in opposition.

By reviewing the elements and principles of design discussed thus far, we can quickly create a long list of potential adversaries, including static/dynamic, smooth/textured, small/large, and curvilinear/rectilinear. When the balance is just right, powerful compositions can be created from any such combination. Many artists and designers devote most of their compositional area to one force and a much smaller amount to a contrasting force. The larger force sets the standard, while the smaller force creates the exception.

Contrast can appear in many forms and in varying degrees. In Arnaldo Pomodoro's *Sphere Within Sphere* (10.31), the imposing spherical form seems to have been eaten away by an external force, revealing a pattern of rectilinear teeth and a second sphere within. This creates a strong contrast between the massive structure and the invading space.

In *Plan, Prepare, Execute* (10.32A and B), Liza Lou also used contrast to suggest the metamorphosis

10.31 Arnaldo Pomodoro, *Sphere Within Sphere*, **1965.** Bronze, 45 × 46½ × 47⅝ ft (114.2 × 118.1 × 121.0 m). Dublin, Ireland.

of an existing structure into a new configuration. It is hard to tell whether the dominant field of dark gray is "eating" or "being eaten" by the colorful patterns around the edge and the lines at the bottom. This uncertainty makes the artwork even more intriguing.

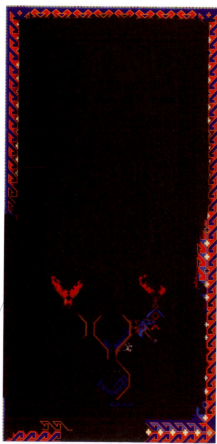

10.32A and B Liza Lou, *Plan, Prepare, Execute*, **2007–08.** Glass beads on aluminum panel, 120 × 60 in. (305 × 152 cm).

A Full View

B Detail

Loops (10.33), by Mary Ann Scherr, presents a contrast between movement and constraint. A curving plane encircles the wearer's throat, providing protection but restricting motion. Below, the suspended rings sway with every movement of the body, creating a dynamic counterpoint to the constraining collar.

Water animates Pol Bury's *Fountains at Palais Royal* (10.34). The design relies on three major elements. The site itself is dominated by the regularly spaced columns so characteristic of neoclassical architecture. The polished steel spheres, poised within the bowl of each foundation, reflect these columns and the shimmering water, the third element in the design. In a sense, the spheres serve as mediators between the rigid columns and the silvery water. Like the columns, they are simple volumes arranged in a group. Like the water, they seem fluid as they reflect the rippling pool and the passing clouds. In this project, unity and variety have been combined to create an elegant and ever-changing sculpture.

10.33 **Mary Ann Scherr,** *Loops,* **1988.** Sterling silver neckpiece, 8½ × 4¾ × 5 in. (21.6 × 12.1 × 12.7 cm).

Key Questions

EMPHASIS

- Is there a focal point in your composition? If not, should there be?

- What is the most prominent form in your composition? Is it the form you most *want* to emphasize?

- What would happen to your composition if you dramatically increased the amount of contrast?

10.34 **Pol Bury,** *Fountains at Palais Royal,* **Paris, 1985.**

REPETITION AND RHYTHM

As noted at the beginning of this chapter, repetition occurs when we use the same visual element or effect any number of times within a composition. **Rhythm** can be defined as the organization of these multiple elements or effects into a deliberate pattern. Just as a musician creates a deliberate pattern by connecting sound and silence, so the artist can create rhythm using positive form and negative space.

Percussive variations also create rhythm. For example, when every fourth beat is accented in a musical composition, a clear rhythm emerges. Repeated accents in an artwork have a similar effect. And the number of beats within a given space creates the **tempo,** or rate of change. In David Watkins's *Torus 280 (B2)* (10.35), the large circular shapes create a slow, regular pattern. Increasing the number of circles would accelerate the tempo.

Rhythm plays an even greater role in figure 10.36. The woven herringbone pattern at the bottom suggests first clockwise then counterclockwise visual movement. A similar pattern at the top accentuates spatial depth. Tapered rectilinear shapes create a border around both the interior and the exterior edges. Like a complex musical piece, three types of rhythm have been skillfully woven together.

The multiple views offered by physical objects accentuate the importance of rhythm. The movement of four women around an exuberant musician creates a joyous dance in Jean-Baptiste Carpeaux's *The Dance* (10.37). Our eyes follow the turning heads, clasped hands, and swirling arms as they move in, out, and around in space. A similar rhythm animates Steve Woodward's *Model of Proposal for Concourse Commission* (10.38). The plywood vortex seems to rise out of the floor to collect in a spinning disk at the top, and then descend again, in perpetual motion.

10.35 David Watkins, *Torus 280 (B2)*, 1989. Neckpiece, gilded brass, 11 in. (28 cm).

10.36 Tanija & Graham Carr, *Untitled*, 2001. Wet-formed leather, acrylic paint, 13¾ × 29¼ × 29¼ in. (35 × 74 × 74 cm).

10.37 Jean-Baptiste Carpeaux, *The Dance (After Restoration)*, 1868–69. Marble, 7 ft 6½ in. (2.3 m).

10.38 Steve Woodward, *Model of Proposal for Concourse Commission*, 1987. Wood, 13¾ × 8 × 7½ in. (34.9 × 20.3 × 19 cm).

10.39 Magdalena Abakanowicz, *Standing Figures (30)*, 1994–99. Bronze, overall 54 ft 3 in. × 19 ft 8 in. (16.55 × 6 m).

10.40 Tomb of Emperor Shih Huang Ti, 221–206 BCE. Painted ceramic figures, life-size.

When combined with the spinning effect, this up-and-down movement gives the design great vitality.

Repetition is often used to increase compositional unity. It can also be used to quantify an elusive idea. For example, the 30 statues in Magdalena Abakanowicz's *Standing Figures (30)* (10.39) are unified by their similarity in size, shape, and solemnity. Variations in each cast bronze surface provide a degree of individuality. Often interpreted as victims of war, the hollow, headless figures seem frozen in time, offering silent testimony to a tragic past. The 6,000 clay soldiers filling the tomb of Emperor Shih Huang Ti (10.40) demonstrate a different use of repetition. As he faced his death, the emperor may have sought companionship or protection from his army. Sherrie Levine's *La Fortune* (10.41) demonstrates a third use of repetition. Our sense of reality is challenged when we encounter these six pool tables. The identical arrangement of the balls seems impossible: the balls would be randomly distributed in six actual games. Here, a very ordinary scene becomes mysterious, even nightmarish, due to the inexplicable repetition.

Key Questions

REPETITION AND RHYTHM

- Try repeating any element in your design. What does this repetition contribute, conceptually and compositionally?

- What happens when simple repetition is changed to specific rhythm?

- Does the rhythm remain constant in your design, or is there a change in tempo? What is the advantage of each approach?

10.41 Sherrie Levine, *La Fortune (After Man Ray)* 1–6, 1990. Felt, mahogany, resin, 33 × 110 × 60 in. (84 × 280 × 153 cm).

SUMMARY

- Through composition, we can combine multiple parts to create a unified whole.

- Grouping, containment, proximity, continuity, repetition, and closure are six common strategies for increasing unity. Difference in any aspect of a design increases variety.

- A grid is created through a series of intersecting lines. A matrix is a three-dimensional grid.

- Symmetry, radial symmetry, and asymmetry are three common forms of balance. A dominant, or primary, form is often balanced by one or more subordinate, or secondary, forms.

- Scale and proportion are two types of size relationships. Proportion refers to size relationships within an image, while scale involves a size comparison with our physical size.

- Emphasis gives prominence to a specific part of a design. A focal point is a compositional device often used to create emphasis.

- Contrast is created when two or more forces operate in opposition. Many artists and designers devote most of their compositional area to one force and a much smaller area to a contrasting force. The larger force sets the standard, while the smaller force creates the exception.

- Repetition occurs when we use the same visual element or effect any number of times within a composition. Rhythm is the organization of these multiple elements or effects into a deliberate pattern. Just as a musician creates a deliberate pattern connecting sound and silence, so the artist can create rhythm using positive form and negative space.

KEY TERMS

anomaly	contrast	human scale	rhythm
asymmetrical balance	dominant	matrix	scale
balance	emphasis	monumental	subordinate
closure	focal point	proportion	symmetrical balance
composition	grid	proximity	tempo
containment	grouping	radial symmetry	unity
continuity	handheld	repetition	variety

STUDIO PROJECTS

To apply the concepts from this chapter in the studio, check out the Projects page in the Online Learning Center at www.mhhe.com/stewart4e. The following is a sample of the chapter-related assignments that are described in step-by-step detail.

Negative and Positive. Creating a dialogue between substance and space.
Three-Dimensional Balancing Act. Increasing compositional complexity, using curvilinear and rectilinear forms.
Myths and Masks. Working with many elements of 3-D design to create a wearable mask for a new ceremonial occasion.

Profile:
Marilyn da Silva, Metalsmith
Metals and Metaphors

Professor Marilyn da Silva is program chair of the Jewelry/Metal Arts Department at California College of the Arts in Oakland. She was selected as "Master Metalsmith 1999" by the National Ornamental Metal Museum in Memphis, Tennessee, and her work has been displayed nationally and internationally, including at the Victoria and Albert Museum in London and the National Gallery of Australia.

MS: What is it that attracts you to metal?

MdS: I really love the resistance and permanence of metal. It only changes when I work it very deliberately: this gives me more control. If dropped, it will dent, but it will not break. It is inherently a "cool" medium, but using patinas and colored pencils, I can make metal appear "warm."

MS: How did you get started in this field?

MdS: From a very young age, I was always making things, such as furniture and clothing for my dolls. Working with my hands just came naturally. Other children enter into art through drawing; I entered through construction.

MS: You studied with Alma Eikerman, a particularly renowned metalsmith. What did you learn from her?

MdS: Alma emphasized both excellent craft and excellent design. She expected impeccable work: there were no excuses for weaknesses in either area. In one assignment, we made a black paper silhouette of our teapot body shape. We then designed 20 variations on handles and spouts using black paper. We then tried different combinations of handles, spouts, and pots, seeking the best solution. It sounds simple, but by generating dozens of variations, we were able to find the ideal combination.

MS: Your designs are charged with meaning. Please take us through your conceptual and compositional development of *Reap What You Sow.*

MdS: I designed this piece for a show devoted to pillboxes. The concept was based on three premises: (1) my recent discovery that I was allergic to penicillin, (2) the alarming amount of antibiotics in the foods we eat every day, and (3) the need for many to go over the border to acquire affordable prescriptions.

I did many drawings and decided to have a bird land on furrows found in fields. The bird would either be stealing a pill in its mouth or be placing it in the furrow. On all of my book pieces, the "leather" of the book turns into something else. In this case, it becomes the dirt and furrows of a field. I then selected the barn swallow as the bird of choice. It was an obvious solution because of its name "swallow" and the fact that this bird often builds its nest in barns, placing it in a farm environment.

The furrows have young plants sawed out of copper. If you look closer, you can see that the leaves look like small hands. The shadows of the hands are grasping at pills lying on the ground.

The book is made from heavy-gauge copper that has been hammered to give it texture. I used red oak flooring for the pages. The bird is carved out of basswood and has wings, feet, eyes, and beak made of metal. All of the metal parts of the book are colored with gesso and colored pencil. The title of the book, *Reap What You Sow: A Prescription for Life*, is etched into a brass plate and riveted to the book spine. Finally, an antique silver spoon with the name "Grove" on it props up the book in the corner. You know, "just a spoon full of sugar helps the medicine go down . . . ."

MS: Conceptually, what do you seek in your work?

MdS: My artworks are layered with meaning. The viewer first sees the basic form and may respond to the beauty of the metal. Upon reflection, he or she may be drawn in by the storytelling and conceptual associations inherent in the work. For example, my *Rock, Paper, Scissors* refers to a children's game that is based on power dynamics and unpredictability. Likewise, *Reap What You Sow* can be read on many personal and environmental levels.

I avoid in-your-face polemics. It is better for viewers to respond to the work on the basis of their own experiences, and then return to the work for a second viewing.

Marilyn da Silva, *Reap What You Sow: A Prescription for Life,* 2004. Copper, sterling silver, brass, wood, plastic, gesso, colored pencil.

Materials and Methods

An incredible range of materials and methods can be used to produce three-dimensional objects. Paper, metal, fibers, clay, and plastic are among the most versatile materials used by artists and designers; folding, casting, carving, weaving, and stamping are just a few of the production methods. A separate course specifically devoted to materials would be needed if we were to explore this subject in depth.

The purpose of this chapter is more pragmatic. As a beginner, you need both practical advice and a basic introduction to the aesthetic implications of various materials. We begin with a discussion of the essential characteristics of all materials, then consider ways in which contemporary artists use both traditional and nontraditional materials. The last section provides an overview of basic materials commonly used in three-dimensional design courses.

CHOICE OF MATERIALS

Each material has specific strengths and limitations. For example, rubber cement is a temporary adhesive for ordinary paper, while white glue is a permanent adhesive for heavier paper and cardboard. Carpenter's glue works well for wood, while hot glue is an effective adhesive for assemblage materials. Misuse of any material can ruin a great design. By understanding the physical characteristics of common materials, we can produce better work in less time and at less cost. The following considerations are crucial:

- *Strength.* How much weight can a given material support? What is its breaking point when it is twisted, folded, or bent?

- *Workability.* How difficult is it to alter the shape of a material? Does it cut and bend easily? Can it be melted and cast or dripped to create a new form?

- *Durability.* What range of forces can this material withstand and for how long? Is it impervious to heat, water, wind, and ultraviolet light?

- *Weight.* A material that is too light for a given purpose can be as problematic as a material that is too heavy. What is the function of the project, and how can material weight best serve that function?

- *Cost.* Can the material chosen be obtained easily and at a reasonable cost? If your budget is limited, you may have to remove expensive materials from consideration.

- *Toxicity.* Many plastics produce toxic gases when they are cut, etched, or burned. Paints and solvents may require the use of masks and gloves and often present significant disposal problems. Is the ventilation of your workplace appropriate for your work process? Are less toxic materials available? How will you dispose of toxic waste?

- *Function.* How appropriate is a given material for a particular purpose? A teapot will be useless if the material used is porous, and a chair that is too difficult to construct can never be mass-produced. The material chosen must serve the structural and aesthetic needs of the object you design.

Increasing Material Strength

Composites

A **composite** is created when two or more materials of differing strengths are fused together. Fiberglass (which combines glass filaments with plastic resin) and ferro-concrete (which is made from metal mesh embedded in concrete) are familiar examples. Foamcore (which is made from a sheet of polystyrene sandwiched between sheets of coated paper) and duct tape (constructed from three layers of "skin") are composites that are commonly used in three-dimensional design classes. Composites are often used when light weight, low cost, and increased strength are required.

Structural Strength

After millions of years of experimentation, nature has developed an amazing array of effective structures. Two major types are skeletons and exoskeletons. A **skeleton** (or **endoskeleton**) provides the internal structure needed by mammals and fish, while insects and many sea creatures rely on an external **exoskeleton** for support.

Architects are masters of both skeletal and exoskeletal structures. In *Guggenheim Museum Bilbao* (11.1), architect Frank Gehry created a complex "skeleton" to support the building's gleaming titanium skin. The Gothic cathedral in figure 11.2 demonstrates the use of an exoskeleton. To increase building height while reducing mass, medieval

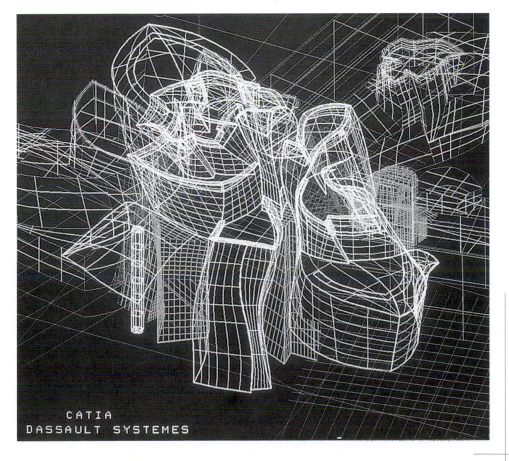

11.1 Computer-generated Catia image used for the Solomon R. Guggenheim Museum Bilbao, finished 1997.

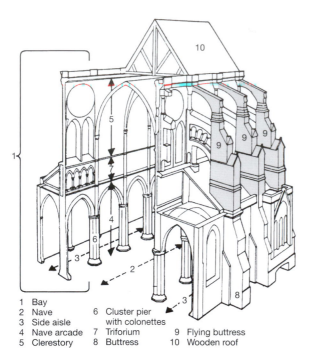

11.2 Perspective diagram and cross-section of Chartres Cathedral, 1145–1220.

1 Bay
2 Nave
3 Side aisle
4 Nave arcade
5 Clerestory
6 Cluster pier with colonettes
7 Triforium
8 Buttress
9 Flying buttress
10 Wooden roof

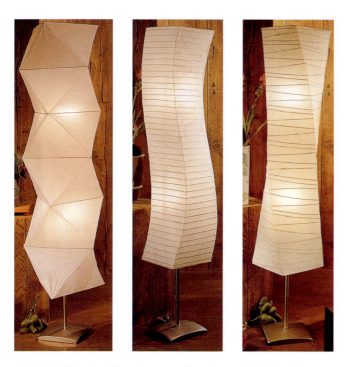

11.3 Shoji Design. Three Japanese floor lamps. Steel, bamboo, paper, size variable.

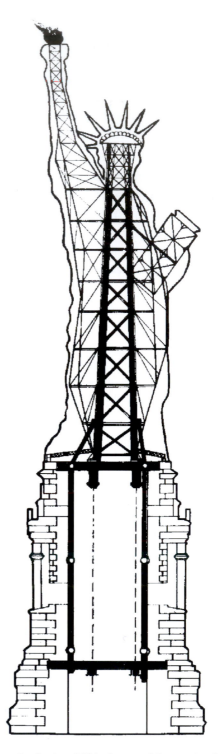

11.4 Alexandre-Gustave Eiffel, diagram of the construction of the Statue of Liberty.

architects developed the **flying buttress** used in hundreds of cathedrals throughout Europe.

Artists and designers often use an **armature** to create internal structure. For example, a wire or wooden armature is often used to support the cloth or paper in lampshades. Designers from around the world have created an amazing range of variations on this simple object (11.3). Engineer Alexandre-Gustave Eiffel developed a much more elaborate armature to support Auguste Bartholdi's *Statue of Liberty* (11.4). Standing over 150 feet tall and weighing 225 tons, this monumental sculpture has to withstand wind, rain, and brisk sea winds. Without a strong internal structure, the statue could never have been built.

Distributing Force

As shown in figure 11.5A–E, the five major forces are compression, tension, bend, torque, and shear. **Compression** occurs when a material is pushed inward; **tension** occurs when a material is pulled outward; direct pressure at one point causes a material to **bend**; **torque** is a twisting motion; **shear** can occur when force is applied to the opposite sides of a material.

The equilateral triangle is the linear shape that best resists deformation caused by each of these forces, and the tetrahedron, or pyramid, is the strongest three-dimensional form. A triangular support, such as a corner brace on the back of a painting, can distribute force effectively and greatly increase strength. On a larger scale, a network of crossbeams in Thorncrown Chapel (11.6) adds both strength and beauty to a sacred space.

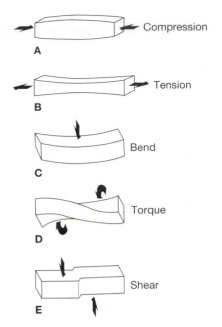

11.5A–E Major physical forces.

11.6 E. Fay Jones & Associates, Thorncrown Chapel, Eureka Springs, Arkansas, 1981.

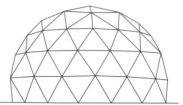

11.7 R. Buckminster Fuller, U.S. Pavilion, Expo-67, Montreal, 1967.

11.8 Joseph Cornell, *Untitled (Medici Princess)*, c. 1948. Construction, 17⅝ × 11⅛ × 4⅜ in. (44.8 × 28.3 × 11.1 cm).

R. Buckminster Fuller's geodesic dome (11.7) expands this idea even further. Typically constructed using hundreds of tetrahedrons, the dome is relatively easy to build and creates a large volume using a minimal amount of mass. A model of beauty and efficiency, the geodesic dome has been widely used for large, open buildings such as greenhouses and exhibition spaces.

Methods of Construction

Compositional choices are strongly influenced by the method of construction. The two most common methods are addition and subtraction.

In **additive sculpture,** the artwork is created from separate parts that have been connected, usually using glues, joints, stitching, or welds. **Assemblage** is one additive method. Using objects and images originally designed for another purpose, Joseph Cornell created a whole series of evocative box structures (11.8). Many of these assemblages were designed to honor specific people, past and present. **Modeling** is an additive process often used by ceramicists. Pinching and pushing the pliable clay, skillful ceramicists can make both functional and sculptural objects of great complexity. To create his *Head Series* (11.9), Jean-Pierre Larocque stamped slabs of clay with various textures from cloth, then

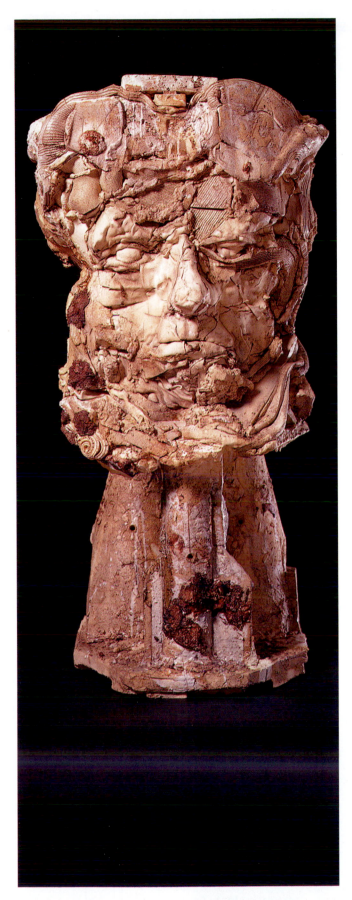

modeled and carved a head that is both activated and imposing.

In **subtractive sculpture,** the artist removes materials from a larger mass. Carving, drilling, cutting, and turning on a lathe are all subtractive processes. The Tlingit man shown in figure 11.10 follows a methodical process, beginning by drawing on the cedar pole, making a rough cut, then refining and finishing the totem pole.

Plastic and metal forms are often produced using two additional methods. In **solidification,** a liquid material is poured into a mold or extruded through a pipe, then allowed to harden. For example, when we squeeze cake frosting through a shaped nozzle, we can create a wide range of extruded forms. This same basic principle can be applied to materials that are more permanent and less tasty. In **displacement,** a solid material is physically forced into a new configuration. The stamping process used to mint coins is a familiar example of displacement.

Key Questions

CHOICE OF MATERIALS

- Test the limits of the materials you plan to use. Note especially their strength, workability, toxicity, and cost.
- Are there "greener" materials that you might use for your project?
- Make a model from an unfamiliar material. Does it offer any conceptual or technical advantages over the material you usually use?

11.9 Jean-Pierre Larocque, *Untitled (Head Series),* **2002.** Stoneware, 36¾ × 21 in. (93.3 × 53.3 cm).

11.10 Tlingit totem carver, 1996. Southeast Alaska.

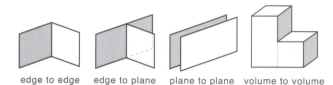

edge to edge   edge to plane   plane to plane   volume to volume

edge to edge   edge to plane   plane to plane   mass to mass

11.11A Examples of connections through contact.

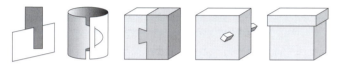

11.11B Examples of connections through junctions.

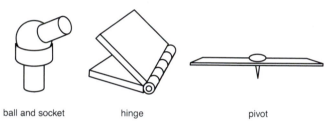

ball and socket   hinge   pivot

11.11C Examples of connections through joints.

CONNECTIONS AND TRANSITIONS

Connections

Physical and visual connections are equally important in three-dimensional design. Visual connections compositionally unify multiple surfaces, while physical connections can increase strength, flexibility, functionality, and stability. Most commonly, connections are made

- Through *contact* (11.11A)
- Through *junctions* (11.11B)
- Through *joints* (11.11C)

Physical connections are especially important to woodworkers. Carpenters and furniture designers learn dozens of specific joints, hinges, and splices. Mary Miss's *Staged Gates* (11.12A) was largely constructed using three types of joints (11.12B). The use of nails, screws, bolts, or glue is required when lap or butt joints are used. Interlocking joints can often create a simple connection without such additional reinforcement.

11.12A Mary Miss, *Staged Gates,* 1979. Wood, 12 × 50 × 120 ft (3.6 × 15.2 × 36.6 m).

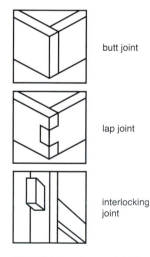

butt joint

lap joint

interlocking joint

11.12B Three types of joints.

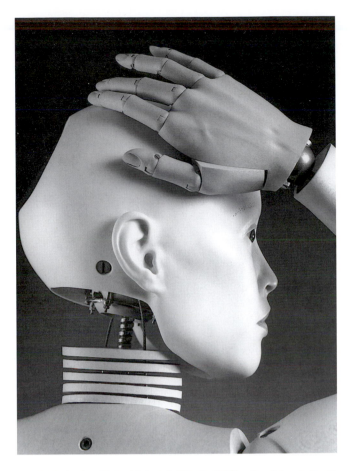

11.13 Katherine Wetzel (photo), Elizabeth King (sculpture), *Pupil* from *Attention's Loop,* **1987–90.** Porcelain, glass eyes, carved wood, brass, one-half life size.

Employed to create functional objects, industrial designers pay particular attention to all types of connections. Because of the various joints used in its construction, a simple camera tripod can be expanded or collapsed, and the top can be rotated and reoriented. A sculpture based on the human figure (11.13) presents an even wider array of possibilities. Ball-and-socket joints at the shoulders and hips create rotating forms, while hinge joints in the fingers, knees, and elbows permit a folding and unfolding movement.

Visual connections are just as important as physical connections. A split yellow-orange circle dominates the center of John Okulick's *Wind Wizard* (11.14). Through closure, we mentally connect the halves, despite their physical separation. A second broken circle echoes the interior circle and creates a dynamic boundary for the composition as a whole. The two gold spheres at the upper left and lower right seem poised for movement. Every form is connected to at least one other form, enhancing overall continuity in the design.

Transitions

Many types of transitions can be created in three-dimensional design. The various angles and joints in Eduardo Chillida's *Asbesti Gogora III* (11.15)

11.14 John Okulick, *Wind Wizard,* **1987.** Painted wood, gold leaf, oil stick, 22 × 25 × 6 in. (55.9 × 63.5 × 15.2 cm).

11.15 Eduardo Chillida, *Asbesti Gogora III,* **1962–64.** Oak, 81½ × 136⅜ × 73⅛ in. (207.3 × 346.4 × 184.2 cm).

11.16 Liv Blåvarp, *Bird,* 1991. Neckpiece, bird's-eye maple, satinwood, whale tooth, 12½ × 10¼ in. (32 × 26 cm).

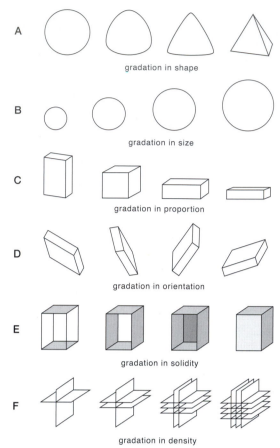

A — gradation in shape

B — gradation in size

C — gradation in proportion

D — gradation in orientation

E — gradation in solidity

F — gradation in density

11.17A–F Examples of gradation.

create an abrupt transition from surface to surface, while a fluid transition helps unify the various sections of Liv Blåvarp's *Bird* (11.16). Fluid transitions are often created through gradual change from one form or surface to another. Such **gradation** creates sequential change within a consistent pattern. Examples of gradation are shown in figure 11.17A–F.

Key Questions

CONNECTIONS AND TRANSITIONS

- How can physical and visual connections enhance the strength of your artwork?

- Which type of transition is most appropriate to the idea or emotion you wish to convey?

- What happens when two or more types of transitions are used in a single artwork?

TRADITIONAL AND TRANSFORMATIVE MATERIALS

Stone

Limestone, basalt, marble, and other dense, fine-grained stones have been used since prehistory to create durable and imposing objects. Handheld stone amulets have been worn to ward off evil, while monumental sculptures, such as Mount Rushmore and the pyramids at Giza, have been constructed to commemorate political and spiritual figures as well as religious beliefs. Using chisels, mallets, and rasps, stone carvers can create remarkably delicate forms with an amazing array of textures.

In *Blind Man's Bluff* (11.18), Louise Bourgeois used traditional methods to make a very contemporary statement. Spherical and cylindrical forms seem to bubble up from the lower half of the sculpture. They are capped by a block of rough stone.

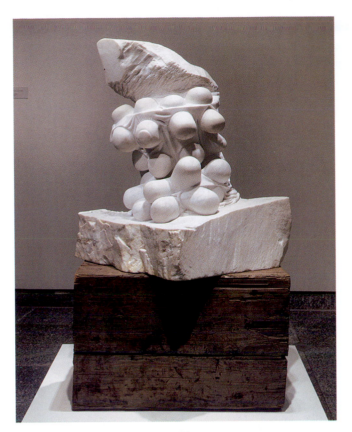

11.18 Louise Bourgeois, *Blind Man's Bluff*, 1984. Marble, 36 × 35½ × 25 in. (91.4 × 90.2 × 63.5 cm).

11.19 Virgil Ortiz, *Untitled*, 2002. Cochiti red clay, white and red clay slip, black (wild spinach) paint, 28 × 29 in. (71 × 74 cm).

This contrast, which Bourgeois describes as "polarization," creates tension between the animated and sexually suggestive forms and the intractable stone cap. Surrounded by sexual promiscuity as a child, Bourgeois has often described the emotional blindness she developed as a coping strategy.

Clay

Clay is perhaps the most basic and versatile of all materials. Essentially made from refined earth, it can be hand-formed using coil, slab, and carving techniques; poured into molds; and "thrown," using a potter's wheel. When fired, it becomes extremely durable and can be decorated with beautiful colored glazes.

All of these qualities are fully exploited by contemporary ceramicists. Born into a family of traditional Cochiti potters, Virgil Ortiz began making pottery at the age of six. Creating a fusion between traditional Native American methods and contemporary life, Ortiz combines bold surface decoration with animated figurative forms (11.19). The malleability of clay is strongly evident in Jean-Pierre Larocque's *Head Series* (see figure 11.9, page 245). Adding and subtracting textural layers, Larocque combined the fluidity of gesture drawing with the solidity of fired clay. Carving into "leather-hard" clay, David MacDonald (see Profile, page 260) activates his simple forms with parallel and intersecting bands of texture.

Metals

Bronze casting, refined during the Renaissance, has traditionally been used for large-scale sculptures of all kinds. Gold, silver, copper, pewter, and brass are more commonly used for jewelry and utensils. Most metals can be cast, forged, soldered, etched, and stamped.

Mariko Kusumoto used copper, nickel silver, sterling silver, resin, bronze, and brass to create *Tansu no Oku* (11.20). A lotus blossom, seashells, butterflies, and an open hand extend out from an etched sheet of

11.20 Mariko Kusumoto, *Tansu no Oku.* Copper, nickel silver, sterling silver, resin, bronze, and brass, 15½ × 14 × 14 in. (39.4 × 35.6 × 35.6 cm) open.

turn-of-the-century advertisements. A plastic resin adds color and sparkle to the butterflies. The structure is based on a children's pop-up book, while the images recall the Victorian fascination with mechanical and natural objects.

John Paul Miller's *Dung Beetle Pendant Brooch* (11.21) was also inspired by nature. Both the lowly beetle and its ball of dung are transformed by exquisite construction and the extensive use of gold.

Wood

Traditional cultures worldwide use wood to create functional structures, such as buildings, furniture, and utensils, as well as sculptural objects,

11.21 John Paul Miller, *Dung Beetle Pendant Brooch*, 1984. Gold fabricated, granulated, and enameled, 2¾ × 1¾ × ⅝ in. (7 × 4.5 × 1.5 cm).

such as masks, ancestor poles, and walking sticks. Readily available in most areas, wood is inherently beautiful, easily painted, relatively lightweight, and surprisingly versatile. It can be carved, steam-formed, and assembled using various hinges and joints. Traditional examples of wood sculpture are shown on pages 246, 247, and 248. Figure 11.22 demonstrates the power of wood in a nontraditional setting. Constructed from pliable strands of bamboo, Patrick Dougherty's large-scale artwork seems to arise directly from nature.

Glass

Glass, which is made primarily from silica, has been used for containers of all kinds since the time of the pharaohs. It can be transparent or opaque and, with the addition of copper, cadmium, cobalt, and other materials, can take on a complete range of colors. In its molten state, it can be poured, blown, pressed into molds, drawn into threads, stamped, and extruded.

The transparency of glass is emphasized in Eric Hilton's *Innerland* (11.23). Constructed from 25 cubes of clear glass, the sculpture appears to shift with each change in the viewer's position. Hilton combined the transparency and brilliance of glass with its density and mass to create an evocative artwork.

Gene Koss's *Hay Loader* (11.24) transforms a piece of farming equipment into a sculpture that is both fragile and imposing. Because we know that the heavy sheets of glass will shatter if the tower topples, the entire sculpture is charged with energy.

Fibers

The term *fibers* covers a wide range of linear materials, including strips of willow, bamboo, and reeds, as well as the more familiar cotton, linen, silk, and wool. Like the other traditional materials, fibers have been used for basketry, quilts, clothing, and other commonplace objects, as well as for prayer rugs and ritual clothing from shrouds to wedding dresses. Most fibers can be painted or dyed and can be worked in many ways, including weaving, braiding, knotting (as with macramé), knitting, and felting. Nick Cave's *Soundsuit* (11.25) combines technical

11.22 Patrick Dougherty, *Untitled*, 1992. Bamboo, height 25 ft (7.6 m), diameter 10 ft (3 m). Temporary installation.

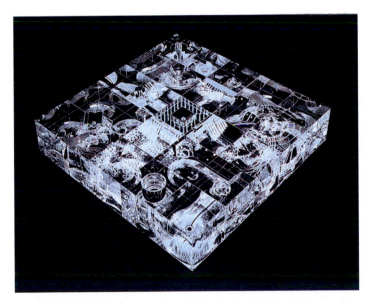

11.23 Eric Hilton, *Innerland*, 1980. Engraved by Ladislav Havlik, Lubomir Richter, Peter Schelling, and Roger Selander, cut by Mark Witter. Cast, cut, engraved, sandblasted, and polished, 3⅞ × 19⅜ × 19⅜ in. (9.9 × 49.3 × 49.3 cm).

mastery with whimsical inventiveness. Used in both solo and group performances, it creates various sounds as the dancer moves.

11.24 Gene Koss, *Hay Loader,* **2006.** Cast glass, steel, and neon, 13 × 2 × 10 ft (4 × 0.61 × 3 m).

11.25 Nick Cave, *Soundsuit,* **2009.** Mixed mediums, 90 × 40 × 32 in. (229 × 102 × 81 cm).

Three qualities most distinguish contemporary fibers. First, the traditional separation between sculpture and fiber arts has largely disappeared. As demonstrated by *Red Forest* (see figure 9.26, page 193), fibers are often used for large-scale designs. Second, the definition of *fibers* has become increasingly broad. For example, Cathy Strokowsky wove together glass, wire, artificial sinew, and horsehair to create *Glass Pod with Hair,* shown in figure 11.26. Third, the relationship between fiberworks and the human body continues to evolve through performance art and installations.

Plastics

Transparent, translucent, or opaque, plastics can be formed into sheets and then cut and assembled. Many types of plastic can also be extruded, cast, vacuum-formed, and stamped. Lightweight, varied in color, and relatively cheap to produce, plastics have fueled a revolution in the design and distribution of household products.

Using a variety of plastics, Ron Mueck has created many large-scale sculptures of human figures. One of the most compelling is *The Boy* (11.27), installed in London's Millennium Dome. The crouching adolescent boy seems vulnerable and defensive, despite (or perhaps because of) his enormous size. As with all of Mueck's work, the details are astounding: every hair is defined, and the eyes seem to glisten with moisture as well as apprehension.

Ephemeral Materials

One of the most notable characteristics of postmodern art is its emphasis on concept combined with a de-emphasis on traditional materials and methods. Many artists today deliberately use **ephemera** (materials that rapidly decay) or trash (which is already in a state of decay). In some cases, the transient nature of the material is part of the concept; in other cases, conceptual punch simply trumps material value.

11.26 Cathy Strokowsky, *Glass Pod with Hair,* **2001.** Blown glass, sandblasted, woven artificial sinew, wire, horsehair, 4¾ × 12½ × 4¾ in. (12 × 31.75 × 12 cm).

11.27 Ron Mueck, *The Boy,* **1999.** Site-specific work installed in the Mind Zone at the Millennium Dome, London, United Kingdom. Mixed media, 16.8 × 16.8 × 7.9 ft (490 × 490 × 240 cm).

11.28 Ernest Daetwyler, *Time Bomb (Im Hölzernen Himmel)*, 2008. Old furniture parts, steel substructure, 11.8 ft (3.6 m) diameter.

Time Bomb (11.28) by Ernest Daetwyler is a dramatic example. Constructed from fragments of broken furniture supported by a steel armature, the nearly 10-foot-tall sphere is ominous and imposing. Precariously balanced and displayed in a lovely forest, this time bomb seems on the verge of exploding.

Tara Donovan uses commonplace materials in a very different way. From hundreds of mass-produced cups, drinking straws, plastic forks, and other lightweight materials, she creates elegant structures and installations that seem to defy their humble origins. The installation shown in figure 11.29 suggests both cloud formations and biological structures.

Rick Paul also used nonprecious materials in many of his installations. *Querschnitt* (11.30) was made from an especially strong type of foam board and translucent fabric supported by a wooden armature. Filling a room nearly the size of a basketball court, this temporary artwork had to be both strong and inexpensive to produce.

Key Questions

TRADITIONAL AND TRANSFORMATIVE MATERIALS

- Research the material you plan to use. How has it been used traditionally? Do contemporary uses expand its physical and conceptual potential?

- What are the conceptual and environmental advantages of ephemera? What are the challenges in terms of construction and longevity?

11.29 Tara Donovan, *Untitled* (Styrofoam Cups), 2008. Styrofoam cups and glue. Installation dimensions variable. Installation view, The Institute of Contemporary Art, Boston.

11.30 Rick Paul, *Vessel at Rest,* 1994. Installation, Gatorfoam™, wood, fabric, 24 ft × 12 ft (7.31 × 3.6 m).

STUDENT MATERIALS

To minimize cost and expedite exploration, three-dimensional design projects are often constructed from common materials, such as bristol board, corrugated cardboard, plywood, wire, plaster gauze, and plaster. This section describes the characteristics of the most basic types of boards and adhesives.

Boards

As noted in our discussion of 11.30 on the previous page, many types of board are remarkably strong as well as inexpensive. *Bristol board* is like thick, stiff paper. It is available in various thicknesses from 1-ply (similar to drawing paper in weight) to 5-ply (similar in weight to illustration board). A *cold-pressed* (or vellum) surface is slightly textured, while a *hot-pressed* (or plate) surface is very smooth. The vellum surface is best for graphite, charcoal, pastels, and colored pencils. The smooth surface is good for felt markers and for pen and ink. Either can be used for model building, book arts, and planar structures.

Chipboard is a dense, gray, uncoated board made from recycled paper. Most drawing pads have a chipboard backing. Single-thickness chipboard can be cut with an X-Acto knife or a heavy-duty paper cutter; use a utility knife to cut all heavier board.

Foamcore is light, strong, and rather unforgiving. It must be cut with a very sharp X-Acto knife or a scroll saw, and dents in the surface or cutting errors are difficult to repair.

Corrugated cardboard is strong, lightweight, cheap, and amazingly versatile. It is often used for large-scale projects. Through careful planning, you can use the grain (corrugation direction) to create curving planes or even expose it to add texture.

Glues

White glue is nontoxic and water-soluble when wet. It can be used with most porous materials, including all the boards described previously. It is not suitable for paper-to-paper adhesion, as most papers will buckle as they dry.

Glue stick is water-soluble, acid-free, and nontoxic. Designed as an adhesive for thin paper, glue stick generally is ineffective for gluing any kind of board.

Rubber cement is a traditional paper adhesive that can be "erased" when misapplied. However, because rubber cement is highly toxic, flammable, and impermanent, it has limited use in three-dimensional design classes.

Hot glue is a wax-based, translucent material that is heated in a gun and applied as a hot, viscous fluid. It is most effective in adhering nonporous materials, and it provides a quick way to create an assemblage. It can also be used to tack cardboard structures together while the white glue dries.

Dry mounting tissue is distributed in sheets of thin, clear plastic. Adhesion occurs when this material is heated, either in a drymount press or using an iron. This is an excellent adhesive for most papers and lightweight cloth, and it is widely used in photography and book arts.

Tapes

Transparent tape ("Scotch tape") is an all-purpose, lightweight, temporary adhesive for paper. It is not an effective adhesive for boards.

Masking tape is tough, flexible crepe-paper tape. It is designed to mask off unpainted areas, as when painting a car. It is a good temporary adhesive for boards, especially during the model-building stage.

Drafting tape and *artist's tape* are like masking tape but have less glue. They can be removed without damaging the surface to which they are applied.

Double-sided encapsulating tape has acrylic adhesive on both surfaces. A layer of thin paper protects one side until the tape is applied. An archival version of this material is sold by bookbinding stores, and it can be used for well-crafted final projects.

Key Questions

STUDENT MATERIALS

- Why did you choose a particular material for your project? Considering its strength, workability, and cost, is it really the best material for your purpose?

- How would a change in material affect the meaning of your project?

- What nontraditional materials might you use? How can they expand meaning?

11.31 **Michele Oka Doner**, *Terrible Table*, **1988.** Bronze and glass, 16½ × 26 × 22 in. (42 × 66 × 56 cm).

MEANINGFUL MATERIALS

The materials used in most three-dimensional design classes are inexpensive, can be easily manipulated, and are conceptually neutral. As you begin to expand your ideas through more advanced assignments, you can more fully explore the meaning of materials.

Every material has unique psychological associations as well as physical properties. Mirrors are fragile, reflective surfaces commonly used for observation of the self and others. A pile of autumn leaves suggests decay and exudes an earthy aroma. Powdered turmeric spice is pungent and suggests both cooking and travel.

Whether we are creating a sculpture or designing a product, materials have meaning. For example, the thorny branches at the base of Michele Oka Doner's *Terrible Table* (11.31) are sure to change the emotional atmosphere of any room this table occupies. The wood and wire Deborah Butterfield used to create *Large Horse #4* (11.32) force us to reconsider our understanding of both horses and nature. A love of materials and an understanding of their characteristics are essential aspects of all three-dimensional work.

11.32 Deborah Butterfield, *Large Horse #4,* **1979.** Steel, wire, sticks, 77 × 124 × 33 in. (195 × 315 × 84 cm).

SUMMARY

- Choice of material substantially affects both the structure and the meaning of a three-dimensional object.
- Strength, workability, durability, weight, cost, toxicity, and function are major considerations when an artist or a designer chooses a material.
- Materials can be strengthened by using composites, by using skeletons or exoskeletons, and by distributing force.
- Common construction methods include addition, subtraction, solidification, and displacement.
- Connections and transitions can increase visual impact as well as structural strength.
- Traditional materials, such as stone, wood, metal, clay, glass, fibers, and plastics, are used by contemporary artists to express a wide range of ideas.
- Ephemeral materials can expand meaning, reduce cost, and minimize environmental impact.
- Student materials, including various types of boards and adhesives, work best when used for the intended purpose.

KEY TERMS

additive sculpture
armature
assemblage
bend
composite

compression
displacement
ephemera
exoskeleton
flying buttress

gradation
modeling
shear
skeleton (endoskeleton)

solidification
subtractive sculpture
tension
torque

STUDIO PROJECTS

To apply the concepts from this chapter in the studio, check out the Projects page in the Online Learning Center at www.mhhe.com/stewart4e. The following is a sample of the chapter-related assignments that are described in step-by-step detail.

Wooden Wizardry. Transforming a standard wooden plank into an extraordinary wizard's staff.
Book Transformed. Transforming an old or used book into a new content-based sculpture.

Profile:
David MacDonald, Ceramicist

A Passion for Pottery

Internationally renowned ceramicist David MacDonald is best known for his work with utilitarian vessels. His work has been included in over 60 exhibitions, including the Torpedo Factory Art Center in Alexandria, Virginia; the Studio Museum in Harlem; and the Afro-American Historical and Cultural Museum in Philadelphia. He is also a renowned community leader, having worked in an adult literacy program, in a summer ceramics intensive program for high school students, and with inmates at the Green Haven Maximum Security Correctional Facility in New York State.

MS: How did you start making art?

DM: Initially, it was a way to create some private space. As the third in a family of nine children, I always shared a bedroom with at least three of my brothers. I would help my parents unpack the groceries, then unfold the paper bags so that I could use the inside as drawing paper. Through hours of drawing, I was able to create my own little world.

MS: In our conversations and in viewing your work, I am struck by your passion for ceramics in general and functional vessels in particular. What is special about clay?

DM: I was introduced to ceramics during my second year in college. I was immediately fascinated by clay: it is responsive to the slightest pressure and can record the finest impression. After my first mug came out of the kiln and I made my first cup of tea, I was hooked. The idea of turning a lump of dirt into a useful object amazed me. Since I grew up with very little material wealth, I loved the idea of transforming nothing into something.

Now, I am drawn to functional ceramics because I like playing with the interaction between the object and the user. Having to produce a functional object makes the creative act much more interesting and challenging for me. When a teapot has just the right weight, balance, and proportions, it makes the act of pouring tea a celebration of the physical world.

MS: What is the source of your ideas?

DM: Anything can become a conscious or unconscious inspiration. I can get lost in the produce section of the supermarket: the shapes and colors of the vegetables give me all sorts of ideas.

On a more scholarly level, I was influenced by Japanese and Chinese ceramics during college, and for the past 30 years I have been strongly influenced by African art and culture.

MS: Yes, I notice that a dramatic change in your work occurred around 1978. Before that time, your work was sculptural, representational, and highly charged politically; afterward, it became more utilitarian and abstract. What happened?

DM: At the opening for a solo show in Syracuse, I was asked a question by an elderly white woman that dramatically changed my attitude about my work. She innocently asked if there was anything positive about being black in America or was it just one frustration and humiliation after another. The question haunted me for months afterward. I realized that my creative work had been based on anger and a feeling of victimization. As I matured as an individual, I realized that my experiences weren't limited to anger—there is much more to my life than that! I then decided to tap the rich and varied cultural and artistic tradition to which I am heir. Now I am most interested in expressing the magnificence and nobility of the human spirit and in celebrating my African heritage.

MS: What distinguishes a great pot from a mundane pot?

DM: There is no simple answer to this question. We can talk endlessly about form, surface, line, and so forth and still not gain any real insight into what makes one pot great and another mundane, yet we immediately feel it when the mixture of physical elements is just right. Out of the 30 similar bowls a potter produces, two or three always seem to stand apart, as something special.

The search for this elemental quality makes my art magical and compels me to make the next piece. Ironically, if I ever identify exactly what it is that makes an exceptional piece, the excitement will be sucked out of the creative process. The search is as compelling as the solution.

MS: Tell me about the vessel pictured here.

DM: *Carved Stoneware Storage Jar* was inspired by the bulbous form of a melon or gourd. The body is full and round and the lid handle is suggestive of a stem. I like the sense of an internal force or energy stretching the outer shell almost to the point of bursting.

First, I considered the function of the jar. To a large extent, the function determines the form. A certain size range facilitates everyday use. If the size is increased, the object is more suitable for ceremonial use, or as a decorative object. Certain shapes offer more storage capacity and better accessibility to whatever is being stored. Finally, the base must be big enough to provide stability.

The surface was carved when the jar was leather-hard, a couple of days after being thrown on the potter's wheel. A form this large can "carry" a fairly complex pattern, composed of smaller shapes in combination with larger design areas. By leaving some areas uncarved, I was able to create an overlapping effect and increase the illusion of space. The slashing diagonal lines help to unify the design and move the viewer's eye around the form, reinforcing the spherical volume.

MS: What were the most valuable lessons you learned from your teachers?

DM: From Joseph Gilliard at Hampton University, I learned the history and technique of ceramics and gained greater patience and self-control. I developed my self-awareness and passion for communication through my work with Robert Stull at the University of Michigan. From Henry Gernhardt, my Syracuse University colleague for 24 years, I learned that teaching is also an art. In nearly 40 years of teaching, Henry's commitment to his art and his students never faltered.

MS: Is there any advice you would like to give to my students?

DM: An artist has to believe in him- or herself. The dedication, courage, and energy my students bring to the classroom are more important than anything I can offer. If you want to stand above the crowd, your passion for your art must be manifest through a willingness to work harder than anyone else. The students who succeed see their art as a way of life and not simply as a way of earning a living. My job as a teacher is to help my students realize their potential and to bring eloquence to their unique voice.

David MacDonald, *Carved Stoneware Storage Jar*, 1997. 15 in. (38.1 cm).

Physical and Cerebral

What is the difference between the pile of wood in figure 12.1 and the sculpture in figure 12.2? The size, orientation, and location of the pile of wood are based on its purpose. It provides the raw material needed for building a house. Positioned at the edge of a construction site, the boards are arranged in a roughly parallel position so that workers can easily grasp and remove individual planks. The pile of wood is purely functional. Its organization has no aesthetic intention.

At first glance, figure 12.2 may seem very much like a pile of wood. The rough planks are clustered together, in close proximity to the house and in a parallel position. On closer examination, we see the perpendicular boards that elevate the structure. Balanced on stilts, the mass of wood seems suspended and in transition. It continues around the house and into the windows. Is the house expelling or inhaling the boards? The entire structure seems poised, ready to shift at any moment.

How and why was this sculpture made? Artist Tadashi Kawamata begins by collecting scrap wood from demolished buildings. He then constructs temporary installations, which he describes as "cancers," on conventional buildings. With no predetermined end point, the structures grow like weeds, often enveloping the building. When the exhibition ends, Kawamata continues onward, dismantling the construction to create another sculpture elsewhere.

12.1 Pile of wood at a construction site.

12.2 Tadashi Kawamata, *Tetra House N−3, W26 Project*, Sapporo, Japan.

Using scrap material to build temporary structures, his work demonstrates the fluidity and circulation of urban structures. His design is based on aesthetic rather than functional criteria.

All three-dimensional work gains power through its physical presence. Sculpture, however, is much more than brute force. It is through the transformation of tangible material into ideas and emotions that a sculpture gains significance. The planks in figure 12.1 begin and end as physical material. A pile of wood is just a pile of wood. By contrast, sculpture, such as *Tetra House N–3, W26 Project*, uses physical material to explore and express ideas.

CONSTRUCTED THOUGHT

From Life to Art

Contemporary sculpture is made from a wide range of materials, including ice, fire, blood, spools of thread, and crushed automobiles. In her *Ceremonial Arch* (12.3), Mierle Ukeles combined the metal and wood used in traditional sculpture with gloves, lights, metal springs, and asphalt to create an artwork that is both visually exuberant and structurally sound. Sculpture is now shown in parks, subway stations, and public plazas, in addition to galleries and museums. Because contemporary sculpture is so reliant on everyday materials and public settings, the relationship between art and life has become especially close.

This can be an advantage or a disadvantage. Connection to life gives art its vitality. Authenticity is essential. For example, when a play expresses actual feelings in a compelling way, it connects to our personal experience. Too direct a connection is deadly, however. A pile of wood is just a pile of wood. For art to have meaning, commonplace

12.3 Mierle Laderman Ukeles, *Ceremonial Arch Honoring Service Workers in the New Service Economy*, 1988. Steel arch with materials donated from New York City agencies, including gloves, lights, grass, straps, springs, and asphalt; overall structure 11 ft × 8 ft × 8 ft 8 in. (3.35 × 2.43 × 2.44 m), plus glove branches ranging from 2 to 4 ft (61 to 122 cm) long.

experiences must be distilled, reexamined, or transformed. It has often been said that a play is "life with the boring parts left out." A play that simply replicates everyday experience can never transport an audience beyond the commonplace. Likewise, sculpture requires a heightened experience *beyond* everyday life. Through a combination of insight and hard work, the sculptor transforms even the most resistant material into compelling communication. When all elements in a sculpture support the central concept, the viewer is simultaneously connected by the reality of the material and transported by the power of the idea.

Degrees of Representation

Representational artworks often depict persons or objects in such exquisite detail that they seem to come to life. Michelangelo's *Pietà* (12.4) is a good example. In this massive sculpture, Mary grieves as she cradles the dead Jesus. Every crease in the fabric is defined, and every nuance of gesture is deliberate. Mary's right hand extends Jesus' flesh as she gently lifts his right shoulder. She tilts her head slightly, and her left hand echoes the position of his feet. Sculptures such as the *Pietà* seem to embody life. They engage our thoughts and emotions through their compelling realism and narrative implications.

Nonobjective artworks can be appreciated for their pure physical beauty. For example, the simple metal rings Sandra Enterline constructed for her *Caged Sphere Bracelet Series* (12.5) work beautifully as ends in themselves. We can appreciate their economy and grace without knowing a story or pursuing any additional ideas they may suggest.

Most sculptural objects fall somewhere between these two extremes. These **abstract artworks** have been distilled down from a recognizable source. Myra Mimlitsch-Gray's *Timepiece* (12.6) simultaneously suggests the mechanism and movement of a clock, a pendulum, and a musician's metronome. By reducing

12.4 Michelangelo, *Pietà,* **1498–1500.** Marble, 5 ft 8 in. × 2 ft 3 in. (1.74 × 0.69 m).

these familiar timepieces to their essential form, she was able to create an economical design that conveys a universal sense of time.

Each approach has its advantages. Nonobjective forms are often used in situations that require universality or simplicity. Barnett Newman's

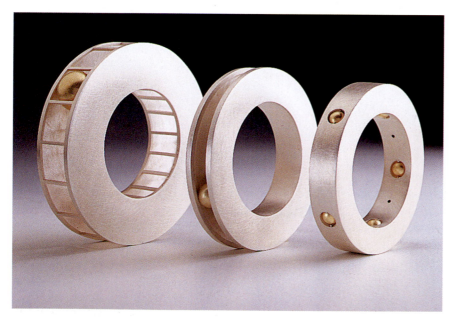

12.5 Sandra Enterline, *Caged Sphere Bracelet Series,* **1992.** Sterling silver, 18-karat gold, hollow-formed, fabricated. Left to right: 5 × 5 × 1⅛ in. (12.7 × 12.7 × 3 cm), 4 × 4 × ¾ in. (10.2 × 10.2 × 1.9 cm), 4 × 4 × ¾ in. (10.2 × 10.2 × 1.9 cm).

12.6 Myra Mimlitsch-Gray, *Timepiece,* **1988.** Kinetic brooch, 14-karat gold, lens, diamonds, abrasive disk. Fabricated, 2¼ × 1½ × ¼ in. (6 × 4 × 0.5 cm).

12.8 Walter Martin and Paloma Muñoz, *Of Bodies Born Up by Water*, 1987. Plaster, oil paint, sheet metal, wood, 111½ × 20 × 16½ in. (283 × 51 × 42 cm).

12.7 Barnett Newman, *Broken Obelisk*, 1963–67. Cor-Ten steel, 26 × 10½ × 10½ ft (66 × 26.7 × 26.7 m).

Broken Obelisk (12.7) is a monochromatic structure constructed from a simple pyramid and an inverted obelisk. The point of contact between the two sections becomes charged with energy, as the top half seems to balance on the top of the pyramid. Caught in this moment of equilibrium, the sculpture is as carefully balanced as a ballerina on her toes.

On the other hand, a representational approach can stimulate the imagination by providing a fresh interpretation of a familiar object. In *Of Bodies Born Up by Water* (12.8), Walter Martin and Paloma Muñoz used a similar structure to create a very different effect. The poised obelisk is now a grandfather clock. When it topples, time, memory, and family history may be erased.

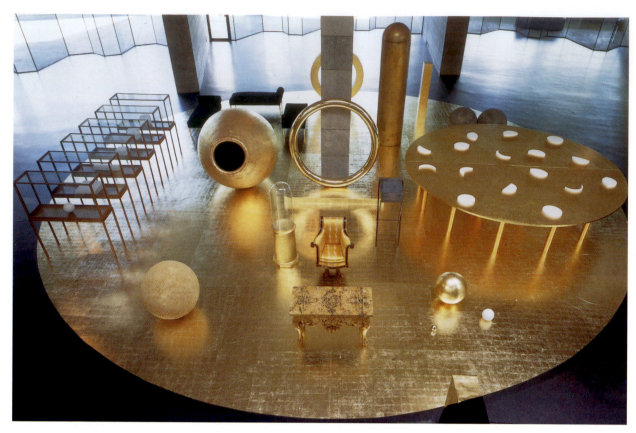

12.9 James Lee Byars, *The Perfect Thought,* **1990 (installation shot).** Various objects covered with gold leaf, composed in one of two circles of gold leaf, large circle 40 ft (12.2 m) diameter, small circle 27 ft (8.2 m) diameter.

Boundaries

Because the art/life connection is so important, sculptors must be especially attentive to the physical and psychological boundaries in each piece. As a dividing line between objects, images, or experiences, the boundary is charged with energy. It can serve three major purposes.

Boundaries Can Connect

A simple shape can create a boundary. To define *The Perfect Thought* (12.9), James Lee Byars placed two gold-leaf circles on the floor. The larger circle enclosed 23 separate works from earlier exhibitions, while the smaller circle remained empty. This simple strategy unified a collection of individual artworks while leaving a second space open, to be filled by the viewer's imagination.

Dwelling (12.10) by Yong Soon Min, deals with psychological boundaries. Born in Korea and raised in the United States, Min explores issues of alienation and disorientation in her artwork. In *Dwelling,* she combined a brightly lit Korean dress with a pile of maps, photographs, and books. A fragment of poetry, inserted in the dress, describes the loss of identity. In this type of sculpture, boundaries between the personal and the public begin to blur.

Boundaries Can Separate

Constructed from nine 12-foot-wide bushes within the median of a busy highway, Maya Ying Lin's *Topo* (12.11) uses a boundary to separate as well as to connect. Enclosed within the mile-long median, the bushes provide a series of visual stepping-stones, inviting us to move down the line diagonally. Shifting circles at either end of the sculpture appear to rotate the last two bushes, directing our attention back down the line. This illusion of perpetual motion activates the simple design.

Psychological separation adds power to George Segal's *The Subway* (12.12). This artwork replicates a commonplace setting, using actual subway seats, handrails, and a window, which flashes with the lights of "passing" trains. The ghostly white plaster figure seems familiar but remains distant, the shell of a living, breathing person. In this installation, a psychological boundary transforms the commonplace into an expression of isolation.

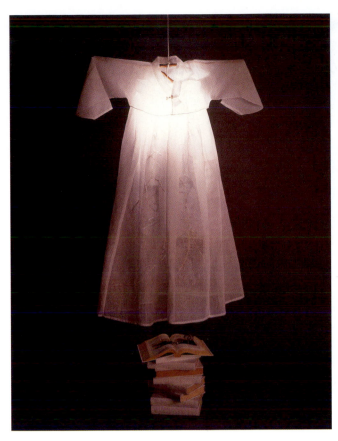

12.10 Yong Soon Min, *Dwelling,* **1994.** Mixed mediums, 72 × 42 × 28 in. (183 × 107 × 72 cm).

12.11 Maya Ying Lin, *Topo,* **1991.** 1,600 × 40 ft (487.7 × 12.2 m).

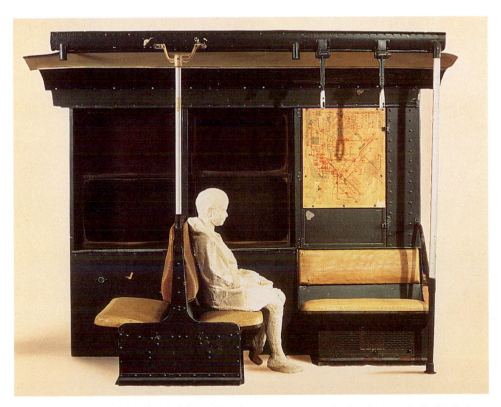

12.12 George Segal, *The Subway,* **1968.** Plaster, metal, glass, rattan, electrical parts with lightbulbs, map. 7 ft 4 in. × 9 ft 5 in. × 4 ft 2 in. (2.25 × 2.88 × 1.3 m).

12.13 Susan Trangmar, *Blue Skies,* 1990. Installation view, size varies.

12.14 Olafur Eliasson, *The Parliament of Reality,* 2006–09. Concrete, stone, stainless steel, water, trees, other plants. Dimensions variable. Installation at The Center for Curatorial Studios (CCS Bard), New York. The Center for Curatorial Studies and the Luma Foundation. © 2006 Olafur Eliasson.

Boundaries Can Enclose

Increasingly, sculptors are using every square inch of gallery space and surface to create complex installations. In *Blue Skies* (12.13), Susan Trangmar used the gallery walls as four large projection surfaces. Surrounded by the projections and by his or her own cast shadow, the viewer becomes a participant in the installation.

The sculpture itself can also envelop the viewer. Olafur Eliasson's *The Parliament of Reality* (12.14) is composed of multiple units, including a man-made island surrounded by a circular lake, grasslands, and two dozen trees. Shown here is a 20-foot-long bridge loosely enclosed by latticework. As visitors cross the bridge, they become part of the sculpture.

Bases and Places

Traditional sculpture is generally mounted on a **plinth,** which provides a horizontal base, or on a **pedestal,** which provides a vertical base. Either can serve three purposes:

- To physically separate the sculpture from the surrounding space
- To provide strength and structural stability

12.16 Edgar Hilaire Germain Degas, *Horse Galloping on Right Foot*, c. 1881. Bronze cast of wax model, 11⅛ in. (30 cm).

12.17 Benvenuto Cellini, *Perseus and Medusa*, 1545–54. Bronze, 18 ft (5.5 m) h.

12.15 Barbara Chase-Riboud, *Malcolm X #3*, 1970. Polished bronze and silk, 118 × 47 × 10 in. (300 × 120 × 25 cm).

- To elevate an object psychologically, distinguishing it from its surroundings and increasing its impact

Seemingly insignificant, the plinth or pedestal is actually a crucial component of sculpture, both physically and aesthetically. In figure 12.15, the marble base adds elevation as well as a marked contrast in material. As a result, Barbara Chase-Riboud's *Malcolm X #3* now has a solid platform from which to speak. The plinth in *Horse Galloping on Right Foot* (12.16), by Edgar Degas, provides a visual context for the galloping horse, as well as physical stability. The sculpture would collapse, physically and aesthetically, if the base were removed. The pedestal for Benvenuto Cellini's *Perseus and Medusa* (12.17) elevates the heroic statue and creates an architectural connection to the surrounding buildings.

For Constantin Brancusi, the base was an aesthetic element rather than a passive support. He used a specific pedestal form to enhance the power and grace of each of his variations on birds (figures 10.25, 10.26, and 10.27, page 230). Seeking dynamism rather than stability, Umberto Boccioni split the base in half

when he composed *Unique Forms of Continuity in Space* (12.18). The abstracted figure strides forward in space, too energetic to be constrained by conventional boundaries.

In contemporary sculpture, the base often extends to include an entire architectural site. Resting directly on the surface of the plaza, the granite boulders in Elyn Zimmerman's *Marabar* (12.19) are intended to suggest continents, while the channel of water suggests the ocean. Combining large scale with a "baseless" design, the artist has dissolved the traditional boundary between the stones and the surroundings. The entire plaza is transformed into a sculptural site.

12.18 Umberto Boccioni, *Unique Forms of Continuity in Space*, 1913. Bronze (cast in 1931), 43⅞ × 34⅞ × 15¾ in. (111.2 × 88.5 × 40 cm).

Key Questions

CONSTRUCTED THOUGHT

- How is your artwork similar to everyday life? How is it different?
- What can a boundary or base contribute to your design?
- How will the meaning change if your project is placed in a specific setting?

12.19 Elyn Zimmerman, *Marabar*, 1984. Boulders (natural cleft and polished granite) and water. Plaza: 140 × 60 ft (42.7 × 18.3 m).

12.20 Dennis Oppenheim, *Device to Root Out Evil,* **1997.** Galvanized structural steel, anodized perforated aluminum, transparent red Venetian glass, concrete foundations, 20 × 15 × 8 ft (6.1 × 4.57 × 2.44 m).

12.21 Antony Gormley, *Learning to Think,* **1991.** Lead, fiberglass, air, five figures, each 68 × 41¾ × 122 in. (173 × 106 × 310 cm).

PHYSICAL FORCES

Weight and Gravity

Of the forces of nature, gravity is the most immediately noticeable when we begin to construct a three-dimensional structure. Lines, spaces, and volumes must be organized according to the laws of physics while simultaneously meeting our aesthetic objectives. Balance is a structural necessity as well as a compositional force. After watching several prototypes collapse, it is easy to conclude that gravity is our enemy, to be conquered at all costs. But is it?

When we begin to analyze the uses of gravity in sculpture, we soon find that it is an asset rather than a liability. Just as a ballet dancer relies on gravity to provide a solid launching pad for each leap and a predictable support for each landing, so the sculptor uses gravity to express ideas and generate emotions.

Downward gravity animates *Device to Root Out Evil* (12.20). The inverted church structure seems to have been propelled aloft, finally driving into the ground upon landing. As noted by sculptor Dennis Oppenheim, this inversion of a familiar structure creates a reversal of content. The steeple is now pointing to hell rather than to heaven. Even without any cultural associations, however, we would still respond to the improbable balance and intense color in this large piece.

A combination of weight and weightlessness gives Antony Gormley's *Learning to Think* (12.21) its impact. Constructed from a mold made from the artist's own body, the hollow lead figures are basically identical. Hovering 10 feet off the ground, they seem weightless. At the same time, because they are suspended from the ceiling, each figure seems as heavy as a convict at the end of a hangman's noose. This paradox gives the sculpture great physical force

12.22 John Chamberlain, *The Hedge*, 1997. Painted milled steel, chromium-plated steel, stainless steel; overall installed 44½ in. × 44½ in. × 46 ft 4 in. (113 cm × 113 cm × 14.12 m); 16 units, each 44½ × 44½ × 12 in. (113 × 113 × 30.5 cm).

and communicates an elusive concept. Clearly, the knowledge embodied in this sculpture is not easy to attain!

Compression and Expansion

Most materials tend to compress as weight increases. As shown in figure 10.21 (on page 228), physical compression can be used to evoke a visceral response. We feel the pressure as the top log pushes down on the log below. Compression plays an especially important role in the works of John Chamberlain, who began making sculptures from crushed automobiles in the 1960s. In *The Hedge* (12.22), crushed pieces of metal have been transformed into an improbable garden. The contradiction between the materials and the meaning suggests a new definition of nature.

Expansion is an equally compelling force. Constructed from the charred fragments of a church that had been struck by lightning, Cornelia Parker's *Mass* (12.23) seems to present the event in suspended animation. Supported by fine steel wire and cotton thread, the hovering sculpture appears weightless, caught at the moment of explosion.

12.23 Cornelia Parker, *Mass (Colder Darker Matter)*, 1997. Charcoal retrieved from a church struck by lightning, suspended from steel wire and cotton thread, 10 × 10 × 10 ft (3.5 × 3.5 × 3.5 m).

Tension and Torsion

Tension can be used to stretch or bend an object, while torsion creates a twisting movement. Either can add physical and cerebral strength to a sculpture. Stretched taut, the steel cables in Kenneth Snelson's *Free Ride Home* (see figure 9.16, page 188) provide the force needed to elevate the aluminum tubes that dominate the sculpture. Tension is equally important for the designer. It is the tension in the bent metal rods that creates the structure in the Peregrine Tent from The North Face (12.24). In Maren Hassinger's *12 Trees No. 2* (12.25), cables and wires have been twisted together, then clamped at the top. Based on our experience in the physical world, we can feel the force in the twisted strands and imagine the explosive result if this power were released.

Presence and Absence

Presence is another important aspect of physicality. When we confront a massive sculpture, like the Olmec portrait on page 197 (figure 9.37), it exudes a strength that is far beyond anything a small photograph can convey. Equally, the space surrounding a sculpture or the absence of an anticipated object can have great impact.

Many sculptors have used this quality of presence and absence to explore the passage of time and the nature of memory. British sculptor Rachel Whiteread explores presence and absence in many of her works. Using hundreds of gallons of cement to create a solid cast from an empty house, she accentuated absence by making the space within the house

12.24 Peregrine Tent by The North Face, San Leandro, CA.

12.25 Maren Hassinger, *12 Trees No. 2*, 1979. Galvanized wire rope, 10 × 150 × 5 ft (3.1 × 45.7 × 1.5 m).

12.26 Rachel Whiteread, *House,* **1993.** Commissioned by Artangel Trust and Beck's (corner of Grove Rd. and Roman Rd., London, destroyed 1994).

very solidly present (12.26). In *The Writing on the Wall* series, Shimon Attie used slide projections to remind us of shops and families destroyed during the Holocaust. Figure 12.27 shows one of the many slides from the 1930s that he projected onto various buildings in Berlin. The actual bookstore depicted disappeared long ago.

Process and Product

In the past 50 years, sculptors have expanded their choice of materials to include many physical and chemical processes:

- *Friction.* The graphite hands in Todd Slaughter's *Grinding Knuckles* (12.28) slowly rotate, grinding the sculpture away every time this artwork is displayed.

- *Condensation.* Sealed inside the Hans Haacke *Weather Cube* (12.29), water evaporates or condenses based on the

12.27 Shimon Attie, *Almstadtstrasse 43 (formerly Grenandierstrasse 7): Slide Projection of Former Hebrew Bookstore, Berlin,* **1930, from the series** *The Writing on the Wall,* **1992.** Ektacolor print of site-specific slide-projection installation, 20 × 24 in. (50.8 × 60.9 cm).

12.28 Todd Slaughter, *Grinding Knuckles*, 1993. One RPM graphite and motors, 12 × 20 × 12 in. (30.5 × 51 × 30.5 cm).

ambient temperature inside the gallery.

- *Oxidation.* Ronald Dahl transformed the familiar ladder when he placed his sculpture in the Nevada desert and set it aflame to create *Seven Windows to a Sky on Fire* (12.30).

- *Filtration.* Located next to a wastewater treatment plant, Lorna Jordan's *Waterworks Gardens: The Grotto* (12.31) purifies up to 2,000 gallons of oil-laced storm water per minute. The 8-acre site includes stone mosaics, natural filtration systems, and colorful bands of sedges, yellow irises, and red-twig dogwoods.

12.29 Hans Haacke, *Weather Cube*, 1963–65. Acrylic plastic, water, climate in area of display, 12-in. (30.5-cm) cube.

12.30 Ronald Dahl, *Seven Windows to a Sky on Fire,* **1982.** Wood/flame, 9 × 12 × 3 in. (22.7 × 30.5 × 7.6 cm).

12.31 Lorna Jordan, *Waterworks Gardens: The Grotto,* **1996.** Third of five public garden rooms in King County East Division Reclamation Plant, Renton, WA.

Key Questions

PHYSICAL FORCES

- How can weight or gravity add meaning to your artwork?

- What are the compressive and expansive limitations of the material(s) you are using? How might these forces enhance your concept?

- Tension and torsion create pent-up energy, like a spring ready to be released. How might these forces add meaning or a sense of suspense?

- What happens when the absence of an object or the residue after an event becomes the artwork?

- All materials and actions eventually decay. Can this process of decay become part of your concept?

12.32 **Covered Effigy Jar with Removable Head.** From Teotihuacán, Mexico. Ceramic, 10¾ in. (27.3 cm).

12.33 Raymond Duchamp-Villon, *The Great Horse*, 1957 version of a 1914 work. Bronze, 39¼ × 24 × 36 in. (99.7 × 60.9 × 91.4 cm).

CONTEMPORARY QUESTIONS, CONTEMPORARY ANSWERS

Building on a Tradition

Traditional sculpture has been characterized by four qualities. First, mass, or solid substance, rather than open space, is the primary concern. Traditional sculptures, such as Michelangelo's *Pietà* (see figure 12.4, page 262), are relatively solid. In this masterpiece, a sense of profound resignation is created through the use of gravity. The mother has fully accepted her grief. The position of the limbs and the folds in the fabric create a dynamic surface on a stable pyramidal mass. Second, the human figure is the primary subject. Sculptors have long sought to capture in wood, metal, or stone the vitality of a living person. Third, as a means to this end, traditional sculpture is overwhelmingly representational. Indeed, attention to detail and the ability to animate marble have long been the hallmarks of Western sculpture, from the Renaissance to Romanticism. Even an expressive pre-Columbian effigy jar (12.32) gains eloquence from the use of representation.

Finally, traditional sculptures often tell stories. Public monuments have frequently been commissioned by kings or by communities of ordinary people to tell national stories. For example, the Statue of Liberty was designed to embody the democratic ideal shared by France and the United States. It was financed through a public lottery, theatrical events, and even prizefights. The poem describing "huddled masses yearning to breathe free," combined with the heroic figure, distills the history of immigration to America into a few words.

Reinventing Sculpture

In Europe, the four qualities of traditional sculpture reached their climax during the nineteenth century. Seeking fresh ideas and new approaches, artists in Russia, Italy, and France then began a process that would transform sculpture forever.

Four major changes followed. First, space became a major concern. Sculpture began to be developed from the inside out, rather than being carved from the outside in. Second, abstraction and transformation became more important than description and representation. For example, Raymond Duchamp-Villon's *The Great Horse* (12.33), constructed from a mix of organic and mechanical parts, bears little resemblance to an actual horse. Third, while the human figure continued to dominate early-twentieth-century sculpture, by mid-century almost any subject matter could be used. Indeed, many significant artworks from this period, including Mark di Suvero's *Ik Ook Eindhoven* (see figure 9.18,

page 189), are nonobjective, having no external subject matter. Weight, balance, and the dynamics of space are the only content such works require. Most important, sculptors began to break down the traditional separation between art and life. Commonplace objects, such as Marcel Duchamp's *Bicycle Wheel* (12.34), were placed in galleries and defined as art. Finding a sculptural idea became as important as forming a sculptural object.

Contemporary Directions

The evolution of sculpture has accelerated in the past 30 years. Earthworks, which transform natural sites into sculptural settings, have become a powerful force in both art and ecology. An installation, which may combine time, space, and sound, can present both artist and audience with new opportunities for communication and expression. Performance art (which is discussed at greater length in Chapter Fifteen), combines art, technology, and theater. The traditional has become the transformative. Four of the manifestations of this change are described next.

Sculpture as Place

Traditionally permanent, sculpture has always been placed in a wide variety of significant settings. Stonehenge (12.35), constructed from massive limestone blocks weighing up to 50 tons, may have been used as a gigantic sundial by its Neolithic builders. The avenue approaching the stone circle is carefully aligned to the summer solstice, while stones within the circle are aligned with the northernmost and southernmost paths of the rising moon.

Likewise, contemporary sculptors add meaning to their work by exploring the physical, psychological, and temporal characteristics of each site. Glen Onwin's *Nigredo* (12.36) is one of four works in a series titled *As Above, So Below*. Placed in an abandoned chapel, this concrete pool, filled with water, black brine, and wax, seems especially ominous in the once-sacred site. In a very different investigation of place, David Adjaye's *Europolis* (12.37) traces transportation networks between the various capitals of Europe. Sandwiched between panes of glass, the brilliant red lines resemble both pulsating blood vessels and a teeming microscopic world.

12.34 Marcel Duchamp, *Bicycle Wheel*, 1951. (Third version, after lost original of 1913.) Assemblage, metal wheel, 25½ in. (63.8 cm) diameter, mounted on painted wood stool 23¾ in. (60.2 cm) h.; overall 50½ × 25½ × 16⅝ in. (128.3 × 63.8 × 42 cm).

12.35 Stonehenge (aerial view), Salisbury Plain, England, c. 2800–1500 BCE.

12.36 Glenn Onwin, *Nigredo,* 1992. Installation view of exhibition *As Above, So Below,* at the Square Chapel, Halifax, May 9–June 15, 1992. Exposed timbers of the roof reflected in an artificial concrete pool filled with black brine and wax.

12.37 David Adjaye, *Europolis,* 2008. Metallic foil laminated in clear float glass, 6 ft × 4 ft × 2 ft.

12.38 Karin Giusti, *White House/Greenhouse*, New York City, 1996. Recycled steel beams, vinyl, Plexiglas, and rosebushes, 40 × 15 × 14 ft (12 × 4.5 × 4.3 m).

The personal and the political were combined in Karin Giusti's *White House/Greenhouse* (12.38). Placed in Battery Park in New York City, the transparent one-quarter scale model of the White House had both Wall Street and the Statue of Liberty in the background. Made of recycled steel beams, clear vinyl, and large paintings on Plexiglas, the structure presented a scathing commentary on American politics while providing a greenhouse for 200 rosebushes.

Sculpture as Journey

As sculptures have expanded in size, the manner in which the viewer enters, exits, and explores the site has become increasingly important. When the audience participates, a sculpture can be transformed from an object into an experience.

Christopher Janney's *Sonic Plaza* (12.39) at Eastern Carolina University is an especially enticing example. Composed of four distinct sculptures, the site offers a variety of sensory experiences. Various melodic sounds greet participants at the *Sonic Gates*. The 64 water jets on the *Percussion Water Wall* spew forth complex patterns of water to a percussive accompaniment. Four smaller sculptures emerge from the large doors of the *Media Glockenspiel* each day. Finally, a cloud of water vapor created by *Ground Cloud* hovers over the plaza, responding to pedestrian movement and wind direction.

12.39 Christopher Janney, *Sonic Plaza,* Eastern Carolina University, 1998. Sound, light, water, and interactive elements, total length 400 ft (122 m). Top: *Sonic Gates;* middle row left to right: *Media Glockenspiel* and *Percussion Water Wall;* bottom, *Ground Cloud.*

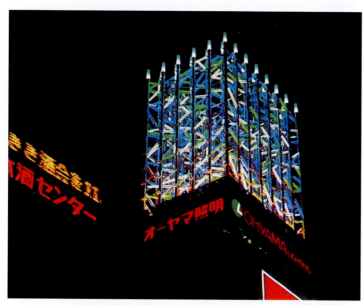

Sculpture as Time

A fascination with time pervades contemporary sculpture. Many sculptures demonstrate the changes that occur as time passes. The amount, frequency, and means of change vary widely. Placed atop the corporate offices of a lighting company, Fumaki Nakamura's *Light Communication* (12.40) presents a simple metamorphosis in a spectacular way. The 88 neon poles gradually illuminate the interior of the structure in three 30-second cycles. The beauty of the light, combined with the hypnotic sequence of change, animates and illuminates the night sky.

Christian Marclay often combines sound with sculpture to expand our experience and understanding of time. In *Amplification* (12.41), he installed large-scale translucent reproductions of six anonymous flea-market photographs in San Stae, a Baroque church in Venice, Italy. Each photograph captures a nonprofessional musical performance. An old woman plays a piano; a small girl plays a recorder; a group of men on various instruments comprise an informal band. Fragments of audio recordings combined with the muted footsteps of each visitor create a somber evocation of the past while simultaneously emphasizing the present.

Sculpture can also demonstrate the impermanence that is an essential characteristic of time. To create *curcuma sul travertino* (12.42, on page 284), Shelagh Wakely covered the entrance hall to a British school with a thin layer of yellow turmeric spice. As visitors passed through the room, they gradually erased the dust. Thus, during the week-long exhibition, visitors were marked by their passage through the room, and, with spice on their shoes, subsequently marked each new room they entered.

12.40 Fumaki Nakamura, *Light Communication,* **Ohyama Lighting.** Installed at Ginza 4-chome (main intersection). Eighty-eight poles on a box frame with 400 flashing lamps and projection lights underneath, front 26 ft 3 in. × 19 ft 8 in. × 29 ft 4 in. (8 × 6 × 12 m), neon tube total length 546 ft 2 in. (1,500 m).

12.41 Christian Marclay, *Amplification*, 1995. Mixed mediums with six found prints and six photographic enlargements on cotton scrim, size varies.

12.42 Shelagh Wakely, *curcuma sul travertino,* **1991.** Turmeric powder on travertine marble floor (smell of turmeric filled the space), swept up after three weeks, 46 ft × 11 ft 6 in. (14 × 3.5 m).

Sculpture as Self

It has often been said that all artwork is autobiographical. This is especially true of sculpture. As the physical manifestation of thought, sculpture has an immediacy similar to that of a living person.

Both traditional and contemporary sculptors have explored this theme in many marvelous ways. The indigenous people of New Zealand, the Maori, have often combined sculpture with architecture to create a genealogical self-portrait. The face of a prominent ancestor is placed on the front gable of the sacred meeting house (12.43). The ridge at the top of the roof is the ancestor's backbone, the rafters form his ribs, and the four corner posts represent his arms and legs. Faces of other ancestors are carved on the exterior of the building and on interior posts. Finally, carvings of the Earth Mother and Sky Father are placed over the porch. Through a combination of representation and symbolism, every aspect of the building is designed to honor the past and inspire the present people.

Attention's Loop (12.44), by Elizabeth King, offers another type of self-portrait. In this installation, six highly detailed mannequins are presented in a variety of poses. Carefully articulated arms and hands in three additional display cases line the back wall of the gallery, while an 11-minute video loop shows the mannequins moving. The combination of supreme craftsmanship, robotic machinery, and fluid animation communicates a complex range of ideas. The mannequins are both fascinating and disturbing. Human consciousness seems to be trapped in a sculptural form.

Kiki Smith infused her *Virgin Mary* (12.45) with a very different energy and insight. Completed during a tragic period in her life that included the death of both her sister and her father, the figure appears flayed and exposed. Built from wax, cheesecloth, and wood, the woman is physically and emotionally fragile.

Eva Hesse's *Laocoön* (12.46) is a more abstract self-portrait. As noted in Chapter Nine, the ancient Greek sculpture *Laocoön and His Two Sons* (see figure 9.22, page 191) depicts a scene from the Trojan War. Laocoön warns against accepting the large wooden horse the Greeks offer as a gift. The Greek goddess Athena sends two serpents

12.43 *Maori Meeting House*, called "Rautepupuke," New Zealand, 1881. 56 ft × 13 ft 10 in. (17 × 4 m).

to attack and kill Laocoön, thereby gaining entry into Troy and victory for the Greeks hidden in the horse. Like the snakes that bind Laocoön and his sons, the cords in Hesse's sculpture are messengers of death. They choke the ladder structure and foreshadow Hesse's own death at age 34 from a brain tumor. As she noted, "My life and art have not been separated."

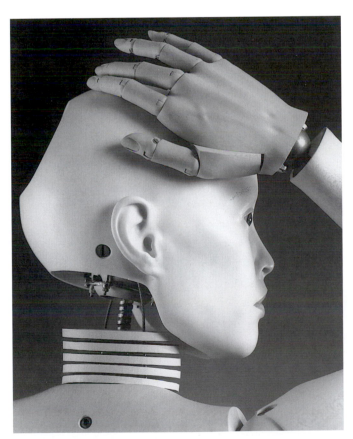 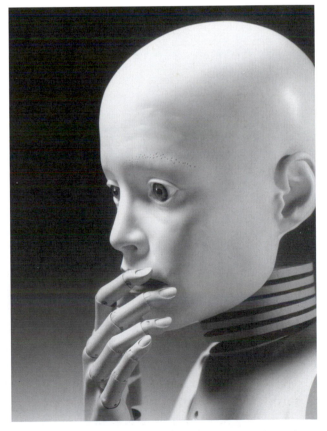

12.44 Katherine Wetzel (photo), Elizabeth King (sculpture), *Pupil* from *Attention's Loop*, 1987–90. Porcelain, glass eyes, carved wood, brass, one-half life size.

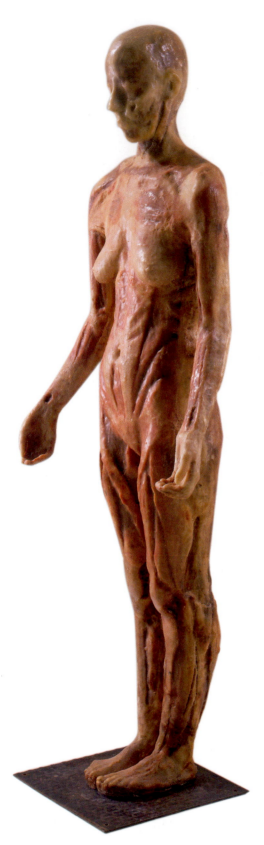

12.45 Kiki Smith, *Virgin Mary*, 1992. Wax, cheesecloth and wood with steel base, 67½ × 26 × 14½ in. (171.5 × 66 × 36.8 cm).

12.46 Eva Hesse, *Laocoön*, 1966. Acrylic paint, cloth-covered cord, wire, and papier-mâché over plastic plumber's pipe, bottom 130 × 23½ × 23 in. (330.2 × 59.7 × 58.4 cm), top 130 × 21½ × 21½ in. (330.2 × 54.6 × 54.6 cm).

Ideas in Physical Form

The combination of tangible material and aesthetic complexity gives sculpture a unique power. Like an alchemist, the sculptor transforms ordinary materials into conceptual gold. Tadashi Kawamata's pile of wood becomes a metaphor for urban change. In Mierle Ukeles's *Ceremonial Arch*, the gloves and lightbulbs used by sanitation workers are transformed into a sculpture. A burning ladder becomes a metaphor for a spiritual passage in Ronald Dahl's *Seven Windows to a Sky on Fire*. Through a miracle of invention, the best sculptures simultaneously embrace and transcend their physical nature.

Key Questions

CONTEMPORARY QUESTIONS, CONTEMPORARY ANSWERS

- What are the historical antecedents for your idea?
- How can contemporary materials and methods strengthen your idea?
- What does your artwork reveal about yourself and the world around you?

SUMMARY

- A pile of wood at a construction site is stacked for convenience and accessibility. A pile of wood in a sculpture is designed to communicate ideas and emotions.

- Art gains power from its connection to life. Through art, commonplace experiences are distilled, reexamined, and transformed.

- Physical and psychological boundaries can connect or separate art and life.

- A base can separate a sculpture from its surrounding space, provide structural stability, and expand aesthetic content.

- Physical forces, such as gravity, compression, expansion, tension, and torsion, can be used to express ideas while providing structural strength.

- The materials a sculptor selects can heighten and deepen the meaning of the artwork.

- Traditional Western sculpture is massive, representational, figurative, and narrative.

- Contemporary sculpture is often more spatial, abstract, and nonfigurative than traditional sculpture. It often breaks down the traditional separation between art and life.

- Many contemporary sculptors use specific sites, audience participation, temporal change, and explorations of the self to create powerful artworks.

KEY TERMS

abstract artworks
nonobjective artworks

pedestal
plinth

representational artworks

STUDIO PROJECTS

To apply the concepts from this chapter in the studio, check out the Projects page in the Online Learning Center at www.mhhe.com/stewart4e. The following is a sample of the chapter-related assignments that are described in step-by-step detail.

Becoming Borg. The skin and skeleton of human and machine.
Time Piece. Expanding upon kinetic time.

Profile:
Samuel Yates, Artist
One Man; 17,860 Parcels

Samuel Yates is known for creating large-scale conceptual art projects that combine performance and minimalism with the structures of government. His artwork is included in numerous public collections, including the San Francisco Museum of Modern Art, Berkeley Art Museum, di Rosa Preserve (Napa, CA), and Ballett Frankfurt (Frankfurt, Germany).

"The Color of Palo Alto" is a public art project commissioned by the City of Palo Alto. The project incorporates technology, contemporary art, environmental protection, and public service into one award-winning public art project. It created a free lexicon of sustainable color and the nation's first photo-assisted 9-1-1 emergency response system.

MS: How did "The Color of Palo Alto" begin?

SY: In the summer of 2001, I installed a seven-story-tall file cabinet sculpture in Napa Valley for a private collector. I had shredded an MG sportscar into tiny pieces, steamrolled each piece flat, and filed the pieces by weight in milligrams from heaviest to lightest inside the cabinet. A public art commissioner from the City of Palo Alto saw the sculpture and invited me to apply for a rotating public art grant, sited in their Civic Center Plaza. I applied for and was awarded the $10,000 grant.

Rather than simply installing a pre-made sculpture in Civic Center Plaza and then taking it away—a practice often called "Plop Art" where you "plop" an existing sculpture in a public space to have it function as "public art"—I tried to consider the concept of public art as an academic exercise or problem to be solved. The fundamental question revolved around the collective group of Palo Alto residents who were funding the project with their taxes: Was there a way to design a public art project that could serve and involve this entire public?

The initial solution I developed, and later expanded, was to digitally photograph all 17,860 parcels in Palo Alto—the entire property tax base—and use the photographs to compute the average color of each parcel, street, and neighborhood, creating "The Color of Palo Alto." On a very basic level, each parcel would contribute one "vote" of color toward the final color of the city; the project would therefore involve the entire public: every resident would necessarily have a relation to the final colors.

MS: How did you expand the public art concept in this project?

SY: I first considered whether I could make the project more public by installing an office in the plaza to function both as a sculpture and as my project headquarters. Many questions emerged: Would this transform my behind-the-scenes studio practice into a public performance and add a layer to the project's "public-ness"?

Next, what if I installed all of the photographs on the front of City Hall for every person in Palo Alto to find their parcel and see their public contribution to the color of their city? City Hall represents the entire city, could we represent the entire city on City Hall? What if my office was solar- and wind-powered so that all the energy I used was renewable, including the energy I used to power my electric scooter around the city every day? Could the project formally promote the city's environmental initiatives?

And, what if the colors could be mixed at any paint store, printed from any computer, or used in any design to freely spread this environmental awareness? What if people could post photographs on a Web site showing how they used the colors, thereby contributing to a larger social canvas—a giant pointillist painting—as a larger public artwork? What if I tied the photographs into the City of Palo Alto database of parcels for use by city staff in planning, public works, emergencies, etc.?

As the project developed, the possibilities appeared endless and taking photos would simply be the beginning.

MS: How do you sustain your interest in the same project year after year to bring them to completion?

SY: I try to keep evolving my projects until hopefully I no longer recognize them, they are something I have never seen before, or they present something I have never thought about before. When I have an idea, I tend to ask myself, "And then what? How can I take this farther? How can I make this more interesting? What can I do to change it? How can I recontextualize it?" Then I ask, "What relation do those changes have to contemporary art discourse? How might those changes affect its possible interpretations and meanings?" Finally, when I come up with the next evolution of that idea, I ask myself the same questions all over again, "And then what?" I try not to settle on an idea for an object too soon.

MS: Are there any pitfalls to this strategy?

SY: Yes and no. I am extremely careful and methodical about my work. Although I work diligently every day, it takes me a tremendous amount of time to complete a project, sometimes years. Some people produce a lot of work very quickly, which is fine. I am not that type of person and I have tried to turn my methodical nature—a trait that could be perceived as a weakness—into a strength.

MS: The whole thing seems so improbable. You were only 26 years old when you began, had little money, and had never done anything on this scale before. Was the sheer size of the project the most difficult part?

SY: Although I generally worked from around 7 A.M. to midnight six or seven days a week, from January to December, the most difficult part was funding the project, rather than executing it. I had to start from scratch, and the $3,000 upfront budget did not begin to cover the expenses. For example, I did not own a computer when I started the project, and I couldn't afford to buy one. Everything had to be donated in one way or another. Leading up to the installation, I lived in my car for over a year (a car donated by a host family), and I stayed with six different host families over five years. It truly was a grassroots, group effort that happened only from sheer force of will.

MS: What advice can you offer to beginning students?

SY: First, I have reached many goals simply by being persistent and consistent. For example, it took

The "portable solar garage" in the Civic Center Plaza served as both a sculpture and "The Color of Palo Alto" headquarters. The garage powered an electric scooter, a digital camera, a GPS, and other computer equipment, turning the colors of the city into intrinsic symbols of ecological awareness because they were generated using renewable energy.

months, and in some cases years, to get permission to do certain projects. When people see that you are serious and committed, they may be more willing to help. I try not to take "no" for an answer and instead try to figure out some alternate route. Ironically, the more difficult path often leads to more interesting and surprising results than the easier path. Second, I try to bite off more than I can chew, so to speak; that is to say, I know that I will be able to finish a project—I am confident that I have the ability—but it will challenge me more in the meantime. It can be good to be naive and not know that something is impossible because you end up doing it anyway. Third, I try not to underestimate my source material. Anything can be material: plumbing, gardening, video games, etc. It just requires noticing it and committing to it. Fourth, if you ever have to sleep in your car, buy a car cover. If you put a cover on your car and then crawl inside, no one can tell you're in there sleeping and you can roll down the windows for air more safely. It's like an urban tent!

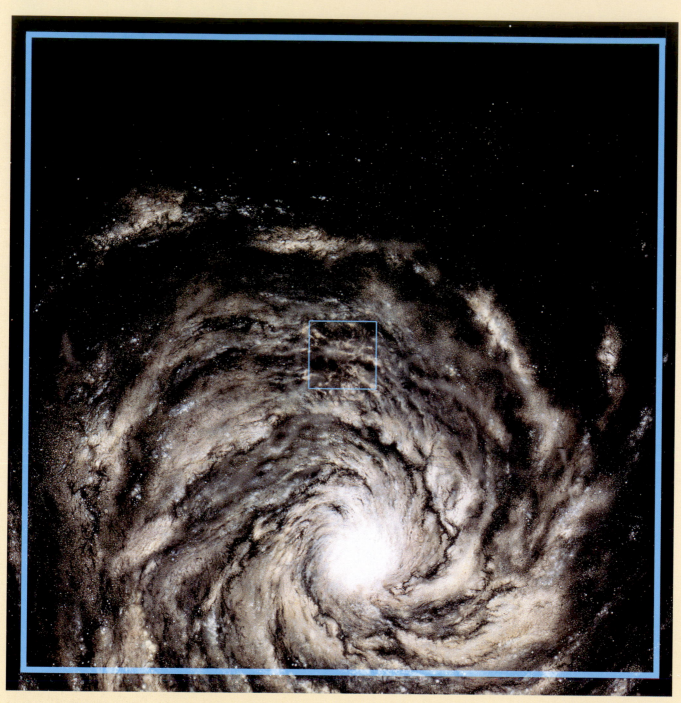

Charles and Ray Eames, *Powers of Ten,* 1977. Film frame.

Time
Design

From prehistory to the present, artists and designers have sought to create images, objects, and architectural works that embody and express the most profound aspects of human experience. Visions of love and hate, life and death, and the beauty of nature fill the walls of any art museum or gallery.

This compulsion to create has always inspired artists and designers to seek new avenues of expression. In contemporary art, innovation and experimentation have become the rule rather than the exception. Amazing new Web-based projects are used to distribute ideas to a global audience. Actions and ideas once considered taboo dominate many exhibitions. Separations among music, theater, and art become blurred when interdisciplinary art-works are presented.

In this final major section, we consider time as a dimension of art and design. While all areas of visual communication are affected by time, it is the sequential arts — such as film, video, computer graphics, visual books, and performance art — that most depend on the manipulation of time.

Chapter Thirteen offers an overview of time design and a description of its basic aspects and elements. Various forms of storytelling are discussed in Chapter Fourteen. We conclude with an exploration of interdisciplinary art and design, including an extended discussion of visual books, installation art, and performance art.

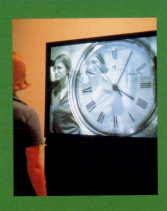

Aspects and Elements of Time

Abe Morell quietly sets up a large camera in an empty New York apartment. Except for a single small opening, he has blocked the light coming in the windows. Ghostly and inverted images of the surrounding city begin to appear on the walls. At just the right moment, he releases the shutter.

In 1998, Nancy Callahan and Diane Gallo created *Storefront Stories* in Cherry Valley, New York. A combination of words, images, and everyday objects was installed in an unused storefront window. Every 10 days, the installation was changed, presenting the next chapter in a story. Over a six-week period, an entire narrative was revealed to the people in the town.

An unusual advertisement was shown during the 1984 Super Bowl. The 60-second commercial begins as gray-faced workers in a futuristic city trudge to a huge theater and shuffle to their seats (13.1). From the screen, a grim "Big Brother" intones: "From today we celebrate the first anniversary of the information purification directions." A woman athlete is then shown, carrying a sledgehammer and sprinting toward the theater, with guards in hot pursuit. On arrival, she hurls the hammer into the screen, which explodes. As the words appear on the screen, an announcer reads, "On January 24, Apple Computer will introduce Macintosh. And you'll see why 1984 won't be like *1984*."

13.1 Apple Computer television ad introducing the Macintosh computer. Shown during the 1984 Super Bowl.

What is the connection? What do these artworks have in common? In each case, an understanding of time is an essential aspect of the work. Like gravity, time itself is intangible. While it is easy to overlook a force that we cannot see, the *effects* of time are critically important in all areas of art and design. An illustrator working on a track meet poster seeks the most dramatic moment in each event. The action shown in a narrative painting such as *Raft of the Medusa* (13.2) is as important as the composition created. And, through variations in texture and color, a ceramicist invites us to examine a bowl slowly, revealing each nuance as we rotate the form.

Photographers, videographers, book artists, and filmmakers are especially sensitive to the importance of time. When news photographer Sam Shere captured the moment at which the dirigible *Hindenburg* exploded, he created an indelible image (13.3). In *The Mysteries of Harris Burdick,* illustrator Chris Van Allsburg suggested a series of complex stories using a single drawing and a fragment of text (see figure 4.21, page 103). Time itself is the subject of Jim Campbell's *Digital Watch* (13.4). An ominous ticking noise accompanies the installation. On the large screen, viewers see themselves twice: in real time to the left of the clock and, after a brief delay, on the clock face itself. The persistent sound of the watch emphatically marks each passing second.

Meanings unfold through the passage of time. By selecting and composing each moment, we can turn the most mundane event into a memorable experience. Connections made through the juxtaposition of images can create a visual rhythm, express an idea, or tell a story. While these aspects of time are most clearly demonstrated through film, video, and photography, the implications for all areas of art and design are profound.

13.2 Théodore Géricault, *Raft of the Medusa,* **1818–19.** Oil on canvas, 16 ft 1 in. × 23 ft 6 in. (4.9 × 7.2 m).

13.3 Sam Shere, *Explosion of the* Hindenburg, *Lakehurst, NJ,* **1937.** Photograph.

13.4 Jim Campbell, *Digital Watch,* **1991.** Watch, camera, video cameras, electronics. Dimensions variable.

13.5A Single frame, close-up.

13.5B Single frame, medium shot.

13.5C Single frame, long shot.

BUILDING BLOCKS

The sequential structures used in film, video, and graphic novels are generally composed using four basic units: frame, shot, scene, and sequence. The **frame** is a single static image. Projected onto a flat screen, a film frame is governed by the same compositional forces as a painting, a poster, or a photograph. As shown in figures 13.5A, 13.5B, and 13.5C, the boundaries of the frame determine the meaning of the image. The **close-up** in the first frame shows the gasoline can that is the source of the fire. The **medium shot** in the second frame shows the parking lot in which the fire has been set. The **long shot** in the final frame shows the fire in a larger context. We now see that this fire at an oil refinery could spark an explosion.

In filmmaking, a **shot** is a continuous group of frames. In figure 13.6, the first shot consists of eight frames, the second shot consists of six frames, and the third shot consists of four frames. In traditional films, the eight-frame shot would last for one-third second, while the six-frame shot would last for one-quarter second.

By combining these shots, we can create a scene. A **scene** is usually constructed from continuous action in continuous time and continuous space. Shots of various length often are combined to strengthen expression.

A **sequence** is a collection of related shots and scenes that constitute a major section of action or narration. To understand the expressive potential of a sequence, we will examine four major ways in which shots can be related.

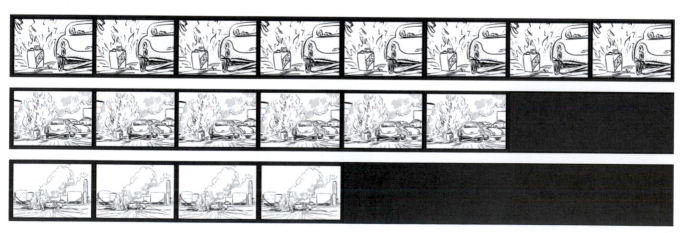

13.6 In filmmaking, a shot is a continuous group of frames.

Relationships

In *Film Art: An Introduction,* David Bordwell and Kristin Thompson describe four types of shot-to-shot relationships.

A **graphic relationship** connects two or more images through visual similarity. Because the images of doves, airplanes, and crosses in figures 13.7A, 13.7B, and 13.7C are graphically similar, a visual connection is made when they are shown together. In this case, a visual connection can be used to communicate a political idea. Doves symbolize peace, bombers symbolize war, and crosses symbolize death. The juxtaposition of these shots shows that the transition from peace to war leads to death.

A **spatial relationship** can expand or compress the stage on which an action occurs. Through a combination of close-ups and distance shots, the filmmaker can imply movement and can increase or decrease the emotional connection between the actor and the audience (13.8A–C).

A **temporal relationship** can establish **chronology,** the order in which events occur. A story may be told through a simple sequence of events or be reorganized using **flashbacks,** which refer to previous events. The 1993 movie *The Fugitive* uses flashbacks extensively. The film begins with the murder of Dr. Kimball's wife. Wrongly accused of the crime and sentenced to death, Kimball must discover the actual killer if he is to clear his name. Flashbacks to the murder, which occur throughout the story, show Kimball's recollection of the event that shattered his life.

When many shots are combined, a deliberate **rhythmic relationship** can be developed. Rhythm is often based on an interplay between static and dynamic, on a contrast between light and dark, or on a combination of shots of different duration.

13.7A Doves symbolize peace.

13.7B Bombers symbolize war.

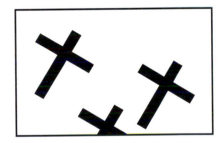

13.7C Crosses symbolize death.

13.8A Long shot.

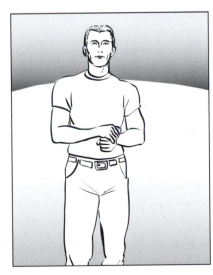

13.8B Medium shot.

13.8C Close-up.

13.9 A–K Alfred Hitchcock, *The Birds*.

In *The Birds*, Alfred Hitchcock used all these relationships to create a suspenseful sequence that builds to an explosive climax (13.9A–K). In *Film Art*, David Bordwell and Kristin Thompson describe this especially impressive example.[1] Melanie, the central character in the sequence, watches in horror as a line of flaming gasoline advances across the pavement, then ignites a gasoline station. The shots of her face create one graphic relationship, while the shots of the flame create a second. By **crosscutting**, or alternating between the two, Hitchcock created a powerful rhythm and established a simultaneous temporal relationship: Melanie is watching the gasoline as it advances toward the gas station. In a final aerial view (13.9K), we shift our spatial position to watch the final explosion from a seagull's point of view. Hitchcock combined graphic, rhythmic, temporal, and spatial relationships to create a cinematic tour de force.

Transitions

Four common transitions in film and video are the cut, fade, dissolve, and wipe (13.10). A **cut** is an abrupt transition that may connect very different images or very similar images, depending on the effect required. Fades and dissolves are gradual transitions. In a **fade,** the shot slowly darkens or lightens. In a **dissolve,** as one shot fades, another appears. Two shots are superimposed briefly in a **lap dissolve.** A **wipe** is more abrupt than a fade but softer than a cut. In a wipe, the first shot seems to be pushed off the screen by the second.

As described by Scott McCloud in *Understanding Comics,* comic books rely on six additional transitions.[2] American comics rely heavily on **action-to-action transitions** (13.11). Capturing sequential moments within an event, the action-to-action transition is clear and straightforward.

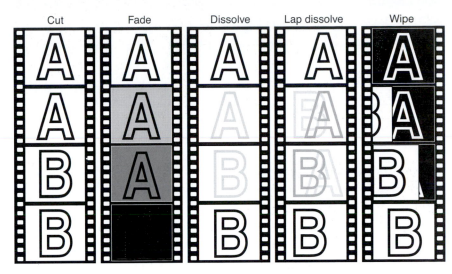

13.10 Common transitions.

In a **subject-to-subject transition** (13.12), two shots within the same scene are juxtaposed. The combination may provide crucial information, as in this explosive story.

A **scene-to-scene transition** (13.13) requires more reader involvement. Depending on the images used, this type of transition can transport us across great distances in time and space.

13.11 Action-to-action transition.

13.12 Subject-to-subject transition.

13.13 Scene-to-scene transition.

A **non-sequitur transition** (13.14) requires even more reader involvement. Because there is no logical relationship between shots, meaning must be invented.

Two additional transitions often appear in Japanese comic books. A **moment-to-moment transition** (13.15) is used when a character or situation is simply being observed over time. An **aspect-to-aspect transition** (13.16) is used to record different views within a scene. The passage of time slows as we scrutinize our surroundings.

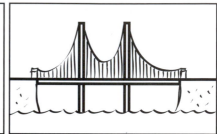

13.14 Non-sequitur transition.

13.15 Moment-to-moment transition.

Key Questions

BUILDING BLOCKS

- Can a graphic or temporal relationship add meaning to your artwork?

- Where are you using close-ups, medium shots, and long shots? What purpose does each serve?

- Would rhythmic variation strengthen your idea? What happens when you accelerate or change the rhythm?

13.16 Aspect-to-aspect transition.

DURATION

Duration refers to three things: the running time of a film, video, or performance; the time covered by the events depicted in the story; and the overall span of time the story encompasses. For example, the viewing time of *Star Wars* is 118 minutes. The **plot duration** (from the capture of Princess Leia to the destruction of the Death Star) is about a month. The overall **story duration,** however, extends back to Darth Vader's betrayal of the Jedi warriors and his alliance with the dark side of the Force.

Matching all three aspects of duration to the intended message is essential. Tolstoy's *War and Peace* cannot be fully communicated in a 15-minute film. Equally, a 10-second rocket launch may lose rather than gain power when the duration is increased. Every moment has its own power. A 15-second soft drink ad uses time just as carefully as a 2-hour film.

Determining the plot duration is especially important. Following the principles of drama described by Aristotle, ancient Greek plays (such as *Oedipus Rex*) generally occur over a one- or two-day period. Even though the characters often refer to previous events, the action on stage is brief. *Hamlet, Romeo and Juliet,* and most other Shakespeare plays are equally brief. By limiting the time frame, the playwright focuses our attention on a few events and thereby increases the impact of the play.

TEMPO

Tempo refers to the speed at which time passes. Despite the apparent constancy of real time, our perception of events in our lives varies widely, depending on the nature of the activity and the rate of change. Consider this story. Six coal miners were trapped by the collapse of a mine shaft. Based on the size of their shelter and the number of trapped men, the miners determined that there would be enough oxygen for a four-hour wait. Beyond that point, rescue would be futile: they would run out of oxygen. A miner with a fluorescent watch was asked to call out the hours as the time passed. He did so but modified his report, cutting in half the actual length of time passed. Six hours passed. All of the miners survived, except the man with the watch. He alone knew that they were out of oxygen.

Tempo is equally determined by the movement of the actors and by the editing of the film. In *Star Wars,* the fight between Darth Vader and Obi-Wan Kenobi began as staged combat between two actors (13.17). To provide director George Lucas with enough raw material, many versions, or **takes,** were filmed, using multiple cameras. The final tempo was determined through editing. By connecting fragments from many different views, Lucas was able to increase or decrease the fight tempo.

Key Questions

DURATION

- What is the actual duration of the event on which your artwork is based? What is the duration of your edited version?

- What did you cut from the raw footage and what did you add? Why?

- What strategies can you use to expand or compress duration?

- Will expanded or compressed duration add meaning to your artwork?

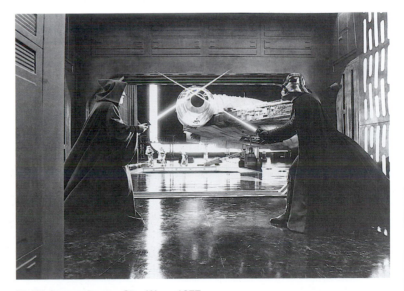

13.17 George Lucas, *Star Wars*, 1977.

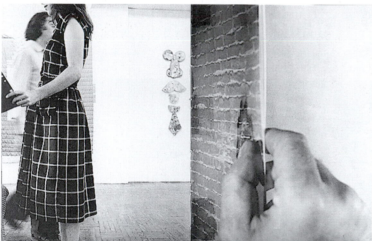

13.18 Michael Snow, from *Cover to Cover*, 1975. Press of the Nova Scotia College of Art and Design. New York University Press.

In a visual book, tempo is commonly created in two ways. First, by increasing the number and frequency of images, the artist can increase the tempo. Second, by turning the page, the reader controls the viewing speed.

In a flip book, actions can pass slowly or quickly, depending on the pace set by the viewer. In a more elaborate book called *Cover to Cover* (13.18), Michael Snow presents multiple views of a room interior and the surrounding landscape. There is no text—photographs of walls, doorways, and streets re-create the environment within the book format. The viewer can run or stroll through the house, depending on the speed with which the pages are turned.

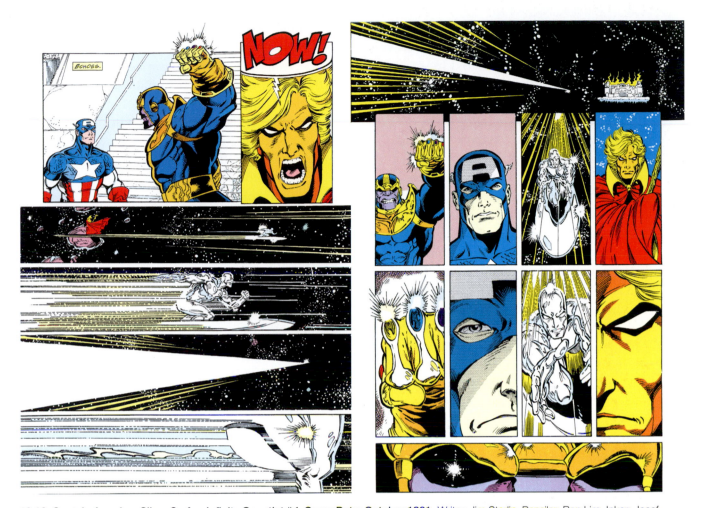

13.19 Captain America, Silver Surfer, *Infinity Gauntlet #4,* **Cover Date: October 1991.** Writer: Jim Starlin. Penciler: Ron Lim. Inker: Josef Rubinstein. Characters Featured: Captain America, Thanos, Adam Warlock, and Silver Surfer. © 2010 Marvel Characters, Inc. Used with permission.

As with film, tempo in a comic book is largely determined by the organization of multiple images. Vertical panels placed in close proximity tend to speed up the tempo, while horizontal panels tend to slow it down. Interactions among various superhero characters are shown in figure 13.19. The horizontal panels emphasize the speed of the flying figures, while the vertical panels slow down the action. Close-ups in the final sequence of images emphasize the fierce determination of each character.

Key Questions
TEMPO

- How quickly does time pass in your artwork?
- What are the advantages of a slow tempo? Of a fast tempo? Of variations in tempo?
- When and why might tempo variations occur?

INTENSITY

Intensity refers to the level of energy in a performance or the quality of observation of an event. For example, to win an Olympic gold medal, an ice skater must spin rapidly, fully extend each move, and exude both athletic skill and emotional conviction. Likewise, even an ordinary glass of water becomes fascinating when observed closely. The glass itself offers a graceful interplay between line and shape, while light passing through droplets of water breaks into a prismatic array of color.

Intensity of performance is an essential aspect of theater. We can feel the concentration the actors bring to the stage, and when a dramatic or dangerous event occurs, we can share their emotion. In *Cleaning the House* (13.20), Yugoslavian artist Marina Abramovic combined intensity with metaphor to make a political statement. Wearing a white dress and sitting in a poorly lit New York City basement, she repeatedly scrubbed the dirt and blood off a collection of massive cow bones. Like the bones, various ethnic groups in her homeland have been "cleansed," bringing trauma and bleached bones to the once prosperous country.

Video is often used first to record, then to intensify everyday experience. In *Migration (Monarch)* (13.21), Mary Lucier photographed a monarch butterfly, which alights on a human hand, then dies. Capable of migrating thousands of miles, the beautiful creature is shown here as fragile and transient. The very act of filming the insect's death focuses our attention on the event, while the subsequent projection of the video in the middle of Manhattan increases its poignancy and significance.

Key Questions

INTENSITY

- What is the intensity level of your artwork or performance? How will a change in intensity affect the expressive power of your artwork?

- How are you communicating this intensity to the audience?

- What is the most important moment in your work? Is it the most intense moment?

13.20 Marina Abramovic, *Cleaning the House*, 1995.
Performance at Sean Kelly Gallery. Duration, two hours.

13.21 Mary Lucier, *Migration (Monarch)*, 2000.
Video projection, Times Square.

SCOPE

Scope can be defined in two ways. Conceptually, it is the extent of our perception or the range of ideas our minds can grasp. Temporally, scope refers to the range of action within a given moment.

The earliest films, such as *The Arrival of a Train at La Ciotat Station* (13.22), are limited in scope. A single event is seen from a fixed viewpoint. By positioning his camera carefully, director Louis Lumière created a dynamic, diagonal composition. The train and passengers seem to come out of the screen and into the theater. Some audience members were so convinced of the illusion that they exited the theater to avoid being hit by the train. In the early days of cinema, any moving image fascinated the audience, and its dramatic composition made this film especially popular.

As directors gained experience, they expanded the temporal scope of their films. In *The Great Train Robbery* (1903), a gang of bandits holds up a train; a telegraph operator alerts the authorities; a posse is gathered from men at a local dance; the posse captures the thieves. Director Edwin S. Porter used only 11 shots, and the editing is quite simple. Nonetheless, it is clear that the robbery, the telegrapher's message, and the dance are roughly simultaneous events.

With *Intolerance,* director D. W. Griffith expanded conceptual scope to the limit. Using intolerance throughout history as a theme, Griffith developed four simultaneous stories: the fall of Babylon, Jesus' final days, the St. Bartholomew's Day Massacre in France, and a labor strike in modern-day America. These stories are intercut throughout the film, with the image of a woman rocking a cradle as a further recurrent theme. Each story concludes in an attempted rescue. Weaving the four narratives together in an accelerating rhythm (13.23A and B), Griffith brought the film to a breathtaking conclusion.

Complex stories often require complex editing, and Griffith became a master of the art. By alternately showing two or more events, he created a connection between simultaneous actions. Comic book artists use many of the same devices. This technique of crosscutting is used repeatedly in *Inhumans* (13.24), by Paul Jenkins and Jae Lee. Moving again and again from cannon fire to a quiet

13.22 Louis Lumière, *The Arrival of a Train at La Ciotat Station*, 1897.

13.23A D. W. Griffith, *Intolerance*, 1916.

13.23B D. W. Griffith, *Intolerance*, 1916.

13.24 Paul Jenkins (Writer) and Jae Lee (Artist), *Inhumans: "First Contact,"* Volume 2, Issue 5, March 1999. © 2010 Marvel Comics, Inc. Used with permission.

13.25 Nicolas Poussin, *The Rape of the Sabine Women,* 1634. Oil on canvas, 5 ft ⅞ in. × 6 ft 10⅝ in. (154.6 × 209.9 cm).

conversation between two men, the artists show that the events are concurrent.

Scope is equally important in traditional narrative painting. In Nicolas Poussin's *The Rape of the Sabine Women* (13.25), a complex event is shown in a single image. Seeking wives, the Romans have invited the Sabines to a festival. They then attack their guests and abduct the women. Many actions occur at once. In the upper-left corner, Romulus raises his cloak as a signal to attack. As the courtyard swirls with struggles between the women and their captors, an old woman and two children at the center of the painting watch in terror.

Key Questions

SCOPE

- Is your artwork limited or broad in scope?
- If it is broad in scope, how can you create continuity among multiple events?
- If it is narrow in scope, how can you make the "small" story become meaningful?
- Consider moving from broad scope to narrow scope within your movie. How does this affect communication?

SETTING

Setting is one of the most complex aspects of time. It includes the physical and temporal location of a story, its props and costumes, and the use of sound.

Physical and Temporal Location

The physical setting of an event has an extraordinary impact on meaning. An action that is appropriate in one context may be appalling in another. As a drum major, you will be applauded when you strut down Main Street during a Fourth of July parade. At a different time of day (such as Monday morning rush hour) or in a different location (such as an airport), you are likely to get arrested.

The temporal setting is equally significant. Most of the action in *Gone with the Wind* is derived from romantic conflict involving Scarlett O'Hara, Ashley Wilkes, and Rhett Butler. While each of the three characters is interesting, the love triangle itself is commonplace. It is the temporal setting of the novel during the American Civil War that shifts the story from soap opera to epic.

Likewise, Nancy Holt's *Sun Tunnels* (13.26) would be meaningless if removed from its site in

13.26 Nancy Holt, *Sun Tunnels*, 1973–76. Great Basin Desert, UT. Four tunnels, each 18 ft long × 9 ft 4 in. (5.5 × 2.8 m) diameter, each axis 86 ft (26.2 m) long. Aligned with sunrises and sunsets on the solstices.

western Utah. Constructed from four 22-ton concrete tunnels, this sculpture is aligned with the rising and setting sun on the winter and summer solstices. The arrangement of stars in four constellations is shown by holes cut in the walls of each tunnel. Designed to heighten awareness of our place in the universe, this work relies on both time and place for its impact.

Props and Costumes

Props and costumes can have an equally dramatic effect in a narrative. The top hat and tuxedo worn by Fred Astaire in many films helped convey a formal elegance, while the leather jacket worn by Michael Jackson in *Beat It* helped place him on a contemporary city street. In Peter Jackson's *The Lord of the*

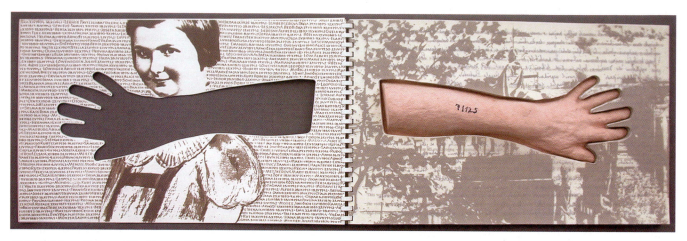

13.27A Tatana Kellner, *Fifty Years of Silence,* 1992. 12.2 × 19.7 × 2 in. (31 × 50 × 5 cm).

13.27B Tatana Kellner, *Fifty Years of Silence,* 1992. 12.2 × 19.7 × 2 in. (31 × 50 × 5 cm).

13.27C Tatana Kellner, *Fifty Years of Silence,* 1992. 12.2 × 19.7 × 2 in. (31 × 50 × 5 cm).

Rings, the one ring of power is as pivotal a character as Frodo himself.

Fifty Years of Silence (13.27A–C), a visual book by Tatana Kellner, is even more dependent on objects and their meanings. The simple pine crate that houses the book seems innocuous until we see the small, five-digit number burned into the lid. When the lid is removed, a papier-mâché arm is revealed, bearing the same number. It is a cast of the arm of Kellner's mother, a survivor of Auschwitz. The book pages, cut out around the arm, tell the story of the family before and during the Holocaust. As the pages are turned, the actual arm and the cutout arm are as inescapable as the repressed memories of a Holocaust survivor. By placing it in such a prominent position in the book, Kellner provides us with a sculptural close-up of the indelible tattoo. The wooden crate suggests a container for expensive wine or a shipping crate for a valuable object. The arm is an even more compelling sculptural object. By using these "props," Kellner gives her book greater immediacy and transforms the story of a Holocaust survivor into a highly personal event.

Setting and Actor

Relationships between an actor and a setting can substantially affect our interpretation of an action or event. As shown in figures 13.28 through 13.34, placement of a single figure within a setting offers a wide range of possibilities.

First, we must decide where to place the dancer within the frame. Three alternatives are shown in figure 13.28. Positioned at the far left edge, she faces an empty stage, which invites her to enter. Positioned in the center, she commands attention. She can move to the right, to the left, forward, or back with ease. She is now in a more commanding position. Facing right, and positioned at the right, she seems ready to leave the frame, perhaps to join other dancers offstage.

What happens when the size of the dancer is varied? As shown in figure 13.29, changing the size of the figure in relationship to the frame helps define the distance between the dancer and the viewer. When the dancer is reduced in size and placed in the upper half of the frame, she seems distant, far from the viewer. When she moves far into the foreground,

with her torso filling the frame, she seems to push past the boundary and into our space.

The addition of an illusionistic setting (13.30) dramatically changes the amount of space available to the dancer. Even a simple line can be used in various ways. It may be the ground, providing a resting place for the dancer. When the dancer overlaps the line, it recedes, suggesting a horizon. The addition of a second line can expand the space even further. We can now show two grounds at the same time: the foreground and the background.

13.28

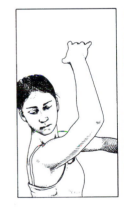

13.29

13.30

In figure 13.31, the addition of perspective lines further enhances the space. A long corridor in one-point perspective gives the dancer an expansive stage that invites movement from the background to the foreground. The space is extended beyond the edge of the frame by the repeating chairs and the lines in the floor. Despite her small size, the dancer's central placement makes her the focus of both images.

The setting can become even more significant when the dancer is viewed from above or below (13.32). Looking up from the front row gives the figure a commanding presence. Looking down from the balcony makes her seem insignificant.

Adjusting the lights (13.33) greatly increases the compositional and emotional possibilities. Sidelighting accentuates the dimensionality of both the figure and the setting. When we back-light the dancer, she becomes a silhouette. We lose information about her volume but gain a striking graphic image and an impressive cast shadow. Spotlighting the dancer can direct attention to a specific part of her body or eliminate the rest of the stage altogether.

Variations in focus (13.34) can affect both spatial location and emotional impact. When the foreground figure is out of focus, she is less dominant,

13.33

13.31

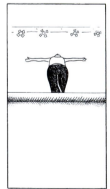

13.32

13.34

and we quickly look past her into the more tightly focused audience. A more traditional use of focus is shown in the middle drawing: clear focus in the foreground gradually diminishes as we approach the distant stage. However, do we really want to focus on the back of the audience? By focusing on the distant stage, we can watch the dancer as she ends her performance and accepts the applause.

Key Questions

SETTING AND ACTOR

- Start with a single actor. Who is this person? An eight-year-old boy? A pregnant woman? A soldier in a wheelchair? What objects relate to this character?
- How many ways can you position the actor in the setting? How does each position affect meaning?
- What is the viewer's position relative to the actor?

Sound: The Hidden Dimension

Two versions of a clip from *Chariots of Fire* were shown during the 1996 Academy Awards ceremony. This story of the British track tream that won many medals during the 1924 Olympic Games showed the transformation of idealistic men into heroic athletes. In the first version, a group of young men ran along a beach, accompanied by the sounds of their feet splashing in the water. It was a pleasant but prosaic scene, showing ordinary men on an ordinary beach. The same footage was then shown as it appeared in theaters around the world. Accompanied by the famous theme music, these Olympic runners became graceful, even godlike. They were transformed by the music.

Despite its invisibility, the soundtrack is as important to a film as the images we see. Sound engages another of our senses and heightens our emotion. A well-written score can set the stage for an action and help unify a complex film. Sound also heightens our expectations. Consider the importance of squeaky doors in any horror movie or our feeling of expectation when the *Star Wars* theme is played. As we begin to study film, we find that the example from *Chariots of Fire* is not an isolated case. Sound can make or break a film.

Four types of sound dominate time design: speech (as delivered by an actor or generated from the audience), music, ambient sound, and sound effects. Each sound has seven qualities.

Loudness is determined by the size of the oscillations in a sound wave. Just as Beethoven varied the volume (or loudness) within his symphonies, so the astute filmmaker or performance artist learns to use a full range of sound, from a whisper to a scream.

Pitch is determined by wave frequency, as compression and expansion occur within the sound wave. The higher pitch of most female voices generally is less threatening than the lower pitch of most male voices. Not surprisingly, the hero is a tenor, while the villain is a baritone in most operas.

Timbre refers to the unique quality of each instrument. For example, a note of the same volume and pitch is quite different when it is generated by a trumpet rather than a violin.

Duration refers to the length of time a sound can be heard. A sound that persists over a long period of time is often used as a bridge between two or more film clips, while a brief, explosive sound may jolt us out of our seats.

Rhythm is determined by three qualities: the **beat,** or pulse, of the sound; the **pace** (or tempo) at which the sound is played; and the **accents,** or areas of emphasis, within the sound. We encounter rhythm in every conversation as we listen to the speed of our friend's speech and note his or her emphasis on particular words. Rap music, which in some ways is a heightened form of speech, greatly emphasizes the beat, through both a rhythmic use of words and the strong definition of each syllable.

In film, **fidelity** refers to the connection between a sound and its source. The arrival of a helicopter at the end of the musical *Miss Saigon* is accompanied by the loud sound of a churning propeller. Here, the sonic information and the visual information match. In *Apocalypse Now*, Richard Wagner's "Ride of the Valkyries" is played as a group of helicopters arrives. As in *Chariots of Fire*, this mismatch between the visual and sonic information substantially changes our interpretation of the event.

Finally, all forms of sound operate within a **spatial context.** The bagpipe, designed to rally troops in war, is an excellent instrument to play outdoors. When played in a small room, the same instrument can very nearly blast plaster off a wall. Likewise, a whispered conversation in a closet may be more compelling than a shouted conversation on a beach. Even when we have no image at all, sound alone can define space and create a sense of anticipation or dread.

In a film, the spatial dimension of sound becomes even more significant. **Diegetic** sound, or sound that is part of the world we see on the screen, can be generated by a visible event or can come from an invisible, offscreen source. Both onscreen and offscreen sound are critically important, and in many cases a director will shift between the two. For example, in *Titanic*, a quartet of musicians is shown playing "Nearer My God to Thee" as the ship sinks lower and lower. The music continues as we see an elderly couple in their cabin, embracing (13.35), and a mother comforting her child. The combination of the music and the images heightens the emotion of the moment.

In addition to his work on ballets (such as *Billy the Kid* and *Appalachian Spring*), symphonies, chamber pieces, and songs, composer Aaron Copland was a master of film music. In 1949, he wrote "Tip to Moviegoers: Take Off Those Earmuffs," an essay describing ways music can enhance a film.[3] While his comments are most applicable to music, they can also be applied to other types of sound. Copland emphasized five points, paraphrased below.

- *Sound can create a more convincing atmosphere of time and place.* For example, harpsichord music may be effective in a film set in seventeenth-century Paris while jazz may be appropriate for a detective story set in contemporary Memphis, Tennessee.

- *Sound can communicate the unspoken thoughts of a character or the unseen implications of a situation.* A cheerful family picnic film can quickly become threatening and claustrophobic if an accelerated heartbeat is added.

- *Sound can serve as a neutral background, filling space between bits of dialogue.* Copland considered this the "composer's most ungrateful task" yet noted its value in helping create a unified film. Background sounds can subtly season the overall temporal stew.

- *Sound can build a sense of continuity.* As noted in Chapter 1, a collage of visual fragments can be difficult to unify. Similarly, a **montage,** or collection of temporal fragments, can quickly

13.35 James Cameron, *Titanic*, 1997.

become chaotic and incomprehensible. The addition of sound helps connect the parts and can add a unifying rhythm.

- *Sound often heralds the beginning of an event or rounds it off with a sense of finality.* John Williams, one of the most successful and prolific of contemporary composers, is renowned for his evocative introductions as well as his grand finales. For examples of his work, watch and listen to *Harry Potter and the Sorcerer's Stone, Jaws, Star Wars, Raiders of the Lost Ark, Superman,* and *Schindler's List.*

For clarity, all these examples are emphatic and familiar. In your own work, consider less obvious and more evocative solutions. The interplay between sound and image is extremely rich, and experimenting with the least familiar combinations may lead you to the most powerful results.

Key Questions

SETTING

- Consider all aspects of setting: sound, props, physical space, and lighting. Have you used each aspect fully?

- How can changes in setting add meaning to your artwork?

- Consider various settings. What will happen if the setting changes during the performance from a deserted train station to a factory? To a doctor's office? To a lecture hall?

CHRONOLOGY

Chronology refers to temporal order. In real time, a foot race begins with the athletes lining up in position (action A), followed by the firing of the starting gun (action B), the running of the race (action C), and the conclusion at the finish line (action D). These actions can be organized in various ways, from a disorienting ABACADA pattern to the familiar ABCD pattern of the actual race.

In *Structure of the Visual Book*,[4] Keith Smith demonstrates the narrative possibilities of multiple images (13.36–13.45, page 312). Changes in chronology completely change meaning. In each case, relationships among the images create the sequence of events needed to tell a story.

Chronology is created when shots are combined. A filmmaker combines shots through **editing.** Editing serves six basic purposes.

First, the film editor must select the most compelling images from the total footage shot. No matter how carefully a scene is rehearsed, variations in performance quality occur, especially when there are many actors on the set. Even more footage is shot for a documentary film. Before editing a film about the 1936 Olympic Games in Berlin, Leni Riefenstahl devoted 10 solid weeks of work to just watching the raw footage. Editing this material down to a 3½-hour film took another two years!

Second, the raw film must be organized into a cohesive whole. Multiple cameras are often used to provide plenty of rough footage. Constructing a coherent composition using both close-up and distant shots is often the first step.

Third, through editing, a temporal framework for the film is developed. Time can expand, contract, or move in a dizzying spiral. When using crosscutting, the editor shifts back and forth between two or more events, thereby suggesting the simultaneous occurrence of multiple actions. *A Tale of Two Cities,* by Charles Dickens, is a literary example of crosscutting. The narrative reaches a climax as Sydney Carton, in Paris, is led to the guillotine, while his double, who was actually condemned to die, is drugged and transported to London. Chapter after chapter, the story shifts between the two men, increasing the sense of urgency while presenting the simultaneous events. This novel offers simultaneous action at its best. Indeed, pioneer film director D. W. Griffith used Dickens as an example when he was challenged for his innovative editing of *Intolerance.*

Fourth, tempo in a film is determined largely by the number of cuts made. For example, an introspective drama may be constructed from 1,000 shots, while an action film may be made of 2,000 shots or more. Variations in tempo help sustain interest. If there is too little variation, a fast-paced film is just as monotonous as a slow-paced film. To develop momentum gradually, many filmmakers use a slow-paced beginning, which builds to a fast-paced climax, which returns to a slow-paced conclusion.

Fifth, connections made through editing can heighten emotion and suggest the real motivation for a character's actions. In a famous experiment, early Soviet filmmaker Lev Kulesov demonstrated the emotional impact of editing. He combined a neutral shot of an actor's face with four very different images: a bowl of soup, scenes from nature, a baby, and a dead woman.[4] When the film was shown, the audience praised the actor's skill: he looked hungry when the soup appeared, longed for freedom when the landscape was shown, was filled with joy at the sight of the baby, and felt grief at the sight of the woman. In each case, however, the shot of the actor's face was exactly the same. The emotions were created by the audience's response to the editing, not by any change in the actor's expression.

Finally, connections made through editing can substantially alter or enhance the meaning of a film. By cutting from a bone spinning in the air to a space station orbiting the earth (13.46, page 313), Stanley Kubrick connected prehistory to space travel in *2001: A Space Odyssey.*

Key Questions
CHRONOLOGY

- Do events in your project occur in a traditional linear (ABCD) order?

- What would happen if this order were changed? Would ADBDCCC be more powerful?

- What would happen if you deleted half the information in your project? Would the artwork as a whole gain or lose power?

- What would happen if you added more material from a different source?

 **13.36**

Start with a door.

  **13.37**

Add a figure. Here, a woman opens the door.

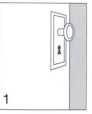  **13.38**

Here, the door opens and we meet a woman.

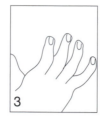   **13.39**

Adding a close-up of a hand creates a confrontation . . .

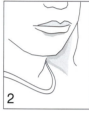 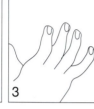  **13.40**

. . . while this order creates a sense of anticipation.

  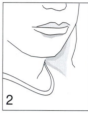 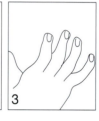 **13.41**

Here, we create a mystery.

 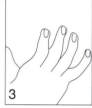  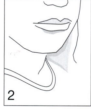 **13.42**

With the introduction of a knife, a new meaning emerges. It is now becoming threatening.

 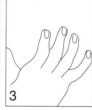    **13.43**

And now even more so. Our imaginations provide a wide range of horrors for panel 5.

 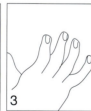  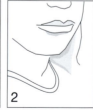   **13.44**

Addition of a loaf of bread, however, diffuses the tension. It is not a murder after all, just a sandwich being made.

 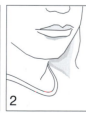 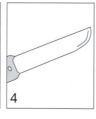 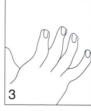 **13.45**

The woman still has to take care, however; this final version suggests that she has cut herself!

13.36 –13.45 Keith Smith, Excerpt from *Structure of the Visual Book,* 1995. Variations in chronology dramatically change the story.

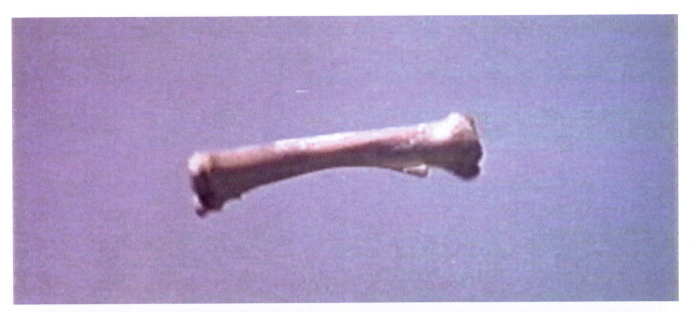

13.46 Stanley Kubrick, *2001: A Space Odyssey*, 1968. Juxtaposing the whirling bone and the floating space station connects prehistory to the space-age.

SCHINDLER'S LIST: CONTENT AND COMPOSITION

All these aspects of editing are used brilliantly in *Schindler's List*. Mixing contemporary images with black-and-white images of wartime Poland, director Steven Spielberg tells a harrowing tale of the survival of over 1,000 Jews during the Holocaust. Based on historical events, the film shows the transformation of Nazi Oskar Schindler from a single-minded war profiteer to a compassionate man who eventually bought the lives of his enslaved workers. It is an incredible story, and any skillful filmmaker could have made a good film based on this event. However, to show the complexities of each character and to turn the story into a truly compelling film required another level of insight. Spielberg and his collaborators had that insight.

The critical importance of editing is apparent from the start. A contemporary scene of a Jewish family at home ends with a trail of smoke rising from an extinguished candle (13.47). We cut to the smokestack on a train in wartime Krakow (13.48) and are transported back in time.

Editing also establishes Schindler's motivation and gives us insight into his personality. When he arrives at a cafe favored by Nazi officers, the maitre d' seats him, then asks a waiter who he is. Neither one knows his name. Schindler carefully positions himself at the center of the room. Through a series of close-ups, we follow his gaze as he notes the SS insignia on an officer's uniform and assesses the importance of the reserved table across the room. Using Schindler as the axis, the camera pans around the room (13.49). Positioned just over his shoulder, we watch Schindler as he observes the soldiers. He did not come to this restaurant to eat. He intends to meet the most influential Nazis in the area and establish himself as a man of consequence.

As the scene continues, Schindler joins the Nazis and leads a song. Finally, the highest-ranking officer asks the maitre d' about this newcomer. He now enthusiastically replies, "Why, that is Oskar Schindler!" (13.50A). Schindler (who entered the restaurant as a nobody) is now well defined: he has become the center of attention (13.50B). The evening has been a success.

Crosscutting is used throughout the film, both to establish a connection and to emphasize separation. Eviction of a Jewish family from their spacious home is immediately followed by images of Schindler surveying the same space, now his new home. He reclines on a large bed and exclaims, "It couldn't be better!" (13.51). We then cut to the evicted family, struggling up the stairs of their new dwelling, which will be shared with many other families. As they sit down in the single room they have been assigned, the wife notes, "It could be worse." Her angry husband replies, "How could it *possibly* be worse?" (13.52). Just then, another large family apologetically moves into the cramped space. It is now worse.

The destruction of the Krakow ghetto is a masterpiece of storytelling. Sound is especially important in this sequence, and variations in pacing substantially increase the visual impact. The sequence begins as Nazi commandant Goeth gives his assembled troops a brief history lesson (13.53). As he describes the arrival of the Jews in Poland in the fourteenth century, we cut from the soldiers to scenes of ghetto families quietly eating and preparing for the day ahead, unaware of the terror to follow. We return to Goeth as

13.47 Steven Spielberg, *Schindler's List.* Extinguished candle.

13.48 *Schindler's List.* Train's smokestack.

13.49 *Schindler's List.* Schindler in a cafe.

13.50A *Schindler's List.* Officer asks maitre d' about Schindler.

13.50B *Schindler's List.* Focus shifts to Schindler as he is identified.

13.51 *Schindler's List.* New home.

13.52 *Schindler's List.* New home, shared by three families.

13.53 *Schindler's List.* Commandant Goeth.

13.54 *Schindler's List.* Staircase.

he concludes his speech, noting that "by this evening, those six centuries are a rumor. They never existed."

An explosion of violence follows. The family at breakfast is now wrapping jewels in bread and eating them, in the hope of retaining something of value when the pogrom ends. Stern, the overworked accountant upon whom Schindler depends, desperately searches his pockets for his identity papers as a soldier screams in his face. The camera is jostled as terrified people are evicted from their apartments. Diagonal staircases and extreme camera angles increase compositional dynamism (13.54).

A contrast between violence and compassion, fast and slow pace, heightens the impact of this sequence. An old woman, walking slowly down a foggy street, is ignored by the soldiers, who run past, determined to clear the ghetto. A doctor methodically adds poison to cups of water, then gently administers it to his patients (13.55) rather than leave them for the soldiers to kill. A young Polish boy, assigned to report any survivors, instead saves the life of a woman and her daughter.

We now see a small girl in a red coat walking through the streets (13.56) and observed by Schindler, who surveys the action from a nearby hill. Accompanied by angelic music, she is the symbol of all the innocent deaths on this horrible day. We last see her as she scoots under a bed, seeking a place to hide. We will not see her again until much later in the film, when her red coat appears as the corpses from the ghetto liquidation are gathered to be burned.

Quiet finally descends on the city. The soldiers are now using stethoscopes to listen for survivors who may have hidden in apartment walls. In a final burst of violence, one soldier plays a vigorous

13.55 *Schindler's List.* Doctor administering poison.

Bach toccata while other soldiers explode into action, firing their machine guns into the walls and commanding their dogs to attack.

The calm before the storm makes this sequence even more frightening. It would be impossible to sustain a fast pace throughout the film. Incessant horror would have simply left us numb. The editing and use of contrast have greatly enhanced the power of the ghetto sequence, leaving an indelible impression.

13.56 *Schindler's List.* Girl in a red coat.

SUMMARY

- An understanding of time is an essential aspect of any artwork. Photographers, filmmakers, and performers use time directly; painters, illustrators, ceramicists, and other artists generally use time indirectly.

- The building blocks of film are the frame, the shot, the scene, and the sequence.

- Shots can be related graphically, spatially, temporally, and rhythmically.

- The cut, fade, dissolve, and wipe are the most common transitions in film.

- Comic books use six additional transitions: action-to-action, subject-to-subject, scene-to-scene, non-sequitur, moment-to-moment, and aspect-to-aspect.

- Duration, tempo, intensity, scope, setting, and chronology are the six major elements of time design.

KEY TERMS

accents
action-to-action transitions
aspect-to-aspect transition
beat
chronology
close-up
crosscutting
cut
diegetic
dissolve
duration
editing

fade
fidelity
flashbacks
frame
graphic relationship
intensity
lap dissolve
long shot
loudness
medium shot
moment-to-moment transition

montage
non-sequitur transition
pace
pitch
plot duration
rhythm
rhythmic relationship
scene
scene-to-scene transition
scope
sequence
setting

shot
spatial context
spatial relationship
story duration
subject-to-subject transition
takes
tempo
temporal relationship
timbre
wipe

STUDIO PROJECTS

To apply the concepts from this chapter in the studio, check out the Projects page in the Online Learning Center at www.mhhe.com/stewart4e. The following is a sample of the chapter-related assignments that are described in step-by-step detail.

Time Observed. Increasing awareness of time through careful attention.
Arrested Time. Implied time and captured moments.
Tempo. Exploring variations in the rate of change.
Chronology. A quick, simple demonstration of the impact of chronology on narrative.

Profile:
Sharon Greytak, Filmmaker
Resilient Spirit

Sharon Greytak is the writer, producer, and director of two award-winning features, *The Love Lesson* (1995) and *Hearing Voices* (1991), as well as the documentaries *Weirded Out and Blown Away* (1986) and *Losing It* (2001). Her films have been screened theatrically and at numerous festivals and showcases.

MS: You studied painting at CalArts and were always interested in literature. How, then, did you become a filmmaker?

SG: Film seemed to suit my personality. I was beginning to feel that art shown primarily in galleries reached a specific audience, but not the general public where discussion and change should occur. I felt an urgency about the social issues I wanted to address, and the unconventional stories I knew only I could tell. I knew as a filmmaker I could reach a very wide audience.

Furthermore, the process of painting is mainly solitary, while filmmaking is absolutely a collaborative art. There's an energy in film production that doesn't exist anywhere else, an energy toward what the mind's eye sees, toward what the camera will record. I guess I'm able to hold an idea and an image in my mind for a very long time. Communicating my vision and staying on track as the piece becomes more refined is the essence of what drives any artist.

MS: You write the screenplay, hire the crew, produce and direct the film, then market the result. Yet it all seems to start with a story you want to tell. What stories interest you most?

SG: All of my screenplays are original. A film is a visual story—very different than a written story. I write pictures. The script is the blueprint, providing the visual and emotional tone as well as the dialogue.

I explore unconventional human relationships in my stories—relationships that are overlooked by the mass media. I am interested in stories that haven't been told. In any film, I am always aware of the facet or angle of a story that is unique. The space between one's public and private identity has always fascinated me. I want to give voice to people whose voices are rarely heard.

MS: You've said that you are good at spotting the nuggets, the most telling images and human interactions. What makes an image or an exchange of dialogue compelling?

SG: It's very hard to explain. For me, it's a combination of all the senses, plus one or two unnamed senses; maybe instinct. I guess you're looking for the essence of what you're trying to communicate, but never naming it precisely. If you name it directly, it's dead. It comes back to trusting the viewer and leaving space for interpretation. When I'm directing actors and doing several takes, I look for something that shimmers, or wavers in the air around them; where all of us, cast and crew, have created an ephemeral moment aside from the actor's lines or anything tangible. It's something that lingers in the air for a moment. It is resonant, yet unsaid.

MS: Film constantly changes, and if the viewer doesn't "get" it the first time, the story can be lost. How do you determine what to say? What is essential?

SG: In any art form, it is so easy to overstate an idea. When I was in my twenties, I studied with painter David Salle. At that time, I was painting and drawing. I showed a series of mixed media works in David's experimental studio class. David cocked his head, stared a long time, then turned and said, "What do you think I am, stupid?" I was stunned. He went on about signs and symbols, the indexical and the iconic, a priori knowledge, and underestimating your audience. He then rattled off a list of books and articles I should be reading.

I made no art for three months. I read. I read aesthetics and politics, semiotics. I skulked around the edges of my classes, listening and watching. It was the turning point in my life as an artist. Exactly the right thing. And I picked up the camera. Super-8 at first. I realized I had been always talking about my abstract drawings in a very narrative way. I wondered what I would do if I had to choose an image in the world. Inspiration had never come from life before. It had always been formal properties of line and color, mark making, and the gesture. It was from that point that my films and drawings began to have an undertone, something of their own, combined with a respect for the intelligence of my audience.

MS: I am impressed by the immediacy of film. A good film draws me in: I feel that I am right there.

SG: A base in reality is essential. When you have that, anything is possible to write. And, small things can illuminate big ideas. When I screened my short films at a festival in Krakow, Poland, we were invited to visit Auschwitz. Since I have a physical disability, I was not able to follow the tour group to the second level of the barracks. The irony of the situation was comical, and powerful. Had it been 50 years earlier, I wouldn't have lasted a day there. Just by fate the scenario would have been very different.

As the rest of the tour went upstairs, I stayed alone on the ground floor of the barracks. In silence I was able to look at the scratches on the door. Scratches that had been made by human hands.

By sitting still, alone, I could touch where so many other lives had been. I could make a more authentic connection through the remnants of a real life, through the energy I did not expect to find.

MS: Tell me about *Losing It*.

SG: *Losing It* is an international film exploring the quality of life for people with disabilities. It's about how people navigate social stereotypes within their culture to carve out a sense of purpose and worth despite physical limitations. I traveled in the United States, Brazil, Hong Kong, Russia, and Italy to interview people about the way they view themselves and the way in which society views them. It's also a story of personal search and human nature with regard to disability.

MS: What advice do you have for my students?

SG: Cultivate a diverse circle of friends and colleagues. Build a career slowly. Making art means a life in the arts. Not a year or two, but a lifetime of observing and questioning in order to create something unique. When I find myself having to do something or go somewhere out of obligation, a thing that at the time seems totally a waste of time, fate often finds a way of adding that experience or person to further my creative work. Most of the time I end up seeing an angle I wouldn't have recognized before. I guess what I'm saying is, stay open enough for life to show you things. Let life take you where you're supposed to go.

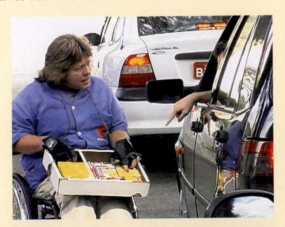

Stills from *Losing It*, documentary film by Sharon Greytak, writer, producer, director, 2001.

Narrative and Nonnarrative

Just as a poet uses a few words to evoke a complex idea, so an artist can communicate complex thoughts and feelings through a single image. By contrast, the sequential artist can act like a novelist. Because the verbal and visual information is distributed over many images, ideas and emotions can be expanded when sequential art is used. In this chapter, we explore the uses, characteristics, and construction of multiple-image structures.

STORYTELLING

Storytelling is one of the most ancient and effective forms of communication. It can serve four basic purposes:

- *Stories can increase self-awareness.* When we record our own story in an autobiography, we become more conscious of the patterns in our lives and can gain a better understanding of the individual events that break or reinforce these patterns.

- *Stories can provide inspiration.* By researching the life of another artist or discussing the past with an elderly relative, we find that our personal problems and conflicts are not unique. Everyone experiences a wide range of emotions, from exhilaration to despair. In reading another person's story, we can learn from his or her solution to a problem.

- *Stories can supply information.* News stories and documentary films provide us with information on current events and analysis of their implications. Art never occurs in a vacuum. Developing an understanding of the world around us can strengthen our ideas.

- *Stories can encourage understanding.* Abstract numbers and dry statistics are rarely as compelling as human experience. When we hear the story of a particular refugee in a specific war, the horrible effect of combat on civilians becomes personal. Such stories can help us understand the emotional meaning of an event.

To increase our understanding even further, we may explore the biggest questions of all, through myths. A **myth** is a traditional story collectively composed by many members of a society. The creation of the world, sources of evil, the power of knowledge, and even the nature of reality may be explained through these grand expressions of the imagination. The *Star Wars* series, most comic books, and many types of performance art are inspired by myths.

Working with Multiple Images

In all forms of storytelling, multiple images can provide many advantages over an individual image. In Jacques-Louis David's *Oath of the Horatii* (14.1), both the action and the emotion must be expressed within a single frame. To avoid mass slaughter, two warring Roman clans, the Horatii and the Curatii, have each agreed to send three warriors into a fight to the death. This heroic moment of self-sacrifice is demonstrated by the three young Horatii warriors on the left. A tragic complication to this plan is borne by the wives of the warriors, who are huddled together in a triangular shape on the right. They are members of the opposing Curatii clan and will lose either their brothers or their husbands in the battle. The children in the background are caught in the middle.

Through skillful composition and careful selection of an emotionally charged moment in the narrative, David created a masterpiece that caused a sensation when it was first shown in 1786, and it continues to be studied today. The use of gesture, composition, and technique in this painting is stunning. Nonetheless, it is difficult to appreciate the painting fully or to understand the story without explanation. Employing only a single image, David had to rely on his audience for some knowledge of the event shown.

14.1 Jacques-Louis David, *Oath of the Horatii*, 1784–85. Oil on canvas, 14 ft × 10 ft 8¼ in. (4.27 × 3.26 m).

By contrast, Jerome Witkin tells a story sequentially in the three paintings that constitute *Division Street* (14.2). Like David, he selected the colors, gestures, and actions most appropriate to the narrative and composed each frame with great care. Unlike *Oath of the Horatii*, however, *Division Street* requires little explanation. The argument in the first frame, the man's explosive departure in the second frame, and the angry woman in the third frame tell the story. This multiple-image narrative can speak for itself.

Multiple-Image Structures

In *Structure of the Visual Book*, Keith Smith describes three multiple-image structures commonly used by printmakers, photographers, and book artists.[1] A **group** is a collection of images that are related by subject matter, composition, or source. In figure 14.3, images of a pyramid, the letter *A*, a meditating man, and a pair of praying hands can be grouped by shape. Each is dominated by a triangle. The three individual illustrations in figures 14.4, 14.5, and 14.6 can be grouped by subject. All are part of the *Frog Folio*, a calendar produced by Dellas Graphics to showcase the work of contemporary illustrators. In a group, the order of the images is unimportant.

A **series** links multiple images together sequentially. Each image builds on the previous image and leads to the subsequent image. As a result, events are linked together like boxcars on a train. *Chance Meeting*, by Duane Michals (14.7 page 324), is a series of photographs. Like a short film, it tells a simple story. Simple narratives, such as fairy tales and fables, often use serial construction. Indeed, numerical repetition may be an essential part of the story. For example, when Goldilocks enters the house of the three bears, she samples three bowls of porridge. One is too hot, the second is too cold, the third is just right. She tries sitting on the three chairs, with a similar result. Finally, when she decides to take a nap, she finds the first bed too hard, the second too soft, and the third just right. As a story for children, "Goldilocks" and other such tales are simple and straightforward. Flashbacks, crosscutting, and other narrative complexities are avoided.

14.2 Jerome Witkin, *Division Street* [A Story Told in 3 Panels], **1984–85.** Oil on canvas, triptych. Top panel 75⅛ × 63¼ in. (190.9 × 160.7 cm), middle panel 81⅛ × 63 in. (206.2 × 160 cm), bottom panel 87⅛ × 63 in. (221.3 × 160 cm).

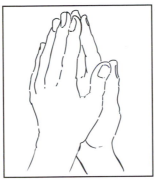

14.3 Grouping by shape.

14.4 Bart Forbes, *Landmark,* **1999.** Oil on canvas, 14 × 19 in. (35.6 × 48.3 cm).

14.5 Charles Santore, Cover of *William the Curious, Knight of the Water Lilies,* **1997.** Watercolor, front cover 9 × 12 in. (22.8 × 30.5 cm).

14.6 Murray Tinkelman, *The Frog Jumps over the Moon.* Colored ink crosshatch, 9 × 12 in. (22.9 × 30.5 cm).

14.7 Duane Michals, *Chance Meeting*, 1969. Six prints, each 4⅞ × 3¼ in. (12.4 × 8.3 cm).

As defined by Smith, a **sequence** is the multiple-image structure used by most popular filmmakers and comic book artists. In a sequence, multiple images are organized by *cause and effect*. In a simple sequence, action two is caused by action one. In a complex sequence, there may be a considerable delay between the cause and the effect. Actions five, six, and seven may all be caused by action one. Rather than film a simple line of boxcars in a train, we may now move among the cars, showing the conductor napping, two passengers playing cards, the engineer steering, and another passenger reading. These human actions may be combined with images of the landscape through which the train is traveling, the setting sun, or even images of the construction of the original train track. To understand a sequence, viewers may have to mentally connect many fragments of information.

From Scene to Screenplay

With a run time of an hour or more, a film or a television show is constructed from many sequences, each building the story using cause and effect. Let's analyze one example.

Jeremy and Angela are spending their honeymoon on the Orient Express. On the third morning of the trip, they awake to the sound of drunken singing in the adjoining cabin. Angela wants to confront the revelers, while Jeremy cautions her against getting involved. They begin to argue. Angela accuses Jeremy of indifference, while Jeremy says Angela is overreacting. Now focused on their own quarrel, they ignore the singers and instead continue their argument over breakfast in the dining car. Finally, Angela threatens to leave. Jeremy ridicules her threat, saying that she isn't capable of traveling alone in a foreign country. Angela punches Jeremy in the nose. Jeremy then shoves his grapefruit into her face. Their fight disrupts the dining car. At the next stop, the conductor throws both of them off the train. Sitting in a deserted train station, they both begin to laugh at their ridiculous response to the drunken singers.

As described in *Story*, by Robert McKee, the **beat** is the most basic element in a story.[2] A beat is an exchange of behavior based on action and reaction. There are six beats in this story.

1. Angela responds to the singers: "I am not going to listen to those drunken louts for one more minute!" Then Jeremy responds to Angela: "Oh, take it easy. Let's get some breakfast; I bet they will be asleep when we return."

2. As they walk to the dining car, Angela says to Jeremy: "You really don't care, do you? If someone punched you in the nose, you would just walk away." Jeremy responds to Angela: "Don't be such a hothead. There is no reason to get angry about every little thing."

3. Over breakfast, Angela retorts: "If you can't take the heat, get out of the kitchen! I suggest we split up at the next station." Jeremy responds: "Are you kidding? You wouldn't last a day on your own."

4. Angela punches Jeremy, who shoves his grapefruit into her face.

5. The conductor reacts by throwing both of them off the train.

6. Sitting on their suitcases in the empty station, they finally respond to the situation by laughing.

Beats build **scenes.** Scenes generally occur in a single space in continuous time. Scenes build sequences. In filmmaking, a sequence is made from a series of scenes, which generally increase in emotional impact. In this story, a minor disagreement escalates into a major battle. Each action results in a stronger reaction, culminating in the couple's ejection from the train. Sequences build **acts.** An act is an even longer sequential structure. The **screenplay,** which is the written blueprint for the film, is constructed from multiple acts.

Key Questions
STORYTELLING

- How many ways might you use storytelling to expand or enhance an idea?

- What are the advantages of a single-image narrative versus a multiple-image narrative?

- How can a series of increasingly powerful beats heighten emotion in your narrative?

BOUNDARIES

When just starting college, few of us have the time, money, or expertise necessary to write a screenplay or direct a film. However, we can use the same principles to develop storyboards, videos, and visual books.

Conceptual Boundaries

It is wise to begin by defining the conceptual breadth of an idea. An idea that is overly ambitious or ill defined will be impossible to communicate well.

You already have extensive experience with conceptual boundaries. Just consider the questions you face when planning a 10-page art history paper:

- *What is the topic?* What historical period interests you most? In a course devoted to Western art from the Renaissance to Impressionism, you have many excellent choices and a dazzling array of images. Choose a topic that is manageable and interesting.

- *How should the topic be approached?* If the paper is on Impressionism, you could

  - Analyze the work of a single artist, such as Mary Cassatt or Edgar Degas

  - Compare and contrast paintings by Cassatt and Degas

  - Explore the impact of photography on Impressionist painters

By focusing on one aspect of a complex topic, you can develop an effective research strategy and complete the paper on time.

Defining conceptual boundaries is equally important in sequential art. Just as Impressionism is too big a topic to explore thoroughly in a 10-page paper, so reality is too vast to record fully in a 10-minute video. The following questions can help you define the conceptual frame of an artwork:

- *What to see?* Start with an interesting and easily accessible site. Explore several of the buildings on campus, then select one and begin your research. Find out the history of the building, look for distinctive architectural details, and find out what happens each day in the building.

- *When to see it?* Each time of day is distinctive, both visually and emotionally. How does the building look at sunset? What is its appearance at midnight? Select the moments in time that are charged with meaning, then watch closely.

- *And then what happens?* To answer this question, you must become a storyteller.

Developing a Story

In 1908, the White Star Line began construction of three identical Atlantic ocean liners. The *Olympic* was launched in 1910; the *Titanic* was launched in 1911; the *Gigantic* was never completed. The *Titanic* struck an iceberg during her maiden voyage and sank on April 15, 1912. She had lifeboat capacity for 1,178 people; there were 2,201 on board. The *Californian*, less than 10 miles away, did not respond to her distress signals. The *Carpathia*, 58 miles away, sped to the scene. Arriving four hours later, *Carpathia* rescued 711 people from the freezing lifeboats. The *Olympic*, *Titanic*'s sister ship, provided reliable service until she was scrapped in 1937.

These are the basic facts. No narrative, however, is limited to facts. Even a newspaper reporter must make choices about the organization of facts and determine the most important aspects of a story. Fiction offers even more options. Using a familiar journalistic device, let's list a few basic questions:

- *Whose story is it?* That of ship designer Thomas Andrews, who perished? Of J. Bruce Ismay, director of the White Star Line, who survived? Of the captain of the *Carpathia*, who became a hero? Of the captain of the *Californian*, who was reviled?

- *When should the story begin and end?* We know that the iceberg was spotted at 11:40 P.M. and that the collision occurred soon after. A storyteller, however, can start at any point in time. How does the story change when we begin with initial planning of the "unsinkable" ship? What happens when we start the story just as a survivor comes to consciousness after being rescued?

- *Where does the story occur?* Each cabin, deck, and lifeboat contains its own specific characters and its own particular story.

- *Why did the tragedy occur?* Was the captain pressured to complete the crossing in record time, causing him to increase the ship's speed, despite the danger? Was faulty construction the cause?

- *What is the story really about?* Courage? Arrogance? Injustice? Sixty-two percent of the 325 first-class passengers survived, while only 25 percent of the 706 third-class passengers survived. Whereas the sinking itself is the most obvious event, this tragedy contains many stories.

Knowing where to start the story is essential. If the story is devoted to the construction of the ship and the arrival of the passengers, the most dramatic events (the sinking itself, the rescue, and the inquiry into the cause) may be lost.

Emotional Boundaries

In theater and performance art, communication often depends on a connection between the imaginary world on stage and the tangible world of the audience. This was demonstrated beautifully in Wole Soyinka's *Death and the King's Horseman*, performed by Syracuse Stage in 1999. The play explores a range of cultural conflicts between the native Yoruba population of Africa and a group of British colonizers. The king has died, and the king's horseman, a powerful leader in his own right (14.8), must commit suicide so that he can guide the king in the world beyond life. Attempts by the British government to stop this ritual are disruptive and tragic.

To feel the full impact of the event, the audience must emotionally connect to the Yoruba world, which revolves around a village market. As we enter the theater, a dramatically lit stage piled with fruit, colorful baskets, and bolts of fabric invites us into this world.

One by one, seven female actors enter, assume the poses of various vendors, then freeze. The play begins with the sound of drumming coming from behind the audience. As the women become animated and the market comes to life (14.9), we are enveloped in the Yoruba world. Additional actors sing and dance down the aisles, finally joining the company on stage.

Establishing an emotional connection between the image and the audience is even more important in filmmaking. When we see a play, the entire stage is visible and each member of the audience frames the scene a bit differently. In a film, the image is created by a flickering beam of light rather than by a live actor. The film frame is defined by the director. By using a close-up, the director can place the actor directly in front of us. A distance shot pushes the actor away, reducing the emotional connection.

14.8 Scene from *Death and the King's Horseman*, 1999. Performed by Syracuse Stage.

14.9 Scene from *Death and the King's Horseman*, 1999. Performed by Syracuse Stage.

Style

In a sense, the style of an artwork provides another boundary. **Style,** the way in which filmic elements are selected and arranged, determines the overall ambience and can help indicate historical setting. Any story can be told in many ways. Three cinematic interpretations of William Shakespeare's *Romeo and Juliet* provide a striking example of the importance of style. Franco Zeffirelli's *Romeo and Juliet* (14.10) is closest to the written play in style and interpretation. There is some editing of the original text, but the lines spoken were written by Shakespeare. While the musical score is a distinctly modern interpretation of Renaissance music, the beautiful settings, opulent costumes, and graceful dancing that fill the screen are based on historical models.

West Side Story (14.11) offers a very different interpretation of the story of Romeo and Juliet. Set in New York City in the 1950s, this film uses warfare between rival gangs to create the tragedy, rather than the familiar conflict between the Capulets and the Montagues. While the story is based on Shakespeare's play, the dialogue is distinctly American. The spirit and emotion of the original were retained, but the dialogue, setting, and specific actions are modern. Even the characters have new names, as Romeo becomes Tony, the leader of the Polish Jets, and Juliet becomes Maria, affiliated with the Puerto Rican Sharks.

An unusual combination of these two sensibilities is found in *William Shakespeare's Romeo and Juliet* (14.12). Now set in contemporary California as a struggle between the skinhead Montagues and the leather-clad Capulets, the film begins with a prologue delivered from a television screen by a newswoman. The words of Shakespeare are often delivered as a scream, and familiar characters are transformed in amazing ways. For example, when we first meet Mercutio, he is wearing high heels, a silver-sequined miniskirt with a halter top, and a white wig. The words of Shakespeare have been retained, but the setting, characters, and action have been shifted to create a bizarre contemporary variation on a sixteenth-century play.

14.10 Franco Zeffirelli, *Romeo and Juliet*, 1968. Romeo and Juliet.

14.11 Robert Wise and Jerome Robbins, *West Side Story*, 1961. Tony and Maria.

14.12 Baz Luhrmann, *William Shakespeare's Romeo and Juliet*, 1996.

BOUNDARIES

- How many ways can you "frame" your story?
- Of these options, which set of boundaries will provide the best balance between focus and richness? Too tight a boundary may result in a constricted story, while too loose a boundary may result in chaos.

- How important is an emotional connection to your audience? How can such a connection be created?
- How many stylistic variations are possible within the framework you have set?
- Of these variations, which style will result in the strongest story?

CAUSALITY

Every story is constructed using a chain of events. In traditional narrative, the first event causes the second, which results in the third, and so on until the conclusion is reached. This chain of events is called **causality.** As in a crossword puzzle, the storyteller presents us with a series of clues, which we construct into meaning.

When the relationship between cause and effect is clear, the puzzle is easy to solve. When there is an extended delay between cause and effect, or when relationships among events seem arbitrary or irrational, the solution becomes much more elusive.

Un Chien Andalou (An Andalusian Dog), by Salvador Dalí and Luis Buñuel, presents such a puzzle. A quarrel between two lovers is presented through a bizarre sequence of illogical events. As the film opens, a man smoking a cigarette calmly sharpens a straight razor. A sliver of cloud passes across the full moon. The man grasps a woman's face (14.13) and slits her left eye with the razor. He then bicycles down the street wearing a nun's uniform. The uninjured woman welcomes him to her apartment. Ants crawl out from a hole in his hand. A severed hand appears on the street below. A crowd gathers. A police-man gives the severed hand to a woman,

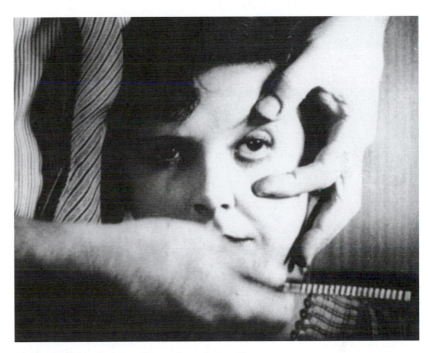

14.13 *Un Chien Andalou.* Woman's eye being slit.

14.14 *Un Chien Andalou.* Mule's head on piano.

14.15 *Titanic.* Young Rose preparing to jump.

14.16 *Titanic.* Elderly Rose at ship's railing.

meet the primary characters. Young Rose is a pampered society woman betrothed to the rich and arrogant Cal. Jack is an independent but impoverished artist who has won his passage back to America in a poker game.

Conflicts between Cal and Rose are apparent from the start. Rose is intelligent and strong-willed, with a love of art and ideas. Cal is arrogant and domineering; he demands obedience. Rose feels trapped, and, in despair, she climbs over a railing on the ship and prepares to jump (14.15). Jack saves her. The resulting romance develops through a sequence of cause-and-effect events and reaches a climax with a battle between Cal and the lovers on the sinking ship. Rose survives, and in a classic **denouement,** or summation, the film ends as the elderly Rose again climbs a ship's railing and flings a diamond back into the sea (14.16). Beautifully filmed and carefully edited, the three-hour film easily sustains our interest. In this case, the traditional narrative structure served the director's purpose. There is no ambiguity: the actions and emotions of all of the characters are shown clearly.

Each film has its own purpose and its own power. *Un Chien Andalou* is suggestive, rather than descriptive; mystery is an essential part of its meaning. *Titanic* gains meaning from the escalating conflict between Cal and Rose. In each case, the director made the right choice for the film content.

who places it in a box. The crowd disperses. The woman, still standing in the street, is then hit by a car.

As the film continues, the man harnesses himself to a piano filled with slaughtered mules (14.14), shoots a double image of himself, and strolls along a beach with the woman, collecting and then discarding debris. While these two characters dominate the story, the film as a whole is as mysterious and disturbing as a surrealist painting.

In contrast, a series of very clear cause-and-effect relationships fuels the lovers' quarrel in James Cameron's *Titanic.* The film begins with a prologue showing a contemporary expedition to salvage a precious diamond from the sunken wreck. Rose, an elderly woman who survived the disaster, then describes the voyage she remembers. Through her memories, we

CHARACTER-DRIVEN NARRATIVE

We strongly identify with the trials and tribulations of others. As a result, character-driven narratives that are biographically based can be especially engaging. *Citizen Kane*, commonly included in lists of the greatest American films, is a classic example of this approach.

The Opening Sequence

Because most narratives are so dependent on the interplay between cause and effect, the first image that is shown substantially affects each subsequent action. As a result, many directors use the opening sequence to create a sense of anticipation that will pull the viewer into the story.

Citizen Kane actually uses three opening sequences to set the story in motion. Each builds on the previous sequence, creating a powerful domino effect. From the very beginning, we are swept into a complex story.

In the first opening, we see the dim silhouette of a castle behind a gate dominated by a "No Trespassing" sign. Through a series of dissolves, we move in closer (14.17), accompanied by slow, ominous music. As the music reaches a climax, a light in a window blinks off. The camera zooms in on a glass globe containing a tiny cabin in a snowy landscape. In an extreme close-up, we now see a man's lips move (14.18) as he whispers the word "rosebud." The globe falls to the floor and shatters. A nurse enters the distorted room and, after taking his pulse, pulls a sheet over the face of the man. Charles Foster Kane is dead.

The second opening is dramatically different in style, narration, and pacing. It is a newsreel, showing the major events in Kane's life (14.19). All the basic information about the man is presented through the narrator's brisk voice-over: Kane's fortune came from a Colorado gold mine, he was a powerful newspaper editor, he had an affair with a shopgirl, and he failed in his attempt to be elected governor. This sequence presents the facts of his life but misses the meaning. A

14.17 Orson Welles, *Citizen Kane.* Castle gate.

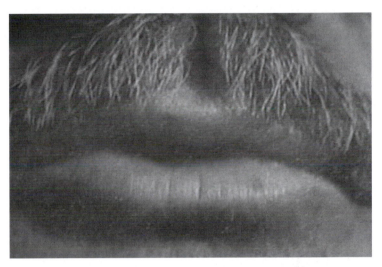

14.18 *Citizen Kane.* Kane's lips.

14.19 *Citizen Kane.* Newsreel.

reporter named Thompson is sent to solve the mystery, to determine who, or what, "rosebud" was.

We get closer to Kane in the third opening. Thompson begins his search at the Thatcher library, a forbidding place of echoing rooms and silent sentries. Walter Thatcher was both Kane's guardian and his nemesis. As Thompson reads Thatcher's journal, the words dissolve into a snowy scene in Colorado. When the scene ends, young Charlie is taken from his parents to begin his new life in Chicago. Each of the openings tells us more about Kane, and each expands the sense of anticipation.

Conflict

Inner conflict or conflicts between characters often generate the cause-and-effect relationships on which a narrative is built. *Citizen Kane* relies on both types of conflict. The pivotal mystery, which is set in motion by Kane's death, is reinforced when Thompson is given his assignment to "find rosebud: dead or alive." Who was Kane, and why was "rosebud" so important to him? As the story unfolds, we are offered a wide variety of opinions.

1. In *News on the March*, Kane is called a communist by Thatcher, a fascist by a man in a labor rally, and finally "an American" by Kane himself.

2. The Thatcher diaries, read by Thompson and shown in close-ups on the screen, include a confrontation between the newspaperman and the banker. Thatcher is appalled by Kane's support for the working class and points out that, as a capitalist, Kane has much to lose if reforms occur. Here, Kane defines himself more emphatically: "You don't realize that you're talking to two people. As Charles Foster Kane, who has two thousand, six hundred and thirty-one shares of Metropolitan Transfer, I sympathize with you. Charles Foster Kane is a dangerous scoundrel; his paper should be run out of town. . . . On the other hand, I am the publisher of the *Inquirer*. As such, it is my duty to see that decent, hardworking people are not robbed blind by a bunch of money-mad pirates." Kane clearly realizes that his motivations are contradictory. Welles uses a series of increasing close-ups to demonstrate the increasing tension between Kane and Thatcher (14.20–14.22).

14.20 *Citizen Kane.* Kane addresses Thatcher jovially.

14.21 *Citizen Kane.* Kane becomes agitated.

14.22 *Citizen Kane.* Kane is enraged.

3. Thompson next visits Bernstein, Kane's business manager. His memories reveal a critical aspect of Kane's character. With the publication of his first edition of the *Inquirer*, Kane inserts a "Declaration of Principles" pledging honest reporting and support for the working man. For Bernstein, Kane was a man of principles.

4. Leland, once Kane's best friend, offers quite a different assessment of the man. Kane, he says, "wasn't a brutal man—he just did brutal things." Kane "never had a conviction, besides himself." Kane "never actually gave you anything—he just left you a tip." At the end of the interview, Leland offers a more compassionate assessment: "He did everything for love. All he ever wanted was love. He just didn't have any to give."

5. Two final interviews complete our picture of Kane. His former wife, Susan, focuses on Kane's attempt to transform her into an opera singer. Susan is initially excited by this prospect but is soon overwhelmed by the gap between her modest ability and the demands of the profession. It is only after she attempts suicide that Kane allows her to end her singing lessons. Raymond, the butler, offers a final memory. When Susan finally walks out on him, the elderly Kane awkwardly lunges around her bedroom, ferociously destroying mirrors and hurling books to the floor. He stops only when he picks up the snow globe seen at the beginning of the film, and for the second time in the film, he utters the word "rosebud." He then departs, endlessly mirroring himself as he walks through his castle (14.23).

While the mystery is revealed to the audience at the end of the film, Thompson never does learn the meaning of "rosebud." Nonetheless, the memories of Kane's associates have deepened his understanding of a complex and contradictory character and provided us with a remarkable film.

The Closing Sequence

Especially with a mystery story, the closing sequence is as important as the opening sequence. A powerful closing can reveal an elusive truth, resolve outstanding conflicts, pose a question, or hammer home an important point.

14.23 *Citizen Kane.* Mirror.

14.24 *Citizen Kane.* Castle chimney.

14.25 *Citizen Kane.* "No Trespassing."

In *Citizen Kane,* three closing sequences mirror the film's beginning. In the first, Thompson summarizes his search for Kane. In the second, the true identity of "rosebud" is revealed to the viewer. The third ending is a reprise of the opening shot. The mysterious outline of Kane's castle is shown, now with smoke billowing from the chimney (14.24). This change is significant. To clear out the castle, workmen are burning most of Kane's possessions, including "rosebud." The camera slowly tilts downward, resting once more on the "No Trespassing" sign (14.25). After two hours of film, the mystery is only partially resolved: we can never fully enter another person's life.

Key Questions

CHARACTER-DRIVEN NARRATIVE

- Whose story is it? A 7-year-old girl's? A 17-year-old boy's? A priest's? A thief's?

- What is the point of view? Does the main character tell his or her own story (first person narrative), or does someone else tell the story? How does this affect meaning?

- What are the strengths and weaknesses of each character?

- What conflicts occur? What causes these conflicts?

- How do the characters deal with conflict?

- To what degree and by what means is the conflict resolved at the end?

NARRATIVE COMPRESSION

Duration, framing, editing, and narration become especially charged with meaning when a television commercial is designed. Lasting only 15 seconds, the ad must immediately command attention, make a favorable impression, and influence consumer behavior. Whether you are selling soap or discouraging smoking, your approach must be clear, concise, and compelling.

Ads must appeal to the emotions as well as the intellect. The **hard-sell** approach, shown in figure 14.26, relies on rational argument and clearly presents one major point. The narrative is linear, and the message is explicit: drinking and driving can kill a friendship. Words underscore the ideas that are being communicated visually.

Soft-sell ads focus on emotion. While the message is still sharply focused, the designer may seek a sensory response rather than a rational response. An ad for a Jeep Cherokee (14.27) shows a car driving through the woods. The song "Row, Row, Row Your Boat" provides the sound track. There is no obvious connection between the song and the car, but the phrase "life is but a dream" certainly implies that a Jeep can provide a carefree vacation.

Feeling good is not enough—the viewer must feel good about the specific product being sold. Because viewer response is triggered by clues rather than by literal content, designers using the soft-sell approach pay particular attention to details, such as the sound track and lighting.

NARRATOR: When friends don't stop friends from drinking and driving

[TIRES SCREECH AND CRASH]

friends die from drinking and driving.

[TIRES SCREECH AND CRASH]

Friends die from drinking and—

[TIRES SCREECH]
Drinking and driving can kill a friendship.

14.26 Agency: Leber Katz Partners, New York. Production: Phil Marco Productions, New York. Editing Company: Cinemetric, New York. Music Production: Roy Eaton Productions, New York. Details: TV, 30 seconds, color. First appearance: December 12, 1983. Advertiser's Supervisor: Eleanor Hanley. Account Supervisor: Susan Wershba. Creative Director: Jack Silverman. Copywriter: Lou Linder. Art Director: Len Fink. Agency Producer: Herb Miller. Producer: Catherine Bromley. Director/Cameraman/Lighting Director: Phil Marco. Editor: Larry Plastrik. Music Director: Roy Eaton. Music Composers: Roy Eaton/Joe Hudson. Performers: Jon Carthay, Laurence White, Bobby Hudson. Voice: Doug Jeffers.

[BIRDS CHIRPING]

CHORUS: Row, row, row your boat,

gently down the stream.

Merrily, merrily,

merrily, merrily,

life is but a dream.

14.27 Agency: Campbell-Mithun-Esty, Southfield. Production: Bill Hudson Films, New York. Editing Company: Editors Gas, New York. Music Production: Elias & Associates, New York. Details: TV, 30 seconds, color. First appearance: October 1, 1988. Creative Director/Copywriter: Mike Belitsos. Art Director: Steve Goldsworthy. Agency Producer: Craig Mungons. Production Company Director: Dickson Sorenson.

[TANGO MUSIC]

Actual cracking time 2 minutes

Nobody's better in cold.

NARRATOR: Nobody's better in cold, than All-Temperature Cheer.

14.28 Agency: Leo Burnett, Chicago. Production: Leroy Koetz Company, Chicago. Editing Company: Cutters, Chicago. Music Production: Colnot-Fryer Music, Chicago. First appearance: 1988. Account Supervisor: Ray DeThorne. Creative Director: Gerry Miller. Associate Creative Director/Copywriter: Alex Goslar. Art Director: Bob Ribits. Agency Producer: Angelo Antonucci. Production Company Producer: George Lakehomer. Production Company Director: Leroy Koetz. Editor: R. J. Music Composer: Cliff Colnot. Casting Director: Bonnie Murray. Performer: Jobe Cerny. Voice: Jim McCance.

All ads rely on a clear message, strong imagery, and simple communication. However, very different strategies can be used to convey an idea, and the skillful designer carefully matches the communication style to the message content. Following are six contrasting strategies.

1. **Rational.** A rational ad provides the viewer with specific information. When the message is compelling in itself or the product is truly unique, a straightforward demonstration can be effective. A 1988 commercial for Cheer detergent (14.28) combined a rational demonstration with deadpan humor, which attracts our attention while conveying the message.

2. **Emotional.** When the product is not unique or the message lacks urgency, an emotional approach may be more effective. For example, to a dog owner, all dog food is pretty much alike. Neither the product nor the message is compelling in itself. When the dog food becomes

[SFX: CLOCKS CHIMING 5 PM]

[MUSIC]

NARRATOR: When you think about the unique joy your dog brings you, why would you ever want to feed him anything less than America's finest dog food? New Reward,

FOR THE VERY BEST DOGS IN THE WORLD

REWARD
Hearty Beef Stew

for the very best dogs in the world. What may just be the very best dog food.

14.29 Agency: Goodby, Berlin & Silverstein, San Francisco. Production: Griner, Custa & Associates, New York. Editing Company: Straight Cut, Los Angeles. Music Production: Piece of Cake, Los Angeles. Details: TV, 60 seconds, color. First appearance: July 18, 1988. Advertiser's Supervisor: Tom Branky. Account Supervisor: Pam Malone. Creative Directors: Jeff Goodby, Rich Silverstein. Copywriter: Jeff Goodby. Art Director: Rich Silverstein. Agency Producer: Debbie King. Production Company Producer: Chris Stefani. Production Company Director/Cameraman: Norm Griner. Lighting Director: William Coleman. Editor: Tom Schacte. Music Director/Composer: Don Pierstrup. Casting Director: Kathy Sorkin.

a manifestation of love for the dog, however, the appeal is heightened. In the ad in figure 14.29, it becomes clear that the emotion of love is more powerful than any rational argument.

3. **Serious.** A serious approach is often best when you have a serious message. Public service announcements dealing with AIDS, drunk driving, or drug abuse are rarely funny. However, the ad will succeed only if it is seen. Horrific images of starving children

or tortured prisoners may so repel viewers that they lose the message. Finding the right balance between serious content and engaging imagery is crucial.

4. **Humorous.** In a society saturated with sales pitches, an ad that makes us laugh is an ad we will remember. Since any ad is designed to encourage a change in behavior, remembering it is important. The advertising message we receive while watching the nightly news must be retained

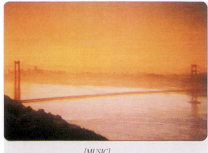

[MUSIC]

WALT STACK: I run 17 miles every morning. People ask

Walt Stack.
80 years old.

me how I keep my teeth from chattering in the wintertime.

I leave them in my locker.

Just do it.

14.30 Agency: Wieden & Kennedy, Portland. Production: PYTKA, Venice. Details: TV, 30 seconds each, color. First appearance: August 1988. Advertiser's Supervisor: Scott Bedbury. Creative Directors: Dan Wieden, David Kennedy. Copywriters: Dan Wieden, Jim Riswold. Art Director: David Jenkins. Agency Producers: Bill Davenport, Elinor Shanklir. Production Company Director: Joe Pytka. Editor: Steve Wystrach.

when we buy a tube of toothpaste two days later. To be effective, however, a humorous ad must truly be funny, without insulting the viewer or demeaning the product. By showing the strength as well as the weakness of an elderly runner, the ad in figure 14.30 strikes just the right balance.

5. **Realistic.** Communication requires connection. For a commercial to succeed, the viewer must feel connected to the ideas and images presented. For example, few adults will pay attention to an ad for the latest rock band, while few teenagers will pay attention to an ad for denture adhesive. In either

case, there is no connection to the message conveyed. Similarly, when we like a character in an ad, we are more likely to listen to his or her argument.

A common form of realism is **testimonial.** In a testimonial, a trustworthy character (often a celebrity) addresses us directly. The 1998 Aleve commercial is a good example. An ordinary-looking middle-aged man wearing blue jeans tells us that two Aleve pills do the same job as a fistful of pills from a competing company. When he ends the ad by saying simply "It works for me," we assume that it will also work for us.

[TRAFFIC NOISE]
TRAFFIC REPORTER: I've never seen traffic like this. The traffic down there today is unbelievable.

[OTHER DRIVERS' VOICES]
NARRATOR: Remember what it was like the last time you drove yourself to the airport. Next time take Massport's

Logan Express Bus from Quincy or Framingham. It's fast, convenient, and comfortable. For more information, call Massport, at 1-800-23LOGAN.

MAN: Move it, buddy!

WOMAN: I can walk faster than this.

1·800·23·LOGAN
massport
We help get you there.

14.31 Agency: Rossin, Greenberg, Seronick and Hill, Boston. Production Company: Cavanaugh & Co., Boston. Details: TV, 30 seconds, color. First appearance: November 1988. Advertiser's Supervisor: Teresa McAlpine. Account Supervisor: Neal Hill. Creative Directors: Gary Greenberg, Peter Seronick. Copywriter: Peter Seronick. Art Director: Gary Greenberg. Agency Producer: Julie Lauerman. Production Company Producer: David Norman. Production Company Director: Steve Cavanaugh. Set Designer: Bob Field. Cameraman/Lighting Director: Dan Stoloff. Editor: George Mauro. Voice: Chris Murney.

6. **Exaggerated.** Exaggeration can be a great strategy when the product is commonplace or the message is uninteresting. To be effective, an ad must be seen and remembered. Exaggeration tends to be memorable. Even if the event shown is ludicrous, the ad can be effective if the basic message is believable. We know that the snails shown in figure 14.31 are not literally stuck in traffic; they represent frustrated drivers who are moving at a "snail's pace." The metaphor is unexpected and, when combined with the voice-over, becomes humorous. Through exaggeration, a mass transit message becomes memorable.

Key Questions
NARRATIVE COMPRESSION

- Which is more appropriate for your concept: a "hard-sell" or a "soft-sell" approach? How might each option be visualized?

- To what extent does your story need to be factual? What facts are most meaningful?

- Can exaggeration or metaphor strengthen the communication?

NONNARRATIVE

Titanic is a familiar type of popular film. It tells a fictitious story, based on a series of actions and reactions. The opening and closing sequences provide an effective framework for the story of Rose, Jack, and Cal. The characters are believable, and the plot is plausible.

Many forms of sequential art, however, are nonnarrative in structure. For example, the elegant contours and gleaming chrome of an expensive car provide both the form and the content in figure 14.32. There is no story: viewers are simply shown a series of beautiful close-ups. Evocative artworks of this kind often require more audience participation and encourage an open-ended response.

Three common approaches to nonnarrative are the categorical approach, the rhetorical approach, and the abstract approach. A **categorical** approach is based on the exploration of a single concept, action, or emotion. *Giving Fear a Proper Name,* a visual book by Susan Kae Grant, uses text from a diary to explore fear. Contained within a clear Plexiglas box, the book itself is like a fet-

ish. Handmade paper and inserted objects cause the book to open on its own, and the tiny toy revolver that dangles from a bookmark string simultaneously suggests self-protection and self-annihilation.

This catalogue of terror begins with kainophobia, the fear of change (14.33). From the diary, we learn that Grant has moved to Detroit, a profoundly foreign environment for her. On the first page of a double-page spread, she writes of "moving forward looking backward . . . I can never say good-bye." On the facing page, she is shown in profile, facing left, with her face pierced by straight pins and accompanied by a tiny compass and a plastic groom, suggesting a wedding cake. Topophobia, the fear of place, comes next. Grant now writes that she "stares in disbelief out smashed vacant beauties/violet oppressive depression surrounds me/people are angry, filled with hate." Her face in the photograph has now become a target. Eremophobia, the fear of solitude, follows. A close-up of her ear is shown, pierced by pins, while a plastic

14.32 Agency: WCRS Mathews Marcantonio, London. Production: Park Village Productions, London. Music Production: Jeff Wayne Music, London. Details: TV, 60 seconds, color. First appearance: June 3,1988. Country: England. Language: English. Advertiser's Supervisor: Martin Hainge. Account Supervisor: Hugh Smiley. Creative Director: Alfredo Marcantonio. Art Director: Paul Garret. Agency Producer: Simon Wells. Production Company Producer: Chris Harvey. Production Company Director: Roger Woodburn. Cameraman: Joe Coe. Lighting Director: Keith Goddard. Editor: Patrick Moore. Music Composer: Trevor Jones.

toy phone dangles like an earring. The book continues, with pages devoted to the fear of sleep, fear of being alone, fear of being observed, and so forth. In each case, increasingly painful words accompany a photographic self-portrait of some kind. The book ends with the fear of infinity. Now in profile facing right, Grant is accompanied by a pair of dice and a map of Texas, which will become her new home. Using fear as a category, then relentlessly exploring various types of fear, Grant transformed her personal experience into powerful communication.

In a **rhetorical** approach, sequential images are used to present an argument. One example is *Powers of Ten*, by Charles and Ray Eames (14.34). This 9½-minute film provides an elegant exploration of "the relative size of things in the universe." The central image is framed by a dark border, which includes information on the spatial position of each shot on the right and its numerical equivalent on the left. Beginning with a shot of a man asleep in a park, the camera gradually moves out to the farthest reaches of the known universe. Physicist Philip Morrison provides the narration, describing the meaning of the image at each step.

The process is then reversed, and the speed is greatly accelerated. Returning to the sleeping man, the camera now moves through his skin, into his blood, down to a cell, and finally into an atom in the man's right hand. The beautiful images entice us, while the mathematical narration teaches us. Moving from astrophysics to nuclear physics, this film presents an analysis of the distance between the largest and smallest spaces known.

14.33 Susan Kae Grant, *Kainophobia, Fear of Change,* from *Giving Fear a Proper Name: Detroit,* The Black Rose Press, 1982–85. Edition of 15, printed letter press with silver prints. Mixed mediums, handmade paper, simulated bulletproof case, 5 × 5 in. (12.7 × 12.7 cm).

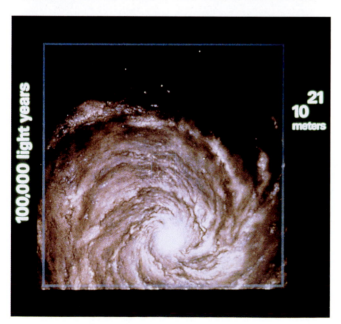

14.34 **Charles and Ray Eames,** *Powers of Ten,* **1977.** Film frames.

Words for the World, by Ed Hutchins, presents a social argument using equally simple means. By filling a small metal pencil box with 16 special pencils, he makes a plea for tolerance and peace. A map of the world is printed on the top of the box. Various texts are printed on the pencils, in languages ranging from Arabic to Zulu, each accompanied by an English translation. The phrases are simple: "It doesn't hurt to listen." "The time is always right for justice." "We all live under the same sky." The message, however, is compelling. What words will we write with these pencils? What words can we say to each other? Hutchins is promoting a change in behavior rather than knowledge of the cosmos.

Finally, sequential art may be purely **abstract.** In a well-designed book or film, changes in color, shape, texture, and movement can provide all the information needed for a compelling piece. *Blacktop,* another experimental film by Charles and Ray Eames, provides one example. An outdoor basketball court has been washed. As the residue is rinsed away, the film records the movement of soap bubbles and water over the asphalt surface. The delicate Bach harpsichord music that is used as the sound track suggests that this act of washing the asphalt is as elegant as a Balanchine ballet. And in the hands of these inventive filmmakers it is.

Key Questions

NONNARRATIVE

- Create rough storyboards exploring categorical, rhetorical, and abstract approaches. Which of these nonnarrative strategies is best suited to the idea you want to express?

- What is the glue that holds your nonnarrative together: an alphabet (as in *Giving Fear a Proper Name*), mathematics (as in *Powers of Ten*), or some other unifying force?

- When using an abstract approach, what aspect(s) of your subject will you accentuate?

SUMMARY

- Storytelling is one of the most ancient and effective forms of communication. Stories can increase self-awareness, provide inspiration, supply information, and encourage understanding.

- Multiple-image structures can be used to express complex ideas using narrative and nonnarrative approaches.

- The group, series, and sequence are the multiple-image structures most commonly used by printmakers, photographers, and book artists.

- The beat, scene, sequence, and act are used by filmmakers and playwrights to create screenplays.

- By establishing effective boundaries, we can develop more effective stories. Common questions include the following: Whose story is it? When should the story begin and end? Where does the story occur? Why did it happen? What is the underlying theme or message in the story?

- A change in style can substantially affect communication.

- Ideas and emotions can be communicated through a straightforward series of causes and effects or through a series of seemingly unrelated images.

- The opening and closing, personal perspective, and characters used can make or break a story.

- Television advertisements can present complete ideas in 15 seconds. Hard-sell, soft-sell, rational, emotional, serious, humorous, realistic, and exaggerated approaches are the most common strategies.

- Categorical, rhetorical, and abstract are common nonnarrative approaches.

KEY TERMS

abstract	emotional (advertising)	rational (advertising)	series
acts	exaggerated (advertising)	realistic (advertising)	serious (advertising)
beat	group	rhetorical	soft-sell (advertising)
categorical	hard-sell (advertising)	scenes	style
causality	humorous (advertising)	screenplay	testimonial (advertising)
denouement	myth	sequence	

STUDIO PROJECTS

To apply the concepts from this chapter in the studio, check out the Projects page in the Online Learning Center at www.mhhe.com/stewart4e. The following is a sample of the chapter-related assignments that are described in step-by-step detail.

Casuality and Duration. An introduction to narrative.
Countdown. Exploring ways to compress, expand, and accelerate time.
Before and After. Understanding narrative implications of objects and interiors.
House of Cards. Exploring nonlinear narrative.

Profile:

Michael Remson, Librettist and Composer

Story and Song

A dual Irish-American citizen, Michael Remson is primarily known as a composer of vocal, choral, and operatic works. He was featured in New York City Opera's Showcasing American Composers series and served as Composer-in-Residence with the Ulster Orchestra in Belfast. Our conversation focuses on Dr. Remson's opera dealing with the life and death of Mary Surratt, the first woman executed by the federal government in United States history.

MS: How did you become a composer?

MR: I grew up in a house filled with music. My father sang in the chorus of the Metropolitan Opera in New York City and I began singing and acting at a young age. At the age of 20, I co-formed a new-wave band and began writing songs. This led me to formal studies at NYU with composer Judy Klein, primarily in the area of electronic music. I then combined my electronic interests with my love of storytelling and soon found myself writing operas.

MS: What is a libretto?

MR: Literally, *libretto* is Italian for "little book." It's the term that describes the story, scene-by-scene breakdown, stage directions and, ultimately, the words that are sung. It's like writing a play that's meant to be sung instead of spoken. Generally, the composer hires or collaborates with a librettist, rather than writing it himself.

MS: What is the advantage of writing both the libretto and the music yourself?

MR: For me, it lets both the libretto and the music evolve more organically. As an aria or scene evolves, my dramatic instincts tell me whether I need more or less text or more or less music. I can then make the additions or sacrifices I feel are best. I'm also a big proponent of American English as a beautiful language for singing. Writing the libretto myself lets me work with the tone, sound, and color of language in tandem with those same aspects of the music.

MS: Tell me about *Mary Surratt*, your new opera.

MR: Mary Surratt was condemned as a conspirator in the plot to kill Abraham Lincoln. Her son, John, was almost certainly involved but historians continue to debate Mary's guilt or innocence. Initially, I left it up to the audience to decide. But I realized that a historically accurate approach weakened the drama. In the next draft, I made a dramatic decision that Mary would be innocent. The compelling question, and therefore the crux of the drama, would become Why was she executed?

MS: How does it begin?

MR: The assassination of Lincoln is the dramatic impulse, the event that sets in motion all of the actions and emotions that follow. So, as soon as the audience is seated and the lights are down, a gunshot sounds. A spotlight focuses on a box above the stage and we see Lincoln dying. The baritone who plays John Wilkes Booth struggles with a guard and leaps to the stage. He shouts "Sic semper tyrannis!" (Latin for "Thus always to the tyrants") and runs off.

After that, the stage fills with eyewitnesses to the assassination, milling about in a fog, despondent and confused. Using actual quotes from people in Ford's Theatre, I am hoping to convey the shock and despair that gripped the nation. So, in effect the theatrical audience becomes the audience in Ford's Theatre on the night of April 14, 1865. Lastly, we see Mary at the gallows, declaring her innocence.

Mary Surratt's story is then allowed to unfold—some through flashbacks and some in real time.

Remember, the question isn't whether she is guilty or innocent but the conditions that would allow her to go to the gallows if she was, in fact, innocent. Mary was pious, retiring, and very devoted to her family; Booth was a nationally renowned actor, vehement in his devotion to the Confederacy and a very charismatic man. In the opera, Mary's actions are motivated by her misguided attempts to protect her son from Booth—regardless of the cost to herself.

MS: Why did you start off with the assassination?
MR: Think of a snowball rolling down a hill. It starts off as a small fistful of snow, but as it rolls along, it gets bigger and bigger. As a librettist, I must set the snowball in motion. And I must keep it in motion and on track; slowing down the action too much or letting the plot become cluttered reduces its dramatic impact. It must be inevitable and unstoppable. Lincoln's death is that snowball. My goal is to have the audience completely caught up in the drama as soon as that first scene is over.

MS: Do you have a technique for working out the pacing and chronology?
MR: I spent at least 18 months working out the chronology and structure. For this particular opera, I needed to keep all of the historical and dramatic events clear in my mind, so I wrote each detail on an index card, then pinned it to a large bulletin board. For example, one card said, "Mary delivers the shooting irons"; another said, "Booth kills Lincoln." By moving these cards around on the wall, I could envision various ways to tell the story and ultimately settle on a chronology that I felt was dramatically compelling.

This technique also helped me see actions I wanted to emphasize and actions or characters I felt I could omit or combine. I try to see everything as a thread. Dates and events are meaningless in the abstract. Drama occurs when the threads come together, like weaving a cloth. Now that I'm working on the music, I can fine-tune the pacing and dramatic impulses that hold the entire opera together.

MS: Your mentors are particularly renowned. Carlisle Floyd is often referred to as "the dean of American opera," and Edward Albee has had a stellar career as a playwright. What were the most valuable things you learned from them?
MR: Mr. Floyd helped hone my dramatic instincts and insisted that I take responsibility for every single word and musical note. Mr. Albee helped me focus on creating individual voices for each character

and on the overall narrative. He helped me look at the forest rather than the trees.

MS: I have only listened to opera on the radio. What are the advantages of live opera?
MR: Opera is more than just music; it's about words, drama, sets, lighting, costumes, and acting on stage. When it's done well, there is nothing more thrilling than sitting in an opera house and being absorbed in that world. Listening to an opera on the radio is like going to a movie with your eyes shut!

MS: Any final bits of advice for my students?
MR: Realize that you can't base a career on talent alone. You must be punctual, prepared, easy to work with, and an asset to the group. In other words, be as good a businessperson as you are an artist. In the arts, people who don't meet deadlines don't get work!

Soprano Kelli Estes performing in the Lone Star Lyric Theatre Festival's recent production of Michael Remson's *Sorry, Wrong Number*, based on the play by Lucille Fletcher.

Interdisciplinary Arts

In this final chapter, we explore three forms of interdisciplinary art. In **interdisciplinary art,** two or more disciplines are fused to create a hybrid art form. The first section focuses on visual books, which combine words and images in a wide variety of structures. The next section is devoted to installation art, which presents an ensemble of images and objects within a three-dimensional environment. The final section is devoted to **performance art,** which can be broadly defined as live art performed by artists.

EXPLORING THE VISUAL BOOK

What is a visual book? A **visual book** is an experimental structure that conveys ideas, actions, and emotions using multiple images in an integrated and interdependent format. Every image is connected in some way to every other image. In a sense, there are no single pages in a visual book. It is the combination of the multiple pages that creates the complete artwork.

Any material may be used for pages, from the bags of tea Nancy Callahan used for her *Daybook* (15.1) to the sheets of lead Anselm Kiefer used for *Breaking of the Vessels* (15.2). Pages may be of any size or shape, from the 3-inch triangles Daniel Kelm and Tim Ely used in *Rubeus* (15.3) to 8-foot-tall screens. The subject matter can be profoundly philosophical, fiercely political, or painfully personal, as in Susan Kae Grant's *Giving Fear a Proper Name* (figure 14.33, page 341). Images can be generated using photography, printmaking, drawing, or other techniques.

15.1 Nancy Callahan, *Daybook*, 1988. Artist's book, screen printing and hand-fabricated tea bags, 16 × 12 × 6 in. (40.6 × 30.5 × 15.3 cm).

15.2 Anselm Kiefer, *Breaking of the Vessels*, 1990. Lead, iron, glass, copper wire, charcoal, and aquatec, 12 ft 5 in. × 11 ft 3 in. × 4 ft 9 in. (378.5 × 343 × 144.8 cm).

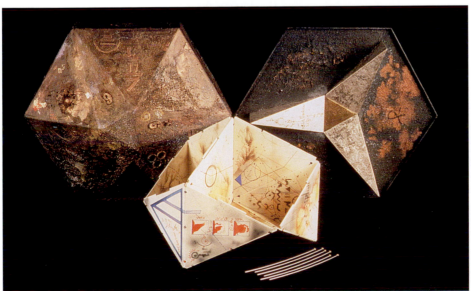

15.3 Daniel E. Kelm and Timothy C. Ely, *Rubeus*, 1990. Book: Flexahexahedron (six cyclically linked tetrahedra with a circular axis of rotation), Arches paper, museum board, stainless steel wire, aluminum tubing, brass beads, cotton-covered polyester thread, with drawings using airbrush acrylics and ink, 5 × 10½ × 10½ in. (12.7 × 26.7 × 26.7 cm). Box: High faceted structure with hexagonal base and felt pad; paper consolidated paperboard and medium-density fiberboard, finished with polymer medium, copper leaf, plastic, metal bits, and sand from sacred sites, 6.25 in. (15.9 cm) high, 13 × 13 in. (33 × 33 cm) base.

15.4 Mary Stewart, a page in *Labyrinth,* front and back view, 1999. Intaglio, 13 × 18 × 39 in. (33 × 45.7 × 99 cm).

15.5 Keith Smith. Bound-edged codex structure.

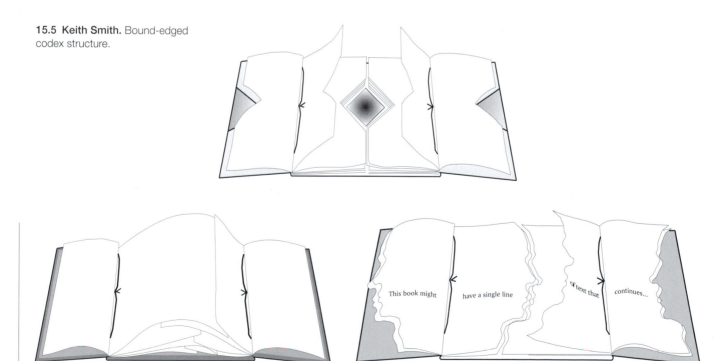

This book might   have a single line   of text that   continues…

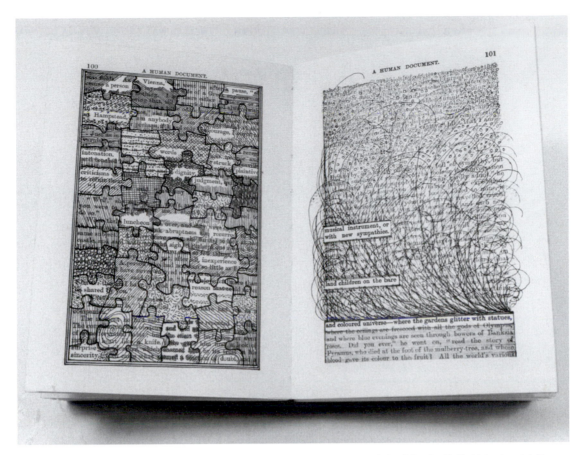

15.6 **Tom Phillips, *A Humument*, 1980.** From *The Cutting Edge of Reading: Artists' Books*, R. R. Hubert and J. D. Hubert. Granary Books, New York, 1999.

Visual books combine two-dimensional composition and three-dimensional structure. For example, each page in my own *Labyrinth* (15.4) was composed individually, then slotted together to create a complex three-dimensional object. Even when a more traditional bound-edged **codex** structure is used (as shown in figure 15.5), variations in the page length and shape can substantially affect meaning.

Visual books may be entirely visual, like Michael Snow's *Cover to Cover* (figure 13.18, page 300); primarily verbal, like Tom Phillips's *A Humument* (15.6); or entirely conceptual, like Keith Smith's *Book 50* (15.7). Generally seen by one person at a time, a visual book can create a very direct connection between the audience and the artist. This contact is especially important with pop-up books, which come to life when the pages are turned and the tabs are pulled.

BOOK NUMBER 50

(Turning the page creates and destroys the image.)
Autumnal Equinox 1974

Construct a Western Codex book consisting of images on thirty transparencies. Process the film-positives by developing, short stop but no fix. Wash, dry and under proper safelight, hand bind as a leather case bound book. Place completed book in light-tight box.

Present the boxed book to the viewer. Upon opening the box and viewing, the entire book will not fog at once. Opening to the first page, the viewer will glimpse the image as it quickly blackens. The black will protect the remainder of the book from light. Upon turning each page, the viewer will momentarily see the image as it sacrifices itself to protect the remaining pages.

KE⊙TH

15.7 **Keith Smith, *Book 50*, 1974.** A conceptual book.

Selecting a Text

Generative Potential

A brief evocative text can act as a springboard for the book artist, while an overly descriptive text may become a trap. More than verbal polish, a text must provide an opening for further development.

The labyrinth book project I assign to my students provides such generative potential, both visually and conceptually. The students begin by developing a labyrinthine drawing of a complex building (15.8). Because this drawing will act as a stage set for the narrative, careful use of lighting, balance, and the illusion of space is encouraged.

After a critique of the initial work, students expand their ideas and refine their images, finally creating two rough drawings, one on the front and one on the back of a 22 × 30 in. sheet of sturdy paper. This sheet is then cut apart to create four 7½ × 22 in. strips, which finally are folded and sewn to create sixteen 7½ × 11 in. pages.

15.8 Emily Frenkel, *Labyrinth Drawing.* Pen and ink, 18 × 24 in. (45.6 × 61 cm).

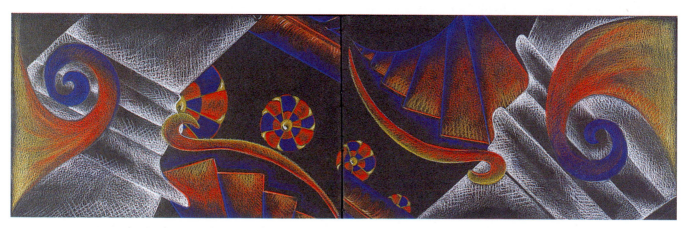

15.9 Emily Frenkel, *Labyrinth Book,* **two double-page spreads.** Colored pencil on black paper, 7½ × 22 in. (19 × 55.9 cm).

The final book is developed from this raw material. We consider dictionary definitions:

lab-y-rinth: 1: a structure full of intricate passageways that make it difficult to find the way from the interior to the entrance or from the entrance to the center (for example, the labyrinth constructed by Daedalus for Minos, king of Crete, in which the Minotaur was confined); 2: a maze in a park or garden formed by paths separated by high, thick hedges; 3: something bewilderingly involved or tortuous in structure: a complex that baffles exploration; 4: a situation from which it is difficult to extricate oneself; 5: the internal ear, or its bony or membranous part; 6: a body structure made up of a maze of cavities and channels; 7: intricate, sometimes symbolic pattern, spec. such a pattern inlaid in the pavement of a medieval church; 8: in metallurgy, series of troughs in a stamping mill through which water passes for washing pulverized ore.[1]

We read the story of Theseus, the Greek hero who conquered the half-man, half-bull Minotaur, and meet the princess Ariadne, who provided him with a ball of golden thread that aided in his escape from the maze. We investigate labyrinths as described by archaeologists, physiologists, and psychologists.

This assignment consistently results in an astonishing array of inventive books. Some students introduce characters into the setting, creating a simple narrative. Others use the illusion of space to move the viewer through mysterious corridors and down precipitous staircases. Light and pattern can be used to create a world of enchantment and beauty (15.9). All are valid solutions to the problem. Because the word *labyrinth* is so open to interpretation, the assignment has great generative potential.

Divisions and Connections

A text that easily breaks apart can suggest connections or divisions between book pages. An alphabet

15.10A Edward Gorey, *A Is for Amy Who Fell Down the Stairs.* Illustration from *The Gashlycrumb Tinies or, After the Outing.*

15.10B Edward Gorey, *B Is for Basil Assaulted by Bears.* Illustration from *The Gashlycrumb Tinies or, After the Outing.*

provides the page divisions in Edward Gorey's *The Gashlycrumb Tinies or, After the Outing* (15.10A and B). Each letter is accompanied by a rhythmic and rhyming text describing assorted accidents and childhood fatalities, beginning with "A is for Amy who fell down the stairs, B is for Basil assaulted by bears, C is for Clara who wasted away, D is for Desmond thrown out of a sleigh," and continuing in like manner. The alphabet provides a sense of anticipation as we wonder what wild expression of humor we will encounter on the next page, while the singsong rhythm and clever rhymes help unify the pages.

15.11 Robert Sabuda, "Nine Drummers Drumming." Reprinted from *The 12 Days of Christmas, a Pop-Up Celebration.* Simon & Schuster.

Similarly, a traditional song provides the structure for *The 12 Days of Christmas,* by Robert Sabuda. This song has become a holiday cliché, and a conventional drawing of the familiar partridge in a pear tree would have been deadly. Sabuda overcame the cliché by combining a lively imagination with elegant and elaborate pop-ups. The "six geese-a-laying" sit atop a slice of gooseberry pie, while the "seven swans-a-swimming" fill a crystal ball. For "eleven ladies dancing," nine ballerinas dance atop a music box and a mirror is used to multiply some of the figures. And the "nine drummers drumming" (15.11) are mice, with their tails tapping out a lively beat! Imagination conquers cliché every time.

Music

Each language has a distinctive aural quality, or music, as well as a distinctive grammatical structure. English, which is dominated by words derived from Latin and the Germanic languages, provides at least two ways to say almost anything. For example, a Viking warrior is *strong* (a word derived from the Anglo-Saxon word for strength), while a Roman warrior is *vigorous* (a word derived from the Latin word for strength). Spanish provides great grammatical clarity and has similar word endings that encourage rhyme, while Chinese is literally musical—the meaning of words changes when the inflection and tone of voice change.

Each text also has music. When words are poorly chosen, the text is discordant and painful to read. When the words are used thoughtfully, however, both the meaning and the music improve. *Kubla Khan,* by Coleridge, uses wonderfully musical language:

In Xanadu did Kubla Khan
A stately pleasure dome decree:
Where Alph, the sacred river, ran
Through caverns measureless to man
Down to a sunless sea.[2]

You simply must read this aloud. A combination of rhyme, repetition, and alliteration makes the words sing.

Rachel Carson's *Under the Sea Wind* provides many examples of musical prose:

> By September the eels of the sound country had begun to drop downstream to the sea. The eels came down from the hills and the upland grasslands. They came from cypress swamps where black-watered rivers had their beginnings; they moved across the tidal plain that dropped in six giant steps to the sea. In the river estuaries and in the sound they joined their mates-to-be. Soon, in silvery wedding dress, they would follow the ebbing tides to the sea, to find—and lose—themselves in the black abysses of mid-ocean.[3]

As with an alphabetic or a traditional song, the music of the text may suggest page divisions while simultaneously providing conceptual unity to the book as a whole.

Writing a Text

At some point, most book artists and illustrators decide to generate their own texts. The ideas and emotions they want to express are not available in a traditional text, and copyright laws may limit the use of a contemporary text.

Taking a creative-writing course is a good place to start. As with art courses, a well-designed writing course can provide a solid base of information and encourage the beginner to try various approaches. Try writing a page or two in response to any of these assignments:

- *Memory amplifier.* Describe an object, a sensation, or a setting that summarizes or epitomizes an event, a feeling, or an idea from your life. Looking at family photographs, childhood toys, or everyday objects is a good place to start.

- *Moment of truth.* Describe an event that clarified or transformed your life.

- *Homeworld.* Describe the physical or psychological place that is your home. Is it a particular house? A forest? The World Wide Web?

- *Build a memory bank.* Triggering questions can help you start. Just fill in the blanks: (a) "The first time I ever____"; (b) "The best day of my life was____"; (c) list memorable events, such as theater offerings, trips, or concerts; (d) list companions in triumph and adversity; (e) consider the greatest gift you ever received or ever gave.

- *Concept generator.* Research a single word, using a thesaurus, a dictionary, an encyclopedia, the Internet, and so on. Collect all the resulting meanings into a book.

Selecting or writing an appropriate text can increase the impact of the book. The best texts are of personal interest, offer room for experimentation in the book format, and are meaningful to your audience. Ask yourself the following questions as you assess the potential of several texts:

- *What is the conceptual, psychological, or political power of the text?* Does it embody ideas and emotions you find personally compelling? The stronger your connection to the text, the more effective the book will be.

- *Does the text include any verbal patterns that can help unify the book?* Rhythm, repetition, and rhyme can be used to create a stronger connection among the pages.

- *How resonant are the words?* Do they gain or lose strength through multiple readings?

- *How accessible is the text?* Is the language comprehensible to the intended audience? How wide an interest is there in the book's subject matter?

- *How long is the text?* Generally, texts of 30 or fewer words are easiest to use effectively. Extended texts can get long-winded and crowd out the images.

Any source, from graffiti to Shakespeare, can be used. Indeed, many visual books derive their power from an unexpected selection of words.

Text and Type Style

After a text is chosen, book construction can begin. Each page you design raises many questions. Let's concentrate on three major questions, using an 11 × 17 in. double-page spread. Ask yourself the following questions:

- *What type style and type size are most appropriate to the ideas expressed?*

Each type style has a significant effect on communication. Let's experiment with a simple phrase: "Footsteps echoed emptiness."

Impact type has an industrial look. Perhaps it is the echo of boots descending a factory staircase that we hear (15.12).

FOOTSTEPS ECHOED EMPTINESS

15.12

Garamond type, especially when italicized, is flowing and graceful. The footsteps we now hear may be those of a child descending a staircase in a Victorian house on Christmas Eve (15.13).

footsteps echoed emptiness

15.13

Madrone type paints a much grimmer picture. A gang war has concluded, and the survivors are slowly leaving the deserted parking lot where it occurred (15.14).

FOOTSTEPS ECHOED EMPTINESS

15.14

- *Can more than one type style be used effectively?*

Multiple type styles are used in many books to communicate the distinctive voices of multiple speakers or to convey multiple perspectives on the same event. *Sticky Buns: An Overnight Roll* uses this approach (15.15). This book was developed by a team of 12 artists during a workshop organized by the Paper and Book Intensive, a national

15.15 *Sticky Buns: An Overnight Roll*, **1996.** A collaborative book developed by 12 artists participating in a letterpress workshop at the Paper and Book Intensive. Kathy Keuhn, instructor.

book-arts group. An actual recipe for cinnamon buns is provided near the top of each page, while a **gloss,** or commentary on the text, is written in italics along the bottom. Words carefully selected from the recipe are thereby reinterpreted, suggesting a romantic afternoon in the kitchen as the emotions (as well as the dough) begin to rise.

- *How should the words be positioned on the page?*

In figure 15.16, position combined with size emphasizes the acute hearing we develop in threatening situations. The mysterious implications of the phrase are emphasized in figure 15.17. With the addition of two more pages, figure 15.18 communicates the loneliness of the journey.

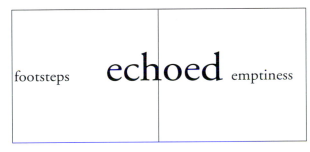

15.16

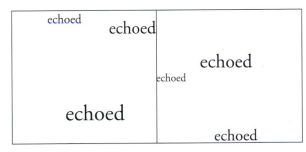

15.17

15.18

footsteps echoed emptiness

15.19

footsteps echoed emptiness

15.20

footsteps echoed emptiness

15.21

Word and Image Relationships

Things get even more interesting when words and images are used together. The organization in figure 15.19 suggests the woman's memory of a past event. The same phrase describes a walk into the future in figure 15.20. Finally, the combination of words and images in figure 15.21 puts us back into a labyrinth.

Advantages of Visual Books

Through a combination of words and images, visual books can convey complex ideas and emotions to a broad audience. In some books, the words provide direct, explicit communication, while the images are more implicit and evocative. In other books, the words are evocative, while the images are explicit and direct. In either case, layers of meaning can be created through a contrast between the visual and the verbal. Instead of overexplaining an image, words can be used to suggest alternative ideas and implications. For artists with big ideas, this interplay between words and images greatly expands communication.

Key Questions

THE VISUAL BOOK

- What thoughts and emotions do you most want to express in your visual book?

- What thoughts and emotions are best expressed in words? Through images?

- What balance between words and images is most effective?

- Will a change in tempo increase impact? Try adding some blank pages to slow down the tempo or putting multiple frames on a single page to speed up the tempo.

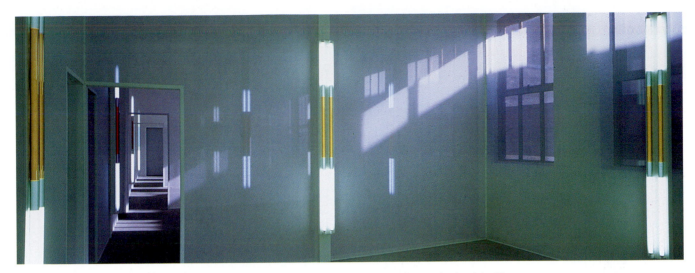

15.22 Robert Irwin, *Part II: Excursus: Homage to the Square³.* Installation at Dia Center for the Arts, New York. September 1998–June 1999.

INSTALLATION ART

An **installation** is an ensemble of images and objects that are presented within a three-dimensional environment. Because we occupy the actual time and space of the artwork, we become physically engaged in an installation. This can heighten the aesthetic experience.

Uses of Space and Time

Some installations are primarily spatial. For example, many installations by Robert Irwin emphasize direct experience within a constructed space. By devising a series of entrances, exits, and environments, Irwin creates a framework that is activated by each visitor. His *Part II: Excursus: Homage to the Square³* (15.22) was installed at the Dia Center in New York in 1998. This structure consisted of nine cubic rooms defined by delicate walls of cloth. The opacity and transparency of the fabric varied depending on the amount and location of the light. Two vertical fluorescent lights illuminated each cube, creating subtle changes in color from room to room.

Entering the installation was both inviting and disorienting. From any point, all the rooms were visible yet veiled. Multiple layers of cloth and the variations in light made the most distant rooms dissolve. The vertical fluorescent lights, which always remained visible, read first as individual, then as mirror images, creating a hallucinatory experience similar to that in a carnival fun house. All activity within the space was created by the visitors themselves, who entered and explored the installation like ghostly silhouettes.

By contrast, *Floodsong,* by Mary Lucier, was primarily temporal. Six video monitors were installed in a narrow room at the Museum of Modern Art in New York. Each showed an interview with a survivor of the 1995 Grand Forks flood. A young girl, an old woman, an old man, a minister, and a farmer told the story of the terrifying event. In the enclosed space, the individual voices were indistinct. They echoed and merged, creating a litany of fortitude and grief, resilience and fear. In sharp contrast to the straightforward interviews, an enormous projection on the back wall of the gallery took the audience through wrecked houses and piles of debris.

Bill Viola's *Hall of Whispers* (15.23) was equally temporal and spatial. In his catalogue for a retrospective exhibition of Viola's work, David Ross wrote:

> Viewers enter a long, narrow, dark room, and must pass between ten video projections arranged in two rows along the side walls, five on either side of the room. The projections are life-sized black and white images of people's heads facing the viewer, with their eyes closed and their mouths tightly bound and gagged. They are straining to speak, but their muffled voices are incomprehensible, and mingle in the space in a low, indecipherable jumble of sound.[4]

15.23 Bill Viola, *Hall of Whispers*, 1995. Video/sound installation.

This installation, while similar to *Floodsong* in layout, created an entry into a nightmare. Lucier's installation evoked a range of emotions: fear, pity, and respect. Viola's *Hall of Whispers* was claustrophobic and terrifying.

The Importance of Context

Installations must be seen in context. Spatial variations from site to site require changes in an installation whenever it is moved. More important, each site adds its own meaning to the artwork. No site is neutral. Each imparts its own emotional and spatial charge.

When the context is used fully, a powerful connection can be made between art and life. For example, our associations with the interior and the objects used in Sandy Skoglund's *Walking on Eggshells* (15.24) are essential to the meaning of the piece. For most of us, there is no place more

private than a bathroom and there are few animals more insidiously frightening than snakes. This combination alone is sure to create tension. The addition of a floor covered with delicate eggshells, nude female figures, and playful rabbits expands the expressive range further. Even the wall tiles are deliberate. Dominated by hieroglyphics from the Egyptian Book of the Dead and other ancient images, they add to the sense of mystery. The women in this space seem like goddesses from antiquity, and the bathroom becomes loaded with conflicting emotions.

A site also may be used to expand the audience for art. In *Storefront Stories* (15.25), Nancy Callahan and Diane Gallo transformed empty shop windows in several small towns into a series of vignettes based on childhood memories. When shown in Cherry Valley, New York, a single window was changed every day over a six-week period. In this project, personal

15.24 Sandy Skoglund, *Walking on Eggshells*, 1997. Cibachrome print, 47 × 60 in. (119 × 152 cm). © 1997 Sandy Skoglund.

experience became public communication through the use of a nontraditional exhibition space.

Through *Truisms* (15.26), Jenny Holzer brought public art to an urban audience for a more political purpose. Printing various proverbs on posters, flyers, T-shirts, hats, and finally electronic signs, Holzer used mass-marketing techniques to convey messages such as "Abuse of power comes as no surprise" and "Raise boys and girls the same way." Shown next to the flashing neon signs in New York City's busy Times Square, these seemingly banal messages took on new importance and reached many viewers unfamiliar with contemporary art.

Advantages of Installation Art

For the artist seeking new and expanded means of expression, installation art offers several advantages:

- *A fresh perspective on a familiar setting or situation.* The site itself is an essential component of the piece. We must see familiar settings afresh. Any aspect of reality can become a staging area for art. Our expectations may be shifted, inverted, or upended.

- *A large scale.* Most installations are made in a scale that invites physical entry. Thus, the distance between viewer and image is eliminated: viewers become one with the artwork. The principles of time, space, and gravity that rule our everyday life can be used deliberately in an installation to heighten impact or to create a sense of disorientation.

- *Increased viewer involvement.* No longer a bystander, the viewer must physically enter and consciously interact with the artwork.

15.25 **Diane Gallo and Nancy Callahan,** *Storefront Stories,* **1999.** Mixed-medium installation, 6 × 6 × 6 ft (1.83 × 1.83 × 1.83 m).

Key Questions

INSTALLATIONS

- What ideas do you most want to express? What emotions do you most want to evoke?

- What is the advantage of a confined space as opposed to an expansive space?

- How much lighting is needed, and what is the most appropriate light source?

- What sounds will you provide? What sounds can be generated by the audience?

- How can you invite viewers into your artwork? What will they discover? What might they know on leaving that they didn't know on entering?

- Will interaction among viewers or between the viewers and the artwork expand meaning or heighten emotion?

15.26 **Jenny Holzer,** *Truisms, 1977–79: Abuse of Power Comes as No Surprise,* **1982.** Times Square, New York. Spectacolor Board No. 1.

PERFORMANCE ART

Mixing dance, theater, music, and art with politics, philosophy, and other disciplines, performance art pushes the possibilities of interdisciplinary work even further. Like any other art form, performance art is designed to communicate ideas and express emotions. Unlike traditional art forms, performance art is immediate and direct. Rather than paint an image on a canvas, the performers generally present images directly—on a stage, in a gallery, or outdoors. The wood, bronze, or marble of traditional figurative sculpture is replaced with the flesh and blood of the artist's own body. For example, in *Indigo Blue* (15.27), Ann Hamilton placed 18,000 pieces of used "blue-collar" work clothes, a seated "attendant," and a desk covered with history books in a large room. The laundered clothes had been meticulously folded by an army of volunteers and carefully stacked. Quietly seated at the desk, the attendant erased the historical texts from back to front, using a pink pearl eraser and moisture from her own saliva. In this performance piece, the worn items of clothing became mute witnesses to the loss of industry and employment in America.

15.27 Ann Hamilton performing *Indigo Blue*, 1991/2007. Cotton clothing, wood and steel platform, wood table and stool, book, eraser. Dimensions variable.

Historical Background

The roots of contemporary performance art may actually extend back in time to the Futurists, a group of Italian poets, musicians, and artists most active from 1911 to 1915. Determined to develop a new approach to art, they created revolutionary paintings and sculptures based on dynamism, wrote inflammatory manifestos, and staged theatrical performances that were both frenetic and shocking. In word and deed, the Futurists rebelled against good taste, traditional subject matter, compositional rules, and established institutions such as museums.

Performance art has become especially prominent in the past 30 years. The current surge in interest is often traced to the Happenings developed by Allan Kaprow and others in the 1950s and 1960s. In a **Happening,** the time, place, materials, and general theme for the event were determined by the artist. Upon arrival, the audience created the artwork through their actions. Unrehearsed, these events often were chaotic as well as exhilarating.

Characteristics of Performance Art

To some extent, contemporary performance art shares many of the basic characteristics of Futurism. Four qualities are especially notable.

Ephemeral

Just as a symphony ceases to exist as soon as the last note fades, so performance art is inherently ephemeral. The performance may persist in the memory of each member of the audience, but the full force of the event disappears as soon as the audience leaves the site. While any well-trained classical violinist can perform a given Beethoven sonata, roles in performance pieces are rarely played by new actors. Generally, a piece written by Laurie Anderson must be performed by her. Even when a new production is planned, difficulty in transferring information about the role may make it impossible to restage the piece.

As a result, time is always of particular importance in performance art. In 1952, musician John Cage deleted pitch, timbre, and loudness from one composition, leaving duration as the only remaining aspect of the music. The resulting work, titled *4 minutes 33 seconds (4'33")* therefore was silent for 4 minutes and 33 seconds.

Time was also a major component of Dan Graham's *Past Continuous Pasts,* installed in a New York City gallery in 1974. The walls were covered with mirrors, and time-delayed video monitors were positioned at each end of the room. Upon entering, viewers first viewed themselves in the present; then, watching the video monitors, they viewed themselves in the past.

Collaborative

Working collaboratively, artists can expand their ideas and explore new modes of expression. Despite their interest in live art, few visual artists have extensive training in dance and theater. It may be physically impossible for them to perform a movement themselves. And, just as an amateur's drawing is very different from a drawing done by a professional, so amateur dance differs greatly from professional dance. By working collaboratively, artists, actors, musicians, and dancers can combine forces to create powerful new pieces.

Furthermore, a collaboration tends to extend the ideas generated by each participant. Despite their similarities, art, theater, music, and dance are also distinctively different. Each has a long and complex history, an extensive theoretical background, and particular aesthetic values. By sharing information and discussing alternative approaches, each participant has an opportunity to rethink his or her own creative process.

Many disciplines have been combined successfully. In *Predator's Ball* (15.28), Karole Armitage

15.28 Karole Armitage, *Predator's Ball,* 1996. Brooklyn Academy of Music. Sets by David Salle, animation videos by Erica Beckman, costumes by Hugo Boss, Pila Limosner, and Debra Moises Co.

combined her choreography with sets by painter David Salle and videos by Erica Beckman. This tale about Wall Street junk bond dealer Michael Milken is both stark in its staging and frenzied in its energy. In *Available Light* (15.29), choreographer Lucinda Childs sought a pulse in the spaces designed by architect Frank Gehry and the music composed by John Adams. And, in *L.O.W. in Gaia* (15.30), Rachel Rosenthal presented a meditation on art, feminism, and ecology.

Blurred Boundaries

During a performance, separations between art and life are often dissolved. For some artists, performance art is a way to work outside the rarefied world of the art museum or the competitive world of the commercial gallery. Viewing art as a creative process and a life-affirming philosophy rather than as a product, such artists seek new venues and new audiences. Separations between high art and mass culture may become blurred. Graffiti, popular music, or television advertisements may provide

15.29 Lucinda Childs, image from *Available Light*, 1983. Performed at the Brooklyn Academy of Music.

15.30 Rachel Rosenthal, *L.O.W. in Gaia.* First performance, Marquette University, WI, 1986.

more inspiration than a masterpiece in a museum. Indeed, in describing his approach to a Happening, Allan Kaprow said that "the line between art and life should be kept as fluid and perhaps as indistinct as possible."

Many contemporary artists pursue this goal with a vengeance. In John Cage's *First Construction in Metal,* automobile brake drums, cowbells, and sheets of metal are used along with conventional percussion instruments in a highly rhythmic piece. In *Imaginary Landscape #4,* Cage broke the concert-hall barrier even more vigorously. Twelve ordinary radios, tuned to various stations, were the major instruments played. Any advertisement, news, or music each radio played became part of the concert.

The Artist and the Audience

When barriers between art and life are removed, separations between artist and audience also become blurred. Indeed, many artists deliberately involve the audience in the work. In *Performance/Audience/Mirror,* Dan Graham confronted his audience directly, describing their appearance and commenting on their participation in the performance. And, with *Pull,* Mona Hatoum created a humorous interaction between audience and artist. Viewers were invited to pull on an actual braid of hair, then watch the artist's reaction on the video monitor. No longer an observer, each member of the audience helped create the artwork.

ADVANTAGES OF INTERDISCIPLINARY ART

Visual books, installations, and performance art all require interdisciplinary integration. The connections created offer new opportunities for creative thinking and complex communication. Ideas and emotions outside the mainstream can become accessible to both artists and audiences. Furthermore, because each of these new mediums requires a substantial amount of audience participation, relationships between artist and audience are redefined. An active audience can contribute more to the experience than a passive audience. When artist and audience share the same time and space, as in a performance piece, this connection is especially strong. With performance art, boundaries dissolve not only between art and theater, but also between art and life.

Key Questions
PERFORMANCE ART

- When working collaboratively, what can you offer your partner and what can your partner offer you?
- What similarities and differences are there in your creative processes? What is the best way to handle differences of opinion?
- How many performers are needed?
- What is the relationship between the performer(s) and the set? Should all the performers appear live, or can some appear via slides, audio, or video projections?
- In what context will your performance appear? A subway station is a very different venue than a gallery and may add meaning to the artwork.
- How can sound and light heighten emotion or expand meaning?
- How much change must occur during the performance? Is repetition a virtue?
- How can you heighten or reduce intensity?
- What is the most powerful beginning you can devise?
- What is the most memorable ending you can devise?
- Who is the intended audience, and what role can the audience play?

SUMMARY

- A visual book is an experimental structure that conveys ideas, actions, and emotions in an integrated and interdependent format. Each page is connected in some way to the preceding page and to the following page.

- Visual books combine two-dimensional composition with three-dimensional structure and may use time and narrative very deliberately. They may be entirely visual, may be entirely verbal, or may mix words and images.

- In selecting a text, consider its potential to generate ideas, how the text will be divided and distributed over multiple pages, the rhythm and music of the words, and the significance of the ideas.

- Every type style has its own distinctive quality, which can add to or detract from the meaning of the book.

- The combination of words and images in a visual book can encourage the development of complex ideas using layers of meaning.

- An installation is an ensemble of images and objects that is presented within a three-dimensional environment. When the viewer enters an installation, he or she is physically surrounded and aesthetically engaged.

- An installation may be primarily spatial, may be primarily temporal, or may use both space and time equally. The context in which an installation occurs can add to, subtract from, or expand its meaning.

- Installation art offers a fresh perspective on a familiar setting or situation, is usually done in large scale, and requires some viewer involvement.

- Performance art is live art designed by artists. Combining aspects of theater, music, art, and dance, it offers both the artist and the audience a laboratory for aesthetic experimentation.

- Many performance artists use time very deliberately, expand their ideas through collaboration, and seek to blur the boundaries between art and life.

- Each of the interdisciplinary arts described in this chapter requires substantial audience participation. As a result, relationships between the artist and the audience are constantly being redefined by contemporary artists.

KEY TERMS

codex	Happening	interdisciplinary art	visual book
gloss	installation	performance art	

STUDIO PROJECTS

To apply the concepts from this chapter in the studio, check out the Projects page in the Online Learning Center at www.mhhe.com/stewart4e. The following is a sample of the chapter-related assignments that are described in step-by-step detail.

Labyrinth Collage and Book. Integrating multiple materials, methods, and structures to communicate a complex idea.

Profile:
Nancy Callahan, Artist, and Diane Gallo, Writer

Storefront Stories: Creating a Collaborative Community

Nancy Callahan (left in photo) is a leader in the field of artists' books and is known for her creative work in screen printing. She has exhibited her work widely, and in 1994 she was one of four artists chosen to represent the United States at the International Book and Paper Exhibition in Belgium. In 1999, she participated in the International Artists' Book Workshop and Symposium in Mor, Hungary. In addition to her full-time teaching at the State University of New York at Oneonta, Callahan has taught workshops at major book centers around the country, including the Center for Book Arts in New York City and The Women's Studio Workshop.

Diane Gallo (right in photo) is an award-winning writer and performance poet, as well as a master teacher. Her film work has received awards from American Women in Radio & Television and nominations from the American Film Institute. Gallo teaches creative writing and life-story workshops at universities and cultural institutes throughout the country and is a visiting poet with the Dodge Foundation Poetry Program, a humanist scholar with the National Endowment for the Humanities Poets in Person program, and cofounder of the newly formed Association of Teaching Artists.

Callahan and Gallo began working together in 1984 as a photographer/writer team for the Binghamton Press. As a result of many years of collaborative teaching, they became the first teaching artist team working with the Empire State Partnership project, jointly sponsored by the New York State Education Department and the New York State Council of the Arts. In 1996, they received fellowships to the Virginia Center for the Creative Arts, where they began working on a major project, which led to their selection by the Mid-Atlantic Foundation for their millennium project. Funded by the National Endowment for the Arts, the project—Artists & Communities: America Creates for the Millennium—named Callahan and Gallo as two of America's 250 most creative community artists.

MS: You've gained a lot of recognition for your recent text-based installations. Please describe *Storefront Stories*.

NC: Over the past two years we've had an extraordinary collaborative experience. As an extension of our writing, we developed a new type of text-based installation. One day as we worked on a story about ironing, we playfully hung a single wrinkled white shirt in the front window of our studio in Gilbertsville, New York. Below the shirt, we placed a small sign that said "No one irons anymore." As

the lone shirt turned, it attracted attention, causing people on the sidewalk to stop, read the window, and react. *Storefront Stories* was born.

DG: Objects became words; words transformed objects. Week by week, using storefront windows as a public stage, we wrote and presented installments of autobiographical stories. In one town, a single window was changed every ten days, creating an ongoing narrative. In another, we used five windows in a row, like pages in a book. Bits of text and symbolic objects were used to tell stories about personal change. Stories and objects—combined with the unexpected street location—sparked curiosity and started a community dialogue.

MS: How did members of the community become participants?

NC: They just began telling us their stories. An elderly woman on her way to the post office stopped to tell us the story of how she had learned to type on an old Smith typewriter, just like the one in the window. Eleven-year-old boys on bicycles stopped by. A mother brought her children to the windows each week to read the story aloud. Couples strolling by in the evening asked, "What's coming next?"

DG: People talked to us easily, asking questions and encouraging us. Many times, we'd return to find handwritten stories, comments, and suggestions. We watched passersby examine the windows and heard them laughing and talking to each other as they pieced together the story. When a viewer made a good suggestion, we incorporated the idea into the next window. When community members saw their ideas so quickly incorporated, they realized they were more than passive viewers. They were now active participants, with a vital involvement in the artistic process. The collaboration which began between two artists quickly expanded, engaging the entire town.

MS: In your household installations you create complete environments to frame your stories. To create these environments, you spend many hours scouting thrift shops and garage sales, searching for just the right objects to evoke an exact time and place. Why are these objects so important?

NC: Household objects are the vocabulary of the everyday world. Everyone feels comfortable with them. The objects are a bridge—they allow the viewer to cross easily from everyday life into the world of our installations.

DG: After the object is safely in the viewer's mind, it becomes a psychic spark which triggers associations and amplifies memories. For example, while we were doing the ironing installation, a delivery man who stopped for a moment to watch us work said, "I don't know anything about art," and began talking deeply and at length about how, when he was a boy, his mother took in ironing to make extra money so that he could have a bicycle.

NC: His narrative then created another layer of collaboration.

MS: When you began creating the installations, did you expect this kind of public reaction?

NC: No. It was a shock. From the moment we hung that first wrinkled shirt in the studio window,

Diane Gallo and Nancy Callahan, *Storefront Stories*, 1999. Mixed-medium installation, 6 × 6 × 6 ft (1.83 × 1.83 × 1.83 m).

people on the street were responsive. The immediate feedback was exhilarating.

MS: What are the characteristics of a good collaboration?

DG: Quiet attention is crucial. We both have to really listen, not only to words but also to the implications.

NC: Always tell the truth. There can be no censoring. If something's bothering you, it's important to talk about it right away. Honesty and careful listening build trust. When you trust your partner, you can reveal more.

MS: When people first see your installations, many are almost overwhelmed. Why?

DG: We're balancing on a fine line between life and art, between the personal and the universal, the public and the private, the conscious and the unconscious. We're working on the edge of consciousness, looking for things you might only be half aware of under ordinary circumstances. It's like watching a horizon line in your mind, waiting for a thought or an answer to rise.

Daniel Sutherland, *I Wish I Could Help You*, 1994. Oil on canvas on wood with hardware, 75 × 84 in. (190.5 × 213.4 cm).

Visual Organization

Arnheim, Rudolph. *Art and Visual Perception: A Psychology of the Creative Eye.* Berkeley: University of California Press, 1974.

Arnheim, Rudolph. *Power of the Center.* Berkeley: University of California Press, 1999.

Berger, Arthur Asa. *Seeing Is Believing: An Introduction to Visual Communication,* 3rd ed. New York: McGraw-Hill, 2007.

Berger, John. *Ways of Seeing.* London: British Broadcasting Corporation, 1987.

Dondis, Donis. *A Primer of Visual Literacy.* Cambridge, MA: MIT Press, 1973.

Two-Dimensional Design

Graham, Donald W. *Composing Pictures.* New York: Van Nostrand Reinhold, 1970.

Kepes, Gyorgy. *Language of Vision.* Chicago: Paul Theobald, 1944.

Myers, Jack Fredrick. *The Language of Visual Art: Perception as a Basis for Design.* Orlando, FL: Holt, Rinehart and Winston, 1989.

Ocvirk, Otto G., Robert E. Stinson, Philip R. Wigg, Robert O. Bone, and David L. Cayton. *Art Fundamentals: Theory and Practice,* 11th ed. New York: McGraw-Hill, 2009.

Color Theory

Albers, Josef. *Interaction of Color.* New Haven, CT: Yale University Press, 1963.

Birren, Farber. *Light, Color and Environment.* New York: Van Nostrand Reinhold, 1982.

Gerritsen, Frans. *Theory and Practice of Color.* New York: Van Nostrand Reinhold, 1975.

Hornung, David. *Color: A Workshop Approach.* New York: McGraw-Hill, 2005.

Itten, Johannes. *The Art of Color.* New York: Van Nostrand Reinhold, 1974.

Kuppers, Harald. *Color: Origin, Systems, Uses.* New York: Van Nostrand Reinhold, 1972.

Linton, Harold. *Color Model Environments.* New York: Van Nostrand Reinhold, 1985.

Munsell, Albert H. *A Grammar of Color: A Basic Treatise on the Color System of Albert H. Munsell.* New York: Van Nostrand Reinhold, 1969.

Norman, Richard B. *Electronic Color.* New York: Van Nostrand Reinhold, 1990.

Creativity

Bohm, David. *On Creativity.* New York: Routledge, 2000.

Briggs, John. *Fire in the Crucible: Understanding the Process of Creative Genius.* Grand Rapids: Phanes Press, 2000.

Csikszentmihalyi, Mihaly. *Creativity: Flow and the Psychology of Discovery and Invention.* New York: HarperCollins, 1996.

Dewey, John. *Art as Experience.* New York: Capricorn Books, 1958.

Gardner, Howard. *Art, Mind and Brain: A Cognitive Approach to Creativity.* New York: Basic Books, 1982.

Gardner, Howard. *Creating Minds: An Anatomy of Creativity Seen Through the Lives of Freud, Einstein, Picasso, Stravinsky, Eliot, Graham, and Gandhi.* New York: Basic Books, 1993.

Gardner, Howard. *Frames of Mind: The Theory of Multiple Intelligences.* New York: Basic Books, 1985.

Lamott, Anne. *Bird by Bird: Some Instructions on Writing and Life.* New York: Anchor Books, 1998.

Le Boeuf, Michael. *Imagineering.* New York: McGraw-Hill, 1980.

Prince, George. "Creativity and Learning as Skills, Not Talents," *The Philips Exeter Bulletin,* 1980.

Shekerjian, Denise. *Uncommon Genius: How Great Ideas Are Born.* New York: Penguin Books, 1991.

Wallace, Doris B., and Howard E. Gruber, eds. *Creative People at Work.* New York: Oxford University Press, 1989.

Concept Development

Adams, James L. *Conceptual Blockbusting.* Reading, MA: Addison-Wesley, 1986.

de Bono, Edward. *Lateral Thinking.* London: Ward Educational Limited, 1970.

Grear, Malcolm. *Inside/Outside: From the Basics to the Practice of Design.* New York: Van Nostrand Reinhold, 1993.

Johnson, Mary Frisbee. *Visual Workouts: A Collection of Art-Making Problems.* Englewood Cliffs, NJ: Prentice Hall, 1983.

Kelley, Tom. *The Art of Innovation: Lessons in Creativity from America's Leading Design Firm.* New York: Doubleday, 2001.

Lakoff, George, and Mark Johnson. *Metaphors We Live By.* Chicago: University of Chicago Press, 1981.

Shahn, Ben. *The Shape of Content.* Cambridge, MA: Harvard University Press, 1957.

Von Oech, Roger. *A Kick in the Seat of the Pants.* New York: Harper and Row, 1963.

Von Oech, Roger. *A Whack on the Side of the Head.* New York: Harper and Row, 1986.

Wilde, Judith and Richard. *Visual Literacy: A Conceptual Approach to Graphic Problem Solving.* New York: Watson-Guptil, 2000.

Critical Thinking

Barrett, Terry. *Criticizing Photographs: An Introduction to Understanding Images,* 4th ed. New York: McGraw-Hill, 2006.

Barrett, Terry. *Interpreting Art.* New York: McGraw-Hill, 2003.

bibliography

Tucker, Amy. *Visual Literacy: Writing About Art.* New York: McGraw-Hill, 2002.

Three-Dimensional Design

Andrews, Oliver. *Living Materials: A Sculptor's Handbook.* Berkeley: University of California Press, 1988.

Bachelard, Gaston. *The Poetics of Space,* trans. Maria Jolas. Boston: Beacon Press, 1969.

Beardsley, John. *Earthworks and Beyond: Contemporary Art in the Landscape.* New York: Abbeville Press, 1998.

Ching, Frank. *Architecture: Form, Space, and Order,* 2nd ed. New York: Van Nostrand Reinhold, 1996.

de Oliveira, Nicolas, Nicola Oxley, and Michael Petry. *Installation Art.* Washington, DC: Smithsonian Institution Press, 1994.

Dormer, Peter, and Ralph Turner. *The New Jewelry: Trends and Traditions.* London: Thames and Hudson, 1985.

Frantz, Suzanne. *Contemporary Glass: A World Survey from the Corning Museum of Glass.* New York: Harry N. Abrams, 1989.

Koplos, Janet. *Contemporary Japanese Sculpture.* New York: Abbeville Press, 1991.

Lane, Peter. *Ceramic Form: Design and Decoration,* rev. ed. New York: Rizzoli, 1998.

Lewin, Susan Grant. *One of a Kind: American Art Jewelry Today.* New York: Harry N. Abrams, 1994.

Lidstone, John. *Building with Wire.* New York: Van Nostrand Reinhold, 1972.

Luecking, Stephen. *Principles of Three Dimensional Design.* Upper Saddle River, NJ: Pearson Education, 2002.

Lynn, Martha Dreyer. *Clay Today: Contemporary Ceramicists and Their Work.* Los Angeles: Los Angeles County Museum of Art; and San Francisco: Chronicle Books, 1990.

Manzini, Ezio. *The Material of Invention: Materials and Design.* Cambridge, MA: MIT Press, 1989.

Miller, Bonnie J. *Out of the Fire: Contemporary Glass Artists and Their Work.* San Francisco: Chronicle Books, 1991.

Nunley, John W., and Cara McCarty. *Masks: Faces of Culture.* New York: Harry N. Abrams in association with the Saint Louis Art Museum, 1999.

Penny, Nicholas. *The Materials of Sculpture.* New Haven, CT: Yale University Press, 1993.

Selz, Peter Howard. *Barbara Chase-Riboud, Sculptor.* New York: Harry N. Abrams, 1999.

Wallschlaeger, Charles, and Cynthia Busic-Snyder. *Basic Visual Concepts and Principles for Artists, Architects and Designers.* New York: McGraw-Hill, 1992.

Williams, Arthur. *Sculpture: Technique, Form, Content.* Worcester, MA: Davis, 1993.

Wong, Wucius. *Principles of Form and Design.* New York: Van Nostrand Reinhold, 1993.

Wyatt, Gary. *Spirit Faces: Contemporary Native American Masks from the Northwest.* San Francisco: Chronicle Books, 1994.

Time Design

Baldwin, Huntley. *How to Create Effective TV Commercials,* 2nd ed. Lincolnwood, IL: NTC Business Books, 1989.

Bordwell, David, and Kristin Thompson. *Film Art: An Introduction,* 8th ed. New York: McGraw-Hill, 2008.

Eisner, Will. *Comics and Sequential Art.* Tamarac, FL: Poorhouse Press, 1985.

Goldberg, Roselee. *Performance: Live Art Since 1960.* New York: Harry N. Abrams, 1998.

Johnson, Lincoln F. *Film: Space, Time, Light and Sound.* Orlando, FL: Holt, Rinehart and Winston, 1974.

Katz, Stephen D. *Film Directing, Shot by Shot: Visualizing from Concept to Screen.* Studio City, CA: Michael Wiese Productions, 1991.

McCloud, Scott. *Understanding Comics.* New York: HarperPerennial, 1994.

McKee, Robert. *Story: Substance, Structure, Style and the Principles of Screen Writing.* New York: HarperCollins, 1997.

Riordan, Steve, ed. *Clio Awards: A Tribute to 30 Years of Advertising Excellence, 1960–1989.* Glen Cove, NY: PBC International, 1989.

Ross, David. *Bill Viola.* New York: Whitney Museum of American Art, 1998.

Vogler, Christopher. *The Writer's Journey: Mythic Structure for Storytellers and Screenwriters.* Studio City, CA: Michael Wiese Productions, 1991.

Zettl, Herbert. *Sight, Sound, Motion: Applied Media Aesthetics,* 4th ed. Belmont, CA: Wadsworth, 2004.

Book Arts

Drucker, Johanna. *The Century of Artists' Books.* New York: Granary Books, 1995.

Gordon, Stephen F. *Making Picture-Books: A Method of Learning Graphic Sequence.* New York: Van Nostrand Reinhold, 1970.

La Plantz, Shereen. *Cover to Cover.* Asheville, NC: Lark Books, 1995.

Lyons, Joan. *Artists' Books: A Critical Anthology and Sourcebook.* Rochester, NY: Visual Studies Workshop Press, 1985.

Smith, Keith A. *Structure of the Visual Book.* Fairport, NY: The Sigma Foundation, 1992.

Smith, Keith A. *Text in the Book Format.* Fairport, NY: The Sigma Foundation, 1991.

bibliography

Chapter Two Works Cited

1. Johannes Itten, *The Art of Color* (New York: Van Nostrand Reinhold, 1974), p. 16.

2. Alexander Theroux, *The Primary Colors: Three Essays* (New York: Henry Holt and Company, 1994), p. 6.

Chapter Five Works Cited

1. Keith A. Smith, *Structure of the Visual Book* (Fairport, NY: The Sigma Foundation, 1991), pp. 17–18.

Chapter Six Works Cited

1. Mihaly Csikszentmihalyi, *Creativity: Flow and the Psychology of Discovery and Invention* (New York: HarperCollins, 1996), pp. 55–76.

2. George Prince, "Creativity and Learning as Skills, Not Talents," *The Philips Exeter Bulletin,* June–October, 1980.

3. Anne Lamott, *Bird by Bird: Some Instructions on Writing and Life* (New York: Anchor Books, 1998), pp. 18–19.

Chapter Eight Works Cited

1. Henry M. Sayre, *A World of Art,* 3rd ed. (Upper Saddle River, NJ: Prentice Hall, 2000), p. 496.

Chapter Nine Works Cited

1. John Beardsley, *Earthworks and Beyond: Contemporary Art in the Landscape* (New York: Abbeville Press, 1998), p. 31.

2. Jonathan Fineberg, *Art Since 1940: Strategies of Being* (Englewood Cliffs, NJ: Prentice Hall, 1995), p. 383.

3. Alexander Theroux, *The Primary Colors: Three Essays* (New York: Henry Holt and Company, 1994), p. 86.

4. Theroux, p. 6.

Chapter Thirteen Works Cited

1. David Bordwell and Kristin Thompson, *Film Art: An Introduction,* 5th ed. (New York: McGraw-Hill, 1997), pp. 277–78.

2. Scott McCloud, *Understanding Comics* (New York: HarperPerennial, 1994), pp. 70–74.

3. Richard Kostelanetz, *Aaron Copland: A Reader: Selected Writings, 1923–1972* (New York: Routledge, 2003), p. 107.

4. Keith A. Smith, *Structure of the Visual Book* (Fairport, NY: The Sigma Foundation, 1991), pp. 102–4.

Chapter Fourteen Works Cited

1. Keith A. Smith, *Structure of the Visual Book* (Fairport, NY: The Sigma Foundation, 1991), p. 106.

2. Robert McKee, *Story: Substance, Structure, Style and the Principles of Screen Writing* (New York: HarperCollins, 1997), pp. 37–41.

Chapter Fifteen Works Cited

1. Jean L. McKechnie, *Webster's New Universal Unabridged Dictionary* (New York: Simon and Schuster, 1983), p. 1011.

2. Maynard Mack, *World Masterpieces* (New York: W. W. Norton and Company, 1965), p. 478.

3. Rachel Carson, *Under the Sea Wind* (New York: Viking Penguin, 1996), p. 23.

4. Bill Viola, *A Twenty-Five-Year Survey* (New York: Whitney Museum of American Art; Paris: Flammarion, 1997).

notes

A

abstract artwork; abstract form 1. an artwork or form derived from visual reality that has been distilled or transformed, reducing its resemblance to the original source. 2. a multiple image structure, such as a film, in which the parts are related to each other through repetition and visual characteristics such as shape, color, scale or direction of movement.

abstract shape a shape that is derived from a visual source, but is so transformed that it bears little visual resemblance to that source.

abstraction the reduction of an image or object to an essential aspect of its form or concept.

accent a specific shape, volume, color, musical note, etc. that has been emphasized. Using an accent, a designer can bring attention to part of a composition and increase rhythmic variation within a pattern.

accent color a color that stands out from its surroundings. Often used to attract attention to a specific part of a design.

achromatic a color (such as black and white) that has no hue.

act a major division in a film or theatrical event. Acts are generally constructed from a group of sequences that increase in intensity.

action-to-action transition in comic books, the juxtaposition of two or more panels showing a sequence of actions.

actual lines lines that are physically present in a design.

actual motion motion that physically occurs in a design.

actual time the duration of an actual temporal event. For example, it takes less than a minute for the bowling ball to roll down the ramps in Jean Tinguely's *Chaos 1*.

additive color color created by combining projected beams of chromatic light. The additive color primaries are red, green, and blue, and the secondaries are cyan, magenta, and yellow.

additive sculpture a physical object constructed from separate parts that have been connected using glues, joints, stitching, welds, and so on.

aesthetics the study of human responses to art and beauty.

afterimage in color theory, a ghostly image that continues to linger after the actual image has been removed.

ambient light the quality of light within an entire space or setting. For example, when we enter an open courtyard on a sunny summer afternoon, we are surrounded by warm ambient sunlight. Everything we see is colorful and bright.

amplified perspective the exaggerated use of linear perspective to achieve a dramatic and engaging presentation of the subject. Amplified perspective is often created using an unusual viewing position, such as a bird's-eye view, accelerated convergence, or some form of distortion.

analogous a color scheme based on hues that are adjacent on a color wheel, such as red, red-orange, and orange.

analogy a similarity or connection between things that are apparently separate and dissimilar. For example, when a teacher describes wet plaster as having the "consistency of cream," he or she is using an analogy.

anesthetic a chemical or action used to induce insensitivity or unconsciousness.

anomaly an obvious break from the norm in a design.

appropriation a postmodern practice in which one artist reproduces an image created by another and claims it as his or her own.

approximate symmetry a form of balance that occurs when roughly similar imagery appears on either side of a central axis.

armature an internal structure created to strengthen and support a three-dimensional object.

aspect-to-aspect transition in comic books, the juxtaposition of two or more panels showing different views of a single setting or event. This transition is often used in Japanese comic books.

assemblage an additive method in which the artist or designer constructs the artwork using objects and images that were originally created for another purpose. Essentially, assemblage can be defined as three-dimensional collage.

asymmetrical balance equilibrium among visual elements that do not mirror each other on either side of an axis.

atmospheric perspective a visual phenomenon in which the atmospheric density progressively increases, hazing over the perceived world as one looks into its depth. Overall definition lessens, details fade, contrasts become muted, and, in a landscape, a blue mist descends.

attached shadow a shadow that directly defines a form.

B

backlight a light source positioned behind a person or object that can either create a silhouette or separate the person or object from the background.

balance the equal distribution of weight or force among visual units.

beat 1. a unit of musical rhythm that creates the pulse of a sound. 2. in acting, the most basic element in a story. A beat is an exchange of behavior, based on action and reaction.

bend one of the five major forces affecting structural strength.

Bezold effect a change in a single color that substantially alters our perception of the entire composition.

boundary the dividing line or edge between objects, images, or experiences.

brainstorming any of a number of problem-solving techniques that are designed to expand ideas and encourage creativity. List making, mapping, associative thinking, and metaphorical thinking are common strategies used.

calligraphic line derived from the Greek words for beautiful and writing, a flowing and expressive line that is as personal as handwriting. Calligraphic lines generally vary in thickness and velocity.

camera angle the angle at which an object or event is viewed. An aerial view can provide the sweeping panorama needed to convey the enormity of a battle, while a low camera angle can provide an expansive view of the sky.

carving the removal of materials from a larger mass, gradually revealing an image or object. Carving is a subtractive process.

cast shadow a dark shape that results from placement of an opaque object in the path of a light source.

categorical (form) in film, a multiple image structure that is based on categories, or subsets of a topic. For example, a film on predators might begin with a discussion of wolves, then move on to lions, and conclude with a discussion of hawks.

causality the interrelation of cause and effect, based on the premise that nothing occurs without cause. Narrative film is based on causality: because the starting pistol was shot, the footrace began.

cause-and-effect critique (or formal analysis) a critique in which the viewer seeks to determine the cause for each visual or emotional effect in a design. For example, the dynamism in a design may be caused by the diagonal lines and asymmetrical balance used.

centricity as identified by Rudolph Arnheim, a compressive compositional force.

characteristic texture the inherent or familiar texture of a material. The gleaming reflective surface of a steel teapot, the transparent and reflective qualities of glass, and the gritty texture of clay are all characteristic textures.

chiaroscuro (from Italian meaning "light-dark") The gradual transition of values to create the illusion of light and shadow on a three-dimensional form.

chroma the purity, intensity, or saturation of a color.

chromatic gray a gray made from a mixture of various hues, rather than a simple blend of black and white.

chronology the order in which events occur.

cliché an overused expression or a predictable visual treatment of an idea.

close-up in film, a type of framing in which the scale of the object shown is relatively large, as in a close-up of an actor's face.

closure the mind's inclination to connect fragmentary information to produce a completed form. Closure is an essential aspect of Gestalt psychology.

codex traditional bound-edged format used for modern books, with separate pages normally bound together and given a cover.

collage an image constructed from visual or verbal fragments initially designed for another purpose.

color harmony use of compatible colors to help unify a composition.

color interaction the way colors within a composition influence one another.

color key a color that dominates an image and heightens its psychological and compositional impact.

color overtone a secondary hue "bias" in a primary color. For example, alizarin crimson is a red with violet overtones, while scarlet is a red with orange overtones.

color theory the art and science of color interaction and effects.

compare/contrast critique a critique in which similarities and differences between two designs are analyzed. Often used in art history classes to demonstrate differences in approach between artists.

comparison recognition of similarity in two or more compositions. Often used in art history to demonstrate connections between images done by different artists or in different periods.

complementary (colors) hues that oppose one another on a color wheel. When paired in a composition, complementary colors create contrast; when mixed, complementary colors produce a wide range of browns.

composite a new material created when two or more materials of differing strengths are fused together. Examples include Fiberglas and foamcore.

composition the combination of multiple parts into a unified or harmonious whole.

compression the forcing or crushing of material into a smaller, denser condition and its visual dynamics and implied psychological effects.

cone of vision in perspective drawing, a hypothetical cone of perception originating at the eye of the artist and expanding outward to include whatever he or she wishes to record in an illusionistic image, such as a perspective drawing. The cone's maximum scoping angle is 45–60 degrees; anything outside the cone of vision is subject to distortion.

containment a unifying force created by the outer edge of a composition or by a boundary within a composition.

content the emotional and/or intellectual meaning or message of an artwork.

continuity degree of connection or flow among compositional parts.

contour line a line that describes the edges of a form and suggests three-dimensional volume.

contradictory texture the unfamiliar use of a texture or the addition of an unusual texture to the surface of an object.

contrast the degree of difference between compositional parts or between one image and another. Contrast is created when two or more forces operate in opposition.

contrasting colors colors that are substantially different in hue, value, intensity, or temperature.

convergent thinking a problem-solving strategy in which a predetermined goal is pursued in a linear progression using a highly focused problem-solving process. Six steps are commonly used: 1. define the problem, 2. do research, 3. determine your objective, 4. devise a strategy, 5. execute the strategy, 6. evaluate the results.

glossary

critique any means by which the strengths and weaknesses of designs are analyzed.

cropping the manner in which a section of an image or a fragment of observed reality has been framed. For example, photographers select a fragment of reality every time they look through the viewfinder of the camera. Part of the scene is included, while the remainder is cut away. Photographs are often cropped further in the darkroom, leaving only the most significant information.

cross-contours multiple lines running over the surface of an object horizontally and/or vertically that describe its surface configuration topographically, as in mapping. This process is much like wire-framing in three-dimensional computer modeling. Cross-contours can also be used in drawing to suggest three-dimensional form through tonal variation.

crosscutting in film, an abrupt alternation between two or more lines of action.

cross-hatching a technique used in drawing and printmaking to shade an object using two or more networks of parallel lines. Darker values are created as the number of networks increases.

curvilinear shape a shape whose contour is dominated by curves and flowing lines.

cut in film, the immediate change from one shot or frame to another.

D

definition 1. the degree to which a shape is distinguished from both the ground area and from other shapes within the design. 2. the degree of resolution or focus of an entire image. Sharply defined shapes tend to advance, while blurred shapes tend to recede.

denouement the outcome, solution, or point of clarification in a story.

density the extent to which compositional parts are spread out or crowded together. Visual connections generally occur easily in high-density compositions, while visual connections may be less obvious in low-density compositions.

depth of field the range of focus in a photographic image, from foreground to background. In a photograph with great depth of field, an object that is 15 feet from the camera is in focus, as well as an object that is 10 feet from the camera.

descriptive critique a critique in which the viewer carefully describes what he or she sees when observing a design.

diegetic describes the world created in a film or video.

directed light localized and focused light, such as a spotlight on a singer.

direction actual or implied movement of an element within a design.

disharmony a combination of colors that clash with one another and appear to be jumping out of the picture.

displacement a forming method in which a solid material is physically forced into a new configuration. The stamping process used to mint coins is an example of displacement.

dissolve a transition between two shots during which the first image gradually disappears while the second image gradually appears.

distribution the manner in which colors, shapes, or other visual elements are arranged within the format.

divergent thinking an open-ended problem-solving strategy. Starting with a broad theme, the artist or designer expands ideas in all directions.

dominant describes the principle of composition in which certain elements assume greater importance than others. Also see **emphasis.**

duration 1. the length of time required for the completion of an event; as in the running time of a film, video, or performance. 2. the running time of events depicted in the story (plot duration). 3. the overall span of time the story encompasses (story duration).

dynamic energetic, vigorous, forceful; creating or suggesting change or motion.

dynamic forms forms that imply change.

dynamic space compositional organization that emphasizes movement or the illusion of movement.

E

earth colors colors made primarily from pigments in soil, including raw sienna, burnt sienna, raw and burnt umber, and yellow ochre.

earthwork commonly, an artwork that has been created through the transformation of a natural site into an aesthetic statement.

eccentricity as identified by Rudolph Arnheim, an expansive compositional force.

economy distillation of a design down to the essentials in order to increase impact.

editing in film, selecting and sequencing the details of an event to create a cohesive whole.

elements (of design) basic building blocks from which designs are made. For example, the essential elements of two-dimensional design are line, shape, texture, color, and value.

elevation in orthographic projection, the front, back, and side views of an object or architectural structure.

emotional in advertising, use of emotion to sell a service, product, or idea. This strategy is often used when a product is neither unique nor demonstrably better than a competing product.

emphasis special attention given to some aspect of a composition to increase its prominence.

engraving a printmaking process in which lines are carved into a metal plate or wooden board, then filled with ink and printed.

environmental work (or environment) an artwork that must be entered physically. Installations (which are usually presented indoors) and earthworks (which are usually presented outdoors) are two major types of environmental works.

ephemera materials that decay rapidly.

exaggerated in advertising, pushing an idea to an extreme to make a point.

exoskeleton an external support structure.

expansion the extending outward of materials to fill more space.

eye level (or horizon line) in linear perspective, the eye level is determined by the physical position of the artist. Sitting on the floor creates a low eye level, while standing at an easel creates a higher eye level. All vanishing points in one- and two-point perspective are positioned on the eye level.

F

fade a gradual transition used in film and video. 1. In a fade-in, a dark screen gradually brightens as a shot appears. 2. In a fade-out, the shot gradually darkens as the screen goes black.

fidelity the degree of connection between a sound and its source. For example, when we hear the sound of a helicopter and see a helicopter on the screen, the sound matches with the image, creating tight fidelity.

figure the primary or positive shape in a design; a shape that is noticeably separated from the background. The figure is the dominant shape in a figure-ground relationship.

figure/ground reversal an arrangement in which positive and negative shapes alternately command attention.

fill light a diffused light used to lower the contrast between light and dark areas in cinematic and theatrical lighting.

flashbacks in film, alternations in chronology in which events that occur later in a story are shown first.

floodlight a softly defined light with a broad beam.

flying buttress a type of exoskeleton commonly used by medieval architects in designing cathedrals.

focal point primary point of interest in a composition. A focal point is often used to emphasize an area of particular importance or to provide a strong sense of compositional direction.

form 1. the physical manifestation of an idea, as opposed to the content, which refers to the idea itself. 2. the organization or arrangement of visual elements to create a unified design. 3. a three-dimensional composition or unit within a three-dimensional composition. For example, a sphere, a cube, and a pyramid are all three-dimensional forms.

formalism an approach to art and design that emphasizes the beauty of line, shape, texture, etc. as ends in themselves rather than as means to express content. Strictly formalist works have no explicit subject matter.

format the outer edge or boundary of a design.

fractured space discontinuous space that is created when multiple viewpoints are combined within a single image.

frame a single static image in film or video.

freestanding work an artwork that is self-supporting and is designed to be viewed from all sides.

function the purpose of a design or the objective that motivates the designer. For an industrial designer, the primary purpose of a design is often utilitarian. For example, he or she may be required to design a more fuel-efficient automobile. For a sculptor, the primary purpose of a design is aesthetic: he or she seeks to create an artwork that engages the viewer emotionally and intellectually.

fusion the combination of shapes or volumes along a common edge.

G

geometric forms three-dimensional forms derived from or suggestive of geometry. Examples include cubes, spheres, tetrahedrons, etc.

geometric shapes shapes derived from or suggestive of geometry. Geometric shapes are characterized by crisp, precise edges and mathematically consistent curves.

Gestalt psychology a theory of visual perception that emphasizes the importance of holistic composition. According to this theory, grouping, containment, repetition, proximity, continuity, and closure are essential aspects of visual unity.

gesture drawing a vigorous drawing that captures the action, structure, and overall orientation of an object, rather than describing specific details. Often used as a basis for figure drawing.

gloss 1. in writing, words of explanation or translation inserted into a text. 2. a secondary text within a manuscript that provides comments on the main text.

gradation any gradual transition from one color to another or from one shape or volume to another. In drawing, shading created through the gradation of grays can be used to suggest three-dimensional form.

graphic relationship the juxtaposition of two or more separate images that are compositionally similar. For example, if a basketball is shown in the first panel, an aerial view of the round free-throw zone is shown in the second, and the hoop of the basket itself is shown in the third, a graphic relationship based on circles has been created.

gravity the force that tends to pull all bodies toward the center of the Earth.

grid a visual or physical structure created from intersecting parallel lines.

grisaille a gray underpainting, often used by Renaissance artists, to increase the illusion of space.

group in sequential structure, a collection of images that are related by subject matter, composition, or source. For example the trombone, trumpet, and tuba are all members of the group known as the brass section in an orchestra.

grouping visual organization based on similarity in location, orientation, shape, color, and so on.

H

handheld a small-scale object that can be held in your hands.

Happening an assemblage of improvised, spontaneous events performed by artist and audience alike, based on a general theme. There is no rehearsal, and any location, from a parking lot to a factory interior, can be used. The Happening is most commonly associated with Alan Kaprow and is a precursor to performance art.

hard-sell an advertising approach in which a major point is presented in a clear, direct manner. The narrative is usually linear, and the message is usually explicit.

harmony a pleasing or soothing relationship among colors, shapes, or other design elements.

hatching a technique used in drawing and printmaking to create a range of gray tones using multiple parallel lines.

high definition sharply focused visual information that is easily readable. High definition creates strong contrast between shapes and tends to increase the clarity and immediacy of communication.

hue the name of a color (such as red or yellow) that distinguishes it from others and assigns it a position in the visual spectrum.

human scale a design that is roughly our size.

humorous advertising use of humor to sell a service, product, or idea. By entertaining the viewer, the designer can make the message more memorable.

hybridity the creation of artworks using disparate media to create a unified conceptual statement.

iconography the study of symbolic visual systems.

imbalance the absence of balance.

implied line 1. a line that is suggested by the positions of shapes or objects within a design. 2. a line that is suggested by movement or by a gesture rather than being physically drawn or constructed.

implied motion the suggested change in location of a figure or object.

implied time the suggested location or duration of an event.

installation an artwork or a design that presents an ensemble of images and objects within a three-dimensional environment.

intensity 1. the purity, saturation, or chroma of a color. For example, fire engine red is a high-intensity color, while brick red is a low-intensity color. 2. in time design, the power, concentration, and energy with which an action is performed or the quality of observation of an event.

interdisciplinary art the combination of two or more different disciplines to create a hybrid art form.

in the round a three-dimensional object that is self-supporting and is designed to be viewed from all sides, as in freestanding sculpture.

invented texture a form of visual texture that has been created without reference to perceptual reality.

joint a physical connection between elements or parts in a three-dimensional object. Some joints are fixed, such as those that are bolted together, while others can be moved, such as a hinge or a ball-and-socket joint.

junction 1. the place at which objects or events meet. 2. a physical intersection between elements or parts in a three-dimensional object.

key light a primary source of illumination.

kinesthetics the science of movement.

kinetic forms forms that actually move.

lap dissolve in film, a dissolve in which two shots are temporarily superimposed.

layered space compositional space that has been deliberately separated into foreground, middle ground, and background.

layering a postmodern practice in which an accumulation of multiple (and often contradictory) visual layers is used to create a single artwork.

line 1. a point in motion. 2. a series of adjacent points. 3. a connection between points. 4. an implied connection between points. Line is one of the basic elements of design.

linear perspective a mathematical system for projecting the apparent dimensions of a three-dimensional object onto a flat surface. Developed by artists during the Renaissance, linear perspective is one strategy for creating the illusion of space.

line weight variation in line thickness.

long shot in film, a type of framing in which the scale of the subject shown is relatively small, as with an image of a human figure within a landscape.

loudness the amplitude of a sound wave; the volume of a sound.

low-definition describes blurred or ambiguous visual information. Low-definition shapes can increase the complexity of the design and encourage multiple interpretations.

maquette a well-developed three-dimensional sketch, comparable to a two-dimensional thumbnail sketch.

mass a solid three-dimensional form.

matrix a three-dimensional grid.

mechanical forms gears, belts, hoses, and other forms suggestive of machinery.

medium the specific tool and material used by an artist or designer, such as brush and oil paint or chisel and stone.

medium shot a type of framing in which the scale of the subject shown is of moderate size, as in a view of an actor from the waist up.

metaphor a figure of speech in which one thing is directly linked to another, dissimilar thing. Through this connection, the original word is given the qualities of the linked word. For example, when we say "She's a diamond in the rough," we attribute to a woman the qualities of an unpolished gem.

metaphorical thinking the use of metaphors or analogies to create visual or verbal bridges.

meter the basic pattern of sound and silence in music or positive and negative in design.

model in three-dimensional design, a technical experiment or a small-scale version of a larger design.

modeling the process of manipulating a pliable material (such as clay) to create a three-dimensional object.

modernism a collection of artistic styles, most prominent from around 1860 to 1960, that emphasized the importance of form, introduced new materials and production methods, and sought to express universal truths.

moment-to-moment transition in comic books, a transition in which a character or situation is simply being observed over time. This transition is used often in Japanese comic books but rarely in American comic books.

monochromatic a color scheme based on variations in a single hue. For example, a light pastel blue, a medium navy blue, and a dark blue-black may be used in a room interior.

montage time-based structure constructed from multiple and often seemingly unrelated sources; a temporal collage.

monumental scale of objects that are much larger than humans.

movement in design, the use of deliberate visual pathways to help direct the viewer's attention to areas of particular interest.

myth a traditional story collectively composed by many members of a society. The creation of the world, sources of evil, the power of knowledge, and even the nature of reality may be explained through these grand expressions of the imagination.

N

negative shape (or ground) 1. a clearly defined area around a positive shape or form. 2. a shape created through the absence of an object rather than through the presence of an object.

negative space space surrounding a positive form or shape.

nonobjective artworks artworks that have no reference to perceptual reality.

nonobjective shapes shapes created without reference to specific visual subject matter.

non-sequitur transition the juxtaposition of multiple frames or shots that have no obvious conceptual relationship.

O

objective criticism the assessment of strengths and weakness in a design based solely on the visual information presented.

one-point perspective a form of linear perspective in which the lines receding into space converge at a single vanishing point of the eye level or horizon line.

opponent theory an explanation for the electric glow that occurs when two complementary colors are placed side by side.

organic forms forms that are derived from nature.

organic shapes shapes that visually suggest nature or natural forces. Also known as **biomorphic shapes.**

organizational lines lines used to create the loose linear "skeleton" on which a composition can be built. Also known as **structural lines.**

orientation the horizontal, vertical, or diagonal position of a composition or design element.

orthographic projection a drawing system widely used by artists and designers to delineate the top, bottom, and four side views of a three-dimensional object. Unlike perspective drawing, which is designed to create the illusion of space, an orthographic projection is constructed using parallel lines that accurately delineate six surfaces of an object.

overlap placement of one shape in front of another to create the illusion of space.

P

pace the rate of change in a temporal event.

pattern a design created through systematic repetition. Many patterns are based on a module, or a repeated visual unit.

pedestal a vertical support for a sculptural object.

performance art a live presentation, often including the artist and usually combining elements from a variety of art forms, such as film, video, theater, and dance.

permanence the degree of durability, or resistance to decay, in a given material or design.

physical texture actual variation in a surface.

picture plane in linear perspective, the flat surface on which a three-dimensional image is mentally projected.

pitch in music, the relative highness or lowness of a sound. Pitch is determined by wave frequency, as compression and expansion occur within the sound wave.

plane a three-dimensional form that has length and width but minimal thickness.

plinth a horizontal support for a sculptural object.

plot duration the running time of the events depicted in a story.

polyhedra (or polyhedrons) multifaceted volumes.

positive forms areas of physical substance in a three-dimensional design.

positive shape (or figure) the principal or foreground shape in a design and the dominant shape or figure in a figure-ground relationship.

postmodernism a collection of artistic styles that arose in the 1970s as a reaction to modernism. Notable characteristics include conceptual emphasis, social commentary, irreverence, and skepticism about universal truths.

primary colors colors from which virtually all other colors can be mixed. The additive (or light) color primaries are red, green, and blue. The subtractive (or pigment) color primaries are yellow, magenta red, and cyan blue.

primary contours the defining edges of a physical object, such as the extremities of a carved sculpture.

principles of design the means by which visual elements are organized into a unified and expressive arrangement. Unity and variety, balance, scale and proportion, rhythm, illusion of space, and illusion of movement are commonly cited as the principles of two-dimensional design.

process colors in four-color process printing, the subtractive primary colors: yellow, magenta, and cyan, plus black.

proportion the relative size of visual elements within an image.

prototype a well-developed model, as with the fully functional prototype cars developed by automobile companies.

proximity the distance between visual or structural elements or between an object and the audience.

pure form a circle, sphere, triangle, cube, or other form created without reference to specific subject matter.

R

radial symmetry a form of balance that is created when shapes or volumes are mirrored both vertically and horizontally, with the center of the composition acting as a focal point.

rational a type of advertising in which logic and comparisons of quality are used to sell a service, product, or idea. A rational approach is most effective when the message is compelling in itself or the product is unique.

realistic in advertising, use of a familiar setting or situation to involve the viewer and relate a product, service, or idea to use in everyday life.

recontextualization a postmodern practice in which the meaning of an image or object is changed by the context in which it is placed.

rectilinear shapes shapes composed from straight lines and angular corners.

reflective light that is bounced off a reflective surface back into space.

refracted light that has been bent as it passes through a prism.

relief sculpture in which forms project out from a flat surface. The degree of projection ranges from low to high relief.

repetition the use of the same visual element or effect a number of times in the same composition.

representational artworks commonly, the lifelike depiction of persons or objects.

representational shapes shapes derived from specific subject matter and strongly based on visual observation.

rhetorical a type of sequential organization in which the parts are used to create and support an argument. Often used in documentary films.

rhythm 1. presentation of multiple units in a deliberate pattern. 2. in filmmaking, the perceived rate and regularity of sounds, shots, and movement within the shots. Rhythm is determined by the beat (pulse), accent (stress), and tempo (pace).

rhythmic relationship the juxtaposition of multiple visual elements or images to create a deliberate pulse or beat.

S

saturation the purity, chroma, or intensity of a color.

scale a size relationship between two separate objects, such as the relationship between the size of the Statue of Liberty and a human visitor to the monument.

scene in film, continuous action in continuous time and continuous space.

scene-to-scene transition in comic books, the juxtaposition of two or more frames showing different scenes or settings.

scope conceptually, the extent of our perception or the range of ideas our minds can grasp. Temporally, scope refers to the range of action within a given moment.

screenplay the written blueprint for a film, commonly constructed from multiple acts.

secondary colors hues mixed from adjacent primaries. In paint, the secondary colors are violet, green, and orange.

secondary contours the inner edges of a physical object, such as the internal design and detailing of a carved sculpture.

sequence 1. in filmmaking, a collection of related shots and scenes that comprise a major section of action or narration. 2. in narrative structure, any collection of images that have been organized by *cause and effect*. In a simple sequence, action number two is caused by action number one. In a complex sequence, there may be a considerable delay between the cause and the effect.

series in sequential structure, a collection of images that are linked simply, like cars in a train.

serious advertising that treats a topic in a somber or solemn manner. Often used for public service announcements, such as drunk driving commercials.

setting the physical and temporal location of a story, the props and costumes used in a story, and the use of sound.

shade a hue that has been mixed with black.

shading in drawing, a continuous series of grays that are used to suggest three-dimensionality and to create the illusion of light; a type of gradation.

shape a flat, enclosed area created when a line connects to enclose an area, an area is surrounded by other shapes, or an area is filled with color or texture.

shear a force that creates a lateral break in a material.

shot in film, a continuous group of frames.

side light a light positioned to the side of a person or an object. Can be used to dramatically increase the sense of dimensionality.

sight line 1. a viewing line that is established by the arrangement of objects within one's field of vision. 2. a straight line of unimpeded vision.

simile a figure of speech in which one thing is linked to another, dissimilar thing using the word *like* or *as*. Through this connection, the original word is given the qualities of the linked word. For example, when we say "He's as strong as an ox," we attribute to a man the strength of an animal.

glossary

simultaneous contrast the optical alteration of a color by a surrounding color.

site-specific an artwork specifically designed for and installed in a particular place.

skeleton (or endoskeleton) a structure that provides internal support.

soft-sell an advertising approach that uses emotion, rather than reason, to sell a service, product, or idea. The narrative is often nonlinear, and ideas or actions may be implied.

solidification a forming method in which a liquid material is poured into a mold or extruded through a pipe, then allowed to harden.

space the area within or around an area of substance. The artist/designer defines and activates space when constructing a three-dimensional object.

spatial context the space in which a sound is generated. A sound that is played outdoors behaves differently than a sound that is played in a small room.

spatial relationship the juxtaposition of two or more images that are spatially different, such as a close-up, a medium shot, and a long shot.

split complementary a complementary color plus the two colors on either side of its complement on the color wheel.

spotlight a light that creates a small, clearly defined beam.

static forms forms that appear to be stable and unmoving.

stereotype a fixed generalization based on a preconception.

stippling a technique for producing an image from multiple dots.

story duration the overall length of a story.

style the recurring characteristics that distinguish one historical period or particular artist's group from another.

subject the person, object, event, or idea on which an artwork is based.

subjective criticism the assessment of strengths and weaknesses in a design based on nonobjective criteria, such as the narrative implications of an idea, the cultural ramifications of an action, or the personal meaning of an image.

subject-to-subject transition in comic books, the juxtaposition of two or more frames showing different subject matter.

subordinate of secondary importance. See **emphasis.**

subtractive color hue created when light is selectively reflected off a colored surface.

subtractive sculpture a forming method in which materials are removed from a larger mass. Carving, drilling, cutting, and turning on a lathe are all subtractive processes.

symbolic color a color that has been assigned a particular meaning by the members of a society. For example, in the United States, the white color of a wedding gown symbolizes purity, while in Borneo white symbolizes death.

symmetrical balance a form of balance that is created when shapes are mirrored on either side of a central axis, as in a composition that is vertically divided down the center.

take in film or video, one version of an event.

temperature the physical and psychological heat suggested by a color's hue.

tempo the pace at which change occurs. A fast tempo is generally used in action films, while a slow tempo is usually used in a dramatic film.

temporal relationship how the shots in a film are related in time.

tension the extension of an object through stretching or bending.

tertiary color a hue that is mixed from a primary color and an adjacent secondary color.

testimonial in advertising, use of a trustworthy character or celebrity to provide endorsement for a product, service, or idea.

texture the visual or tactile quality of a form. Texture can be created visually using multiple marks, physically through surface variation, or through the inherent property of a specific material, such as sand as opposed to smooth porcelain.

three-point perspective a form of linear perspective in which the lines receding into space converge at two vanishing points of the eye level (one to the left of the object being drawn and one to the right of the object being drawn) plus a third vanishing point above or below the eye level. Used when the picture plane must be tilted to encompass an object placed above or below the eye level.

three-quarter work a physical object that is designed to be viewed from the front and sides only.

timbre the unique sound quality of each instrument. For example, a note of the same volume and pitch is quite different when it is generated by a flute rather than a violin.

tint a hue that has been mixed with white.

tone a hue that has been mixed with black and white.

torque the distortion of an object through a twisting movement. Also known as **torsion.**

transition the process of changing from one state or form to another; for example, the surface of a metal sculpture as it shifts from a smooth to a rough surface or the manner in which a computer drawing morphs from one form to another.

translucent a surface that partially permits the passage of light.

transparent a surface that permits the passage of light, such as clear plastic or glass.

triadic describes a color scheme based on three colors that are equidistant on a color wheel.

tromp l'oeil a flat illusion that is so convincing that the viewer believes the image is real. A French term meaning "to fool the eye."

two-point perspective a form of linear perspective in which the lines receding into space converge at two vanishing points of the eye level (or horizon line), one to the left of the object being drawn and one to the right of the object being drawn.

type style the distinctive quality of the letter forms within a given font. For example, Helvetica has a very different look than Palatino type.

unity compositional similarity, oneness, togetherness, or cohesion.

V

value the relative lightness or darkness of a surface.

value distribution the proportion and arrangement of lights and darks in a composition. Also known as **value pattern.**

value scale a range of grays that are presented in a consistent sequence, creating a gradual transition from white to black.

vanishing point in linear perspective, the point or points on the eye level at which parallel lines appear to converge.

variety the differences that give a design visual and conceptual interest; notably, use of contrast, emphasis, differences in size, and so forth.

viewing time the time an audience devotes to watching or exploring an artwork.

visual book an experimental structure that conveys ideas, actions, and emotions using multiple images in an integrated and interdependent format. Also known as an **artist's book.**

visual movement use of continuity to create deliberate visual pathways. Often used to direct the viewer's attention to areas of particular importance in the composition.

visual texture texture created using multiple marks or through a descriptive simulation of physical texture.

visual weight 1. the inclination of shapes to float or sink compositionally. 2. the relative importance of a visual element within a design.

vitalistic sculpture a sculpture that appears to embody life in an inanimate material, such as fiberglass, stone, or wood.

volume 1. an empty three-dimensional form. 2. in two-dimensional design, a three-dimensional form that has been represented using the illusion of space. 3. in time design, the loudness of a sound.

volume summary a drawing that communicates visual information reductively, using basic volumes such as spheres, cubes, and cylinders to indicate the major components of a figure or object.

volumetric three-dimensional in nature.

W

weight the visual or physical heaviness of an object.

wipe in film, a transition in which the first shot seems to be pushed off the screen by the second. Wipes were used extensively in *Star Wars.*

Introduction

Page iv: Courtesy of Rusty Smith, University School of Architecture.

xvi T: © Bill Viola. Collection: Edition 1: Museo Nacional Centro de Arte Reina Sofia, Madrid. Edition 2, Los Angeles County Museum of Art, Modern and Contemporary Art Council Fund. Photo by Gary McKinnis. Courtesy of artist and James Cohan Gallery.

xvi BR: Collection Toni Greenbaum, NY. Photo courtesy of Keith E. LoBue.

xvii T: Designers: Bill Cannan, Tony Ortiz, H. Kurt Heinz. Design Firm: Bill Cannan & Co. Client/Mfr. NASA Public Affairs.

xvii B: Hans-Jurgen Syberberg, Parsifal, 1982.

xviii: The Museum of Modern Art, Film Stills Archive.

xix B: Designers: James E. Grove, John Cook, Jim Holtorf, Fernando Pardo, Mike Boltich. Design Firm: Designworks/USA. Client/Mfr: Corona Clipper Co.

xx B: Funds from Helen Dill bequest, 1935.1, Denver Art Museum Collection. Photo courtesy of the Denver Art Museum.

xxi: © 2010 Sam Francis Foundation, California/Artists Rights Society (ARS), NY.

xxii: Collection, University of Illinois at Urbana, Champaign. Photo courtesy of the artist © Alice Aycock, 1994.

xxiii: TM & © 2005 Marvel Characters, Inc. Used with permission.

xxiv: Vasily Kandinsky, *Several Circles (Einige Kreise)*, January–February 1926. Oil on canvas, 55 1/4 x 55 38/8 inches. The Solomon R. Guggenheim Museum, New York. Gift, Solomon R. Guggenheim, 1941. 41.283. © The Guggenheim Foundation, New York. © 2007 Artists Rights Society (ARS), New York/ADAGP, Paris.

Chapter 1

Page 1 T: Collection of David Geffen, Los Angeles. Art © Jasper Johns/Licensed by VAGA, New York, NY.

1 B: Courtesy Scott Hull Associates.

3 L: The Sidney and Harriet Janis Collection, Digital Image © The Museum of Modern Art, NY/Licensed by SCALA/Art Resource, NY. © 2010 Succession Giacometti/Artists Rights Society (ARS), NY.

3 R: AP/Wide World Photos/© Disney Enterprises, Inc.

4 TL: © 2010 The Barnett Newman Foundation, New York/Artists Rights Society (ARS), New York.

4 TR: Iris & B. Gerald Cantor Center for Visual Arts at Stanford University. Gift of Dr. and Mrs. Louis J. Rattner.

4 CR: Collection of David Lebrun, Courtesy of Koplin Gallery, Los Angeles.

4 B: © The Trustees of The British Museum/Art Resource, NY.

5 TL: Attributed to Tawaraya Sotatsu, Japanese (active c. 1600–1640) and Hon'ami Koetsu, calligrapher, Japanese (1558–1637), *Flying Cranes and Poetry*, Edo Period (1615–1868). Handscroll section mounted as a hanging scroll. Ink and gold paint on tinted paper, 7 5/8 x 6 9/16 inches. The Nelson-Atkins Museum of Art, Kansas City, Missouri. Gift of Mrs. George H. Bunting, Jr., 73–27. Photo by Mel McLean.

5 TR: © Wu Guanzhong.

5 C: © Jerome Witkin, Courtesy of Jack Rutberg Fine Arts, Inc. Palmer Museum of Art, The Pennsylvania State University.

6 C: Minor White, *Columbus Avenue, San Francisco*, 1949. Gelatin silver print, 7 5/8 x 9 7/8 inches. Reproduced with permission of the Minor White Archive, MWA 49-78.1. Princeton University Art Museum. © Trustees of Princeton University.

6 B: Vatican Museums, Vatican State. Scala/Art Resource, NY.

7 TL: Gift of Victor S. Riesenfeld. The Museum of Modern Art, New York. Digital Image © The Museum of Modern Art/Licensed by SCALA / Art Resource, NY. © Artists Rights Society (ARS), New York.

7 TR: Courtesy of David Mach.

7 B: Musée du Louvre, Paris. © Réunion des Musees Nationaux/Art Resource, NY.

8: The Museum of Modern Art, The Sidney and Harriet Janis Collection. Digital Image © 2001 The Museum of Modern Art/Licensed by Scala/

Art Resource, NY. © 2010 The Pollock-Krasner Foundation/Artists Rights Society (ARS), New York.

9 TL: PATH Station Maps, Louis Nelson Associates Inc., NY. Artist: Jennifer Stoller, Louis Nelson. © Louis Nelson Associates for the Port Authority of New York & New Jersey.

9 TR: Courtesy of Joel Peter Johnson.

9 B: Courtesy of Pentagram Design, NY.

10: Schomburg Center for Research in Black Culture, The New York Public Library/Art Resource, NY.

11 T: Diego M. Rivera, *Detroit Industry*, North Wall, 1932–1933. Gift of Edsel B. Ford, Photograph © 2001 The Detroit Institute of Arts. Bridgeman Art Library, NY.

11 L: Carin Goldberg, Cover of *Ulysses*, by James Joyce, 1986. Random House Vintage Books. Art Director: Edith Loseser.

11 C: Courtesy of Bantam Books, a division of Random House.

11 R: Galleria Moderna Venice, Italy. Cameraphoto Arte, Venice/Art Resource, NY.

12: © The Murray-Holman Family Trust. Courtesy of PaceWildenstein Gallery. Philadelphia Museum of Art: Purchased with the Edward and Althea Budd Fund, the Adele Haas Turner and Beatrice Pastorius Turner Memorial Fund.

13 TL: Bill Brandt @ Bill Brandt Archive Ltd.

13 TR: Erich Lessing/Art Resource, NY.

13 B: M.C. Escher, *Metamorphosis II*. © 2007 The M. C. Escher Company-Holland. All rights reserved.

14 T: © 2010 Sam Francis Foundation, California/Artists Rights Society (ARS), NY.

14 BL: The Department of Theater Arts, California State University, Los Angeles, Courtesy of David McNutt, 1985.

15 T: The Stapleton Collection. The Bridgeman Art Library, NY.

15 B: Art © Robert Rauschenberg/Licensed by VAGA, New York, NY.

16 T: Art © Valerie Jaudon/Licensed by VAGA, New York, NY.

16 B: Helen Frankenthaler, *Interior Landscape*, 1964. Acrylic on canvas, 104 7/8 x 92 7/8 inches. San Francisco Museum of Modern Art, Gift of the Women's Board, © Helen Frankenthaler. © 2011 Artists Rights Society (ARS), New York.

17 TL: Vasily Kandinsky, *Several Circles (Einige Kreise)*, January–February 1926. Oil on canvas, 55 1/4 x 55 38/8 inches. The Solomon R. Guggenheim Museum, New York. Gift, Solomon R. Guggenheim, 1941. 41.283. © The Guggenheim Foundation, New York. © 2007 Artists Rights Society (ARS), New York/ADAGP, Paris.

17 R: Courtesy Joseph Helman Gallery, New York (#BH 1912).

17 BL: Photograph © Ansel Adams Publishing Rights Trust/CORBIS.

18 T: Charles Demuth, American, 1883–1935, *...And the Home of the Brave*, 1931, Oil and graphite on fiber board, 74.8 x 59.7 cm (29 1/2 x 23 1/2 in.), Alfred Stieglitz Collection, gift of Georgia O'Keeffe, 1948.650, The Art Institute of Chicago. Photography © The Art Institute of Chicago.

18 B: Courtesy of William Klein and Howard Greenberg Gallery, New York.

19 T: Sidney Goodman, *Man Waiting*, 1961. Charcoal on paper, 25 x 5/8 x 19 1/8 inches. The Museum of Modern Art, New York. Gift of Mr. and Mrs. Walter Bareiss. Digital Image © The Museum of Modern Art/Licensed by Scala/Art Resource, NY.

19 B: Courtesy Marian Goodman Gallery, New York.

20: Art Director & Designer: Gary Goldsmith, Copywriter: Neal Gomberg, Agency: Goldsmith/Jeffrey, Client: Citizens Against Cocaine Abuse.

21: The Museum of Modern Art, New York. Blanchette Rockefeller Fund. Digital Image © The Museum of Modern Art/Licensed by Scala/Art Resource, NY. Art © Romare Bearden Foundation/Licensed by VAGA, New York, NY.

22: Collection of David Geffen, Los Angeles. Art © Jasper Johns/Licensed by VAGA, New York, NY.

campaign that left thousands of Ndebele dead and the area traumatised. Photomontage: Chaz Maviyane-Davies.

60 B: Hiroshi Senju: Haruka Naru Aoi Hikari, Sundaram Tagore Gallery, New York, December 2007.

61 TL: Courtesy of Museum of Northern Arizona Photo Archives, (Negative number 83C.45) (Catalogue number E561).

61 TR: The Museum of Modern Art, New York. Gift of the Celeste and Armand Bartos Foundation. Digital image © The Museum of Modern Art/Licensed by Scala/Art Resource, NY. Art © Jasper Johns/Licensed by VAGA, New York, NY.

61 B: Staatliche Kunstsammlungen der DDR. Kupferstichkabinett Dresden. © 2010 Artists Rights Society (ARS), New York/VG Bild-Kunst. Bonn.

62 L: Staatsgalerie Stuttgart. © 2010 Artists Rights Society (ARS), New York/VG Bild-Kunst. Bonn.

62 R: Kathe Kollwitz, *Self-Portrait as a Young Woman*, c. 1900. Pastel on laid paper, 18 7/16 x 14 3/8 inches. Gift of Robert and Chris Petteys. Image courtesy of the Board of Trustees, National Gallery of Art, Washington. 1956.1 © 2010 Artists Rights Society (ARS), New York/VG Bild-Kunst. Bonn.

64–65: Courtesy of Ann Baddeley Keister.

Chapter 3

Page 67 TL: Courtesy Scott Hull Associates.

67 TR: Viga Celmins, *Untitled (Ocean)*, 1969. Philadelphia Museum of Art: Purchased with a grant from the National Endowment for the Arts and Matching Funds.

67 BR: Staaliche Museen zu Berlin. Photo: Jorg Anders, Preussiher Kulturbesitz, Nationalgalerie/NG57/61. © 2010 Artists Rights Society (ARS), New York/VG Bild-Kunst. Bonn.

68 B: The British Library, London.

69 B: Courtesy of Larry Moore, Winterpark, FL.

70 T: © Aaron Macsai.

70 B: Vatican Museums. Photo: A. Bracchetti-P. Zigrossi. Scala/Art Resource, NY.

71 T: Toledo Museum of Art, Toledo, OH. Purchased with funds from the Libbey Endowment, gift of Edward Drummond Libbey (1972.4). © 2010 Frank Stella/Artists Rights Society (ARS), New York.

71 C: Musée du Louvre, Paris. © Réunion des Musées Nationaux/Art Resource, NY.

71 B: Musée du Louvre, Paris. © Réunion des Musées Nationaux/Art Resource, NY.

72 T: © Devorah Sperber. Photo by Aaron Deetz.

72 R: Art Resource, NY. © 2010 The Andy Warhol Foundation for Visual Arts, Inc./Artists Rights Society (ARS), New York.

72 BL: © 2010 Morla Design, Inc. San Francisco.

73 L: Syracuse University Library, Department of Special Collections, Syracuse, NY.

73 R: Faith Ringgold © 1988. Solomon Guggenheim Museum, New York. Gift, Mr. and Mrs. Gus and Judith Lieber, 1988. 88.3620.

74: Courtesy of Kevin Sprague.

75 L: © Berenice Abbott/Commerce Graphics Ltd, Inc.

75 R: Kathryn Frund, *Radical Acts*, 2008. Mixed media, 48 x 48 inches. Courtesy of Chase Gallery, Boston, MA.

76: © Ansel Adams Publishing Rights Trust/CORBIS.

77 TL: © Anthony Kersting/AKG Images.

77 B: © Richard Estes. Courtesy of the Allan Stone Gallery, NY.

78 BL: The Ella Gallup Sumner and Mary Catlin Sumner Collection Fund. Wadsworth Atheneum, Museum of Art, Hartford, CT. Wadsworth Atheneum, Museum of Art/Art Resource, NY.

78 TR: Judy Chicago, *Rejection Quintet: Female Rejection Drawing*, 1974. Prisma color and graphite on board, 40 x 30 x 1 1/2 inches. San Francisco Museum of Modern Art, Gift of Tracy O'Kates. © 2010 Judy Chicago/Artists Rights Society (ARS), New York.

80 T: Hirshhorn Museum and Sculpture Garden, Smithsonian Institution, Washington, DC. Gift of Joseph H. Hirshhorn Foundation, 1972 (HMSG 72.205).

80 B: Interaction/Motion: A poster for the 2006 "Exposed" lecture series sponsored by the Graphic Design Department, The University of the Arts, Philadelphia. Concept and Design: Hans-Ulrich Allemann, Principal. Allemann Almquist & Jones, Design/Strategic Communications, Philadelphia.

81 T: © 2010 Banco de México Diego Rivera Frida Kahlo Museums Trust, Mexico, D.F./Artists Rights Society (ARS), New York.

81 B: Courtesy of the artist and Mary Boone Gallery, NY.

82 C: Michael Bierut, Design Firm: Pentagram, NY. Client: Designing New York Committee. © Pentagram.

83 BL: Gift of Seymour H. Knox, 1967. Albright-Knox Art Gallery, New York/Art Resource, NY.

83 BR: Courtesy of Sue Benner, Dallas, TX.

84: Philadelphia Museum of Art. The Bridgeman Art Library. © 2010 Artists Rights Society (ARS), New York/ADAGP, Paris/ Succession Marcel Duchamp.

85 TL: Publisher: Art Center: College of Design, Pasadena, CA. Emphasis by isolation. Design Firm: Pentagram, NY.

85 TR: Photo by Doug Yaple.

85 BL: © Jacey, Debut Art Ltd.

86 T: Ella Gallup Sumner and Mary Catlin Sumner Collection, Wadsworth Atheneum, Museum of Art, Hartford, CT. Wadsworth Atheneum, Museum of Art/Art Resource, NY.

86 B: © Robert Crawford.

88–90: © 1998 by Bob Dacey from MIRIAM'S CUP by Fran Manushkin. Scholastic Inc./Scholastic Press. Reprinted by permission.

Chapter 4

Page 91: Bildarchiv Preussischer Kulturbesitz/Art Resource, NY.

92: Stanza della Segnatura, Vatican Palace, Vatican State/Scala/ Art Resource, NY.

94 L: Image provided by the author.

94 R: Charles Sheeler, *Delmonico Building*, 1926. Harvard University Art Museum, Gift of Paul J. Sachs, M3188. © 2005 The Estate of David Smith/Licensed by VAGA, NY. Photo: Allan Macintyre © President and Fellows of Harvard College.

95 T: Museo del Prado, Madrid. Bridgeman-Giraudon/Art Resource, NY.

95 B: The Metropolitan Museum of Art, Rogers Fund, 1907 (07.123). © The Metropolitan Museum of Art/Art Resource, NY.

96: National Palace Museum, Taipei, Taiwan.

97 L: Courtesy of the Burrell Collection, Culture & Sport, Glasgow.

97 R: David Hockney, *Henry Moore Much Hadham*, 23rd July, 1982. Composite Polaroid, 21 x 14 inches. Photo by Steve Oliver. © David Hockney.

98: Robert Stackhouse, *Inside Running Animals/Reindeer Way*, 1977. Watercolor and charcoal on paper, 59 3/4 x 39 1/4 inches. From the Collection of the John and Maxine Belger Family Foundation.

99 T: Courtesy of Ann Strassman and Kidder Smith Gallery.

99 B: Courtesy of Mark Messersmith.

101: © Disney Enterprises, Inc.

102 TL: Albright-Knox Art Gallery/Art Resource, NY.

102 TR: Museo Nazionale Romano delle Terme, Rome, Italy. Scala/Art Resource, NY.

102 BL: Henri Cartier-Bresson/Magnum Photos.

103: "Under the Rug" from THE MYSTERIES OF HARRIS BURDICK by Chris van Allsburg. © 1984 by Chris van Allsburg.

photo credits

104 T: The Historical and Interpretive Collections of The Franklin Institute, Philadelphia, PA.

104 B: Edgar Degas, French, 1834–1917, *Frieze of Dancers*, c. 1895. Oil on canvas, 70 x 200.5 cm. The Cleveland Museum of Art. Bequest of Leonard C. Hanna, Jr., 1946.83.

105: © 2010 Marvel Characters, Inc. Used with permission.

106: George A. Hearn Fund, 1956. © The Metropolitan Museum of Art, New York. Art Resource, NY/DC Moore Gallery.

108–109: Photo by Don House. Courtesy of Ken Stout.

Chapter 5

Page 110: Courtesy of Georgiana Nehl.

111: Courtesy of Jason Chin.

113 TL: Gift of Gary Laredo. Cooper-Hewitt National Design Museum, Smithsonian Institution/Art Resource, NY.

113 TR: The Museum of Modern Art, New York. Gift of Edgar Kaufman, Jr. Digital Image © The Museum of Modern Art/Licensed by Scala/Art Resource, NY.

114 L: The Museum of Modern Art, New York. Gift of Herman Miller Furniture Company. Digital Image © The Museum of Modern Art/Licensed by Scala/Art Resource, NY. © 2007 Eames Office/www.eamesoffice.com.

114 R: Photo courtesy of Knoll, Inc.

115 C: Courtesy of Ray Rogers.

115 B: Vera Liskova (Czech, 1924–1985), *Porcupine*, c. 1972–1980. Flameworked, h. 10.8 cm. (81.3.11) Gift of Vera Liskova, Collection of The Corning Museum of Glass.

117: © The Trustees of the British Museum/Art Resource, NY.

120 T: The Museum of Modern Art, New York. Mrs. Simon Guggenheim Fund. Digital Image © The Museum of Modern Art/Licensed by Scala/Art Resource, NY. © 2007 Estate of Yves Tanguy/Artists Rights Society (ARS), NY.

120 B: © 2010 Artists Rights Society (ARS), New York/SIAE, Rome.

124 L: Courtesy of Peter Forbes.

126: Photo by Jeanne Hilary.

Chapter 6

Page 133: M.C. Escher, *Metamorphosis II*. © 2010 The M. C. Escher Company-Holland. All rights reserved. www.mcescher.com.

134 C: Courtesy of Mary Stewart.

134 B: Honolulu Academy of Arts, gift of James Michener, 1991 (21.971). Photo © Honolulu Academy of Arts.

135 T, C: Honolulu Academy of Arts, gift of James Michener, 1991 (21.971). Photo © Honolulu Academy of Arts.

135 BL: © Eddie Chiu, courtesy of the Noguchi Museum.

135 BR: © Deborah Tan, courtesy of the Noguchi Museum.

136 L: Courtesy of Sergio Silva.

136 R: Courtesy of Rusty Smith, University School of Architecture.

138–139: Courtesy of Suzanne Stryk.

Chapter 7

Page 142–143: Gustave Caillebotte, French, 1848–1894, *Paris Street. Rainy Day*, 1877. Oil on canvas, 83 1/2 x 108 3/4 in. (212.2 x 276.2 cm). Charles H. and Mary F. S. Worcester Collection, 1964.336, The Art Institute of Chicago. Photography © The Art Institute of Chicago.

144: Courtesy of Rodger Mack.

145: Stanza della Segnatura, Vatican Palace, Vatican State. Scala/Art Resource, NY.

146: Courtesy of the author.

150–151: Courtesy of Jason Chin.

152 T: The Kansas City Sculpture Park at The Nelson-Atkins Museum of Art, Kansas City, Missouri including *Shuttlecocks* (two of four), 1994 by Claes Oldenburg, American (b. Sweden, 1929) and Coosje van Bruggen, American (b. The Netherlands, 1942). Aluminum, fiberglass-reinforced plastic, paint, 230 9/16 x 191 7/8 inches. (585.63 x 487.36 cm). Purchase: acquired through the generosity of the Sosland Family, F94-1/3-4. Photograph by Louis Meluso.

152 B: Photo by Lynn Whitney.

153 B: Photo by Harry Shunk. Art © Robert Rauschenberg/Licensed by VAGA, New York, NY.

154 R: Moderna Museet, Stocklholm. Art © Robert Rauschenberg/Licensed by VAGA, New York, NY.

154 L: Art © Robert Rauschenberg/Licensed by VAGA, New York, NY.

156–157: Courtesy of Kendall Buster.

Chapter 8

Page 158: Collection of the National Palace Museum, Taipei, Taiwan.

159 T: Detail of William Kentridge, *Black Box/Chambre Noire*, 2005, miniature theater with mechanized objects, projections and sound, commissioned by Deutsche Bank with the Guggenheim Foundation for the Deutsche Guggenheim, Berlin. Photo courtesy of Moderna Museet, Stocklholm. Courtesy of the artist and Marian Goodman Gallery, NY.

159 B: Courtesy of the author.

160 L: Courtesy of Milton Glaser Studio.

160 R: The Menil Collection, Houston. © 2010 C. Herscovici, London/Artists Rights Society (ARS), New York.

161 TL: Designed by Noon, San Francisco. Courtesy of the ODC, San Francisco.

161 TR: Los Angeles Ballet, Serenade. Balanchine ® is a Trademark of The George Balanchine Trust. Photo: Reed Hutchinson. Graphic Design: Catherine Kanner. Permission granted for LA Ballet.

161 BR: Michael A. Mello, *Dead Wrong: A Death Row Lawyer Speaks Out Against Capital Punishment*. © 1997. Cover design and illustration by Mark Maccaulay. Reprinted by permission of The University of Wisconsin Press.

162: Courtesy of Markus Schaller, Berlin.

163: Ruhr/Paragon, Minneapolis.

164 T: Courtesy of the artist and Chambers Fine Art.

164 B: Courtesy of Kim Martens.

165 T: Courtesy of Richard Saul Wurman, wurrmanrs@aol.com and Pentagram.

165 L: Art © Robert Rauschenberg/Licensed by VAGA, New York, NY.

165 R: Kiki Smith, *Virgin Mary*, 1992. Wax, cheesecloth and wood with steel base, 67 1/2 x 26 x 14 1/2" (171.5 x 66 x 36.8 cm). © Kiki Smith. Photo by Ellen Page Wilson, courtesy of PaceWildenstein, New York.

166 TL: Margaret Bourke-White/TimePix/Getty Images.

166 TR: Alfred Eisenstadt/TimePix/Getty Images.

166 CR: Michael Bierut & Tracey Cameron, Design Firm: Pentagram, NY. Photo: Don F. Wong.

166 B: Courtesy of Sean O'Meallie. Photo by Ric Helstrom.

167: © 1999 Iomega Corporation.

168 T: Courtesy of Jimmy Margulies.

168 B: Museo Nacional Centro de Arte Reina Sofia, Madrid. The Bridgeman Art Library, NY. © 2010 Estate of Pablo Picasso/Artists Rights Society (ARS), NY.

169: Photo provided by the author.

170: © Anthony Kersting/AKG Images.

171: Barbara Kruger, *"Untitled"* (We don't need another hero), 1987. Photographic silkscreen/vinyl, 109 by 210 inches. © Barbara Kruger. Collection: Fisher Landau Center for Art, Long Island City, New York. Courtesy of Mary Boone Gallery, NY.

172 TL: Mona Hatoum, *Doormat II*, 2000–2001. Steel and rubber, 1 x 28 x 16 in/2.5 x 71 x 40.5 cm. Photo by Orcutt & Van Der Putten. Image courtesy of Alexander and Bonin, New York.

photo credits

208 B: Photo by Satoshi Yamamoto. Courtesy of Stephen Knapp.

209 T: © Krzysztof Wodiczko, Courtesy Galerie Lelong, New York.

209 B: Edition 1: Collection of Marion Stroud Swingle. Edition 2: Collection of the Artist. Photo by Roman Mensing. Courtesy of artist and James Cohan Gallery.

210 BL: Courtesy of Fisher-Price.

210 BR: Courtesy of Toshiyuki Kita/IDK Design Laboratory, LTD, Japan.

211 TL: Do Ho Suh, *Reflection*, 2004. Nylon and stainless steel tube. Courtesy of the Artist and Lehmann Maupin Gallery, New York.

211 TR: © Keith Edmier. Courtesy of Sadie Coles HQ, London.

211 BL: Courtesy of Michael Graves & Associates. Photo by William Taylor.

212 T: © Philippe Caron/Sygma/CORBIS.

212 B: Photo by Robert Stave, 1989. © Adele Linarducci, 1989.

213 TL: George Segal 1924–2000, *Walk, Don't Walk*, 1976. Plaster, cement, metal, painted wood and electric light, Overall: 109 x 72 x 74 3/8 in. (276.9 x 182.9 x 188.9 cm. Whitney Museum of American Art, New York. Purchase, with funds from the Louis and Bessie Adler Foundation, Inc., Seymour M. Klein, President, the Gilman Foundation, Inc., the Howard and Jean Lipman Foundation, Inc. and the National Endowment for the Arts 79.4a–f. © The George and Helen Segal Foundation/Licensed by VAGA, New York, NY.

213 TR: Museo del Templo Mayor, Mexico City. Instituto Nacional de Antropologia e Historia (INAH).

214 TL: Courtesy of Ned Kahn.

214 CL: The Kansas City Sculpture Park at The Nelson-Atkins Museum of Art, Kansas City, Missouri including *Shuttlecocks* (two of four), 1994 by Claes Oldenburg, American (b. Sweden, 1929) and Coosje van Bruggen, American (b. The Netherlands, 1942). Aluminum, fiberglass-reinforced plastic, paint, 230 9/16 x 191 7/8 inches. Purchase: acquired through the generosity of the Sosland Family, F94-1/3-4. Photograph by Louis Meluso.

214 R: © Kim Karpeles/Alamy.

216: Courtesy of Todd Slaughter.

217: Overlooking the Straits of Gibraltar. Commissioned by the port city of Algeciras, Spain. Courtesy of the artist.

Chapter 10

Page 218 L: Courtesy of Humanscale, NY.

218 R: Martin Puryear, *Seer*, 1984. Water-based paint on wood and wire, 78 x 51 x 45 inches. Solomon R. Guggenheim Museum, Purchased with funds contributed by the Louis and Bessie Adler Foundation, Inc., Seymour M. Klein, President, 1985. 85.3276. Photograph by David Heald. © The Guggenheim Foundation, New York.

219: Courtesy Marian Goodman Gallery, NY.

220 T: Courtesy of Hauser & Wirth, New York.

220 BL: Giraudon/Art Resource, NY. © 2010 Estate of Louise Nevelson/Artists Rights Society (ARS), New York.

221 L: © Aaron Macsai.

221 R: Zac Freeman, *Steve*, 2006. Found objects on board, 60 x 48 inches. Photo courtesy of J. Johnson Gallery.

222 T: Photo by Timothy Hursley. Holocaust Memorial Museum, Washington, DC.

222 B: Collection, University of Illinois at Urbana, Champaign. Photo courtesy of the artist © Alice Aycock, 1994.

223 TL: Photo by Don Cole. Courtesy of Fowler Museum of Cultural History, UCLA.

223 TR: Eva Hesse, *Accession II*, 1968. Galvanized steel, vinyl, 30 x 30 x 30 inches. Detroit Institute of Arts, Founders Society Purchase, Friends of Modern Art Fund, and Miscellaneous Gifts Fund, 1979. © The Estate of Eva Hesse. Courtesy Hauser & Wirth, Zurich, London.

223 B: Art @ Judy Pfaff/Licensed by VAGA, New York, NY.

224 T: Courtesy of Mary Boone Gallery, NY.

224 B: Superstock.

225 L: © David Becker/Reuters/CORBIS.

225 R: Courtesy the Library, American Museum of Natural History, New York. AMNH Trans. #2104(2).

226: Courtesy of Theodore Gall.

227 L: Ludovica Canali De Rossi, Milano, Italy.

227 R: Santa Maria degli Angeli, Rome, Italy/Mauro Magliani/Superstock.

227 C: Courtesy the Library, American Museum of Natural History, New York. Trans. #2104(2).

228 T: Kurkje Gallery, Chrong Ku, Seoul, Korea.

228 B: Courtesy of Patricia A. Renick.

229: Designers: James E. Grove, John Cook, Jim Holtorf, Fernando Pardo, Mike Boltich. Design Firm: Designworks/USA. Client/Mfr: Corona Clipper Co.

230 L: Solomon R. Guggenheim Foundation, Peggy Guggenheim Collection, 1976. 76.2553.50 Photo: David Heald. © Solomon R. Guggenheim Museum Foundation, New York. © 2010 Artists Rights Society (ARS), New York/ADAGP, Paris.

230 C: Constantin Brâncusi, French, born Romania, 1876–1957, *Golden Bird*, 1919/20 (base c. 1922), Bronze, stone, and wood, 86 x 11 3/4 x 11 3/4 in. (217.8 x 29.9 x 29.9 cm), Partial gift of The Arts Club of Chicago; restricted gift of various donors; through prior bequest of Arthur Rubloff; through prior restricted gift of William Hartmann; through prior gifts of Mr. and Mrs. Carter H. Harrison, Mr. and Mrs. Arnold H. Maremont through the Kate Maremont Foundation, Woodruff J. Parker, Mrs. Clive Runnells, Mr. and Mrs. Martin A. Ryerson, and various donors, 1990.88, The Art Institute of Chicago. Photography © The Art Institute of Chicago. © 2010 Artists Rights Society (ARS), New York/ADAGP, Paris.

230 R: The Museum of Modern Art, New York, given anonymously. Digital Image © The Museum of Modern Art/Licensed by Scala/Art Resource, NY. © 2010 Artists Rights Society (ARS), New York/ADAGP, Paris.

231 TL: Fratelli Alinari/Superstock.

231 TR: Digital Image © The Museum of Modern Art/Licensed by Scala/Art Resource, NY. © 2010 Succession Giacometti/Artists Rights Society (ARS), NY.

231 BR: Photo by Doug Yaple.

232 T: © Destinations/CORBIS.

232 B: © Liza Lou. Courtesy of L & M Arts, New York.

233 T: Courtesy of the National Ornamental Metal Museum, Memphis, TN. Collection of the artist.

233 B: © 2010 Artists Rights Society (ARS), New York/ADAGP, Paris. Photo © CNAP Command Publique, Ministére de la Culture, Paris.

234 T: Courtesy of Museum fuer Kunst und Gewerbe, Hamburg.

234 B: Courtesy of Tanija & Graham Carr. Photo by Victor France.

235 TL: Musée d'Orsay, Paris. Réunion des Musées Nationaux/Art Resource, NY.

235 TR: Collection Walker Art Center, Minneapolis. Acquired with Lannan Foundation support in conjunction with the exhibition Sculpture Inside Outside, 1991.

235 B: Magdalena Abakanowicz, Polish (b. 1930), *Standing Figures (Thirty Figures)*, 1994–1998. Bronze, 74 x 23 x 16 inches each. The Nelson-Atkins Museum of Art, Kansas City, Missouri. Gift of the Hall Family Foundation, F99-33/1 A-DD. Photo by Jamison Miller. © Magdalena Abakanowicz, courtesy Marlborough Gallery, New York.

236 T: Siegfried Layda/Getty Images.

236 B: © Sherrie Levine. Courtesy of Paula Cooper Gallery, NY.

238–239: © Marilyn da Silva. Photo by M. Lee Fatherree.

Chapter 11

Page 241: Guggenheim Bilbao © 1997, The Solomon R. Guggenheim Foundation, Bilbao. © FMGB Guggenheim Bilbao Museoa, 2001. All rights reserved.

242: Courtesy of Shoji Design.

243: Photo by Whit Slemmons. Courtesy of Thorncrown Chapel.

286 L: Kiki Smith, *Virgin Mary*, 1992. Wax, cheesecloth and wood with steel base, 67 1/2 x 26 x 14 1/2" (171.5 x 66 x 36.8 cm). © Kiki Smith. Photography by Ellen Page Wilson, courtesy of PaceWildenstein, New York.

286 R: © Allen Memorial Art Museum, Oberlin College, OH. Fund for Contemporary Art and gift of the artist and the Fischbach Gallery, 1970.

288 T: Photo by Shelby Duncan, 2006.

288 B: Courtesy of Samuel Yates.

Chapter 13

Page 290: © 2007 Eames Office/www.eamesoffice.com.

291 T: San Francisco Museum of Modern Art. Doris and Donald G. Fisher Fund. © Jim Campbell. Courtesy Hosfelt Gallery, San Francisco/New York.

291 B: Courtesy of Lucinda Childs.

292: © Apple Computer, Inc. Used with permission. All rights reserved. Apple ® and the Apple logo are registered trademarks of Apple Computer, Inc.

293 T: Musée du Louvre, Paris. © Réunion des Musées Nationaux/Art Resource, NY.

293 C: Sam Shere/Hulton/Archive/Getty Images.

293 B: San Francisco Museum of Modern Art. Doris and Donald G. Fisher Fund. © Jim Campbell. Courtesy Hosfelt Gallery, San Francisco/New York.

299: Photofest.

300: Michael Snow, *Cover to Cover*, 1975. The New York Public Library, Astor, Lenox and Tilden Foundations.

301: © 2010 Marvel Characters, Inc. Used with permission.

302 L: © 2010 Marina Abramovic. Courtesy of Sean Kelly Gallery/Artists Rights Society (ARS), New York.

302 R: Mary Lucier, *Migration (Monarch)*, 2000. Astrovision Board, Times Square, New York. © Mary Lucier. Photo by Charlie Samuels. Courtesy of Lennon, Weinberg, Inc., New York.

304 T: © 2010 Marvel Characters, Inc. Used with permission.

304 B: Harris Brisbane Dick Fund, 1946, The Metropolitan Museum of Art, New York. © The Metropolitan Museum of Art/Art Resource, NY.

304–305: Art © Nancy Holt/Licensed by VAGA, New York, NY.

306: Courtesy of Tatana Kellner and the Syracuse University Library, Department of Special Collections.

318: © Joanna Eldredge Morrisey.

319: From *Losing It*, documentary film by Sharon Greytak.

Chapter 14

Page 321: Musée du Louvre, Paris. © Réunion des Musees Nationaux/Art Resource, NY.

322: © Jerome Witkin, Courtesy of Jack Rutberg Fine Arts, Inc.

323 TR: From *Frogfolio 10*, Dellas Graphics, Syracuse, NY. © Bart Forbes, 2005.

323 BL: Courtesy of Charles Santore.

323 BR: From *Frogfolio 10*, Dellas Graphics, Syracuse, NY.

324: © Duane Michals. Courtesy of Pace/MacGill Gallery.

327: © Douglas Wonders.

328: Photofest.

329 T, B: © 2010 Salvador Dali, Gala-Salvador Dali Foundation/Artists Rights Society (ARS), New York.

333: Photofest.

335 T: Used with permission Greenberg, Seronick, O'Leary & Partners, Boston.

335 B: Used with permission Jeep/Daimler Chrysler.

336: Used with permission Procter & Gamble.

337: Used with permission Goodby, Silverstein & Partners.

338: Used with permission Nike and the estate of Walt Stack.

339: Used with permission Greenberg, Seronick, O'Leary & Partners, Boston.

340: Used with permission BMW and WCRS Matthews Marcantonio, London.

341: © Susan Kae Grant, Black Rose Productions.

342: © 2007 Eames Office/www.eamesoffice.com.

344: Photo by Mark Rubin, Courtesy of Michael Remson.

345: Soprano Kelli Estes performing in the Lone Star Lyric Theatre Festival's recent production of Michael Remson's Sorry, Wrong Number, based on the play by Lucille Fletcher. Photo by Buck Ross. Used by permission.

Chapter 15

Page 346: © Nancy Callahan, 2005.

347 T: Anselm Kiefer, *Breaking of the Vessels*, 1990. Lead, iron, glass, copper wire, charcoal, Aquatec. 12' 5" x 27' 5 1/2" x 17". Saint Louis Art Museum, Funds given by Mr. and Mrs. George Schlapp, Mrs. Francis A. Mesker, the Henry L. and Natalie Edison Freund Charitable Trust, The Arthur and Helen Baer Charitable Foundation, Sam and Marilyn Fox, Mrs. Eleanor J. Moore, Mr. and Mrs. John Wooten Moore, Donna and William Nussbaum, Mr. and Mrs. James E. Schneithorst, Jain and Richard Shaikewitz, Mark Twain Bancshares, Inc., Mr. and Mrs. Gary Wolff, Mr. and Mrs. Lester P. Ackerman Jr., the Honorable & Mrs. Thomas F. Eagleton, Alison and John Ferring, Mrs. Gail K. Fischmann, Mr. and Mrs. Solon Gershman, Dr. and Mrs. Gary Hansen, Mr. and Mrs. Kenneth S. Kranzberg, Mr. and Mrs. Gyo Obata, Jane and Warren Shapleigh, Lee and Barbara Wagman, Anabeth Calkins and John Weil, Museum Shop Fund, the Contemporary Art Society, and Museum Purchase. Dr. and Mrs. Harold J. Joseph, estate of Alice P. Francis, Fine Arts Associates, J. Lionberger Davis, Mr. and Mrs. Samuel B. Edison, Mr. and Mrs. Morton D. May, estate of Louise H. Franciscus, an anonymous donor, Miss Ella M. Boedeker, by exchange.

347 B: Courtesy of Daniel E. Kelm and Timothy C. Ely.

348: Courtesy of the author.

349: © Tom Phillips, 2010 Artists Rights Society (ARS), NY, DACS, London.

350 T: Courtesy of Emily Frenkel.

350 B: Courtesy of the author.

351 T, B: Illustration from *The Gashlycrumb Tinies or, After the Outing*. © 1963 and renewed 1991 by Edward Gorey, reproduced by permission of Harcourt, Inc.

352: Reprinted with permission of Little Simon, an imprint of Simon & Schuster Children's Publishing Division, from *The 12 Days of Christmas*, a Pop-up Celebration, by Robert Sabuda. © 1996 by Robert Sabuda.

357: Robert Irwin, Part II: *Excursus: Homage to the Square3*, installation at Dia Center for the Arts, New York City. September 13, 1998–June 13, 1999. Photo: Thibault Jeanson. Courtesy Dia Art Foundation. © 2010 Robert Irwin/Artists Rights Society (ARS), NY.

358: Photo by Roman Mensing. Courtesy of the artist and James Cohan Gallery.

359: © 1997 Sandy Skoglund.

360 T: © Nancy Callahan and Diane Gallo.

360 B: © 2010 Jenny Holzer/Artists Rights Society (ARS), New York.

361: Ann Hamilton, *Indigo Blue*, 1991/2007. Cotton clothing, wood and steel platform, wood table and stool, book, eraser, dimensions variable. San Francisco Museum of Modern Art, Accessions Committee Fund purchase. © Ann Hamilton.

362: Photo © Dan Rest. Courtesy of Brooklyn Academy of Music. Courtesy of Armitage Gone! Dance, New York.

363 T: Courtesy of Lucinda Childs.

363 B: Courtesy of The Rachel Rosenthal Company, Los Angeles, CA.

366–367: © Nancy Callahan and Diane Gallo.

index

G

Index

index

Index

index

index

index

Index